龍頭

The Dragonhead

The True Story of

the Godfather

of Chinese Crime—

His Rise and Fall

The *Dragonhead*

John Sack

Crown Publishers • New York

Grateful acknowledgment is made to the following for permission to reprint previously published material:

Universal Music Publishing Group: excerpt from "California Dreamin'," words and music by John Phillips and Michelle Gilliam. Copyright © 1965 Universal-MCA Music Publishing, Inc., a division of Universal Studios, Inc. (ASCAP) International copyright secured. All rights reserved.

Warner Bros. Publications, Inc.: excerpt from "Don't Stand a Ghost of a Chance With You," by Bing Crosby, Ned Washington, and Victor Young; and an excerpt from "Diana" by Paul Anka. All rights reserved. Used by permission of Warner Bros. Publications U.S., Inc., Miami, FL 33014.

Published by Crown Publishers, New York, New York.
Member of the Crown Publishing Group.

Random House, Inc. New York, Toronto, London, Sydney, Auckland
www.randomhouse.com

Crown is a trademark and the Crown colophon is a registered trademark of Random House, Inc.

Printed in the United States of America
Design by LENNY HENDERSON
Calligraphy by WANG K. LAU

Library of Congress Cataloging-in-Publication Data
Sack, John.
The Dragonhead / by John Sack.
1. Kon, Johnny. 2. Criminals—China—Hong Kong—Biography. 3. Organized crime—China—Hong Kong. 4. Organized crime—United States. 5. Chinese American criminals.
I. Title.
HV6248.K624 S17 2001
364.1'06'089951073—dc21
00–047476
ISBN 0-609-60353-1
10 9 8 7 6 5 4 3 2 1
First Edition

DEDICATION

You were born today. Your lips
At every exhalation towards
My own create what didn't exist
Until this very day. Your words

Emerge, and all those freshly-formed
New molecules coalesce
As smithy-sparks that never burned
My heart until today. Your kiss

That lingers like ellipses where
Your tender sentence melts away
Was brewed of earth, air, water, fire
In your retort today. And I

Am what I never was till you
But breathe and I am newborn too.

Contents

Crofton

PART ONE

1
Coolie
Gongjalu . . . Shanghai . . . Shanghai . . . Shenzhen

2
Outsider
Hong Kong . . . Hong Kong . . . Hong Kong . . . Canton . . .
Hong Kong . . . Hong Kong

3
Blue Lantern
Hong Kong . . . Saigon . . . Danang . . . Danang . . . Saigon . . . Vungtau . . .
Saigon . . . Hong Kong . . . Saigon . . . Hong Kong

4
Vietnik
Vungtau . . . Saigon . . . Danang . . . Danang . . . Saigon . . . Saigon . . . Hong Kong

5
Number Four Nine
New York . . . Bangkok . . . Nhatrang . . . Saigon . . . Phnom Penh . . .
Hong Kong . . . Hong Kong

PART THREE

17

Runner

18

Ash Carrier IV

19

Hand-Tied Man

20

Cincinnatus

21

Peacemaker

22

Coke Carrier

The Dragonhead

CROFTON

Our home is our castle, people say, our sanctuary from all the muggers, mayhem-makers and murderers running amok on Main Street. Our home, built of bricks they cannot blow down, secured by a lock they cannot pick, surrounded by a socially contracted moat, is the one place on the planet where we can live according to our own pleasures, untroubled by sociopathic intruders. Or so people say, but in the new millennium thousands of homeowners in the U.S.A. have discovered otherwise.

One such initiate was a man in the green-grass suburb of Crofton, Maryland, a man in his seventies whose name (and whose temperament) was Young. His home, half brick, half wood, showily fronted by Colonial columns, was just alongside the Walden Walking Path and just behind tee number one at the Walden Golf Course. Lilies, all yellow, flanked his heavy front door. In the late afternoon of Tuesday, February 15, 2000, old Young was in his two-story living room, sitting on a black leather loveseat waiting for the five o'clock news when the doorbell rang, *ring, ring*. Getting up, he went to the foyer and, in the five little windows that ran in a column beside the double-locked door, saw a seeming deliveryman—a Chinese deliveryman—with a brown cardboard box. "I have a package for you," the Chinese man said through the stylish windows.

"Who from?" said Young.

"It's from a Mr. Wong."

"I don't know him."

"Well," said the Chinese man and looked at Young's door, then down at the cardboard box, "this is the right address."

Mr. Young! Don't open that door! No one was home to give that warning, and when he unlocked the double lock, opened the door minimally, and said, "Put the package here," the Chinese man did—then pushed the door open, pulled out a 9-millimeter pistol, and with two other men, both Chinese, both pulling pistols, burst into Young's former castle. A home invasion, that's what police across the U.S.A. call incursions like this by gangs of Chinese criminals. In this part of Maryland, invasions had happened recently in Linthicum, Cockeysville, Westminster, Elkridge and Abingdon, Abingdon where a month earlier three Chinese men had irrupted into a many-gabled home, tied up the old woman homeowner, beaten her up and, shouting, asked her, "Where is your money?" Had they mugged her on an Abingdon street, they'd have had a few seconds, perhaps, to rob her beaded purse and her $40, but in the privacy of her shuttered home they took their sweet time and left with a necklace and $40,000.

The leader in Abingdon (and Linthicum, Cockeysville, Westminster and Elkridge) was the same seeming deliveryman who told Young today, "Well, this is the right address." His nickname was Chickenhead, he'd been born close to Hong Kong, and like thousands of fellow gangsters in the Big Circle, the world's largest gang of Chinese, Russians, Italians or any other ethnicity, he'd come as an illegal alien to what the Chinese called the Golden Mountain: the United States. This morning, driving a Toyota, he'd picked up his two confederates, born in China, at 11:15 in Chinatown in New York, taken the Holland Tunnel and the Pulaski Skyway to the New Jersey Turnpike, and played cassettes of Mandarin music while he drove down to Baltimore and its Crofton suburb. Now and then he'd turned to one confederate, a man whose nickname was Pig (in Cantonese, Good-for-Nothing Pig) who owed him one month's interest on a debt of $2,000, contracted at a baccarat table in Atlantic City, and had asked him in Cantonese, "When will you pay me?"

"I have $400 now."

"It isn't enough."

At 4:45 they got to Young's sumptuous home, which their "brothers" in the Big Circle in Baltimore had already scoped out. As they walked to his door, they carried the empty cardboard box and, in a black briefcase, a jiffy invasion kit: a hammer, screwdriver, crowbar, box cutter, glass cutter, butcher's knife, flashlight, can of Mace, rope, duct tape, handcuffs. As they barged in, Chickenhead told Young quite matter-of-factly, "This is a stickup," and Pig and the third man used the rope to tie his hands behind him and the duct tape to tie a blue sweatshirt around his frightened face. "Oh, my heart!" cried Young through the sweatshirt, hoping to chase the Chinese off (or, at least, to convince them *don't beat me*) by feigning a heart attack, but Pig and the third man trotted him to the cellar, seated him on the floor, tied him to a bench-press bench, and told him, "Don't move." Then, using intelligence from the Big Circle in Baltimore, the three uninvited guests went to Young's bedroom to get the wads of $10,000 to $20,000 that Young had hidden in Ziploc bags in towels in his dresser drawers and in pockets in his clothes closets—to get those and a $200 gold ring, a $500 jade ring, and a $2,000 diamond ring and to leave unhurriedly in the Toyota, no sounds of sirens disturbing the golfers' concentration on the Walden Golf Course.

Since then, the three have done no invasions in quaint little towns like Birdsville or anywhere else in Maryland. But their brothers in the Big Circle (and other wheels within wheels in tongs, triads, secret societies) have put a more sulfurous face on crime in America by supplanting the Mafia in gambling, extorting, usurious lending, pandering, counterfeiting, hijacking, carjacking, dealing in heroin, running guns, and—most notably nowadays—smuggling stowaways from Asia into America for as much as $80,000 per man (men who, once here, often join the Big Circle) and, yes, by invading people's homes and by kidnapping, mayhem-making and murder from Maryland to California. They're public enemy number one, says the California attorney general. "They'll make the Mafia look like Sunday-school kids," "They'll make the Mafia look like wimps," say the police chiefs elsewhere. A memory from the seventies are the Chinese who, when encountered, could be counted on to be inoffensive, obeisant, benign. Who are the new Chinese criminals? Why did they leave their ancestral land? Why did they come to make mischief in the United States? Don't ask the FBI, it doesn't know but in the beginning—the early eighties—the Chinese were sent specifically to *destroy* the United States. Were sent by their wide-smiling leader, their Godfather, their Dragonhead, a man who operated from a vast marble-topped desk on the thirteenth floor of a building in Hong Kong, a man whose nickname was Johnny Kon. This book, whose sources are the most knowledgeable ones, the Chinese criminals, is about him and them.

Part One

I
Coolie

GONGJALU

Ants. Army ants. A column of creepie-crawlies, advancing like a wobbly pencil line across the paddies south of Shanghai, that's what these people look like. It's winter, 1959, on the paddies a cracking crust of ice reflects the sky and its gloomy clouds, clouds like mole holes, clouds like icicle-sided caves, and the ten thousand coolies are cold in spite of their ankle-length underwear, cotton-padded outerwear, scarves (muddy towels) around their necks, caps with flaps around their ears—caps with shiny stalactites of frozen sweat. On their shoulders the women and men carry yokes: crosspieces of crucifixes: finger-to-finger bamboo poles: at every end is a rice-stem rope and a basket of wet and stinking mud, for at this freezing season (as in the past hundred? thousand? who in Gongjalu ever counted? years) the Chinese are dredging the Gongjalu Canal. On their callused feet are the rice-stem sandals that Mao, their venerated chairman, has rather untenably approved as the proper attire for the Great Leap Forward.

Above them the seagulls screech. On one boy, aged sixteen, the sandals are scratchy, the thong is a saw between his toes, his toes are bubble-gum bubbles: red, spherical, shiny-skinned, his toes are the source of shooting pains that run to his straining shoulders, *oh,* the boy thinks, *my tortured toes!* And squatting, slipping the sandals off, sinking into the mud to his

7

ankles, wrenching them out, the mud making sucking sounds like an underground octopus, *wup, wup,* the boy climbs the twenty or thirty steps that men with shovels have sculpted into the canal's embankment, climbs with his crucifix, baskets, mud. His name is Kon. His home ten miles from here is a stone-walled room in the morgue of the Heaven Eternal Cemetery. Allotted to him by his commune, the pad isn't home sweet home for Kon, who, having cleaned the grimy windows, cleared the pawing cobwebs, and hauled off the one dozen coffins, is still afraid of the prowling ghosts, afraid of going outdoors at one, two, three in the morning (the door going *creak,* the wind whipping down from Mongolia, the door going *bang,* then *creak,* then *bang*) to pee off the porch on one of those probably offended apparitions. Most days, Kon is in his commune, standing at a hot cauldron, dropping in hundreds of Chinese weasels—of Chinese weasel skins—and making the meaningless salary of one half penny per day by stirring the weasels, stirring the weasels, moving his paddle in figure eights, dyeing the weasels "jewel black" or "jasmine white" like the American minks they'll be sold in America as. At noon there's a bell, at the mess hall he trades his red coupon for his eight ounces of rice: not enough, and in the evening he uses his adze to scratch out one or two peanuts the farmers have missed, to fish with a spear and to crab with his bare right hand, his hand going gallantly into a hole, his wrist, elbow, armpit following it, his arm on a hazardous recon patrol till Kon triumphantly says in his Shanghai dialect, "I got it! It didn't get *me!*" At night he attends the commune's self-criticism sessions ("You did something wrong," "Yes, I ate one peanut," "You still aren't red") but on this special dredging day he's merely an *Anomma* species ant, another anonymous dot advancing across the paddies, dumping the stinking mud, and descending the slippery steps to the Gongjalu Canal.

The canal's without water today. On its bottom are muck and mire, sewage and garbage, a wasteland of all that's inedible: of bones of skin-nibbled fish, of roots of digested vegetables, of shiny ceramic shards: of soup bowls, rice bowls, soy-sauce bowls, of Chinese household gods, why not? the squalor excreting an odor that in an instant drops from Kon's nose to Kon's queasy throat. Still barefoot, he steps inadvertently onto a broken bottle, says, "*O,*" the Shanghai dialect for "*Ow,*" and

extracts a couple of blood-reddened shreds that the boss of this operation disapprovingly notices. *"You,"* says the man, his uniform blue, his
armband red, his belt just a yellow rice-stem rope—"you don't have sandals on. Why not?"

"Comrade, I can't walk with them."

"You've got to wear them anyhow."

"Comrade," says Kon, his words turning solid, turning to cap-strap stalactites. "Without them I can walk faster, and I can carry more mud for
the People's Republic." He flashes his summery smile at the boss, practically melting the stalactites.

"Good boy, Yu," the boss approves—Yu is the boy's first name,
though soon (while trying, trying to climb from this wasteland, climb
from this wretched poverty) the nice but, oh, so nimble fellow will ask
to be known as Johnny, as Johnny Kon.

SHANGHAI

Flat on its face falls the Great Leap Forward. Unnourished by eight
ounces daily of rice or by barbecued dogs, cats and rats, some twenty
million citizens of China have died. In Gongjalu the Chinese weasel-
works (founded in the 1920s by Kon's go-getting father but in the 1950s
expropriated by Mao: they're capitalism, they're feudalism, they're pup-
pets of American imperialism)—the mink-works have flopped. At eighteen years old, Johnny (we'll call him Johnny) is staying alive by straying
from the precepts of Mao and peddling string in the shadows of the
Szechwan Street Bridge. "Fishing line! Fishing line! It's *green,"* cries
Johnny, the former weasel-dyer, the boy who earns two hundred times
what he did in Gongjalu by dyeing his fishing line the color of the
Yangtze River. "The fish won't see it!"

Uh-oh, the communist cops. His brother on the corner signaling him,
Johnny closes his ragged satchel, wraps it with slices of inner tube, ties it
to his rusted bicycle, ceases to peddle but pedals swiftly into the noodle-
shop-smelly streets.

Shanghai

Johnny sells out. His miles of river-colored strings sell out, the man who sold him the raw white string (a man who'd presumably stolen it) is also unstrung these days, and Johnny's nouveau-impoverished father sits in their slatted home on a tattered sofa saying in Shanghai dialect, "There are no jobs in Shanghai, you must resettle in Hong Kong," to somewhere so far from anywhere that Johnny has ever remotely known that Johnny can't picture where it is.

"Yes, daddy," says Johnny, an obedient son, a Buddhist, a boy who prays every day at the Buddhist temple, prays to a black-bodied god who if Johnny is bad and doesn't observe the Buddhist commandment to honor his father and mother may resurrect him as an *Anomma* ant, and who prays every day to a white-bodied god who if Johnny is good will terminate all these tiresome reincarnations. "I'll go where you say," says Johnny, a boy who knows that the Kons (three sisters, three brothers, the oldest is Johnny) must live on his gleanings in, where was it? Hong Kong? and who, before departing, visits his grandfather's garden to tell the old man goodbye.

The garden has four impressive levels. On each are mountains, waterfalls, rivers, across every river arches a scarlet bridge, trees as gorgeously gnarled as India filigrees grow on each bank, behind them hundreds of thoroughbred horses graze. But the garden envelops an area smaller than a vegetable patch—it's a miniature garden, a rock, water, plant, and glass-horse menagerie, and as Johnny enters it his grandfather is using manicure scissors to trim it. "I hear you're going to Hong Kong," his grandfather says in Shanghai dialect, then sits down in a straw-colored rattan chair.

"Yes, grandfather," says Johnny deferentially, then sits down on a bamboo stool.

"Do you want some tea?"

"Yes, grandfather." And raising a flower-decorated pot, the grandfather pours some for Johnny while he himself drinks from the spout, the Shanghai way. "I tell you," he whispers. "You mustn't say I told you, but you mustn't forget it. In Hong Kong," he whispers, staring at the garden's bamboo wall, a wall that pedestrians walk by, pedestrians who might overhear him and tell the Shanghai authorities that he isn't red, that he's due for a reeducation camp—"in Hong Kong it's like the old days here in Shanghai." Saying *the old days,* the old man sighs, raises his hand, and points a cigar-stained finger over his shoulder at what apparently are the 1920s and 1930s, are fond recollections of opium dens, of pai-gow dens, of dens full of sing-song girls: of girls whose finger-sized feet a man could caress, could smell, could lick: a man could nibble the almonds between the nipple-sized toes or put his penis between the two Lilliputian feet till *yes!* he abandoned himself to the Time of the Rain. The sing-song houses (and in Shanghai, one house in every twelve was one) of course were run by organized crime: by gangs, by secret societies, by what would someday be known as the Mafia, Chinese Mafia, by organizations as well-connected as New York's Tammany Hall, on their long rosters were Sun Yat-Sen, the founder of the Republic of China, and Chiang Kai-Shek, China's leader in World War II. And now Johnny's grandfather whispers, "They still have these gangs in Hong Kong. They still run the opium, morphine, heroin, the pai-gow, fan-tan, mahjong, the delicate sing-song girls—they run all the illegitimate *and* legitimate businesses in Hong Kong. They—"

His grandfather stops. His eyes become narrow, and Johnny turns around thinking, *He sees someone listening.* From under his rattan chair, the grandfather draws a scissors that's more like a shears, stands up, moves forward like a stalking animal, *snap!* then snips an imperfect leaf off one of his miniature pine trees. He sits down again and tells Johnny imperturbably, "These gangs run Hong Kong. You must respect them. You needn't," he says, shaking his brown-stained finger, his almost hypnotic metronome, *whatever I tell you, you will do*—"you needn't *join* them." He knows that in 1948 another of Johnny's grandfathers was in the Green Gang, the biggest gang in Shanghai, and that the other grandfather kidnapped a VIP, was caught, and was killed by a firing squad, and that he lay in his coffin as Johnny's father stared at the red that edged every hole in his ashen face. "Don't join the Green Gang. Don't, don't, don't," Johnny's still-shaken father told Johnny, Johnny who promised him, "Daddy, I won't," this, too, the man in this flawless garden knows, and he says emphatically, "You needn't join them. But you must make friends with them. Don't think, *I'll wait till I need them.* By then it's too late. You'll tell them, 'Hey, I have trouble,' and they'll just shrug and say, 'Who are *you?*' Then who will you turn to? The Royal Police? *Ha,*" the old man half-laughs, then he uses some gangland slang, "the *oafish officers* are in the gangs themselves. But if the gangs are your friends, they'll tell you, 'Trouble with who? What name? What address?' *Listen,*" the old man interrupts himself, meaning listen to the sparrow that's perched in one of his miniature trees. "Listen, that bird sings well!" He stands up, scatters some seeds to the sweet-sounding sparrow, and says to Johnny, "Don't forget what I've told you."

"I won't forget," says Johnny obediently. And bowing goodbye, going to the sooty station, standing in line three days, buying a dirt-encrusted seat on a train to Shenzhen, the city in China closest to Hong Kong, then riding, crying, telling himself, *I'll never see my mother again*—and truly he never will—he steams past the paddies, the sprouting stalks, and the penniless proletariat, steams to the Chinese border at Shenzhen three days away.

SHENZHEN

What famished man in China wouldn't rather escape to Hong Kong? None, but one billion people is more than the British have flats for, and Johnny has two unauthorized options to get to that beckoning wonderland: to (1) climb across mountains, guarded by Dobermans, or (2) swim across water, guarded by great white sharks. But after a month making friends (some of them gangsters, some in the Green Gang) in the corridors of the Peace Hotel, he learns of another nefarious option, to (3) pay the riches of Solomon, that's $125, for one little six-inch shred of thread, and he has eagerly bought one.

The thread, which is red, dangles from Johnny's passport as he walks anxiously onto the bridge to Hong Kong. All this month he's watched the men crossing it, the businessmen in their fresh white shirts, their slant-striped ties, their pin-striped suits, their Rolexes glinting in Shenzhen's sun, and he's thought, *These fools. If I had their money I'd send so much to Shanghai. And someday I'll have it.* That day seems nearer as, on this narrow bridge, the little red thread (like a flaw in some fabric) impresses the Royal Police as a pair of blue knickers impresses a Dodger fan if the man who's wearing them is rounding third in Dodger Stadium. "Go this way," the tan-hatted police tell Johnny enthusiastically, but one policeman counsels him, "Go slower. Go slower. Or *they*," the police who consider themselves above their corruptible colleagues, above what the Chinese call the biggest gang in Hong Kong, the gang named the Royal Police—"or they will notice you." At the border a British policeman walks casually off for coffee, not tea, and a Chinese policeman wielding a great rubber stamp goes *blop!* not on Johnny's passport but on some scrap paper near it, a *blop!* that echoes authoritatively as the Chinese policeman waves Johnny on. Then, Johnny boards a train, and, not speaking at all, for Cantonese is the unintelligible language here and Johnny's own Shanghai dialect could alert a virtuous cop, he points to a vendor's orange juice, buys it, and rides past the sunny paddies into the Promised Land.

2
Outsider

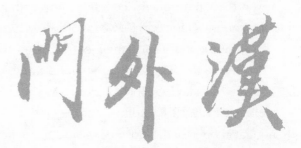

Hong Kong

He rides into El Dorado. Nothing in China prepared him for the people in rainbow-colored clothes, in China the rainbow was blue, blue, blue (just the flag and the posters of Mao were red), but the clothes in this flourishing colony range from the edge of infrared to the edge of ultraviolet. The crowds in this splendid stuff (as Johnny, just spellbound, can see) are trotting along at double time on high-priority missions of making money or spending it with alacrity on watches, bracelets, brooches, rings, on cigarette lighters that look like Marlboros, Players, Salems, Kents, on lighters that look like hand grenades or .45 automatics. The choicest items that Johnny observes (Johnny who's also walking faster, double-clutching, shifting to second gear) end up inside him: rice, fish, pork wrapped like crêpe suzettes in semitransparent tofu—"skin of tofu"—watercress soup, he even enters a movie theater, purchases popcorn, exits. At the market, the food still in cages, still alive, he doesn't waste precious money on ducks, monkeys, raccoons, snakes (*"O,"* he says in surprise, confronting one) but doesn't stop eating, either, at the market it's steaming noodle soup. "You," an old woman asks him in his schoolroom language of Mandarin, a woman who's perched like a sparrow, her feet up on Johnny's bench, her hips on her ankles, that's how the Cantonese do it, "do you want a lovely girl?"

"No," says Johnny. His money isn't for him but his Shanghai family. "She costs ninety cents." The woman works for the Green Gang.

"No. But thank you," says Johnny politely.

In front of Siberia Furs, the mannequins blue-eyed blondes, the mannequins wearing minks, weasels, silver foxes, exotic things like lynxes and sables that Johnny doesn't recognize, in front of it Johnny resolves, *I'll have a store someday.* In front of the Shanghai Bank (till now he's been on the mainland, known as Kowloon, but after his first-ever trip on water, aboard a green ferry, he's now on Hong Kong Island)—in front of its proud stone lions Johnny thinks, *I'll have a bank account someday,* not all of his money will go to Shanghai. On the Island he gets a job as a kindergarten custodian, pressing a little black button-bell at 8:30, 9:30, etcetera, at 5:30 saying in English, "Bye-bye," then washing the blackboards, picking up crayons, mopping the crayon-dotted floors, cleaning the toilets with Comet, well, Johnny's a janitor, basically. He isn't paid, but the principal tips him, buys him breakfasts of soybean soup, invites him to homemade dinners, then lets him sleep like Bartleby on an inch-thick mattress on top of a kindergarten desk. It's summer now (it's 1962, incidentally)—it's hot and the school is a sweat lodge, and Johnny in his pajamas sometimes stands in the alley cooling himself, sipping a Coke, watching the Daimlers arrive at a nightclub run by the Green Gang, and watching the valet parkers open the car doors celeritously to let out the linen-suited men and slit-skirted girls, exquisite girls who glance at Johnny with eyes that say, *Are you begging from us? Someday,* thinks Johnny, *I'll have a girl like that,* a girl whose dress is slit to her thigh, a girl he intends to send not at all to Shanghai.

One month in Hong Kong, and Johnny has doubts about his father's philosophy. "Why buy something expensive? Someone will steal it," his father has said, his father who once wore a Mandarin hat that someone snatched as he rode in a rickshaw to his struggling weasel-works. His father also lent the equivalent of $10,000 to men who didn't repay it but who he magnanimously forgave, telling Johnny, "Maybe they need it." "Daddy," Johnny said then, Johnny just ten years old, "our family's hungry, we need money too," and now in this affluent colony where no one cares of transcendent things, of art, music, literature or God, where (said

Kipling) everyone smells of money, where tourists ask, "Where do I go if I'm not buying something?" and where the measure of man is his Rolex, Cerruti, Daimler, or the carats in his girlfriend's earrings, now Johnny thinks, *No, daddy, you're wrong. Why must I be the one man without money?*

HONG KONG

Under his belt like a .45 is Johnny's secret weapon: twenty pages of his father's weasel recipes (1,000 weasels, 300 gallons water, 4 pounds dye—heat this to 85 degrees, stir 4 hours, let dry) as well as his father's recipes for lamb, rabbit, fox, for dog, cat, rat. These secrets get Johnny a job at James Fong Furs in Kowloon, where for 40 cents per day he holds a paddle in both of his hands, and, as his shoulders rock like a drummer's, moves it in figure eights to brisk transistor music like *She Loves You, Yeah, Yeah, Yeah.* Johnny does this till two a.m., sends out for boiled dumplings, then wakes up at eight to dress in a shirt and tie, a sober red-striped tie he bought from a cart (eschewing the ties depicting dolphins and Daffy Ducks) for 12 cents. With enormous effort, one of the weasel salesmen taught him to tie it, telling him in Cantonese, the weird language that Johnny's learning, "No. You pull down the narrow end," as Johnny groped like a music student learning the clarinet, "and you pull up the wide end. No. You pull down the *narrow* end and you pull up the *wide* end. No." "Maybe," said Johnny thoughtfully, "in the mirror the tie looks backwards." "Yeah, maybe," the salesman agreed, and now while selling weasel coats he tells him in Cantonese, "Get me the brown one. Get me the palomino one. Get . . ."

One summer day, everyone in cotton, an Australian couple comes into James Fong Furs, and Fong (the owner) tells Johnny dubiously, "You can try," can try selling fur. Fong doesn't know, but Johnny was a supersalesman when he was eight in China, catching cicadas and crickets, selling cicadas for "singing" and crickets for fighting on tea-house tables as cricket-promoters egged them on. "This cricket," Johnny would say, "is my general," then Johnny would sell it, display his second-best cricket, and say with instant honesty, "This cricket is my general," and today in

Kowloon he's far from bashful as he approaches the Australian couple. "Welcome," says Johnny in English. He's studying English, too, the weirdest language of all, one that discriminates for no detectable reason between *he, she* and *it,* between *I, my* and *me,* between *long, length* and *lengthen,* between *is, was* and *will be,* between (well, why do the English say, "On the radio," but also say, "On TV"?)—between *a, the,* and nothing at all. "Madam," says Johnny, whose night-school teacher told him to choose an English name, who'd recently seen the Mafia movie *Johnny Cool,* and who told the teacher excitedly, "I got good name. I'm Johnny Kon"—"Madam, can I help you?"

"Oh, I'm just looking."

"You are most welcome. Where are you from?"

"I'm from Australia."

"Oh, beautiful country," says Johnny, who'd say the same if the woman had said Albania or Algeria. "Can I get you Coca-Cola? It's hot."

The woman says yes. She and her camera-wrapped husband sit down, a salesman runs off for the Cokes, and with Christ-on-the-Cross-like widespread arms Johnny shows her a $630 weasel whose almond color is totally wrong for a woman her age, as Johnny well knows.

"We call this the Chinese weasel. Madam," says Johnny, who's still unsure if the English call it the Chinese weasel, a Chinese weasel, or just Chinese weasel, "would you stand up?" She does and Johnny swaddles her in the mammal, straightens her off-color collar, tells her, "It's like wild mink."

"It's nice," her husband says.

"But this," and Johnny enfolds her in a darker, call it coconut, weasel, "is more quality but is $660."

"That's better," her husband says.

"And *this,*" and Johnny enfolds her in a coat of the coffee color that a woman of sixty requires, "comes from China near Russia. Is colder winter. Is thicker fur. You," sighs Johnny, running his fingers along the sleeve as if he's caressing his true love's tresses, "can *feel* it," and, sighing, the woman does. "But costs more," says Johnny. "$830."

"It's higher quality," the woman sighs.

"It's your choice," says her husband.

"I like this best . . ."

"Yeah, I do too . . ."

"But honey, it's too much money."

"No. Is now in Australia winter," says Johnny knowledgeably, "but is hot summer in Hong Kong, so I give summer discount," the accent is on the *count,* dis*count,* "for $660."

"*Okay!*" the Coke-sceptered husband says. A salesman runs for the box, Johnny pops the weasel into it, and Fong (who'd gladly have sold it for $500) murmurs in Cantonese, "Good job." Not troubled by Johnny's hypocrisy, he does what any American from a shoe-store owner to a brokerage owner would: he promotes him to permanent salesman, and Johnny joyously splurges his two-weeks' salary of $15 on the Beatles, live at the Princess Theater, *Yeah, Yeah, Yeah!*

HONG KONG

"You must make *friends,*" said Johnny's finger-wagging grandfather, and Johnny dutifully buddies up to the gophers, groupies, goodfellas, wiseguys-in-waiting, in Cantonese slang the *yellow cows* (a cow is said to eat its food twice: to eat it, regurgitate it, and eat it)—the yellow cows of the Green Gang. One day Johnny visits a friend of a friend who (although it's illegal) admits that he's *in* the Green Gang and who asks Johnny in Shanghai dialect, "Do you know what a gang is?" A man whose tummy's a pot, whose hips are a cauldron, and who the whole colony knows as Fatty, he lives in a zoo of birds, tigers, dragons and flowers, all painted on ancient china such as Johnny has never seen except in the Gallery of Ancient Chinese Ceramics at the Shanghai Museum, the fat man wallows in opulence though he has no job that people like Johnny know of. "You know what a *pang* is?" asks Fatty, sitting in his sumptuous apartment at a table inlaid in mother-of-pearl, sipping tea from a chinaware cup on a cloisonné tray.

"A little. My father told me," says Johnny, avoiding the grisly particulars, the red-edged holes in his grandfather's face.

"The greatest one was the Green Gang. It had," says Fatty, installing himself as Johnny's mentor, "a hundred thousand members just in Shanghai. The boss, and I knew him, was Big Ear. Do you see fungus on tree trunks, sometimes? His ears were like that, were Big Ear's. He was illiterate, but he became a major general in the Chinese army. He became a director of the Cotton Exchange and the Chinese Central Bank."

"But how?" asks Johnny longingly.

"The Cotton Exchange: He had his gangsters attack it. The Bank:" continues Fatty. "He sent an ornamented coffin to the Minister of Finance. One time in Shanghai, I marched (as did the police and the boy scouts, too) in honor of Big Ear. I marched three days. Oh, the magnificent fireworks! Oh, the acrobats and the actresses from the Peking Opera! At the river were boats with pennants to take us (all eighty thousand of us) to his ancestral temple on its whole quarter acre. And Johnny? You know what the temple was for?"

"His ancestors, uncle?"

"And also for opium. In his ancestral temple, he distilled it to morphine, then he distilled it to heroin. And that was the source of his fortune, his $40,000,000. And that was the Green Gang in Shanghai." As two contradictory voices, both of his real-life father, quarrel in Johnny's mind, one saying, *We need money,* the other saying, *Don't join the Green Gang,* Fatty continues. "In Hong Kong, at one time three-fourths of the population were in the Green Gang. We're fewer now, but it's still easy money."

"Money," says Johnny wistfully.

"Lots of it. I don't work hard."

"I work every night until two."

"Not me."

"Uncle?" says Johnny hesitantly. "What work do you *do?*" and Fatty laughs, waddles to his rosewood bedroom, returns with a manila envelope, unwinds the little red string, and on the table of mother-of-pearl (the ocean floor, about to acquire a pirate chest) dumps what Johnny concludes are Fatty's latest profits: a wobbling pile of $100 bills from America, 100-baht bills from Thailand, 100-naira bills from Nigeria, red, orange, yellow bills, bills with engravings of kings, queens, panjandrums, bills that Johnny has never seen until now. *Fatty,* thinks the innocent country boy, *is Fatty distributing heroin?*

"Feel them!" Fatty exults.

"Uncle?"

"Use your fingers! Feel them!" and Johnny, a bit embarrassed, for Chinese as well as Americans consider it crass to flaunt their wealth until it has been transmuted to something more tasteful, like a Rolex or Rolls, chooses a $100 bill and pats the long-haired head of Benjamin Franklin. "You know what that is?" asks Fatty shamelessly.

"Yes, it's a $100 bill."

"I made it," says Fatty.

And *gasp!* Johnny inhales explosively, like the Hoover he runs at eight every morning over the dust motes marring the carpet at James Fong Furs. The words *I made it* in Shanghai dialect aren't ambiguous, and Fatty doesn't mean he earned these bills but he printed them, he perpetrated what Johnny didn't think people did, for in China counterfeit currency is the entrance fee to a firing squad. "Uncle? Do you make *money?*"

"You want some? For $100, I'll sell you $1,000."

"No! I don't want it! Maybe," says Johnny, thinking of blood-crusted craters left by merciless firing squads but, as the "nephew" in this discussion, minding his manners—"maybe in the future sometime."

"Do you want to join the Green Gang?"

"Maybe in the future." *No, never,* thinks Johnny, the filial-pietistic son, the boy whose father ordered him to remain what the Mafia calls a *civilian* and the secret societies call an *outsider.* He leaves, but in a red envelope he leaves a real bill, a traditional tip for Fatty's cloisonné-carrying maid.

CANTON

It's three years later and Johnny's in China, where chickens in wicker baskets, chickens in plastic bags, and chickens in the altogether hang on one-speed bicycles on every dust-ridden street. With real money ($4,000 saved and $4,000 borrowed) he buys five hundred minks born in Russia and raised in China that he'll bring to Kowloon—legitimately, for Johnny's become a legal resident. In an apartment whose door says JOHNNY KON FUR, he'll paddle, paddle the five hundred minks (and one thousand lambs and one thousand weasels) like a weird sister, *double, double, skin of mink, stir it in the kitchen sink,* until he has two hundred elegant coats that he'll then rubber-stamp as American. Will this be committing consumer fraud? No, thinks Johnny, a furrier doesn't sell fur, he sells self-esteem, a sense of *I'm not who I fear I am,* a sense of *I'm wearing American mink,* a sense of *so I'm okay.* It matters not if a mink never saw Minnesota as long as the woman who's wearing it is strolling the boulevards sure of it, and there's not a furrier in Kowloon who doesn't embellish the already ostentatious by using a rubber stamp like Johnny's. Johnny's disingenuous coats, he'll take to the great hotels escorted by yellow cows from the Green Gang, by men who'll tell their clients (their *pieces,* their pieces of meat) that Johnny supplies every eminent store in Kowloon, who'll tell them in English, "No store. No rents. No expenses." And except for the ten percent kickback, they're right.

HONG KONG

"I've someone to introduce you to. A very, very important person," a friend of Johnny's promises, then they walk to the Astor Hotel. It's wedge-shaped: it sits at a triple intersection like a master switching station, like a great loudspeaker telling cars, *Turn onto Carnavon Avenue! Turn onto Cornwall Avenue!* At its door the air-conditioner condensation drips into Johnny's hair, and in its lobby a clamor unheard of in four-star hotels assaults his ears. At the bar are fifty boisterous men, all talking, shouting, ordering beers, all punching each other playfully like at a reunion, *hey, how you doin'?* all wearing identical haircuts: *short,* as short as the stubble on welcome mats. All wear American uniforms and all are American soldiers, sailors, airmen, marines, to Johnny they look like invaders and his first anxious thought is *Do the authorities know about this?* One man cries in English, "Quiet!" and Johnny sees that this drastic command didn't come from any American but from a Chinese, a man of an army colonel's age, a man who is crew-cut but is in a harmless suit and tie. "Quiet! Quiet!" the Chinese cries to Johnny's amazement.

"Yes sir," an American colonel says.

"My name is V.C. Kan. Just call me V.C.," the Chinese says.

"That's *him*," whispers Johnny's friend as a blast of laughter emanates from the Americans, from the GIs (it's now 1965) who clearly came from Vietnam, for they seem elated to see their evasive enemy in such a sociable incarnation. "V.C.! V.C.!" they roar. "Viet Cong!"

"Yes, welcome to Hong Kong," says V.C., the very important person who Johnny is at the Astor to be introduced to. "I'm in charge of R&R," of Rest & Recreation, of one-week vacations on pavement in Asia that every grunt relishes in the course of his Vietnam tour. "I'm in charge of the tours, shopping, restaurants, nightclubs, bars—"

"Girls!" the GIs all cry like the chorus of *South Pacific*.

"Yes, there'll be girls," continues V.C., who wangled this pivotal job from the Pentagon, "but certain girls and certain stores you people won't want." A sudden sobriety fills the bar, the GIs concluding that only by V.C.'s generous guidance can they avoid straying against directives into a communist girl or a communist clothing store. More sensibly Johnny concludes, *Oh god! Every store they shop at, V.C. will have sent them to!* "You don't want to go anywhere if I don't approve it. In Hong Kong," says V.C. considerately, "the money's in Hong Kong not U.S. dollars. Please take your U.S. dollars—"

"Sir?" an American officer asks. "What is a U.S. dollar worth?" and V.C. points to the white plastic letters, numbers and $-signs on a board on the Astor's reception desk.

"There you'll get the official rate," says V.C. as Johnny observes, *No, you won't.* "Now, please take your money, put it in one of these envelopes, write your name on it, and write what's in it. I'll check it, seal it, and put it in the safe-deposit box," says V.C. as Johnny concludes, *Oh god! He'll know how much money everyone has! He'll know what price they can pay!*

"Sir? How much money will I need?"

"To start with? Change about $200. All right, I'm finished. Whatever you want," says V.C. as herds of yellow cows assail the GIs, "ask my people for it."

"Girls!"

"Don't worry. You'll get them," says V.C., and as the GIs empty their wallets, build their paper castles of currency, yell, "Are those tens?" "No, they're twenties!" and vie with each other like the Chinooks to show who's prepared to lose the most money in one rowdy week in Kowloon, and as Johnny thinks, *If I can make friends with V.C., I'm rich,* the yellow cows commence mooing, "You want Chinese girl? Australian? British? . . ."

V.C. sits down with Johnny and Johnny's friend. He falls down into their booth as if some disorderly soldier has shot him. "I get here," he moans in Cantonese, "at five every morning, and all day the GIs come and do I get any rest? no, all night I entertain them at the Golden Crown. Coffee," he moans to a white-shirted waiter.

"You're busy," says Johnny, compassionately tapping V.C.'s wrist. "That's good."

"*Oyo,*" says V.C. He's shorter and skinnier than Johnny, and his word means *Oy.*

"This boy," says Johnny's friend, "runs Johnny Kon Fur. Can you help him?"

"Whoever wants fur," says V.C., too drained to discuss it, "I'll send to Johnny."

"Thank you, V.C.," says Johnny. "I'll do for you as I do for the other people."

V.C. looks shocked. He knows that Johnny means "I'll give you the ten percent kickback," and tells him, "Oh no!" But he's not sincere, for that afternoon when a colonel comes to Johnny's eighth-floor apartment, when the colonel says, "My," and points to himself, and then says, "Wife," and punches his heart, when Johnny says, "Yes. You want fur for wife," and shows him an, er, American mink, when the colonel counts out $750 in eye-popping piles of $20 bills and a $10 bill, counts out the equivalent of one and a half years' salary for Johnny at James Fong Furs—that afternoon at the Astor when Johnny offers V.C. an envelope of American-currency size, well, V.C. doesn't return it but wedges it into his jacket pocket. "Thank you," says V.C., whose bulging pocket has $100 or more for every soldier, sailor, airman, marine in Hong Kong.

"No, thank *you,*" says Johnny.

HONG KONG

It's two years later and Johnny, now twenty-four, is prodigally supporting his father, mother, brothers and sisters in their famished city of Shanghai. He's also supporting a good-looking wife in Hong Kong: a Chinese who's Christian, who tells him in Cantonese, "Jesus will save you," and who sings spirited hymns with him like *God, Our Help In Ages Past* in Cantonese ("I'm Buddhist," says Johnny, "but for you I'm also Christian") in church on Sundays. The boy who slept in a morgue with grudging ghosts like a character in *The Good Earth* has moved to a smart three-bedroom (one for him and his wife, one for the baby, one for the maid) apartment on Prince Edward Road in the Capital of Capitalism.

Johnny is seldom home. He's usually at his almond-carpeted store near the ferry to Hong Kong Island, he's happily selling self-esteem to British, Australians, Americans, he's showing them identical minks while asking, "You can tell difference?" "No . . ." "You confidence in me?" "Yes . . ." "So buy the $200 more expensive." But often Johnny (moonlighting for V.C., the Chinese in charge of Rest & Recreation) and American captains, colonels, generals are in a Pentagon limousine twisting up to the summit of Hong Kong Island, or they're at a floating restaurant exploring the shark's-fin soup ("I don't eat sharks," an American says. "It just like fish," says Johnny)—exploring sweet-and-sour pork that Chinese serve to Americans who imagine that Chinese eat it, or lobsters whose mammoth antennas probably pick up Mazatlán and whose luminous eyes are lit up by Energizers, or green gelatinous geodes that Chinese with slight hyperbole call 1,000-year eggs, or they're at a ritzy nightclub watching magicians, maraca-rattlers, dancers in lion costumes, drummers, slit-skirted singers with songs about marmalade skies, marshmallow pies, kaleidoscope eyes ("I want that girl," an American says. "You can't afford her," says Johnny. "I want her for *free!*" the American says)—this last at the Golden Crown, a welcome relief from Hamburger Hill. Or, almost every night, Johnny and a dozen captains, colonels, generals are at the Oriental Club, where Johnny naughtily orders up a dozen good-looking girls (and a thirteenth for Johnny) and when they come mincing in presents them to the Americans, saying, "Chinese hospitality." Some nights

Johnny's wife discovers him and asks him in Cantonese, "What are you doing?" and Johnny says accurately, "I'm working for V.C."

He now wears a Rolex worth $20,000. Unlike a Timex, a watch that's off by a second every century, the diamond-studded machine under one of Johnny's gold cufflinks is off by a second every *day* but, hey, it's a Rolex. Oh, the rewards of making money as Johnny does! Making money is like climbing up a mainmast, where a one-foot ascent extends the horizon by ten thousand shining square feet. The higher that Johnny shinnies on the luxuriant money tree, the farther he sees and the more he's engrossed by the good things money can buy. By now his shoulders, which long, long ago in Gongjalu supported a burdened bamboo pole, bear $500 suits, $20 shirts and $2 flawless ties that Johnny with little finger-flicks can *tie,* can *tie,* can anyone ask for anything more?

Yes, every magnate in Hong Kong (and in America, too) who's high enough on the mainmast to see to Milan and its $1,000 crocodile shoes and to see to the century's end and its $100,000,000 homes can ask for more, and Johnny one night goes to V.C.'s apartment full of jut-jawed generals' photographs to ask him something intriguing. "The GIs," says Johnny in English, then switches to Cantonese. "We send them to clothing stores. So why don't you and I open one? And send them *there?*"

"No, I'm too busy," says V.C.

"And send them to our jewelry store?"

"No, I'm too old," says V.C., who's forty.

"We won't get ten percent, we'll get *forty.*"

"No, I haven't time," says V.C.

Oh, how like a Cantonese! thinks Johnny. Men from the South, and V.C. is one, are men who won't cross a street until all four traffic lights are green. Men from the South, if they have $10 they will gamble $1, but men from the cold crude country like Johnny, if they have $1 they will borrow $9 and gamble it all. "You're right, V.C.," says Johnny diplomatically. "But we'll have employees. A company has many employees."

"No, I'll lose control," says V.C.

"I promise I can control them."

"No, they will steal," says V.C.

"So they'll steal. And I'll get everything back," says Johnny, who's thinking that he'll confront the dishonest employees and say, "Mother-fuckers! Either you pay or I'll break your legs," who's thinking, *What? Do I mean it? Am I a confederate of Fatty's? Am I really contemplating join-ing the Green Gang?*

"No, I'm too busy," says V.C.

"I *promise* I can control them."

"Let's look at my photographs."

3
Blue Lantern

HONG KONG

"Is summer here," says Johnny to a British couple, cotton for her, striped serge for him, "so I give summer dis*count*," but two dozen communists interrupt him. They run by his store in their flip-flops pursued by the yellow-skinned dogs (the Chinese police) and the white-skinned pigs (the British police supervisors) in their preposterous porcine masks, and a mist like a London fog comes spookily through the store's open door. "Ah," says Johnny, the mist stimulating his mucous membranes like Szechwan eggplant. "Police make smoke."

"It's teargas!" the British gasp.

"Stay inside," says Johnny immediately, closing the door, then locking it, then serving his captive customers his Coca-Cola and selling his summer-discounted mink for $1,400. In time the customers escape, but the communist riots in Hong Kong in 1967 continue. One day there's another bomb every hour. The British, Australians, Americans, even the GIs stop coming, mannequins are the only humanoids in Johnny's gold-walled, multi-mirrored, almond-carpeted store, and Johnny is one more motionless torso till V.C. suggests that if the mountain won't come to Johnny, then Johnny should go to the mountain, should sell his fur to the GIs right in Vietnam. *Well,* thinks Johnny, *nothing ventured, nothing gained,* he drives with V.C. to Kai Tak International Airport, and, sitting in business class with

V.C. and clenching the armrests as if they were anchored to all of Asia, asking V.C. in Cantonese, "Is this noise normal?" he takes a rattling plane to . . .

Saigon

Sell fur in Vietnam? In this sauna whose heat seems a permanent attribute of the air around him? Never was Johnny so hot as when he steps onto the taxiway at Tansonhut International Airport. The asphalt is almost gelatinous, it may have been laid thirty seconds ago, *pop pop,* bubbles of air burst audibly through it, trumpeting dinosaurs wallow in it, sinking, becoming extinct—better believe what the Vietniks say, Vietnam is a quagmire indeed. His shoes going squish, Johnny takes off his jacket, loosens his suffocating tie, unbuttons his collar, tells V.C. in Cantonese, "It's very hot."

"Yes, very hot."

"Fur coats. I'm not sure I can sell them here."

"You can try."

"If I can't sell them, maybe I can sell ice cream."

"Maybe," says V.C., and the entrepreneurs fly to . . .

Danang

Up north just a hundred miles from the border, they're met by a man they befriended back in Kowloon, a marmalade-marshmallow pal from the Golden Crown, a Chinese-hospitality pal from the Oriental. He's the commander of all the U.S. marines in Vietnam, but his three shining stars are eclipsed today by the starless and barless suited shoulders of Johnny's partner V.C. Remember the old Luigi joke? Luigi who stood with the Pope on the balcony of Saint Peter's and all the people below them said, "Hey, who's the guy with Luigi?" Today amidst potted palms at the upper-echelon officers club, the colonels come crowding up to V.C. extending their hands as though they were in the Pacific reaching for life preservers, saying, "V.C.! Hello!" and "V.C.! How are you!" and "V.C.! I've heard about you, sir!" and paying no never-mind to Lieutenant General Robert Cushman, Jr.

V.C. says hello, then sits down with Johnny at *semper fidelis* chinaware and *semper fidelis* silverware at a white-linened table. At one end (raising his cabernet, saying, "To our guests from Hong Kong") is General Cushman, to his right is V.C., to his left making small talk is Johnny, then come the two-star and one-star generals, then the ambitious colonels, then well below the salt some forgettable lieutenant colonels—to the rear standing rigid as Nubian slaves, wearing holsters with .45s, are four lowly privates who Johnny keeps wondering about. *Who are they? Why are they standing there? Are they,* thinks Johnny, who hears the distant *bang* of American or VC rifles through the romantic bamboo walls, *there to protect the generals and me if the VC attack?* Like many an American man who watches the honor guard at the Tomb of the Unknowns, in Washington, he stares, even waves, at one of these statues to try to ensnare its eye: he doesn't succeed, the marine is a marble bust of Washington crossing the Delaware, is someone whose gaze is crazy-glued to the trunk of a potted palm, and the man whose concentration cracks isn't him but Johnny. "Sir?" a black steward suddenly asks him. "How do you want your steak?"

"Um, medium ware."

After the ice cream, the mints wrapped in silverfoil, the after-dinner liqueurs like B&B, and the after-dinner cigars that Johnny politely pockets, the two Chinese and their star-shouldered hosts go out past canvas sandbags as tight against one another as stones in the Great Wall of China, go to banks of the River Danang. The *bang bang* is nearer now, the marines are firing at floating twigs in case the VC are swimming behind them, but V.C. (the Chinese businessman) doesn't let the small talk falter. "How's the war going, general?" V.C. asks General Cushman.

The commander of 160,000 warriors frowns. A poster-perfect marine, a broad-shouldered, barrel-chested, ramrod-postured marine ("I'm tired. He's too much for me," a girl from the Oriental reported after a night with him), Cushman says candidly, "Well, we're near the DMZ," the border with the Vietnamese communists. "They keep coming here but I can't go there. If," he says ruefully—"if I could cross the DMZ, I could win this war. But my hands are tied."

My god. He's saying that America can't win, thinks Johnny, who now knows more about this war than America's press, America's people, and the 55,000 who'll die do. He whispers his terrible insight to V.C. in Cantonese.

"The war will last many years," whispers V.C., who's recalling the Chinese proverb that if you put your hand in wet rice flour, the flour will never come off. "The soldiers will do their job. And you and I, we'll do ours."

He's saying that we'll make money, thinks Johnny, who tells himself, *Well, why shouldn't we? So will General Cushman. So will McDonnell Douglas. So will Boeing.*

Correct. This year in Vietnam, Johnny will make many millions, but the pernicious source of his riches—the war, the deplorable war—will eventually torture his conscience, twist his whole consciousness, push him (it's paradoxical, yes) into a Chinese secret society: into the Green Gang. Read on.

DANANG

Mink-Coats-in-Calcutta Day. It starts as Johnny anticipated. On tables amidst somewhat scrawnier palms (brown spots on their fronds) at the lower-echelon officers club, Johnny has spread out his minks, foxes and weasels when *screech,* a second lieutenant comes through the spring-hinged plywood door. "Oh, great," the lieutenant exclaims, as though on Johnny's three tables he sees a practicable array of VC-seeking death rays. "We have *fur* in Vietnam." Next through the door comes a captain who the lieutenant tells, "Hey, sir, we have fur."

"What did you say?"

"We have fur!" And laughing, the lieutenant turns to Johnny and tells him, "I'm listening. Why do I need fur in Vietnam?"

Now even when Johnny was training crickets, feeding them Szechwan peppers, stabbing them like a mad picador with an excruciating straw— even when he was selling crickets in Shanghai his greatest asset was his endearing smile, his ear-to-ear crinkles, and now Johnny shines it on the lieutenant, saying in English, "Christmas coming! You send to United States!"

"Who to?"

"You got wife?"

"No."

"You got girlfriend?"

"No."

"You got," and Johnny cocks his head mischievously, lifts his eyebrows inquisitively, implies that the answer's axiomatic—"you got *mother?*"

"Yeah," the boy laughs, "I've got one."

"You buy for mother for Christmas!"

"Hey, I'm just a second lieutenant."

"So?"

"A second lieutenant can't afford fur."

"What you say?" says Johnny, looking aghast. "We got $25 here. We got $25 hat," and Johnny seizes a pillbox fashioned from weasel's tails that in Gongjalu he'd have contemptuously thrown out. "You buy $25 hat!"

"Well . . ."

"We don't know about fur, sir," the captain explains.

"You don't need to. Your woman knows and *I* know."

By now more marines are at Johnny's tables, crowding around as if Johnny were General Cushman and his weasels represented the hills and dales the marines would cross at 0500 when they attacked the DMZ.

"Sir?" one asks him. "How much is this coat?"

"In catalog $750, but I give twenty percent dis*count.*"

"The coat is $600, sir?"

"Is $600. It comes different colors, matches hair."

"What if my wife always dyes her hair?"

"Don't worry," laughs Johnny. "You buy pastel."

"I'll buy the hat," the lieutenant says.

"Yeah, and I'll buy the coat," someone says.

And ten seconds later the officers club is the bargain basement at Macy's, the marketplace at Marrakech, the street of cigarette-lighter carts in Kowloon—ten seconds later the boys storm up Suribachi, shouting, "Hey, I got *that* one!" and "Hey, I got *that* one!" and Johnny is making more money than in a month in Kowloon. No need to sell ice cream, though he could sell it to Eskimos if (like these marines) they're paid at the end of each month and if in the Arctic there's nothing to buy except ice-cream cones. One day later he opens a branch at the PX (the post exchange, as vast as a Wal-Mart) and he flies south to . . .

SAIGON

An infantryman he's not, but he flies east in a combat chopper, a Huey, his tie (colored crimson) going flop-flop in the wind that refreshingly enters the Huey's open doors. The helicopter, worth $300,000, is courtesy of a full colonel who Johnny once took to the Oriental, in Kowloon, and is a loud-mouthed machine that has Johnny absolutely shouting. *"Why fly low?"* Johnny shouts as the rotors trim the mahogany trees.

"What?" shouts the gunner, a flak-jacketed black man.

"Why fly low? Maybe hit trees!"

"You ever in a Huey?"

"What?"

"You in a Huey ever?"

"No!"

"Don' worry! We fly higher, the VC will snipe us!"

"What you say? The VC will shoot us?"

"Yeah, but I shoot 'em back!"

"What?"

"Enjoy yoursel', and I'll watch the VC!"

And from behind his machine gun the gunner glares down at the Vietnamese: at men cutting rice, at women tending buffalo, at people wearing black like the Ninjas and looking up at the deafening helicopter exactly as Johnny, age three, hiding in bushes in China, looked up at Japanese bombers, Johnny who muses today about the folly that's war, *The farmers think that we'll shoot them, and we think that they'll shoot— us,* Johnny wearing MacArthur shades, Johnny riding this Osterizer to . . .

VUNGTAU

"You come, I give dis*count,*" says Johnny, jumping out of the helicopter like a GI at a hot lima zulu, giving the gunner high five. At the
pad, the rotors blowing dirt onto Johnny's suit, Johnny's shirt, the grateful colonel welcomes him and lo! at the PX there's soon a lead pipe festooned in minks, foxes, weasels, there's soon a third branch of Johnny
Kon Fur. A bewildering thing is the bookkeeping there. A soldier buys a
$600 fur, and Johnny writes a receipt for $600, keeping the carbon copy.
A soldier buys nothing, but Johnny writes a receipt for $600, crumpling
it, chucking it out, and keeping the carbon copy. A soldier walks by, he
has three stripes and a "Smith" tag, and Johnny writes a receipt for
Sergeant Smith for $600, crumpling it, are you following me? chucking it
out, and keeping the carbon copy. "Do what I'm doing," says Johnny in
Cantonese to his Chinese employees.

"Whose names do we write down?"

"Anyone's."

"Like him? The guy over there?"

"Yes, him."

"But he's never bought any fur."

"I don't care. Write his name."

"How many names do we write?"

"$12,240 worth," says Johnny, who deposits the carbon copies and the
$12,240 (it's from his own pocket) with the PX, then takes $12,240 of
duty-free furs to his fan-humming suite at the Pacific Hotel and sells them
for double the money to Vietnamese middlemen. All right, is Johnny
felonious? Is he on the primrose path that leads as surely as A, B, C to
smuggling, drug-running, murder? Maybe so, but then so is everyone in
Vietnam, for except at the market called "black" a man who's not an
American can't buy any watches, cameras, cars or (without preposterous
effort) even any Vietnamese currency here. *The profit,* thinks Johnny, and
like businessmen everywhere thinks no further—*the profit is high at the
PX but higher at the Pacific Hotel,* and Johnny orders more fleecy furs
from Kowloon. He then boards a little bubble helicopter (*Who is this pas-*

senger? a Vietnamese cabinet minister? the pilot probably wonders) and flies at tree-trimming level to . . .

SAIGON

And into adversity. In his briefcase are letters from a dozen generals, but the "I recommend"s don't get him the smallest alcove at the PX at Tansonhut International Airport, the busiest in Vietnam. "Johnny, Johnny," says a Chinese man who manages one of the clothing stores in a spacious alcove at Tansonhut and sells $20,000 worth every day. "The PX is being bribed by Siberia Fur. No one sells fur at Tansonhut unless he's Siberia Fur."

Johnny is at the Chinese man's magnificent villa. It's night, above him the crescent moon is oven-baked emmentaler, the tips are practically melting and the moondrops coat the banana, papaya and coconut trees, coat them with pale moonglow. In the same silver light is a pool flat as glass, a man who jumps from the diving board would crack it before he splashes into the water below. The air is Tahiti balmy. In the great mansion where Johnny is, a picture window embraces all this serenity, inside on the parquet floors and the Persian rugs are rattan chairs and mahogany tables, the longest is almost bowed by the weight of hors d'oeuvres, of shrimp, chicken, blood-red beef, of fresh bananas, papayas, pears, of Jim Beam, Jack Daniels, Johnny Walker: and eating and drinking these (in addition to Johnny, who's nursing some beer) are Vietnamese girls dressed like porcelain dolls and American captains-through-colonels who run the PXs throughout Vietnam. "What sign are you?" the girls ask these tipsy military men, and on being told that it's Aries, Bacchus, whatever, they look at the men adoringly and say, "Oh, very romantic."

It's Friday. It's party time at the Chinese concessionaire's. Excusing himself from Johnny, the man moves from one to another flush-faced captain-through-colonel, invites him into an office whose ceiling is an Amazon canopy, graciously hands him an envelope whose flap is about to pop, and if (as sometimes happens) the mortified officer says, "Oh, no," the Chinese man smiles emolliently and says, "Just you know and I know it," or gives him a Rolex instead. At the sour-mash-and-scotch-loaded table, Johnny introduces himself ("I do the fur in Danang, Vung-tau") but he feels like a whippersnapper here, sure, Johnny's a half-millionaire but the host is a multi-multi and it's just human nature to want to emulate humans around us, whoever they are, whatever they do. Like everyone at this soirée and everyone else in Vietnam ("We got a good body count today," say the Public Affairs Officers), Johnny has now suc-cumbed to our civilization's great imperative: more. The twelve o'clock curfew approaching, the Americans in their green uniforms and the Viet-namese in their pastel dresses disappear in each other's company ("Please," the host tells a colonel who's about to depart alone, "let one of my Vietnamese drive you") and Johnny and his regular chauffeur depart in Johnny's Mercedes. Speeding away, they see the dry, brown, fallen fronds of palm trees skittering from them. The pale street lights are like stroboscopes, disclosing a Johnny who's angry, his mouth twisted into a W, his eyes sending lightning bolts to the back of Nguyen's shad-owed neck. He's angry at the Americans who run the PXs: not for accept-ing heavy bribes but for not accepting them from *him*.

HONG KONG

Back in Kowloon, his store without customers, his wife with another child, his search for an outstanding bribe has Johnny in a shop full of Chinese antiques, of Chinese gods made of ivory, mahogany, teak, of gods holding scepters, orbs, long wooden poles on their shoulders and, at the ends of the poles, bandanna-bags like American hobos, of gods who are drumming, fanning themselves, giggling while children tickle their ears, tickle their tummies, steal their hats. "This man, who is he?" asks Johnny in Cantonese, looking at a Chinese god who's old, bald, bearded to his waistline like Confucius, a god who's enigmatically hold-ing a very labial-looking peach, *do I dare eat it? do I dare touch it?* The person who Johnny is talking to is the owner of this phenomenal attic.

"He's the God of Long Life."

"What is he made of? Ivory?"

"Yes." He's half an elephant tusk.

"Why is he colored brown, then?"

"He's from the Ch'ing Dynasty."

"How much are you asking for him?"

"$5,000. But," the congenial owner says, "I'll give you a discount, fifty percent."

"I'll take him, please box him," says Johnny.

SAIGON

"Happy birthday," says Johnny in English, handing the God of Long Life to an American man who doesn't run the PXs but runs another chain in Vietnam: the USOs, the United Service Organizations, the stage-door canteens that "*I left my heart at*" in the lyrics of a popular song in World War II. Once again, Johnny in his mind isn't being wicked, the Chinese in all their history thought of bribes as the perquisites of government service, often as the very *raison d'être* to enter it, in the 1700s in twentieth-century dollars one unappeasable cabinet minister made more than $1,000,000,000. To rise above bribery in China (as against in America, where presidents, senators, congressmen wouldn't dream of accepting *anything*) was to rise above appetite, and Johnny isn't ashamed to tell the American man, "Please open box."

"Oh, no. What's in it?"

"I hope you liking it."

"No no. But thank you," the American says, opening the four-foot box and practically gasping, "*Oh!*" He sets the redwood stand on one of his gleaming mahogany tables—he's in his home, and Johnny is visiting him—and sets the time-stained ivory onto the redwood stand. He's now eye-to-eye with the wrinkled god. Arms folded, head tilted, eyes focused like a connoisseur's, he says to Johnny, "I love it. What's it worth?"

"No, I got very cheap."

"And this old man is—?"

"Long-Life God," says Johnny. "I wish you long life," and lo, the American (a fat and iguana-wattled civilian) has scarcely lived another day when he discovers an alcove for Johnny Kon Fur on the grunt-multitudinous floors of the Tansonhut USO and the USO in Nhatrang, Johnny gratefully tipping him the normal ten percent ("No no"). The rule at the USOs is, Johnny Kon Fur can sell nothing but fur, so Johnny establishes eighteen more companies and is soon selling fur, wood, paper, pewter, brass, jade, jewelry, watches, cameras, photos, tablecloths, wigs for the wives, etcetera: $10,000 worth every day, and Johnny is indisputably out of the whippersnapper class.

HONG KONG

Could it be? An actual customer? A man from Korea comes into Johnny Kon Fur and converses with Johnny in their common language of Pidgin English. "I saw the generals," says the Korean, pointing to the hard-jawed officers whose photos fill Johnny's windows. "So you are sell fur to the U.S. military?"

"Yes. I sell the PXs and USOs."

"I same. Have gift shop Korean PX."

"Korean PX? Never heard of."

"You know our Korean army?"

"Korea is in Vietnam, yeah, yeah."

"Also our PX is was many years."

"And you selling what kind gifts?"

"Watches, cameras, jewelries—"

"Oh, you selling everything."

"You name it, we sell it. Furs."

"How you bring into Saigon?"

"I'm smuggling," says the Korean, says it as nonchalantly as if he were saying, "I'm using United Parcel." His voice doesn't drop, his shoulders don't hunch, his eyes don't dart to the windows to see if he's being observed by lip-reading agents of Interpol—the Korean is just an Asian to whom what lawyers call smuggling isn't a criminal act but a cost-conscious one.

"Oh, smuggling. How do?" asks Johnny.

"I paying Vietnamese customs inspector."

"Who customs? I'm never got trouble."

"No, never you," the Korean laughs, his gold tooth coruscating, "you working for American. American PX no never pay Vietnamese customs inspector. American PX easy, but," the Korean sighs, "Korean PX many difficult."

"Oh, many difficult," muses Johnny.

"Yes, many danger. We paying the Vietnamese inspector, but sometimes the *big* inspector coming. And everything taking."

"Ah," says Johnny compassionately.

By now the two men are seated on Johnny's wallowing sofa. "I wondering," the Korean says, sipping from one of Johnny's flower-enameled teacups, "if you can maybe supplying me," he says this and Johnny becomes distressed, distressed at his own ineptitude, snapping his head back as if he has just remembered something important.

"Oh, I never thought about!"

"You can supplying for me?"

"Why not? We split fifty," says Johnny, and soon he's into the age-old smuggling business, packing up diamonds and jade, leather and crocodile, cameras and dirty movies in boxes he labels either PX or USO and sends for free to Vietnam via America's philanthropic wild-blue-yonder force, then in Vietnam he diverts it to the Korean, who ("I sell more high in Seoul") often diverts it right to Korea. Once more, is Johnny's conscience clear? It's adjusted for worldly reality, sure, but Johnny believes that to bring his own lawful possessions from this to that latitude without any robber barons ripping him off is scarcely unscrupulous. He doesn't think he's a criminal and doesn't suspect that Fatty, his cauldron-shaped mentor in Kowloon, considers him a top candidate for the Green Gang. In the old days in China when someone died (and was therefore reborn as a gangster, whatever) the Chinese left a blue lantern above the dear departed's door, and Johnny from Fatty's standpoint is what the Chinese secret societies call a *blue lantern* and the Mafia calls a *connected man*.

4
Vietnik

VUNGTAU

"All the leaves are brown," the girls in their shimmy-stringed miniskirts sing in sight of the China Sea,

> *And the sky is gray,*
> *I've been for a walk,*
> *On a winter's day!*

The girls are high on an outdoor stage looking down at thousands of hellishly howling soldiers and Johnny. At bases like this one he's now a familiar figure, sleeping in tents, streaking behind the sandbags when *ooo,* the rockets come in, grouching like any GI, "Fucking rockets, waking us up," driving his Jeep, watching the GIs put missiles on fighter-bombers, thinking, *if I were a Chinese spy I'd know absolutely everything,* stopping his Jeep at an MP's command, complaining, "Me look like VC?" "No, sir, but who are you?" "You want I call general? And general tell you?" listening to shimmy-stringed girls sing, *"I'd be safe and warm,"*

> *If I was in L.A.,*
> *California dreamin',*
> *On such a winter's day!*

the girls twisting, the skirts squirming, the GIs screaming, the GIs like at Victory Day in Times Square, the GIs drinking, waving their Buds, ripping their shirts off, waving these too, waving their pants, oh, no, not those, and Johnny waving his Bud and his white linen handkerchief, a wreath of embroidered violets around its K monogram. One boy climbs into a tree, another jumps onto the stage to twist with the sweating girls, *hey hey,*

> *California dreamin',*
> *On such a winter's daaay!*

"That's the last song!" the girls announce.

"No!" the GIs reprove them, shaking their Buds. "One more!"

"One more!" cries Johnny and empties his Bud on a black soldier's head.

"Hey, Johnny," the boy laughs, licking a crinkled cigarette. "You want one?"

"No, I'm no smoking."

"It's marijuana, Johnny."

"I'm no smoking either."

"Whatever you say."

"That shit, why you want it?"

The black soldier draws on his J. "We smoke it, we forget everything," he says, smiling paradisiacally, then after the encores the girls couldn't avoid without a secret tunnel to Honolulu, the soldier and Johnny go past the grapefruit trees, the pineapple trees, the telephone-pole-like palm trees into the Pacific Hotel. "I'm Airborne," the boy proclaims, drinking a Bud with Johnny at the Pacific Bar.

"A-Bonn? What mean?"

"You know parachute?" The boy drops his hand like a jellyfish descending onto a minnow, and Johnny remembers the one thousand parachutes he saw in Kowloon in *The Longest Day.*

"Yeah, I saw the movie."

"Airborne! We're tough!"

"You tough. That's good."

"The toughest there are!" the GI says. But soon his high degenerates, his cockiness goes limp, he stares at the little triangular hole in the top of his can as if he's puzzling out the Pythagorean theorem, *which side is the hypotenuse? why?* or as if his other eye has fallen into the blackness beyond it. "I got six more months in 'Nam," the boy says melancholically. "I'm worried I'm gonna die."

Now, Johnny is in Vietnam to add many multi-multis to his millionaire classification, but he's not oblivious to the Americans dying untimely around him. On his first day in Danang, he saw a stone house and, outside it, a pile of narrow aluminum bins, and he asked a nearby marine, "What that?" "The morgue," the boy answered, and Johnny said with embarrassment, "Oh. It's cold storage for the dead bodies." And once in Chulai a mournful soldier told him, "I came to Vietnam with twelve other guys, and now I'm the only one left." "I sorry," said Johnny sincerely, and far from the jungle at Johnny's bright store in Kowloon an air force colonel bought a fur coat once and Johnny mailed it to the United States. Back from the colonel's wife came a letter saying that he'd been shot down: that he'd died, and it was with more embarrassment that Johnny wrote her, "I sorry. I hope your fur will be souvenir for your dead husband." As awkward as Johnny's vocabulary is, he isn't callous about the deaths (on the average, at age nineteen) of the GIs who are enriching him, and at the palsy-walsy bar he tells the Airborne boy, "No, VC not see you."

"Why won' they?"

"You black. In jungle they see the white people easy than you."

"You bullshittin' me."

"No, you the same fuckin' color than tree. Nobody see you."

"My buddy, the VC kill' him last week!"

"He white?"

"He black. The gov'men' send a telegram."

"Teregram?"

"To his mama to tell her he's dead. Oh, Johnny," the gloomy soldier says, still staring into his black hole of Bud. "I don' wanna die."

"Maybe you lucky."

"Yeah . . ."

"Maybe not die."

"I hope not," the boy says totally hopelessly. "Well," he continues, his eyelids rising, eyes at last looking at Johnny, one dim glimmer of hope inside them, a candle flame miles away—"well, that's what the marijuana's for. We smoke it an' we forget we gonna die." He stands up and steps outside, and he rolls himself another reefer.

SAIGON

"Johnny, I need you."

"For what?"

"I need white powder."

"What that?"

"It's heroin," the American lieutenant says. A skinny, blue-eyed, blond-haired boy, the leader (or so he claims) of a platoon of thirty soldiers in the suburb of Longbinh, he's sitting tonight with Johnny on a red velvet cushion in an oak restaurant booth, enjoying ("I love it, I'll cut some for *you*") some fish with Bernaise sauce as Johnny has garlic-roasted prawns. In the pink light the lieutenant's fatigues appear to be swat-team black. "I need two kilos of it," he says imploringly. By now Vietnam is a haunted house where the VC, those invisible poltergeists—invisible snipers, invisible miners—are very visibly killing the personnel of every platoon, and a good many nervous soldiers move up from marijuana to stronger stuff, to super-nepenthe, to heroin cigarettes. The drug, the GIs buy from the Green Gang or from the bartenders, shoe-shiners, prostitutes who've bought it (or kept it on consignment) from the Green Gang, the GIs then smoke it even while standing guard in slit-windowed hooches. "I need two kilos," the skinny lieutenant tells Johnny.

"Lieutenan', I'm not white powder dealer."

"But you have friends who are. Yes?"

"Anyhow, why you want this shit?"

"To sell it to my GIs. At cost," the lieutenant quickly adds. His voice is cotton soft, and to accentuate the *cost* he says it still cotton-softer.

"You sell that many? Two kilos?"

"Yes, Johnny. A lot of guys want it."

"Are they allowed to using it?"

"No, they have to use it secretly."

"What happens MPs coming?"

"MPs use the white powder too."

"But why Americans want this shit?"

"Johnny, Johnny," the lieutenant says, the lieutenant says *Johnny* profusely though he has barely met him, "Johnny, you just don't know. We use it, we aren't scared."

"Why you scared? You supposed soldier."

"I tell you, Johnny, *you* would be scared if you're on patrol and the guy in front of you's killed and the guy in back of you's killed. You wouldn't get scared?"

"You right, lieutenan'. I get scared."

"You're laying there," the lieutenant continues. "The medics come bringing body bags. But sometimes the guys aren't dead yet. Sometimes," he says, his voice growing loud, as though he didn't comprehend that Johnny has just conceded, that Johnny has said, "I get scared," "the guys are still screaming, the screaming's the only sound around. One day one of my guys lost one of his legs, oh, god, the blood was just spouting out and the guy was rolling around like a pig and was screaming like hell. We held him down. We gave him morphine. We," and his fist slams the table, *whack*, the people at the next table glance up—"Johnny! We don't know what we're doing here! We're fighting, *kkk*," his throat constricts, to clear it he swallows some Bamouba beer, "we're fighting we don't know why! My soldiers just hate this war! Just hate it! When I see them dying, their bodies distorting the plastic bags, their blood in the mud, I feel—I feel—" The lieutenant stops. He stares over Johnny's shoulder, and Johnny turns to see what he's raptly staring at. In the next booth, the Vietnamese man? Or with him, the Vietnamese woman? No, the lieutenant's attention is on something recollected, on something in some moist mind's eye, on something unutterable and "Johnny," the boy simply says. "So that's why we're scared. And why we're using white powder. We use it, our brains aren't sharp, they're in slow motion and we just forget we're in Vietnam. We're *sleepy*."

Johnny is picturing it. In the back alleys of Kowloon, he has seen addicts chasing the dragon: taking some opium, sprinkling it onto aluminum foil, jiggling it like saucepans over a kerosene stove: the opium melting, the smoke ascending, the addicts sucking on soda straws, chasing the curling smoke. "Why are you doing this?" Johnny has sometimes scolded them in Cantonese, Johnny whose father's father's father was an incorrigible addict too, Johnny whose father sat telling him, "Never smoke opium! Never!" his father's arms crossed, his legs scrunched up, "or you'll sleep in the street like *this,*" Johnny who's promised him, "Daddy, I'll never smoke it." In Kowloon, Johnny sometimes brought rice to the hungry and haggard addicts, telling them, "Eat it, it's better for you," but he commiserates with the woeful lieutenant, too, the American sitting opposite him, his eyes wet, his ice cream uneaten, his ice-cream spoon limp in his fingers, his Bamouba drained. *But what,* thinks Johnny, *what if he isn't who he alleges? what if he's an undercover cop? why should I take this risk?* "I tell you, lieutenan'," says Johnny, who sanguinely thinks that if he does good for his fellow man, the man won't be so unchivalrous as to do evil for *him,* "I think you're nice guy. I help you."

Then, Johnny in Cantonese (*"Ngo bei chen"*) and the lieutenant in English ("It's mine") fight for the $100 check and Johnny capitulates, and the next day to his Batdat Hotel, a relic of old Indochina, all dusty and decadent elegance, the glass in the chandeliers cloudy gray, as though it's preserving precious soot, to the lobby comes one of Johnny's acquaintances, scanning the black-capped bellboys as if they might be Vietnamese plainclothesmen. A member of the Green Gang, the man brings a brown plastic shopping bag to Johnny's fifth-floor suite. He takes out a little packet, takes off a rubber band and a Chinese newspaper, takes out two white-colored bricks whose paper labels say GLOBE, bricks that on America's streets would sell for $100,000 apiece.

"White powder?" asks Johnny in Cantonese.

"Yes," says the man in the Green Gang.

"I never saw it," says Johnny and, knocking his knuckles on it, *hello? hello? is anyone home?* continues, "It's very hard. How come?"

"For transport. It comes from Bangkok."

"But how can Americans use it?"

"They mince it. They hammer it into powder. They smoke it or chase the dragon," the gangster explains, and the next afternoon the skinny lieutenant (he wasn't pretending, he isn't an army policeman) comes to the Batdat and buys the two bricks for $800 apiece, we're not on America's streets today.

"I do you favor, lieutenan'. I no make money from this. I no make penny from this," says Johnny completely truthfully. To profit from addicts: his father would surely disapprove.

DANANG

At two in the morning there's an explosion—*boom!* it's six on the Richter scale at Johnny's hotel. The bed that he's sleeping in rattles as if some brawny sergeants were at its corners, shaking them, screaming at Johnny, "*Wake up,*" and the window explodes onto Johnny's body, forty-pound frame and all. Aching, bleeding, winner of a purple heart if fate hadn't made him a Chinese civilian, Johnny is in his underwear shorts as he stumbles downstairs in the darkness to an eerie candlelit lobby full of people chattering in the *nya-nya* staccatos of Vietnamese. And *boom,* from afar come more great explosions that the Vietnamese crouch at, the Vietnamese but not Johnny. Johnny sits unperturbed, listening to a transistor radio and the U.S. Armed Forces Network. His baptism of fire this isn't, for in Shanghai at age three he was bombed by the Japanese and at age six by the Nationalists, the Chinese of Chiang Kai-Shek who'd fled to Taiwan, he's also been rocketed in his insubstantial tent in Danang. But his first bloody wounds are now.

The month is January 1968. The radio says it's a major offensive: the Tet Offensive, the New Year's Offensive, the VC exploding our ammo dump in Danang and closing our "You know parachute" bar in Vungtau and capturing part of our embassy in Saigon. At daybreak Johnny, his body tattooed by red, blue and black blemishes but his $800 suit now decorously concealing them, goes via Jeep to the U.S. marines, passing the very first soldiers he's seen in Vietnam who haven't the circumspection to be Americans. A company of VC, mostly men, partly women, most about twenty, some maybe twelve, they're sprawled in their black shirts, shorts and longies, sprawled as though from an awful flash flood along the bank of the River Danang. Like pickup sticks, the VC point north, east, south, west and all the directions in between, including downhill. All the VC are dead, perhaps from divine retribution for clubbing a sleeping capitalist with a forty-pound window frame. "The bodies," Johnny asks a marine there. "What they from?"

"They came last night. They tried to blow the bridge up. They," the boy answers, his words flowing out, his feelings bolted inside him— "they killed one of us."

"I sorry," says Johnny, who tactfully doesn't add that he's sorry for the VC, too, for the children who (like Johnny when the Japanese and the Nationalists bombed him) were on their ancestral land and not ten thousand miles away like the rigid marine he's talking to. "The war not good," says Johnny.

The boy just shuts his eyes, saying nothing.

DANANG

One night an American pilot (there is an air force base in Danang, the planes taking off with terrible roars like pneumatic drills and *arr!* roaring north to the DMZ)—an American fighter-bomber pilot tells Johnny, "I have this movie, let's see it." Sitting in his metal trailer sipping a Bud, the pilot threads up an eight-millimeter projector, the pilot is Colonel Frederick Blesse, Jr., and Johnny is here with a Coca-Cola. "It's something you've never seen," says Blesse, and turns off the trailer lights.

And whirr. On the small screen in black and white (or rather in something in between: in rain-cloud gray) are lots of amorphous blobs that if they appeared to a man's naked eye, a doctor would diagnose as posterior vitreous detachment and put the unfortunate fellow on Mydriacyl. Like fleecy clouds, the blobs drift by except for a blob that stays on the screen like a stain, never stirring, and Johnny asks Colonel Blesse, "What that?"

"My baby. The nose of my F-4."

"How you make movie this nose?"

"We mounted my camera near it. Okay," says Blesse, "we're entering communist country. And down we *go,*" as on the screen there appears a non-blob-like bridge that Blesse is diving at and sending missiles at. And then intermission: the clouds reappear, the clouds like during a typhoon, the clouds hell-bent for the Philippines, apparently, then the bridge reappears on the seasick screen. The missiles explode and Blesse crows, "Did you see? Did you see? I hit that bridge!"

"You did good job," says Johnny softly.

"Now watch my buddy," cries Blesse, and from the left comes another fighter-bomber. It too sends missiles, each of them swoops like a sparrow hawk onto a big cylindrical thing that Johnny infers is an oil, gas or water tank and that Johnny observes is next to a Vietnamese home. The tank explodes, then Blesse dives at a train that's cravenly backing into a tunnel, it's halfway in as Blesse's implacable missiles hit it. The projector drones on as the train explodes.

"You hit train, too?" asks Johnny softly.

"Yeah, I got the new Bullpup missiles."

"You did good job," says Johnny, the lights are out and Blesse can't see the torment in Johnny's squeezed-shut eyes. *And who,* thinks Johnny, *was on that unhappy train? was it VC? commuters? women with nursing babies? colonel, did you consider this?* In Shanghai when Johnny was seven an American fighter-bomber piloted by a Nationalist dropped several tons of American bombs on Shanghai's water chlorination plant. A half hour later, the people imprudent enough to live near the plant came streaming by Johnny's home. They were wheeling barrows, *clop clop,* full of children, husbands or wives, mothers or fathers, all with unnatural-looking holes, most without hands, feet, arms or legs, most of them bleeding (as were the men who were wheeling them) into bandages made of T-shirts, T-shirts imprinted with communist slogans or Mao's beneficent photograph. Weeping and wailing, the cortège went to a Catholic hospital, and Johnny followed it spellbound like someone behind a Pied Piper. In the hospital the nuns/nurses soared from barrow to barrow, laying the bloody contents on bedsheets spread on the floor, promising, "A doctor's coming," or whispering a Hail Mary. One bloody woman stood in the corridor looking as if she'd forgotten the standard procedure for getting from sunrise to sunset, *what do I do? where do I go?*

who do I talk to? what do I ask? and cuddling against her bloody breasts her horribly bloody baby. "Hurry," Johnny implored her in Shanghai dialect. "Go to the doctor," but someone told Johnny the baby was dead and the woman should be at the funeral parlor and not at this under-staffed hospital. In time Johnny left, but for years he woke up with sweat pasting him to his sheets and a panicked question inside him: *am I alive? am I dead?* and often he turned on the ceiling light to peruse every inch of his body, *is it or isn't it bloody?* And today at the colonel's movie, he wonders if on that flame-filled train was a bloody, screaming, squawking baby and, if there were, if the colonel knew it. If so, did Blesse behave like so many imperturbable military men (like those next month in My Lai) and did he enter the bloody baby into his VC body count? "You did good job," says Johnny politely.

"Yeah, I've got good weapons."

Better than in Shanghai, thinks Johnny.

"Do you want to see another reel?"

"No, I got appointment for fur," lies Johnny, and the next morning he runs down a taxiway chasing an air force cargo plane, facing its scorch-ing exhaust, obsessing, *I've got to get out of Danang.* His face almost toasted, he runs up the tailgate to a red nylon sidewall seat, he sits down amidst the crates like so much styrofoam stuffing, then *arr!* the tailgate rises and Johnny takes off. Beside him a GI starts sniffing. "Hey, man," the GI tells him, "your hair's on fire," and the two start swatting away at the exhaust-caused conflagration as Johnny escapes to Saigon.

SAIGON

Johnny will meet today with General Creighton Abrams, the new supreme commander in Vietnam. A captain in a Lincoln picks up the Chinese moviegoer ("Good morning, sir") and drives him in air-conditioned splendor past the gray-tinted crowds to Tansonhut Interna-tional Airport and what's often called the Saigon Pentagon. In its lobby is a Vietnamese hut, it's built of crooked bamboo and of curled yellowed bamboo leaves, its walls aren't there and Johnny can see the Vietnamese (wooden mannequins) doing their things: talking, listening, reading, writing, crawling through traps to an ill-lit underground tunnel. "These people, they're the VC," the captain explains, but Johnny isn't convinced of it, *maybe,* thinks Johnny, *they're simply civilians, maybe they're hiding out from American fighter-bombers,* and Johnny broods about this as he steps into Abrams' imposing office. "Hey! Mr. Kon!" says Abrams, seated at his paper-freighted desk.

"General! You got this important job!"

"Mr. Kon, I'll tell you," says Abrams. A massive man, he behaves like a giant grizzly bear who's convening the Goldilocks criminal trial. "Breaking, entering, porridge-snatching," he practically says to Johnny, "I think you're guilty. Six months." One night in Kowloon, Johnny procured a slit-skirted girl for the then three-star general but Abrams said gruffly no. "A friend of mine was in Hong Kong," Abrams growls at Johnny today. "He saw your windows there. He saw the generals' photographs there. He saw the photograph there of *me.*"

"Yes, general. We want the GIs know," says Johnny disingenuously, "that we aren't communist store."

"Well, I don't like it," Abrams growls, holding his palm up. "Don't put my photograph there."

"I sorry, general. I'll take it down," says Johnny while thinking, *But why? The other photos, the generals like them. Only this motherfucker doesn't.* "I'll put it in photograph album."

"Okay," growls Abrams, sitting back, and for the next twenty minutes (or so it seems to Johnny) the two say nothing at all. A clock on Abrams' desk goes *tick.* A dust mote descends like a spider onto a paper stamped SECRET. The paper turns yellow, as if the desk were a stove, and it's practically sepia when the ghastly silence expires. "So how is your trip to Vietnam?" Abrams asks.

"Oh, very good!" blurts Johnny. "I visit lotta bases. One time I no can come to Saigon. I heard from GIs, the VC inside Saigon." *Oh no,* thinks Johnny immediately, *I shouldn't have said that.*

But the provocative words are out, and Abrams reacts like a sleeping bear that Johnny has poked with a cattle prod. Not quite roaring, Abrams leans forward, using his palms like plows to clear a route through his numerous secrets. "Mr. Kon, I'll tell you," says Abrams in a condescending tone of "I'll tell you, Chinaman." "We had information," says Abrams, Abrams who never shared this secret with the American press or American people. "We *knew* the VC were coming. We *knew* exactly when and where. We *trapped* 'em," says Abrams, and his palms come together, *clap,* as if he's crushing an annoying gnat. "And we *destroyed* 'em," says Abrams, making a fist like a fighter who's telling a cheering crowd, "I am the greatest."

Johnny isn't cheering. He's thinking, *terrible, terrible,* thinking that Abrams has slaughtered the VC like flies, the VC on their ancestral land, the VC in sandals resisting the white invaders in fleece-lined fighter-bomber boots, *and Abrams slaughters civilians, too. Why,* thinks Johnny, *does Abrams do it? Why doesn't Abrams stop it? Why did Abrams come to Vietnam?* Fly here from the antipodes, fly ten thousand tiresome miles, *sir, is your seat belt fastened?* sleeping while sitting up, midnight becoming noon, oh, Lord, for dinner the man had scrambled eggs, what was Abrams' intention then? To kill three million civilians? To wage a war that his own marine commander said that America can't win? Or was it Abrams' ambition to be a big grizzly general? To sit behind secrets, to plow a path through these mysteries like a 35-ton tank clearing mines, to growl at visiting furriers to dress their windows like *so?* to insinuate, *I am the greatest, I kill? Abrams,* thinks Johnny, *is a war criminal,* is the Tojo of Tonkin, and if Johnny were a judge in the Hague he'd give this sentence to Abrams: *life,* and ten years to Colonel Blesse and thirty years to General Cushman and death to President Johnson, to Mr. Hey-Hey-LBJ-How-Many-Kids-Did-You-Kill-Today. Johnny wants to yell at Abrams, "Murderer! Murderer!" but Johnny tells him more temperately, "I not want to waste your time."

"Yes, I'm very busy," says Abrams.

"Thank you for your valuable time."

SAIGON

Back to the Batdat comes the white-powder lieutenant. His two kilos blown, he now needs another two, and Johnny (an unpaid middleman) sells them to him and also sells him $2,000 of counterfeit money from Fatty, the tire-tummied gangster in Kowloon. The heroin is $800 per key and the $2,000 of funny money is $500, but now it's Johnny's emerging philosophy that the Americans (who even move heroin on the CIA airline, Air America, at the request of Chiang Kai-Shek) are the most heinous criminals around, and Johnny says, "In future, lieutenan', if you buy more than five key it's $600 per key. We give dis*count*."

"Thank you, Johnny!"

"So more soldiers sleeping."

"What?"

"So less soldiers fighting."

"Ha ha! You didn't forget!"

"I not forget, lieutenan'," says Johnny, Johnny the proud philanthropist and not just the profiteer today.

HONG KONG

"It's daddy!" says Johnny in Cantonese, rejoining his son, daughter, wife in their gorgeous apartment on Prince Edward Road. He hugs them, takes off his tailored jacket, takes off his jade-jeweled necktie-clip, takes off his rose-striped necktie, then takes $100,000 from inside the tie, $100,000 that Johnny (not thinking of *The Purloined Letter,* by Poe, but of a similar story from China, the cops searching everywhere but the most obvious place)—that Johnny has blatantly smuggled past the Vietnamese customs inspectors. By now he's doing everything a genuine gangster does: smuggling, counterfeiting, drug-dealing, bribery, blackmarketeering, everything but the strong-arm stuff he eventually does this week at a Kowloon restaurant. Over iced tea at the Ritz, he purposely shouts at a cringing tailor in Cantonese, "My friend Michael says you owe him $900!"

"It's true but—"

Wham! And the two scowling men with Johnny (both from the Green Gang, one also from the Royal Police) have jumped up and grabbed the tailor's neck, and as they impatiently strangle him Johnny says, "No, there's customers here," and like two clinching heavyweights that a referee is pushing apart the gangsters grudgingly let go. "*No,*" Johnny sternly tells the restaurant owner, a man who's phoning what Johnny assumes are the Royal Police in and out of the Green Gang. "We aren't fighting. We are just arguing. *You,*" he then shouts at the tailor, a man who's probably thinking, *If they're like this in the Ritz, how are they in the alley behind it?* "You gambled the $900, didn't you? And lost every cent."

"Oh no. I've been sick."

"Pay the 900 tomorrow."

"Well—"

"Pay the 900 tomorrow! *No, don't,*" Johnny tells the restaurant owner, whose diners are tiptoeing out and whose fingers are at the phone again. "We're almost done. And *you,*" to the terror-ridden tailor. "I won't beat you. Not here. Not yet," and the tailor pays $900 to Michael the following day.

Man ist was man tut, said Goethe, men are what men do, and Johnny at age twenty-six is for all practical purposes now in the Green Gang. All that remains is to raise his right hand, scratch his right ear, and say, "I solemnly swear." Or whatever it is that postulant gangsters do.

5
Number Four Nine

NEW YORK

"Oh, yes, the minks are American," a wholesale dealer tells Johnny. It's Johnny's first trip to the Big-Nose Nation, but his passport already looks like a children's coloring book. It's two hundred pages of scribbles on red, brown, blue and green visas from Vietnam, Cambodia, Laos, from Taiwan and Thailand and from Japan and Korea, from temple-bell nations where Johnny has woken at noontime, worked in the afternoon, sat in a nightclub saying in English, "What your name?" "That nice name," and "You with me," and escorting one or more lissome girls to his grand hotel and (*viva la dolce vita*) sleeping again until noon. An hour ago he awoke in a room whose towels professed that he was at the Americana, in Manhattan. He went down for scrambled eggs, then walked by *Mame* and *Cabaret* and the treadmill headlines high in Times Square (408 AMERICAN SOLDIERS KILLED), then ventured onto the obstacle course of Seventh (or Fashion) Avenue: the dollies, the dresses on dollies, the boys propelling the dollies as if they were battering rams, *coming through,* and Johnny is now at the showroom for Mayfair Fur. "Oh, yes," says the short, skinny, skullcapped owner, a man who's spreading a thousand skins beneath a glaring fluorescent light. "Yes, all my minks are American."

"I like Canadian, too," says Johnny.

"I go to Toronto often. Leningrad too."

"Oh, yeah? Why you go Leningrad?"

"To go to the auction there."

"Oh, yeah? No Leningrad labels here."

"I—I—I've sold them out."

"You sell me Russian mink?" asks Johnny, who in his green visor looks like a mild accountant and not like a debutante gangster. "You put in American label?"

"Oh, no!"

"You sell as American mink?"

"Oh, no! I wouldn't with *you*."

"I don't mind," Johnny laughs. His philosophy is that rules are rules, never break them, and that in the furrier business the rules are to lie, dissemble, deceive, they're like the rules of the Green Gang in every credulous city in Asia. Johnny buys one thousand dubious skins for $40,000 and has them shipped to Hong Kong. He walks crosstown, then goes to the top of the Empire State, lo, Johnny is King of America, then, that night, goes to his orchestra seat at *Mame,* starring Janis Paige.

BANGKOK

Today's the day. Coincidence puts Johnny and Fatty (his gangster mentor from Kowloon) together in this exotic city, one to sell weasels and one to sell counterfeit bills with the bespectacled face of Thailand's King Bhumibol. "Remember?" asks Johnny one day in Fatty's musty hotel room in Bangkok's Chinatown, asks Johnny in Shanghai dialect. "You asked if I'd join the Green Gang? All right, I'd like to."

"Tomorrow you'll do it."

"I'm glad."

It's not as if Johnny will be a stranger to tomorrow's initiation. In grade school in China he ran a lightweight gang, a half-dozen "gangsters" that he took home after school one day (his father was working, his mother was shopping) and led through an ancient ceremony that he had gleaned from a Chinese comic book. At the family altar (a couple of shelves of ceramic gods) the children knelt in front of Kuan Kung, the God of Loyalty, and Johnny lit two red candles and a fistful of sandalwood incense that he then solemnly passed around, three to each beginner gangster. The aroma of sandalwood burdened the air as though they were in a Buddhist temple. "Now we must pray," said Johnny, and with their knees on the rug and their palms around incense the children bobbed to and fro like children on rocking horses as Johnny quoted the comic book, saying, "Now we are brothers. We're always together, richer or poorer, better or worse. We weren't born together but we will die together," and lo! the children were members of, as they called it, Our Gang.

Alas, that innocent ritual was far more impressive than the one in 1969 in Fatty's twin-bedded room at the New Empire Hotel. On its floor is a navy-blue rug, in its ceiling an O-shaped fluorescent light such as we encounter in an automobile mechanic's customer waiting room. To this economical venue comes a white-haired gangster who Fatty introduces as Mr. Chow. In the old days in Shanghai, he worked directly with Big Ear, the fungus-eared boss of the Green Gang: he bought opium in Turkey (exactly as Al Capone in Chicago bought scotch, bourbon and gin in England) and smuggled it to the God-walled ancestral temple, there to refine it into morphine, then into heroin, then into a $6,000,000 profit every month for the Green Gang. But when Johnny was six, the communists took Shanghai, and Big Ear (an addict himself, his eyes lifeless, teeth decayed, chin receded, legs inoperable) fled to his death in Hong Kong, and Mr. Chow, his lieutenant, fled to another source of this corrosive opium: to Bangkok. For twenty years he bought it in navy-blue-rugged rooms of the New Empire Hotel (he bought several pounds several minutes ago) and had a whole school of Chinese chemists in flask-filled laboratories in Bangkok refine it. His end-product, heroin, either of two-thirds purity to be smoked in a cigarette or of absolute purity to be shot through syringes into a man's bulging veins, he smuggled to addicts through all Asia and, most recently, to the forty thousand tenderfoot addicts in the American army in Vietnam. He *doesn't* smuggle it to the home front itself, to America, whose heroin comes from Istanbul to Marseilles (to the fabled docks of the French Connection) to Montreal to New York and the rest of the country through the good graces of the Italian Mafia and not any Chinese secret society. No war, please, with the Cosa Nostra!

A man of the *ancien régime* is Mr. Chow. In the hotel room he moves slowly, as though he's still wearing a gown with a column of silk-covered buttons, his hair isn't in a queue anymore but his eyes still focus on something inside his forehead, on some tender recollection from the 1920s or 1930s. Not spotting an armchair, he sits down on a bridge chair, and Johnny brings him a red-banded cup of tea and also brings from a jacket pocket (it's hot today, and the jacket is in the closet) a red envelope that he bought at a Chinatown bookstore. Inside are a lucky number of 100-baht bills, $108 of noncounterfeit bills, and Johnny uses two hands like a priest with the Eucharist to offer it to this white-haired man. "Uncle Fatty has said you'll accept me," says Johnny in Shanghai dialect. "If you accept me, I'll be very happy."

The old man sighs. He reaches out like a toll collector taking another fifty cents, and he puts the envelope listlessly into his crinkled jacket pocket. "Back in Shanghai," says Mr. Chow, "we would have had a great ceremony," then he pauses to picture it as he might picture a childhood sweetheart, *come back, little nectarine, come back.* "The ceremony was— The ceremony was— Ah, but that was Shanghai and we're in Bangkok today. I don't dislike it in Bangkok. We have many excellent chemists here. They make very pure white powder. Of course it's too hot in Bangkok, wouldn't you say? It isn't pleasant like in Shanghai, where Fatty tells me you're from. And the great ceremony (it was quite striking, really) is one that we don't have in Bangkok, alas. But," the old man continues, sighing, "you know Fatty and many American generals (or so Fatty tells me) and I accept you," and with no flourish of trumpets the blue lantern enters the Green Gang, the boy whose father said *"Don't"* has half-ambivalently done it. Johnny in Mafia slang is now a soldier, a wiseguy, and in Chinese secret society slang he's a *student,* a proud disciple of Mr. Chow's. He hasn't raised his right hand, and he hasn't taken an oath, though if he'd had the good fortune to be in Shanghai in the 1920s or 1930s he'd have unfailingly taken it and (as it happens) he'll take it several months from now. But now the old gangster simply says, "Never tell secrets. Never betray anyone. If ever your brothers," your fellow gangsters, "need your help, never refuse them. Never betray them. Never talk to police about them."

"I never will," says Johnny, who's thinking, *Of course I'll talk to police about the Green Gang. The police are in the Green Gang,* but who's also thinking excitedly that he's in the very gang among whose less homicidal alumni were the founder of the Republic of China and its leader prior to Mao. "Thank you, master," says Johnny, the dutiful student, then he and the others take the thin elevator down to the lobby, fluorescently lit, and to the main street of Chinatown, the one street in Bangkok (a city whose drivers sit in stalled traffic a total of one day every week) where automobiles roar by like at Indianapolis, *zoom,* a one-way street, a half-dozen lanes, a minute a thousand cars, then he and the others celebrate over goose feet, goose wings, and goose breast with salty garlic salt at a Chinatown restaurant.

From now on, Johnny's life as a gangster will be almost indistinguishable from his civilian life. Tomorrow, like yesterday, he'll sit and drink pineapple juice at the pool of his President Hotel and he'll grope at the Japanese singers there ("No, *giggle,* no," the Japanese girls will say). He'll take one Japanese to his room—avert your eyes—then next week he'll meet an American woman in one of the passenger lounges at Kai Tak International Airport in Hong Kong. "Excuse me," he'll say and display a Salem, "do you have a light?" and by prearrangement the tall, thin, long-haired, good-looking, yellow-dressed woman will tell him, "Yes." She'll slip him $5,000, he'll slip her some counterfeit ID cards for the U.S. Defense Department, and she'll spirit them to the man who, without ever saying why, has requisitioned them from Johnny: the Saigon white-powder lieutenant. But (like a man in the Mafia) practically everything Johnny will do will be on his own initiative and not as a man, made man, in the Green Gang.

NHATRANG

And now Johnny falls in love, though not with his wife in Kowloon. Having come to this place in Vietnam, a port full of bowl-shaped fishing boats, of palms and poinsettias, having checked out the PX here and partied all night, he's weary while buckling up on the plane to Saigon, and a Chinese girl sitting near him asks him in Cantonese, "Are you sick?" Her tone couldn't be more compassionate if Johnny were groaning aloud, if Johnny were grasping a barfing bag, if Johnny were turning seaweed green. She herself is a tall, thin, big-eyed (those eyes! a man who tripped on her lashes would plummet right in)—a beautiful girl in silky white trousers, silky white blouse.

"No, I'm just tired," says Johnny, falling in love instantaneously.

"I have some medicine for you." And from her handbag the girl withdraws a sweet-smelling vial of White Flower Oil and offers it to Johnny.

"Thank you."

"All you need do is inhale it. Then put it inside your nostrils and on your forehead. And then you'll feel fine."

"Thank you."

"I have many medicines with me. They aren't for me but for other people. Whenever I travel I carry them. That way I can help other people. My mother and I are Buddhists."

"Thank you," says Johnny. "May I also have your address?"

SAIGON

At night he calls on this kind-hearted girl. He escorts her—her name is Jonquil—and her mother, sisters, uncles, aunts, to the French, Vietnamese and Chinese food and the Japanese singers at the best nightclub in this still spirited city: the Club Maxine. Like froth on a peaceful pond is Jonquil's light laughter, and Johnny takes her and her chaperones to dinner night after night, then he has coffee alone with her. She says that though she's Chinese, she comes from Phnom Penh, Cambodia, and Johnny reports he's from Hong Kong.

"Oh, my," says Jonquil with sorrowful eyes. "I've heard about people from Hong Kong."

"What have you heard about them?"

"That they entice girls. And take them to Hong Kong. And sell them to houses of ill repute."

"It's sad, but some people do it."

"They don't let the poor girls out. They don't let them telephone. They beat them if they tell their clientele."

"Of course I'm not like that."

"The girls write, *Please help me, I'm kidnapped,* and throw the desperate messages down to the passersby."

"Myself, I don't kidnap people."

"My own best friend was kidnapped to Hong Kong. And now she's ruined and no one will marry her."

"I'm an established furrier."

"But how do I know that?" asks Jonquil, looking forlorn. "How do I know you won't lure me to Hong Kong? To sell me into depravity?"

"That just isn't me. I'm married."

"You're married?"

"Yes, I have two little children."

"Oh," says Jonquil gently. Her teacup floats on her fingertip like a magician's bewildering trick. A few days later, Johnny comes calling and Jonquil's gone—she's fled to a room in a grocery store, then to a room above a barber shop, then to a room above a clothing store. Saigon is as big as Chicago, Saigon is an intricate city, but Johnny pays off her uncles and aunts to pinpoint her. And every time Johnny finds her, Jonquil says, "No, I won't see you," and Johnny says, "But I love you," and Jonquil says, "No, you're married, you're going to sell me in Hong Kong."

Ah, love. No one has claimed that a man accords it to the most rational woman around. Jonquil's incessant subtext of "Please reassure me" and "Please re-re-reassure me" arouse compassion or call it obsession in Johnny, *She's frail. She's fragile. She needs a man to protect her. Me.* Her past, Johnny knows, is full of near-mortal wounds that Jonquil doesn't attempt to heal by transferring them to her neighbors, no, all she unloads on other people are her White Flower Oil, her lavender, chamomile, frankincense, and her Wan Hua Oil. Her mother is her foster mother, her birth mother died while delivering her, her father just vanished that day, her grandmother sheltered her but died, her sisters, uncles and aunts are foster people too, she fled to Saigon last year when rape, pillage, plunder, death were all a girl could expect in Phnom Penh, in Saigon she earns just a dollar a day doing baby-sitting, yet on her face there isn't a wrinkle, ripple, line, her face is sunrise-serene even when she's on one of her tormented audio loops.

"I worry you'll sell me in Hong Kong."

"Don't worry. I'll marry you."

"But you're already married, aren't you?"

"Yes, but I am Chinese."

"What does that have to do with it?"

"I can have another wife."

"You can?" asks Jonquil, tilting her head perplexedly. She and Johnny are having tea in the lobby of the Ambassador Hotel.

"Yes. You didn't know? A man who's a Moslem can have four wives and a Chinese man can have two, sometimes three. That's the law from the Ch'ing Dynasty. You don't have that law in Vietnam?"

"No, I've never heard of it."

"Well, Mao," says Johnny correctly (everything Johnny has said, it's correct), "had two wives and so will I. You'll be my wife in Saigon, and Isabel," his existent wife, "will be my wife in Kowloon. Isabel will have seniority, so you must respect her."

"And Isabel? Will she accept *me?*"

"Yes," says Johnny incorrectly.

"What if she comes to Saigon?"

"You'll be her little sister. But when she's here, she'll still have seniority and I'll be living with her. And when she's gone, I'll be living with you."

Jonquil considers Johnny's inventive proposal. She sips some invisible steam from her tea—a Western woman she isn't. "You'll always love me?"

"Both her and you, I'll love forever."

"You won't sell me in Hong Kong?"

"No. I'll never leave you, I'll never hurt you. As long as I live I'll care for you—this I promise. If you or I die, we'll die in each other's arms."

"You promise you won't sell me?"

"I promise I won't."

PHNOM PENH

They're married in Cambodia, that tranquil place (the rape, pillage, plunder have halted) where the tinkling of temple bells settles around them as softly as cherry blossoms. In their hotel room, Jonquil in her red flower-embroidered sarong is as flesh-meltingly beautiful as someone from Bali Hai. A man from room service brings them a breakfast of oranges, mangoes, papayas and Johnny in his blue suit and in Cantonese tells her, "I marry you."

"And Johnny, I marry you."

"And now you're married," says Jonquil's foster mother in her black sarong, concluding the short sweet ceremony. But married they're not, for at the city license bureau a clerk in slacks, not sarong, tells them in the Cambodian language, "No. It's not like in China. You need to be dressed in Cambodian clothes, and I need a photograph of it." So off in their limousine past the saronged civilians, the yellow-robed monks, the olive-uniformed soldiers, off to a photo studio equipped like one at Disneyland go Jonquil and Johnny to dress in the proper ceremonial costumes: a golden sarong for Johnny, a golden gown for Jonquil, a lei of red-banded white silk like a king snake on each of their necks. On Jonquil's head is a high silver coronet.

"You look like the king of Cambodia," Jonquil laughs.

"And you, like the beautiful queen," laughs Johnny.

"Say cheese," the photographer says in English.

HONG KONG

Oh no. Johnny must tell his Wife Number One of her little sister, his Wife Number Two. But how can he phrase it? "Oh, Isabel, I haven't mentioned—" "Oh, Isabel, I keep forgetting—" "Oh, Isabel. By the way—" No, the whole concept is one that cannot be rendered in Cantonese felicitously, though Johnny has paced around month after month attempting to parse it while out of Isabel's earshot. Thwarted by language's limitations, he then attempts it in body language: call it a Freudian slip, but Johnny starts wearing a baby-blue shirt that Jonquil gave him in Vietnam ("Where did you get it?" asks Isabel. "In Vietnam," says Johnny honestly) and Johnny, God help him, once even wears the wrong wedding ring ("What's this?" "Oh, this? A sample for the GIs. You want it?" "Uh, no"). Something not quite adding up, Isabel scratches her head, but she doesn't suspect that Johnny has gallantly wedded another wife in another port. How many women would?

Suddenly life is chop suey for Johnny, chop suey whose morsels don't blend. In town now is Jonquil, hoping to hug her dear counterpart and the mother of her two children? stepchildren? children-in-law? her niece and nephew? whatever. The communists in China think that Johnny's an American spy ("You don't know who I am," a telephone caller says, "but I'm warning you") and the British in Hong Kong think that Johnny's a communist spy ("You're being watched," says a friend in the Royal Police) and even Johnny muses, *Well, maybe I should become one.* And now as if life weren't jumbled enough . . .

HONG KONG

He now joins another gang. A student for three instructive years in the Green Gang, he adds another entry to his *Who's Who in the Under-world* by joining, what else, the Red Gang. In the Mafia a man can't claim a dual citizenship in Gambino and Genovese, say, but in the Chinese secret societies it's a philosophical principle that if trees, apples, straw-berries go from green to red, then gangsters who go from the Green to the Red (though certainly not from the Red to the Green) are in eurythmy with Nature's Way. This is true although "green" and "red" are simply puns in Chinese and although dozens of autonomous gangs, often at odds with each other, comprise the Green Gang and Red Gang. Both Greens and Reds arose in the 1600s, but the Greens (who started as sol-diers and sailors, transporting rice, and who progressed to smuggling salt) had an eminently forgettable history. Not so the Reds! Their annals are Camelot matter! A certain man in the Red Gang, a master chemist in Bangkok, a man who can transmute a tar-brown opium straight from a suppurating plant into a white, white heroin pure as Ivory, outmaneu-vering Midas, is Johnny's best friend in Bangkok. At dinner with him he's often enthused about the Reds' wondrous history, starting in the 1600s: the monks, the poisonous wine, the supernatural sword, the sword went into the wine and lo! it changed color, the sandal became a boat, the tree became a sword, blah-blah, the book went into a chest, the chest went into the sea, blah-blah, the White Tiger Pass, the White Stork Grotto, and did we forget the Precious Lamp from Persia? The man has told endless apocrypha that Johnny's heroically heeded, then he's recruited him into the roughest and toughest (although, at ten thousand members, or five times more than the Mafia, by no one's census the largest) gang in the Red Gang. Long ago, its founders worked for the Soda of Tranquil Happiness, Incorporated, so its name is the Gang of Tranquil Happiness and its nickname is Soda.

Johnny accepted alacritously. And one night outside of Kowloon the gang performs the great ceremony that the old fogies fossilized in the Green Gang don't even attempt in Shanghai anymore. The site is a well-curtained fifth-floor living room by the Chinese border, a room full of candles, sandalwood incense, censers, inscriptions in Chinese characters like

> *Six calls from the rooster,*
> *And six from the hen,*
> *Six times six*
> *Is thirty-six,*

and Δs, deltas, logos whose sides represent the heaven, earth, and man and account for the Reds' appellation in English: the Triads. The witnesses are a few "brothers" from the ten thousand ones in the Gang of Tranquil Happiness, are men whose occasional duties as robbers, extortionists, counterfeiters, kidnappers, muggers, mayhem-makers and murderers in much of Kowloon won't be alluded to in this quite pastoral ceremony. In black robes, officiating, isn't the Dragonhead (the mysterious godfather, seen as infrequently as the Wizard of Oz) but the chief priest, a skinny old man whose official title in Cantonese is Incense Master. As he commences, his first awful words to Johnny (words three centuries old) are so unspeakably secret that to write them is death and to read them isn't especially healthy—caution, proceed at your own risk.

"Tonight you will die," the priest tells Johnny in Cantonese.

Johnny says nothing, a silence that's also three centuries old.

"After that you will be reborn," the priest says in Cantonese.

Johnny still says nothing. But for his impending rebirth, the erstwhile king of Cambodia takes off his suit, shirt, undershirt, shoes and socks, all but his Jockey shorts, and on his naked knees he kneels on the scratchy carpet.

The priest resumes. "Which is of harder matter? My sword," he says in Cantonese, "or your neck?" Not having a sword tonight, the priest taps a kitchen knife on Johnny's neck, taps it as though he's knighting him.

This ceremony, thinks Johnny, *is scarier than I expected.* "My neck," says Johnny nevertheless, answering as he's been taught to, implying that he'd rather die than spill these unspeakable secrets. "I'll honor my father and mother," says Johnny, commencing a series of thirty-six oaths, "and if I don't may I drown, and may my bones remain on the ocean floor." He says the next thirty-five oaths, like "I won't steal. If I do, may I be eaten by tigers," and "I won't commit adultery. If I do, may I drown," and "I won't sell heroin. If I do, may I be hanged." To listen to all these noble pledges, a man might assume that Johnny is joining the YMCA. Next, Johnny walks under a yellow blanket, then through a red-decorated hoop, then over a kitchen pot ("the Fiery Pit") with flaming paper inside it, then on three papers inscribed *I'm floating, on calmer, water,* then past a pair of ribbons, one white, one red, all these perambulations reenacting in microcosm what the five founding fathers of all the Triads (the monks who the master chemist lectured about) did in the 1600s. Then the priest gives a succulent date to Johnny, and Johnny recites a poem he's been taught, a poem that doesn't at all refer to the muggers, mayhem-makers and murderers who he's becoming a brother of.

> *In the first month are the long-life fruits,*
> *In the second the peach and plum flowers bloom,*
> *In the third the sugar cane ushers in spring,*
> *In the fourth the nuts of the lichee ripen,*

In the fifth the honeydew melons ripen,
In the sixth . . .

etcetera, until in December come mandarin oranges and

And all this belongs to the Red Gang,

all this belongs to the Triads.

There's more. The priest takes a living chicken, cuts off its squawking head, and says, "Be loyal, or you will die like this chicken," then takes a pin, pricks one of Johnny's fingers, dips the finger into wine, and puts it in Johnny's mouth.

"It's sweet," says Johnny, as he's been taught to.

"You will live ninety-nine years," says the priest, pricking another brother's finger, dipping it into the wine, then serving the blood-tinged wine to Johnny. "If you live nine more, you'll live 108."

For three hundred years they have said this, thinks Johnny, impressed. He bows to the priest, gives him the lucky number of $108 in American dollars, takes some fire-tipped incense, recites another idyllic poem,

I worship my father heaven,
I worship my mother earth,
I worship my brother the sun,
I worship my wife the moon,
I worship . . .

then Johnny snuffs out the incense and lo, Johnny (who's still in the Green Gang) has flowed smoothly with Nature's Way by joining the Red Gang, the Triads, specifically the Gang of Tranquil Happiness. No mere student, in secret society slang he's now a number 49, a number *four nine* and not *forty-nine,* since four times nine is thirty-six and Johnny has taken thirty-six solemn oaths.

Nowhere in this great ceremony was Johnny told, "Oh, yes, and we'll commit crimes." But that night at a good restaurant where all the brothers (except for the mystery man, the Wizard of Oz: the Dragonhead) eat roasted duck, barbecued pork, and scallops, the smallest and skinniest senior member tells Johnny, "A tree grows branches. The branches grow other branches, and the tree becomes stronger. Already the Gang has many branches in Europe: in Paris, Brussels, Amsterdam, London. I hope someday you'll open branches in the United States."

"Someday," says Johnny, who isn't especially thinking of mugger-and-murderer dens but of honor-your-father-etcetera dens—"someday I'll open many."

6

Has-Been

Washington

He starts reconnoitering. He tours the Nixon White House. He makes an appointment with General Robert Cushman, Jr., the former marine commander in Vietnam and now the Deputy Director of Central Intelligence—the broad-shouldered, barrel-chested, ramrod man who right around now is procuring a wig for Howard Hunt, the Watergate burglar.

Quantico

He has steak and potatoes at the home of Lieutenant General William Thrash, a tall, white-uniformed, medal-resplendent friend from Vietnam ("Oh, general! You look great!") who now commands the U.S. Marine Education Center in Virginia. On the general's reading stand is *The Art of War*, a far-from-secret book by a Chinese author of 500-something B.C. that Johnny peruses. "Let your plans be as dark as night," says *The Art of War*.

Langley

Johnny does a U-turn. In his hotel near the CIA, he calls off his appointment with General Cushman and his appointment with Major

General James Galloway, the commander at Fort Knox, Kentucky, and books himself onto the first flight to Saigon. "What's wrong?" asks Isabel, his senior wife, who's in America with him.

"I don't know," Johnny lies.

DANANG

What's wrong isn't Johnny's other wife but Isabel's younger brother. In the all-in-the-family spirit of all Chinese, he manages a concrete warehouse full of $500,000 of fur, cloth, clothes, watches, brooches, bracelets, rings, of Buddhas made of mahogany, amber, brass, of X-rated movies that Johnny has smuggled into Vietnam—he managed it, that is, until yesterday, when he was put in a wet-walled jail as the most heinous smuggler in Vietnam's history.

SAIGON

Crime doesn't pay. Arriving on Pan American, Johnny forks out $50,000 to the police, jailers and judge to get his wife's brother out and get his own fur, etcetera, back, though the Vietnamese won't relinquish the X-rated movies unless Johnny pays so much money that, if the Vietnamese wanted to, they could shoot several sequels to *Behind the Green Door*. Also while in Saigon, Johnny has baked clams and barbecued prawns with Jonquil, his junior wife.

HONG KONG

And now from Vietnam comes the fat and bribe-baited man who runs the American USOs. "I got some problems, Johnny," he says, swilling iced coffee in an air-conditioned café and yet sweating, using his handkerchief like an athlete's towel. The café, at the Hyatt Regency, is inside a shopping mall: it's surrounded by strolling shoppers looking at rings, earrings, bracelets, the diamond-encrusted usual, and the American man almost whispers, "The Department of Defense is investigating me."

"No! I protect you!" cries Johnny, his fist hitting his shoulder twice. "The investigator come to me, I not talk! I making money from you? And I going to hurting you? I going to snitching you? No way! No way! I Johnny Kon!" Not finishing his iced tea, Johnny stands up, and all this week he leans on the other concessionaires at their glorious stores in Kowloon, asking them in Cantonese, "Has anyone questioned you?"

"Yes, some Americans did."

"What did they ask you?"

"If I ever paid the USO."

"What did you tell them?"

"No, I didn't pay them."

"Good answer," says Johnny, whose eyes are two drills doing frontal lobotomies on the Chinese concessionaires. Johnny doesn't feel he's obstructing justice. Far from it: he feels he's *obtaining* justice for his iguana-wattled friend, feels he's doing his bounden duty as a number four nine, feels he's obeying one of his thirty-six oaths, "I won't betray anyone. If I do, may I be killed by five thunderbolts." "You keep your motherfucking mouth shut," he tells the Chinese concessionaires, aiming his index finger, flicking his thumb like a pistol cock.

"I know," say the men ingratiatingly, and the DOD never gets the goods on the double-chinned director of the USOs.

N HATRANG

But troubles come in battalions, it's said. At this Vietnamese port, Johnny sells fur, wood, paper, pewter, etcetera, and also jade apples, bananas and grapes through a pig-faced, puffy-faced front man, a Filipino, who now rips off $80,000 and absconds with it to Manila. "We'll kill him," say Johnny's new gangster brothers in Cantonese, slapping their hips as if they were packing guns (and maybe they are)—it wouldn't be expensive, they say, it would be $5,000, but their voices aren't as loud as Johnny's father's in Johnny's own inner ear, and Johnny says no.

BANGKOK

And what's wrong with Fatty, Johnny's vat-tummied mentor? He's standing in fiery-furnace heat at Don Muang International Airport, he's paid off the entry people, customs people, airport police, he's paid them $5,000 but now he's surrounded by *special* police who tell him in Thai, "Forgive us. We cannot accept your bribe."

"But think of your needy children."

"No, too many people will see us."

Catastrophe. The special police open Fatty's two bags, inside are ten thousand drawings of their bespectacled king engraved on counterfeit currency, and the police go "*Ooh*" and "*Ahh*" as Fatty discreetly ambles away. He takes a taxi downtown, buys a monk's orange robes, pulls up the orange hood, rides in the back of a Daimler north. At the checkpoints he prays without words to imply that he's under a vow of silence, lest the police detect his Shanghai accent.

CHIANG MAI

Up north, close to Laos, Burma and China is the hub of the opium-morphine-heroin business in Thailand. To stroll around in Chiang Mai is to be hit upon endlessly, sometimes by heroin dealers in their forties, sometimes by heroin dealers under ten: by barefoot, blackfoot, dirt in their toenails, relentless children who ask you in English, "You want smoke?" "You want smoke something good?" "You want enough all day?" "Oh, you want maybe pure?" "It knock your head off, I swear it!" To duck into your hotel isn't respite, for the source of this heroin—the poppies, growing farther north—are depicted as if they were fleur-de-lis on the wallpaper, carpets, and T-shirts of tourists around you, on Asians, Europeans, and GIs from Vietnam with pinpointed pupils, as if they were watching the world through punctuation periods.

Eschewing the city's best nightclub, the Poppy Club, Fatty enters a Buddhist temple smelling of sandalwood, sounding of gongs. He waddles through its gold corridors looking like Buddha, changes to arctic-weather clothes, and, escorted by friends from the Green Gang and from the Chiang Mai Police, climbs the cloud-shrouded mountains (the clouds almost frozen there, like in a Chinese painting)—the mountains and valleys north of Chiang Mai. He's now in Indian Country. No constituted authorities, no men in official capacities, no Thais, Laotians or Burmese enter these thousand square miles of red-petaled poppy fields, enter what's been for the past twenty years a totally lawless land. In charge since the Chinese communists ousted them are Chinese divisions loyal to Chiang Kai-Shek, on Taiwan, Chinese divisions that, with help from the CIA, dream of damming the twentieth century and of irrupting again into China, welcomed, bewreathed, triumphant. Chinese divisions that, by order of Chiang, and with help from the CIA, buy out every poppy crop, pay the poppy growers salt, sell everything in Chiang Mai, and send the enormous profits to Chiang.

This poppy-basket of Asia, this sanctuary for Fatty, is known as the Golden Triangle. It's cold as the Himalayas here, it's night and Fatty's escorts, using flashlights, follow the trail through the forest when *click!* in the darkness they hear some rifle bolts and say to Fatty, "Don't worry. These people, they're friends." In time Fatty gets to a chilly valley and to a shack whose décor (a bamboo roof, bamboo walls, nonexistent floor: a bamboo bed, mosquito net, tumbledown table, chair: on the table a small bowl of oil, on the oil a small wooden raft, on the raft a small burning wick) is a comedown from the birds, tigers, dragons and flowers in his Kowloon apartment but is his new permanent environment. One day to this hideout in suit, shirt and tie (and wool sweater, while Fatty's in striped pajamas like a prisoner's clothes) comes Johnny, Johnny who's just had his own little climbing-and-clicking trek. "Are you all right?" asks Johnny in Shanghai dialect.

"I'm happy. You've come to see me."

"But uncle, these living conditions."

"The conditions don't bother me."

"Why are there no electric lights?"

"Ha ha, there is no electricity."

"You mean you don't have TV?"

"No, but I have this radio."

"What does the radio run on?"

"On batteries from Chiang Mai."

"You can't get batteries *here?*"

"I can't get *anything* here!" laughs Fatty. "The people here, they produce nothing except," and he points to an escort wearing an army jacket, enjoying a cigarette—"except white powder. You want some? It's cheap," says Fatty, and from his pajama pocket he takes a Marlboro cigarette, pulls out a half inch of tobacco, takes from his pocket a small plastic bottle, shakes some white powder into the gap in the Marlboro, replaces some of the tobacco, packs it, and offers it to Johnny.

"Thank you, Uncle Fatty. But no."

"It's very cheap. It's produced here," says Fatty, who then holds the cigarette to the wick, lights it, sucks it, and blissfully blows out the smoke as though it tasted like amaretto.

His indulgence distresses Johnny. Shades of the Kowloon dragonchasers! Shades of the Saigon GIs! Johnny knows from *Sing Tao,* his daily paper in Hong Kong, that half the world's heroin starts as lovely red poppies here in Fatty's backyard. He knows that it's here that the poppy growers cut the fat poppy pods, here that like resin the opium oozes forth, here and in Thailand that master chemists in Chinese secret societies—the Green Gang and the Red Gang, the Triads—use their unpleasant chemicals (charcoal, chloroform, sodium carbonate, alcohol, ammonia, acetic anhydride, hydrochloric acid, sulfuric acid, lime) to extract from the opium, morphine, and from the morphine, heroin. He knows when in Rome, do as Romans do, but he'd happily snatch the cigarette from Fatty if his respect for his mentor didn't stay him, and to keep conversation aloft he asks him, "How cheap is it?"

"The bottle was 100 baht."

"What? That's $5," gasps Johnny, who knows from the skinny lieutenant in Saigon that a bottle of fresh white powder is worth about $25,000 on any American street. "A bottle is how many cigarettes?"

"Maybe 100. Maybe 150."

"That's five cents apiece!"

"It's less than my Coca-Cola."

"It's less than your *cigarette!* But Uncle Fatty," asks Johnny, still grieved by the man's self-abasement. "Why do you use it?"

"Not for its cheapness," laughs Fatty. He taps his ashes into his Coke and says, "It's cold here, it's damp here, the oxygen's thin—the heroin is like medicine for me. Without it I'd have arthritis."

"Uncle? Do you need money?"

"Well, I lost a lot in Bangkok."

"That's what I heard," says Johnny, and from his jacket pocket he pulls out $5,000, enough for a lot of Aleve but also enough (as Johnny sadly computes) for one quarter million heroin trips.

"Thank you," says Johnny's old mentor.

SAIGON

Broke. Johnny's broke. His fur, cloth, clothes, watches, brooches, bracelets and Buddhas businesses have shut down, for it's 1972 and at the behest of the Nixon White House the GIs have withdrawn from Vietnam. A hundred thousand GIs, to be sure, haven't withdrawn physiologically, for now they're addicted to the white powder they got for $800 per brick from Johnny, from bartenders, shoe-shiners, prostitutes, from Chinese secret societies—addicted to what they smuggled (in duffel bags, even in body bags, even in *bodies* in body bags) to the United States, to what they squandered in the United States, to what they're paying the Mafia much, much more for. Also withdrawn from Vietnam are the GIs' alpha-omegas, their PXs, their OCs for Officers Club, their USOs for United Service Organization, their places where Johnny made his $10,000 daily gross. In Kowloon the lights are lit at Johnny Kon Fur, but the business belongs to Johnny's first wife: to Isabel, who finally wised up and acquired it in their inevitable divorce, and Johnny's so broke that Jonquil must sell a diamond ring for $1,000.

Once again Johnny starts at go. He buys ten thousand audiotapes in Minneapolis, smuggles them into Saigon, slices them, winds them in plastic cassettes, labels them SONY, FUJI, HITACHI. Every cassette costs him eighteen cents but Johnny sells it for fifty cents in Saigon, Bangkok, Phnom Penh. The profit! It's almost double!

PHNOM PENH

"Honey," says Jonquil in English, then switches to her newest language, to Shanghai dialect, "I worry about the communist army." It's three years later, it's 1975 and Jonquil and Johnny are at a twinkling control board in Johnny's audio studio, watching the counterfeit tapes go around as little electromagnets rearrange their molecules into the same configurations as those on the Beatles' *White Album*. Standing near Jonquil and Johnny, his feet tapping to *Ob-La-Di, Ob-La-Da,* his hips swinging, his red sarong pleating, unpleating, is the older of their two baby boys, and Johnny takes off his earphones to address him in Cantonese.

"You love the Beatles?"

"Uh!"

"You love your mommy?"

"Uh!"

"You love your daddy?"

"I'm daddy's boy!"

"Honey," says Jonquil again, for with earphones on Johnny didn't hear her, "I worry about the communists." She means the soldiers of Pol Pot, Cambodia's despot-to-be.

"Sweetheart, don't worry."

"They're ten miles away. We hear them shooting. What if they capture this city?"

"They probably will. But when I was six in Shanghai the communists captured *that*. They were well-mannered. They wore rubber sandals. They sat on the sidewalk in front of our home but not in front of our door. I told them, 'Come in, I'll get you some tea,' and they said, 'No, thank you. We mustn't go into anyone's home.' I told them, 'I'll bring the tea outside,' and they said, 'No, thank you. We mustn't accept anything.' The communist soldiers, they're decent people."

"I needn't worry about the babies?"

"No," says Johnny, watching the one in the red sarong rocking to *Rocky Raccoon.*

"Then why do I worry about them?"

Poor lovely Jonquil. The girl is addicted to answers, answers, as early as breakfast she's reaching for answers, *will they? will you? will I? why?* but the more she's served them, the more she needs them. She needs them now, but now Johnny wraps, then he dispatches the Beatles (and also the Rolling Stones) by go-go smuggling ships to Saigon, then he buys airplane tickets to Saigon to pick up the $10,000 profits. He and Jonquil ride to the airport, ten miles away, as at the front of their bus the stewardess practically parodies the airline announcements that you and I are so fond of. "Ladies and gentlemen," the stewardess says in English, says so exquisitely calmly that no one would think (without looking) that in front of the bus is a Jeep of gun-slinging soldiers, helmets down to their eyebrows, eyes peering out like mice under stones, peering at empty paddies flashing by like leaves in a great tornado, "at Pochiton International Airport go to the aircraft directly, please. Go on board quickly. Sit down quickly."

"Honey? Why quickly?" asks Jonquil in Shanghai dialect.

"She's being cautious," says Johnny—he's wrong, for as soon as they're inside the terminal, *boom!* a communist rocket explodes outside it, some plaster comes down and Jonquil drops gracefully to one of her white-trousered knees. "Don't worry," says Johnny, kneeling beside her.

"I just worry about the babies."

"I'm glad they aren't here with us."

"But shouldn't they come to Saigon?"

"No, sweetheart, there's a *war* in Saigon."

And *boom!* another rocket explodes, and "Ladies and gentlemen," the stewardess says in English exquisitely calmly, "the flight is temporarily canceled," and the bus, the Jeep, the scowling soldiers, and Johnny and Jonquil return to Phnom Penh. "In two hours," the stewardess promises, "we will depart again to Pochiton," then to this downtown terminal come Jonquil's foster mother and Johnny and Jonquil's cherubic sons, Jonquil kissing and kissing them as though she's going to Jupiter and won't be kissing them again until 2001. In her purse are two children's tickets to Saigon, tickets she doesn't tell Johnny about, Johnny she's constantly thinking about, *He is my husband. He is my master. He is someone like this,* her eyes looking upward, *and I am like this,* her eyes looking downward, *and I must obey him.*

"Husband," says Jonquil respectfully, "shouldn't the children come to Saigon?"

"No, mommy, they're safer here," says Johnny, and Jonquil's mother takes them home as Johnny and Jonquil practically flee on the bus to the airport, double-time to the runway, climb up the mobile stairway, board the already-roaring jet, and listen empathically to the at-last-amok stewardess.

"Quick! Quick! Do not sit where you're supposed to! Sit *anywhere*," the stewardess cries in English, disclosing that in her arteries there isn't iced lemonade but the more traditional human blood. "You sit *there!* And you sit *there!* Fasten your seat belts! We're taking off!" And with some passengers standing, the plane does indeed achieve V_2, then climbs to the sky like a Roman candle. "Ladies and gentlemen," the stewardess says in English exquisitely calmly, "welcome to Air Vietnam."

"Honey," says Jonquil in Shanghai dialect, looking down worriedly at the rapidly shrinking city. "It's dangerous there. Shouldn't the children have come with us?"

SAIGON

An hour later they're at Tansonhut, it's frantic, it's just frenetic, everyone's running north and south simultaneously, three years ago the Americans left and now it's the Vietnamese GHQ, and Johnny and Jonquil visit a friend who's a Vietnamese general. "Johnny! Why you here?" the man says in English despondently. "Up north there's a VC offensive! We've just lost Hue! We've just lost Danang!" He looks at his watch as though it's a 21st-century pager with a new message for him and says, "And now lost Dalat, pretty Dalat! I have vacation villa there!"

"I not know," Johnny winces.

"One month we'll lost Saigon!"

"I not know," says Johnny, then he and Jonquil ride to the Batdat Hotel, Johnny to its musty restaurant to talk to a friend about the coming catastrophe and Jonquil (who's pregnant again) to a fifth-floor suite to worry about her children in Phnom Penh.

The coming catastrophe. It's not cataclysmic to Johnny's friend, a Chinese who smuggles clothes to the officers club in Can Tho. An addict to Chinese poker (one card up, one card down, one card up), the man is now doing daring gambling at the Batdat Restaurant. While snacking on Marlboros, lighting them at his red-and-white-checkerboard tablecloth like so many crêpes flambés, he's whispering conspiratorially to one or another of dozens of Chinese men, men who rush off and soon rush back with shoeboxes wrapped in newspapers wrapped in rubber bands—with shoeboxes full of American dollars. "Money! Money! I'm making money!" he crows to Johnny in Cantonese.

"How are you making it?"

"I don't smuggle anything into Vietnam!"

"I don't understand."

"I smuggle everything *out* of Vietnam!"

"Like what, exactly?"

"Like gold! It's heavy and the Vietnamese generals don't want it. I buy their gold for $150 and sell it in Hong Kong for $300. And generals themselves! For $2,000 apiece, I smuggle the *generals* to Hong Kong. But the most money-making item," the man says excitedly while he lips a Marlboro, lights it, and lays it uninhaled in a steel ashtray, its smoke slowly rising, "is motorcycles, is motorcycles, hey, Johnny? You want to go into that business with me?"

"What motorcycles?"

"They're in Danang," the man continues excitedly, and he lights another cigarette. "There's thousands of them in Danang. They're abandoned on every street in—"

"Danang is full of VC."

"So what? You and I, we'll charter a freighter and sail to Danang and dock—" He stops. He peers around the restaurant for any Cantonese eavesdroppers. He detects none and says, "We'll dock in Danang and—"

"The VC will fire at us."

"No, Johnny! We'll be on the deck, we'll be raising our hands, we'll be waving white flags," and the man waves his hand energetically, the waiters turning and probably thinking, *Is he beckoning us?* "and the VC will know we're friendly. And they'll—"

"Arrest us for spying?"

"No, because we're Chinese! You and I! And the captain! And crew!" and on his four fingers the man ticks these people off. "We're all Chinese communists, we're on the VC side!"

"We work with Americans."

"Yes, but I work with them in the Delta and not Danang! The VC up in Danang don't know about me."

"But they'll find out."

"No, not this month," the man exults—the month is April 1975, and the VC are coursing down to Saigon. "They haven't taken the Delta yet. They haven't seen my dossier yet."

"All right," says Johnny, softening somewhat. He sips his coffee thoughtfully and says, "So the VC don't kill us or jail us. They stop us and ask us, 'Who are you?' What then?"

"We tell them we're businessmen. We tell them we're exporting motorcycles. And then we pay them off."

"What if the VC refuse?"

"If they refuse $5,000, we raise it to $10,000. If they refuse *that,* well, hell—we raise it to $15,000."

"What if a VC general—"

"We pay him $20,000."

"You're taking chances," says Johnny. "This isn't the Vietnamese army, this is the VC. They might even be afraid of $1."

"*What?*" the man practically yells. "I'm talking money, American money! You think these people don't want it? Ten, fifteen, twenty years at war and now they don't want it? And now the war's over? And now they don't want it? Money? Green money?" He grabs Johnny's hand, and he shoves his other hand close to Johnny's nose, rubbing his thumb and index finger together. "You think the VC aren't human beings?"

"Maybe you're right," muses Johnny. To him, the thumb-finger gesture is so seductive that he can't imagine it wouldn't convert a simple, sandal-shoed soldier, especially if in those fingers are $5,000, $10,000 or $15,000. Money, money—to Johnny (and not just Johnny) it's practically incandescent, it's full of electrified neon, it blinds him to practical realities. His only acquaintance who is above pecuniary temptations is Jonquil, his saintly wife. Once, when wooing her, Johnny generously gave her $500, her salary for a whole year, but Jonquil returned it and sweetly said, "No, I don't work for you," and Johnny was suddenly speechless, thinking, *I don't know anyone like her.* "Maybe," he tells his companion today, "we pay the VC counterfeit currency. What would the profit be?"

"Let's see. The freighter is $50,000. The bribes are $50,000, perhaps. Five thousand motorcycles, smuggle them into Singapore, sell them for $200 apiece, that's $1,000,000. The profit," the man computes, his eyes shining like Long John Silver's in a Chinese illustrated edition of *Treasure Island* that Johnny once read in Shanghai, like Silver's on seeing the sequins, the double guineas, and the doubloons in the cave on Skeleton Island—"the profit is $900,000. Nine hundred percent."

"Wow," says Johnny in Cantonese.

"Shh," says the man, his hand flat, his fingers apart, his hand wagging meaningfully, his eyes surveying the restaurant for any obstinate eaves-droppers. He picks up his half-burnt cigarette stub, sucks it like a bee taking nectar, whispers to Johnny, "You with me?"

"I'll ask Jonquil," says Johnny, then goes to his suite to get his wife's imprimatur, his wife whose brains aren't fried.

"Honey," she tells him, gazing straight through his eyeballs, gazing at his very retinas. "We don't need $900,000. We need our babies and we need each other. What do we need after that? Just rice." Her voice is like lavender and eucalyptus, the constituents of her White Flower Oil, and Johnny decides to forgo his *Soldier of Fortune* adventure. His friend at the restaurant sails to Danang stoutheartedly. He doesn't get any motor-cycles there, but he gets many empty cannon shells—he gets many glit-tering tons of brass, and he makes millions of mint-green dollars.

SAIGON

"My babies! My babies!" cries Jonquil, her fingers on her temples lest they explode and her gray matter splatter the Batdat Hotel. It's still April 1975, and on TV she's heard that the communists have taken Phnom Penh and established a Reign of Terror, not chopping off heads but hammering nails into them: into doctors, lawyers, intellectuals, urbanites. "When will I see my *babies?*" cries Jonquil in Shanghai dialect.

"Don't worry," says Johnny, the man who assured her at Pochiton International Airport, "I'm glad they aren't with us." "Your mother will spirit them here to Saigon. She knows the way."

"But when will I *see* them?"

"You'll see them."

"When?"

And round and round in this circle game go Johnny and Jonquil. Then, Johnny picks up his Beatles profits, converts them to crinkly leaves of gold, puts some in his wing-tip shoes, puts more in his false-bottomed baggage, trudges by customs at Tansonhut, boards a plane to Hong Kong. His plan is, Jonquil will follow him, but the shifting sands of the war intercept her: the VC attack Saigon, the VC in their green helmets, the VC not shooting but shaking hands with Vietnamese civilians, the VC fusing the North and South into the unified communist country of Vietnam. Still at the Batdat, Jonquil calls up Hong Kong and Phnom Penh but the overworked operator tells her, "We're not getting through." Alone, apprehensive, sleepless, pregnant, Jonquil miscarries. She becomes ill, but she boards a bus to the border to wait for her mother and her beloved babies.

THIEN NGON

Deep in the Vietnamese jungle, Jonquil's bus leaves the rutted road, rolls down the wet embankment, and smashes against a mahogany tree, and Jonquil smashes against the window at twenty or thirty mph. Many hours later, the communist soldiers come to pull the dead passengers out.

DA CAO

Deep in the Cambodian jungle, Jonquil's mother, Jonquil's little sister, and Jonquil's sick children lie on the soggy ground, asleep. Perhaps there's a moon above them, but if there is there's no way to know it in this lightless cathedral. A month ago the communists came to Jonquil's family's apartment, acting unlike the communists at Johnny's door in Shanghai: they leveled some rifles, crying like Nazis except not in German, "Get out! Get out!" "Where do we go?" *"Get out!"* And seizing a ragged rice bag, the rice quickly trickling out, Jonquil's mother and Jonquil's sister carried the children into the jungle, then day by day they walked toward the Vietnamese border. They drank from the muddy rivers, ate the squash, pumpkin, banana leaves, told the communist soldiers, "Please feed us," instead got beaten by two-by-fours, stole a sweet-meat squash from a farm although a man who'd been walking with them and who'd stolen some corn had been tied to a sturdy mahogany tree and fed to a prowling tiger. At night Jonquil's mother built huts, but always the communists torched them, so tonight she, the sister, and the two babies sleep on the jungle mulch near Da Cao.

They wake before dawn. But now the younger baby has diarrhea, and, to treat him, the mother feeds him some guava leaves. The baby also has fever, and the mother feeds him some cotton leaves—the two folk remedies work for a while but the baby inevitably dies, and Jonquil's mother buries him in the sodden mulch. For another four months she, Jonquil's sister, and Jonquil's other baby ("I'm daddy's boy") walk east, or west when the communists order them to, but then diarrhea overtakes that baby too. "I want to see daddy," he cries in Cantonese, his hand (as always) holding his daddy's handkerchief, his hair almost touching his shoulders: no one but daddy must cut it.

"You'll see him soon. But first," says Jonquil's mother, "I'll cut your hair."

"All right," the baby says, his hair gets cut, the guavas don't work, he pathetically dies, and Jonquil's mother buries him in the all-consuming mulch. For two more months, she and the sister (eleven years old) go east and west, she soon develops a fever herself, and one night in the black jungle she wakes up and thinks that Buddha is smiling upon her.

"Hee-hee-hee," Buddha giggles, Buddha kneeling behind her, his face floating right above her, his face appearing upside-down. "Don't worry, daughter, you'll get to Vietnam."

"But how?"

"Hee-hee-hee. Walk east for 280 kilometers."

"Why 280?"

"*Hee-hee-hee.* Walk it and then you'll know."

"Thank you, Buddha," says Jonquil's mother, and in the morning she and the sister start walking determinedly east. The sun is a red-hot hammer, beneath it the road is like melba toast, and at a checkpoint they pass some gun-toting communist soldiers.

"*You!*" one communist cries to Jonquil's mother in the Cambodian language. "*Who are you?*"

HONG KONG

Johnny is living with Isabel, his very tolerant ex. "You're broke," she's told him in Cantonese. "You should stay in the guest room," and Johnny is doing so, waking at midnight, walking to the living room, sitting, thinking, *Why doesn't Jonquil phone me? cable me? write me? Why doesn't Jonquil's mother? Why doesn't Jonquil's sister?* thinking about his babies, the red-saronged one and the younger one, *They're not in Kowloon, I didn't bring them out, I brought out my gold instead, now I see it: I cared about money more than I cared about them.* At night sometimes, Isabel joins him and asks him, "Why aren't you sleeping?"

"I'm thinking . . ."

"I understand." At breakfast this good Christian woman mixes some eggs, flour, soybean milk, and sesame seeds into Chinese pancakes for Johnny, then Johnny takes the ferry to Hong Kong Island and walks by Gucci, Tiffany, Louis Vuitton, by the glitzy golden pagoda of King Fook Jewellery, its windows full of $300,000 watches, its Sikhs with shotguns guarding them, then all day Johnny sits in a friend's export-import office. When the telephone rings (and it does every minute) he looks up desperately and asks, "Is it her?"

"Not yet."

At night he walks, takes the ferry, walks back to Isabel's apartment. A half year passes, there's no news of Jonquil or Jonquil's mother, Jonquil's sister, the *Ob-La-Di* baby, the younger one, and Johnny senses, *I'm cracking up, I'm falling apart, I've got to do something other than this.* Never was Johnny a man who just lounged around, lounged on a beach until one or another random mango took it upon itself to fall within reach. As empty as Johnny's world is, his Vietnam gone, Cambodia gone, fortune most of its zeroes gone, as empty as his Jonquilless, childless world is, Johnny at last becomes proactive. He borrows $5,000, then opens a rabbit-fur factory near the old kindergarten where he once washed the blackboards, mopped the floors, cleaned the toilets with Comet, slept on the desk, and watched the slit-skirted women go mincing into the Ritz, the nightclub run by the Green Gang. At age thirty-two, Johnny is starting again at square one.

7

White Paper Fan

HONG KONG

One day there's a knock at the factory door, and a man in white slacks, white jacket, delivers a telegram to Johnny. Written in English, its words are "ARRIVING ON AIR FRANCE TONIGHT," its startling signature is JONQUIL, but when Johnny in near delirium rushes to Kai Tak International Airport he learns that the airplane left Saigon but then went methodically west, not east, went on a heading to Paris, and all night it doesn't come in as Johnny sits twisting in a passenger lounge in a chair of poinsettia red. A man who's falling, falling, reaching for any random branch, any tangible thing to grab at, Johnny returns to his factory (its name is Imperial Fur, he's divorced from Johnny Kon Fur) and topples asleep in his office when *ring!* on the phone it's Jonquil, saying in Shanghai dialect, "I'm here!" By taxis they rush to a small hotel on Great George Street, Johnny in pinstripes and Jonquil in rippling white, an angel dispatched by God to this needy terrestrial. She rushes to Johnny's arms and sobs, "I love you!"

"Finally! I got you back!"

"Did you get my letters?"

"No, they never came."

"I went to Thien Ngon. It's on the Cambodian border. My bus crashed and lots of passengers died and I was terribly injured. My teeth were knocked out. I climbed out the window, and I got porcelain teeth in Saigon. But Johnny—"

"The teeth look good."

"—Our *babies*. Did you hear anything from Phnom Penh?"

"No. But they'll come to Hong Kong."

"Are you really sure?"

"Yes, I am."

"You *really* are sure?" asks Jonquil the next afternoon as they stroll in Victoria Park, the one great traffic island, the one great grassy oasis in Hong Kong, a place where instead of high-rising steel are palm trees, eucalyptuses, flower-bearing trees like the flame-of-the-forests, pizza-leafed trees like the elephant-ears, coconut, candlenut, almond trees, peltophorums whose leaves are like exquisite lace fans. Two years ago the older son ("*Ob-La-Di, Ob-La-Da*") was playing in this very sanctuary, was sprawling on its silver-dragon benches, riding its coil-footed hobby horses, swinging on swings, sliding on slides, calling *hello* to the red-eyed cranes as Jonquil led him protectively past the poisonous chin-aberry trees, and now Jonquil asks Johnny, "You *really* are sure?"

"Yes, mommy. The babies will come to Hong Kong."

"We'll have enough babies then. We won't need more."

Johnny says nothing. Near them a man is doing tai chi.

"More babies," says Jonquil, "would be burdensome to me."

Tai chi. It's like addressing a golf ball for sixty minutes.

"I've started taking pills," says Jonquil.

"What pills?" Johnny asks.

"For birth control."

"Sweetheart," says Johnny carefully. "And while you're taking them, what will you do? Sit home alone? Worry about the babies in Phnom Penh? Wait for the babies to come to Hong Kong? I work hard, and I want to come home to my children and you. What if," says Johnny carefully, for he's never told his virtuous wife that he's an accredited gangster, a man who might be murdered someday, be shot, be stabbed, be stowed on an ocher-sailed junk and fed to the great white sharks—"what if something happens to me? You won't want to be left alone. You'll want children around you."

"I love you," whispers Jonquil.

PARIS

Pregnant again, Jonquil now lives with Johnny on the Avenue de Choisy near the Place d'Italie in Paris's Chinatown, they live in a left-bank picture-windowed apartment so that their coming child will be a French citizen. Johnny drinks Burgundy, with gusto devours *escargot,* with great effort says *"Bonjour,"* but even beneath a guillotine he couldn't order *civet de lapin à la française.* A bunny? A cuddly bunny? Even when he was starving in Gongjalu, Johnny couldn't eat a rabbit, nor can he now endure *fromage*—his countrymen aren't omnivorous, the Chinese relish a cat, rat, snake (they fry it with pickled tofu) or the brains of a living, shivering, shrieking monkey, but Gorgonzola is something else.

In Paris in the Year of the Dragon, Jonquil delivers another *bébé,* and Johnny says in Shanghai dialect, "Good. A brother for the babies in Phnom Penh."

BUDAPEST

Like a black shihtsu, a mass of black hair is romping on top of a wild violin at the Old Orszaghaz Restaurant. *"She was a Transylvanian,"* a gypsy sings in his language to Johnny and his Hungarian associates, Hungarians who have used cattle prods to kill ten million rabbits that Johnny won't eat but will buy, eviscerate, ship halfway around the world to Kowloon—his fur factory and his four hundred workers are now in Kowloon—dye, cut, stitch, euphemistically label *fun fur,* ship halfway around the world to Hamburg, and sell to European teenyboppers. *"She laughed as she read my palm,"* the gypsy continues, and Johnny in English sighs, "So nice. So romantic. I wish Jonquil with me."

VALENCIA

"Macho, macho man," sing the Village People. Johnny, who's come to Spain to buy more electrocuted rabbits, is disco-dancing at the beach tonight with the French, German and American women tourists, with the men-conscious women. *"Bonjour,"* he says to a French one, her

panties peeping out from her miniskirt, her bra from her V-necked top, her hand often hoisting her red Cinzano.

"*Bonsoir,*" she corrects him playfully.

"You tourist?" Johnny asks in English.

"*Oui oui.* You not speak French?"

"My wife in Paris speak well," Johnny says. "I go to school in Paris, but I no learn it. But maybe if I have French girl, then I learn fast."

"Ooh! You are naughty man!"

"You are beautiful woman," Johnny says, then he lifts his rare alcoholic drink (a scotch) and tells her, "Cheers." Above him the moon is a piece of eight on a velvet-covered countertop. "Come. We go dancing," Johnny says, and he and his *jeune fille* disco-dance to the sounds of the Village People,

> *You can best believe that*
> *He's a macho man!*
> *He's the special godson*
> *In anybody's land!*

Like pennies from heaven, the moonlight dapples their twinkling toes.

PYONGYANG

Here people march to a different drum. "*You dirty Korean, I'll kill you,*" a big-nosed basso sings in Korean at a chandeliered opera house in North Korea. His costume a suit, shirt, and tie, the basso whips out a pistol and *bang!* a tenor falls to the boards intact: the tenor then pulls out a pistol and *bang!* and kills the impertinent basso. "He killed the American spy," a Korean companion whispers to Johnny in English, Johnny in the coveted front row, the footlights forming his bib, the gunpowder pricking his nostrils, the *bang!* and the *bang!* boxing his ears. "The opera has ended now," the Korean whispers.

"I liked it. I loved it," says Johnny, who's come to this communist country to buy more unfilleted fun fur. In spite of (or maybe because of) his epic tour of Vietnam, he feels that the big-nosed basso who sang, "*I'll kill you,*" has captured the quiddities of American soldiers. In grade school one day in Shanghai, Johnny portrayed an American black man who American soldiers assaulted, yelling at him in Shanghai dialect, "You're black! We'll kill you!" Like someone in Chinese opera, Johnny wore a curly black wig, and his face was blackened by shoe polish blended with Vaseline—his face in this greasepaint felt like a hippopotamus's, a hippo's that's rolling in an African wallow. "Don't kill me!" Johnny the actor implored the American soldiers, raising his hands and his hoe, but after his one fleeting line the callous soldiers commenced to club him and Johnny died on the grade-school stage. His eyelids down, he couldn't see, but his classmates portraying the Chinese army snatched the hat off and shot Uncle Sam, a dénouement like the one tonight at the Pyongyang opera house. "Such beautiful story," says Johnny in English, applauding. "Such beautiful music."

One shouldn't say, but the fun furs that Johnny is shopping for in Korea are dogs. Once Johnny owned a dog in Shanghai, a mutt that he often tossed a red rubber ball to. Sometimes in Shanghai the beggars wore dog fur, but not till the mid-1970s did the European bourgeoisie adopt its Fidos in place of minks, lynxes, and Chinese weasels. One day at Imperial Fur, in Kowloon, a German importer asked Johnny in English, "Do you carry dogs?" "Yeah, yeah," Johnny answered nimbly, "I also carry cats," and within days he was buying dogs in China, Australia (dingo dogs) and now North Korea. Arriving at Sunan International Airport, Johnny was met by the managers (all wearing pinstripes, all wearing buttons with pictures of Kim, their permanent premier) of the North Korean Animal Attribute Corporation. Johnny was taken to a great hotel whose other clients consisted of prowling plainclothesmen, and he was served a dinner of spherical buns that the Koreans declined, explaining in English, "We aren't allowed to dine with foreigners." He was taken to the gory opera, and now (the next day) he's taken to an enormous doghouse, where he buys 200,000 pooches for $2 each that he'll ship to his new factory in Shanghai, dye, cut, stitch, and call fun fur.

"I like a Kim button, too," says Johnny.

"You aren't allowed one," say his hosts.

CANNES

Lined up like corpses at a county morgue, their heads pointed north, their feet pointed south, their shoulders abutting one another, lined up on yellow chaises longues at the Carlton are hundreds of motionless topless women. Not one reincarnates herself to walk to the Mediterranean, to wade, splash, float upon it, or to swim to Sardinia, not one stands up to get herself a Bollinger champagne, a liquid that waiters in short white pants might as well inject in their stomachs through needles. The air is almost impenetrable from the stench of Lancaster suntan oil. On the beach walking by this ghastly tableau is Johnny, who misadvisedly came here to enjoy the Mediterranean. He eyeballs a topless woman who yes! who moves! who waves two fingers at him! and Johnny replies with the same vague cub scout salute. Then, faithful to Jonquil, he slowly walks on.

OSLO

"*Rudoph*," sings Johnny in English,

> *Rudoph the Red-Nosed Reindeer*
> *Had a wary shiny nose,*
> *And if . . .*

It's winter, there's snow in the trolley-car tracks, and Johnny (who's come to Norway to buy something orthodox: minks) is singing what his Year of the Dragon son and his new Year of the Monkey son (who was born in Meriden, Connecticut, an American citizen) somewhat imperfectly taught him. He segues from *Rudolph* to *Jingle Bells* and then asks in Shanghai dialect, "You know about Santa Claus?"

"Um," says the girl who's riding with him. A bright-eyed Chinese, she recently implemented the obviously inevitable by having sex in Oslo with Johnny.

"Santa Claus. He led the reindeer all the way. He put the presents in children's beds. The story of Santa Claus comes from Norway."

"Oh," says the Chinese girl. They pass a brick building with a black-and-white mural of Munch's *The Scream*. "I love you, Johnny," says the Chinese girl.

"I love you too."

"Will you get divorced? Will you marry me?"

"No. I told Jonquil that I'd never leave her."

Subdued, they continue to Akershus Castle.

BANGKOK

Oh no. Not more dogs. At six a.m., the sun is scrubbing the golden cones on Bangkok's fairyland temples and Johnny in his Toyota is tailing the rumbling truck of Bangkok's accredited dogcatcher—*woof!* On the long-shadowed street, the catcher descries one of man's best friends, one of Bangkok's ten million derelict dogs. The dogcatcher stops (and Johnny stops too) and silently steps to the street, extends a long pole, pulls a long rope, nooses the mongrel, *woof woof,* then takes it (and three hundred more, as Johnny still trails him) to Bangkok's monumental pound. Inside it as Johnny watches, a man in a lab coat empties a bottle with a jolly-roger label into some Alpo, something like that, then feeds the wet Alpo to his menagerie, feeds it to dogs that half an hour later are wincing, writhing, not going *woof* but howling, wailing, looking at Johnny with eyes that ask, "Are you behind this? You and your fun fur? You and your chichi teenyboppers?" *Oh god,* Johnny thinks as packs of the pets emeritus collapse around him. *It's cruel! It's uncivilized! They're dying like Jews in World War II!* Turning to his manager in Bangkok, a Chinese man who's escorting him, Johnny says in Mandarin, "But we're supposed to be Buddhists."

"We are," says Johnny's manager sadly. "And that's what's costing us. The people in this pound don't like this. They want more money for it. And our own factory workers, they work for a day and can't take it. And quit."

"They can't take *what?*"

"Come, I'll show you," says Johnny's cadaverous manager, and off they go to Johnny's secluded factory well past Don Muang International

Airport. A grove of bamboo poles covered by bamboo roofs, the factory reeks of something so stomach-inverting that Johnny must take out his handkerchief and use its linen, embroidered violets, and K monogram to filter the air around him. He presses this to his nose while watching the factory workers (all Buddhists, and all as devoutly drunk as the SS at Auschwitz) carry dead dogs in, hook them onto the bamboo poles, cut holes in their pendulous legs, put rubber hoses into these holes as you and I do into tire valves, then turn on an air pump, *sssss!* As the dogs blow up like balloons in the Macy's Parade, Johnny almost chokes on his papaya breakfast.

"What's this?" Johnny almost gags.

"I invented it," says his proud manager. "At first we used kitchen knives, but we needed several minutes per dog and now we use air to sever their skins from their meat. We have mass production now. I'll show you," the man continues, and he escorts his handkerchief-clasping boss to an even smellier shed. In it the boozy workers are dumping the innards of two dozen bowwows into a vat of boiling water, cooking them, scooping them out, and tossing them into a pond of unfastidious fish, of big, fat, omnivorous fish. "Unlike us Chinese," explains Johnny's manager, "the Thais have no stomach for dogmeat. But they like fish."

"So do I," says Johnny, "but I wouldn't eat *those*."

"Don't worry. I don't disclose how I feed them."

For several seconds, Johnny reflects on his fun-fur process in Bangkok. Is it unethical? Is it against the golden rule as well as the Buddhist commandments? A silken mink from Norway, is its trip from the farm to Imperial Fur, in Kowloon, any less ghastly than this? In the end, Johnny, now known in Europe as the King of the Dogs, can conceive of no capitalist protocol that he's in violation of, and he orders his innovative manager to ship fifty thousand skins to Kowloon. Not till they're there will Johnny learn that his $2,500 business expense ($2,500: five cents per dog) was grossly exorbitant, for in Bangkok he distanced himself from the Grand Guignol des Chiens and didn't take into his calculations that dogs in this tropical heat don't have hair. They don't have fur, and they can't be fashioned into fun fur.

HONG KONG

There's trouble in the Gang of Tranquil Happiness. It's trouble with a capital T, for the Gang is at war with thirty thousand bloodthirsty men, the members of the largest (though not the roughest and toughest) secret society, the Gang of Loyal Tranquillity. A war of words this isn't—it's fought with machetes, the sort of machetes civilians use to cut apart watermelons and the Gang of T.H. and Gang of L.T. carry inside their trouser legs. Every night in Kowloon, a man in one gang encounters a man in the other, there's no provocation but he unsheathes his trusty machete and *zap!* he swipes at the other man's neck. That man instinctively raises his arm and instantly loses it or, after an S-shaped machete move and a sound like a chastening slap in the face, loses his neck. The *casus belli* among these irascible men is the turf in the tourist part of Kowloon, is ten twisted streets full of tailors, jewelers, restaurants, glittering nightclubs, and bars whose inveterate customers (all fat, all forty, all women) tell any American tourist in English, "Hello, lover." The ten streets belong to the Gang of Tranquil Happiness, the merchants pay $1,000 to $5,000 per month for the Gang's essential protection, essential because if a merchant rejects it, the Gang will beat him or break his windows or torch his whole uncooperative store. But one month ago a club in this neon-resplendent part of Kowloon was cockily bought by the Gang of Loyal Tranquillity.

And that meant war. A number four nine, Johnny would be expected to wear his sharpened machete under his pin-striped trouser leg if his brain didn't surpass his brawn and if, as the war raged on, his brain wasn't sorely needed by the Gang of Tranquil Happiness. For thinkers like Johnny, a better weapon would be a white paper fan, one constructed with thirteen ribs, one inscribed with two geometric peonies—one peony red, one peony white—and one indecipherable poem, a fan that for three hundred years was the "scepter" of any adviser, any *consigliere,* in the Gang and the Gang's ancient antecedents. A man who wields a white paper fan (and whose formal title is White Paper Fan) is the Dragonhead's Cardinal Richelieu, and one hot night at a restaurant in

Kowloon the rank of White Paper Fan is offered to the top intellectual in the Gang of Tranquil Happiness: is offered to Johnny.

The man who proposes this (now you don't see him, now you *do*) is none other than the Dragonhead, the maximum leader of the Gang of Tranquil Happiness. A ringer for President Truman, his jaw square, his glasses owlish, the Dragonhead joined the Gang twenty years ago and achieved his preeminence through a career of S-shaped machete moves. Until now he's never met Johnny, but tonight he has graciously left his lair (a room in a grocery, probably) to materialize in this restaurant, to sit quite like a stone pharaoh, and to eat crab meat in shark's fin soup, goose with special soy sauce, chicken with oyster sauce, shrimp, pork, duck, and scallions with cabbage. While sharing this with the Dragonhead, Johnny hands him (it's mandatory, like a bottle of vintage wine to the host of a dinner party) a red envelope with the lucky number of $108 inside.

"I accept you," the Dragonhead says in Cantonese.

"Thank you, Big Brother."

"Now you're a White Paper Fan," the Dragonhead says. "But there'll be no ceremony for you. The hats," the police, "mustn't know about you."

"I understand, Big Brother."

"Congratulations," the Dragonhead says, then drinks green tea, then disappears from the table like a dirty dinner plate. But later he sends word to Johnny: don't let the hats discover it, but you're in command of the war with the Gang of Loyal Tranquillity.

So be it. A few nights later, Johnny waits in a dark parked car in the tourist part of Kowloon as along the crowded street like a group from a British cruise ship come two hundred men from the Gang of Tranquil Happiness. Creasing their trouser legs are machetes, and clenched in their teeth are white soda-straws (from the Gang's nickname of Soda)— straws that identify every man but accord him a Wally the Walrus look. Up this same street to confront them come two hundred men from the Gang of Loyal Tranquillity, men who are wearing machetes and, for ID, white armbands instead of white soda-straws, and in front of each army company is a man appointed for brawn, not brain, a man whose formal title is Red Pole. Also on hand (in addition to Johnny, who's simply wearing a jacket) are hundreds of Royal Police who have been alerted by squeamish members of the Gang of T.H. and the Gang of L.T.

The two hordes meet in front of the nightclub recently bought by the Gang of Loyal Tranquillity and grunt, grimace, and paw the suffering asphalt as Americans merrily enter the beckoning club and as Chinese scatter. "This club," says the Red Pole for the Gang of Tranquil Happiness, says after taking out his inexpedient straw, says to his rival on Johnny's instructions, and, all things considered, says in Cantonese quite courteously, "is on our territory, and you must pay us $5,000 per month."

"I know it's your territory, but," says the Red Pole for the Gang of Loyal Tranquillity, says equally courteously, his head nodding agreeably—"but we're your cousins in Loyal Tranquillity. Can you give us a special discount?"

"Yes, I can give you ten percent."

"Thank you, but we want fifty."

"No, fifty is much too much."

"How about forty, then?"

"Maybe twenty," says the Red Pole for the Gang of Tranquil Happiness on Johnny's instructions, and the two meet halfway at thirty percent. Attention, whoever dreams of climbing the dangerous rungs on the ladder of organized crime: the fur business is a good training ground.

HONG KONG

One day another telegram comes from Saigon. It's from Jonquil's long-lost mother and says in English, "ARRIVING TOMORROW CATHAY PACIFIC." And hallelujah, think Johnny and Jonquil, with her will be their children, the one who said, "I'm daddy's boy," and the one who still hadn't spoken, and so joyous are Johnny and Jonquil that they're bouncing as if they're on trampolines and, like in shampoo commercials, their hair is bouncing with them. "*Finally,*" Jonquil exclaims in Shanghai dialect.

"When they come, I'll *kiss* them," Johnny exclaims.

"And me, I'll *bite* them. They're bigger now."

"Oh, yes! We may not recognize them."

"Let's buy them something."

"Some monkeys!" Johnny exclaims, and off to a toy store go Johnny and Jonquil in search of spring-driven monkeys shaped like the living gibbon that Johnny once bought in Bangkok for "I'm daddy's boy." Once he'd received it, the boy behaved like an organ grinder with an ever-present companion. He cuddled his white-bodied, black-faced pet, his "baby" he called it in Cantonese, he fed it bananas it promptly peeled, peanuts it promptly cracked, walnuts it promptly walloped with one of Johnny's handmade shoes. "Monkey see, monkey do," Johnny cautioned his son in Cantonese, and Johnny never lit a match in the presence of the vigilant gibbon lest it imitate him and burn down his new apartment on Austin Avenue. But today in Kowloon, Johnny and Jonquil spot so many spring-driven monkeys that Johnny proposes, "Let's let the children choose one."

"Tomorrow," Jonquil exclaims, and she buys candy and Pampers instead.

The next day, the happy parents are in a lounge at Kai Tak International Airport. They're sitting on the red chairs as, with tear-wetted cheeks, the passengers from Saigon come wheeling their tattered baggage out, the passengers from Saigon but not Jonquil's mother nor Johnny and Jonquil's monkey-loving children. "Don't worry," an airline man assures them in Cantonese. "There are more people coming," but when after thirty racking minutes the mother at last materializes, she is a standing skeleton, her skin is old yellow paper, her eyes are black inkblots, her body depends from a stewardess like a coat from a coat rack, inanimate, limp. Back in Cambodia when the communist soldier asked her, *"Who are you?"* she assumed he'd decapitate her if she confessed she was Vietnamese, and she despondently asked him, "Why are you asking me?" The soldier said politely, "If you're Vietnamese, I'll let you go to Vietnam," the mother prayed to Buddha and said, "Let me go to Vietnam," and the soldier said, "Go." Subsisting on possibly poisonous frogs, the mother hobbled to Vietnam (it was 280 kilometers east, just as Buddha had told her) and boarded the perilous bus to Saigon and the flight to Hong Kong. From customs she's guided into the red-chaired lounge, she and Jonquil's sister but not Johnny and Jonquil's much-missed babies. "Mother!" cries Johnny in Cantonese, startled. "What happened?"

"I'm very sick."

"Why aren't the babies with you?"

"They're dead."

"What did you say?" asks Jonquil.

"They're dead."

"My two babies, they're where?"

"They're buried somewhere."

"They're buried?"

"Somewhere in Cambodia."

"Why are they buried?"

"They're dead."

"No! No! It's not true!" cries Jonquil, at last comprehending her mother's meaning. "No, I don't believe you!" Her eyes are like sponges being squeezed, and as Johnny and his embarrassed chauffeur help her, her sister, and her swooning mother out of Kai Tak, she wails like a woman at an Asian funeral. "No! No! Not my two beautiful babies! No!"

HONG KONG

Nor does Jonquil improve. The next day, her mother in the hospital, her sister in the children's bedroom, convalescing, and she herself looking as if she subsists on poisonous frogs, she's in the apartment moaning, "My babies . . . My beautiful babies . . ."

"I loved them too," says Johnny unhappily.

"Then why didn't you bring them to Saigon?"

"I thought they'd be safer in Phnom Penh."

"But why did you *think* so? You and I went to the airport, remember?" says Jonquil with lifeless eyes. "The communist rockets came in, and I said the babies should come to Saigon."

"And you were right. And now I'm so sorry."

"Then you and I went downtown, remember? My mother brought us the babies, and I said again they should come to Saigon."

"And I said no, they shouldn't come."

"Well, why did you say that awful thing?"

"I thought they'd be safe in Phnom Penh."

"Safe? With all those rockets exploding?"

"Mommy," says Johnny, biting his lip, thinking, *I mustn't cry.* "What if we'd brought them to Pochiton Airport? And what if a rocket had killed them and *us?* Our babies in Paris and Meriden wouldn't have been born. And," says Johnny, gesturing at Jonquil's altar and her red statue of Khun Ying Mo, the Goddess of Good Fortune, "our babies are the Cambodian babies, reborn." He hugs her, and tears appear in her otherwise taxidermist eyes.

All morning Johnny and Jonquil circle like this. But then Jonquil's character flaw (Jonquil's *re-re-reassure me*) completely consumes her, and she can't absorb what Johnny says even if Johnny repeats it, reiterates it, reprises it like the lyrics of *Row, Row, Row Your Boat,* even if Johnny could chant it all evening like a Tibetan monk during prayers. "I told you," says Jonquil, "the babies should come to Saigon. Didn't I tell you?"

"You did and I told you no. I was wrong."

"So why didn't you listen to me?"

"Mommy, this hurts me."

"If you had listened, they wouldn't have died." In agony Johnny reaches to Jonquil, his arm is a life preserver on her stiff shoulders but Jonquil jerks herself away. "Don't touch me!" she suddenly shouts. "You killed them and now I don't have them!"

"I don't have them either."

"But you never loved them!"

"Believe me, I loved them."

"No, you never loved them!"

"Mommy, I loved them."

"No, you never loved them!"

"Sweetheart—"

"No, you never loved them!"

For months Jonquil agonizes like Job and scratches at every obstinate sore in the hope that in its imprisoned pus is the *why* of her life's latest

tragedy. In her anguish, her two alive babies aren't as real as her two recollected ones in their root-perforated graves in the jungles somewhere
east of Angkor Wat. At home, at Johnny's bustling office, at lunch with
him at the Chiu Chao Restaurant, at parks derisively full of pink-cheeked
toddlers ("Please," asks Jonquil, "may I pick him up?"), at dinner at the
Marseilles she's either talking, sobbing, or shouting like in a crazy-house,
her pitch soprano, her tempo prestissimo, her lyrics always "We went to
the airport, remember? The rockets came in . . ." And though he's struggling not to, Johnny sometimes reacts and says, "Stop, I can't listen anymore!" And then Johnny pushes her and Jonquil bursts into tears and
says, "You hurt me! You promised you wouldn't ever hurt me!" and
Johnny, mortified, reaches out to embrace her and Jonquil cries, "Don't
touch me!"

By now the woman is half-demented. But now is Johnny a little
demented too?

HONG KONG

One night there's a quarrel like this in Johnny and Jonquil's king-
sized bed. Johnny feeds her a Seconal, and while she's asleep he trudges
into the living room, lights the table lamp, slumps in the armchair, stares
out the window, watches the Dippers revolving, the Big one chasing the
Little, broods. *Jonquil,* thinks Johnny, *is saner than I am. Why didn't I listen to her in Phnom Penh? Why didn't I see what she saw: the war in Vietnam had trickled into Cambodia? Her two babies, why didn't I bring them
to Hong Kong? Did I really kill them? Did I really kill them? Did I—*

Or did someone else? Under the Dippers, Johnny would see to China
tonight if, in between, there weren't a thousand apartment houses, a
thousand towering oblongs, and Johnny observes that in some of these
stacked apartments other table lamps are lit, lit although it's well after
midnight. He wonders, *Why are these people awake?* Are they people like
him? Are they sitting, staring at circling stars, brooding on loved ones lost
in a war inflicted on powerless people in Vietnam, Cambodia, Laos? *Of
course,* thinks Johnny, *there are others like me*—if millions of innocents
died, if millions of relatives miss them, then millions like him are griev-

ing tonight at one-man memorial services from the ghost-ridden huts of Cambodia to the high-rises of Hong Kong, are tormenting themselves with *Why did I do it? Why was I home that calamitous day? Why wasn't I in the family tunnel? My wife, my parents, my precious children, why weren't they in the tunnel with me? Why did I say they were safe where they were? The people who killed them that day, were they me?* And Johnny in his eighth-floor eyrie thinks, *No,* the people who pushed this war from the China Sea to the Gulf of Siam weren't tonight's insomniacs, weren't the feeble émigrés, weren't even the communist soldiers of Vietnam, Cambodia, Laos who Johnny had never met and therefore couldn't deplore. No, the villains who secretly dropped bombs on those halcyon countries were Johnny's old friends the Americans, the war criminals like Colonel I-Have-This-Movie, like General Thrash, General Cushman and General I-Am-the-Greatest, and like Mr. Hey-Hey-LBJ.

The evil American imperialists. That's what Johnny's grade-school teachers in Shanghai consistently called them, and Johnny himself once won a red box of pencils for a vehement speech about an American jingoist during the Korean War. A fighter pilot, the man found himself in a dogfight with a Chinese pilot named Chang Quin-Wei. "Now, Chang," said Johnny, his rostrum the grade-school stage, his two hands swooping like Chinese kites, ascending, descending, doing a fan dance around one another, "went *this* way and *this* way and," one hand ascending like a surfacing shark, "up *under* the American imperialist. The way Chang felt was *I don't care if I die but I'll get him,* and he went *this* way and *this* way and got him, and from the American plane came fire, and," one hand like a corkscrew now, "the American imperialist crashed!" *"Ha!"* cried Johnny's red-neckerchiefed schoolmates, in Shanghai dialect that is *"Good!"* and tonight in his Kowloon watchtower Johnny thinks, *I don't care either, I don't care if I die but I'll get the Americans,* the soldiers, sailors, civilians who in their insolent quest to run other people's homelands impassively murdered his and Jonquil's adorable children. Americans, go to your cursed ancestors! May your bones rot on the ocean floor! And the avenger who'll send you is Johnny Kon!

Now, Johnny has often heard about terrorists when he's been in England, Germany, Italy, heard about them when he was at American air-force bases in Vietnam, for isn't an American a terrorist if he's throwing bombs at civilians while he's a half-mile above them? Johnny decides that he'll visit an American base in Manila or in Kadena, Okinawa, or in Iwakuni, Japan, or in Tongduchan, Korea, or, *yes yes,* in Quantico, U.S.A. And there he'll toss powerful bombs (he'll have bought them in Bangkok and smuggled them into Quantico, wherever) and get his well-deserved revenge: surely he won't destroy all the wicked imperialists but, as a Chinese proverb goes, if one small stone is removed from a mountain by each of ten thousand men, the mountain in time disappears, becomes an immaculate plain. *I don't know exactly what I'll do, but I'll do it,* Johnny resolves as dawn encroaches upon the Dippers and daylight extinguishes them. Johnny in his own teleology won't be committing crimes in America—no, Johnny feels, he'll be stopping them.

8
Murderer

Hong Kong

His first priority will be an office in the United States. A presence on enemy territory will be no particular problem for a man who sells fun fur to Macy's, Gimbel's, Alexander's, Broadway, Bullock's, Penney and Sears, but Johnny will need an office manager, too, an English-speaking Chinese criminal. One summer night in Kowloon, his quest for a loyal lieutenant takes him to dinner at a round-tabled restaurant called the Great Shanghai, to dinner with a sui generis gangster known as the Northerner.

Nowhere in organized crime is there anyone else like the Northerner. The pug-nosed man doesn't murder, kidnap, rob, or even pester civilians, he doesn't hit on anyone but his secret-society brothers. All over Asia his M.O. is to sit down alone in a restaurant like the Great Shanghai, to put the teapot in front of him and four teacups behind it: to put the dinner-ware in a sergeant-and-soldiers formation. If on his table is one lone teacup, then his M.O. is to *fill* it, put the teapot in front of him, and put the teacup behind it. On seeing the Northerner's setting, you and I and most restaurant patrons in Asia aren't especially apt to undergo an anxiety attack, but a patron from a secret society sees it as an SOS, an SOS as plain as Morse code, an SOS that means "I'm your brother, and I'm broke." "Where are you from?" the patron then asks the Northerner, and the Northerner answers, "I'm from the East," *correct,* that's the proper answer, and in compliance with one of the thirty-six oaths ("Or may I die in the street") the patron graciously hands him $100 to $1,000. One night in Saigon, Johnny himself gave him $2,000, and often in Hong Kong Johnny coughs up his $200 rent, for the Northerner wallows like a wanton son on a father's unselfish allowance, hitting on his Chinese brothers, living like a Chinese tycoon.

He doesn't do any dish designs tonight at the Great Shanghai. He uses his coral-colored shears (his thumb in one handle and his four fingers in the other handle) to cut the claws off his Shanghai crab and his chopstick to dig out the succulent meat. Johnny, who's treating tonight, doesn't try to recruit him as manager in the United States, but he's trusting enough to ask for his recommendation. "I've got one," the Northerner answers in Shanghai dialect over the din that ricochets off the walls of the Great Shanghai. "My nephew in New York City. Everyone calls him Mahogany. He's the man for you."

"I'll interview him," says Johnny.

"I'll guarantee him," the Northerner says, devouring the ghastly green organs that the Chinese call crab's eggs. Alas, the Northerner's breaking another of the thirty-six oaths: to never cheat his secret-society brothers ("Or may I be blasted by lightning"). He never reports that Mahogany, among his one thousand rackets, works as a secret agent for the DEA, the Drug Enforcement Administration. He never reports that Mahogany entraps his Chinese acquaintances, never reports that he then informs against them.

NEW YORK

At his office at 15 Park Row, near City Hall, at his paper-inundated desk sits the Northerner's nephew, a man whose color accounts for his name of Mahogany. He's short, mustached, bearded, built like a Mexican peasant. Above all he's fat: his face is a sagging basketball, his stomach a medicine ball, his weight is two hundred pounds, his swivel chair sounds like the creaking sides of a schooner in an Atlantic gale. His tie entwines his multiple chins but his jacket is off, and Johnny (on one of the visitor's chairs) is impressed by Mahogany's brown leather shoulder holster and, squatting inside it, his Colt .45.

"Is it officially licensed?" asks Johnny in Shanghai dialect.

"Yes. I've got this friend in the NYPD," the New York Police Department. "Hey, Johnny," Mahogany says, commencing his favorite entrapment routine. "Do you want a gun yourself? Do you want a license for one?"

"You get people licenses?"

"Yes. My friend in the NYPD and I. For civilians it's $2,000, for criminals maybe $5,000." And speak of the devil, even as Mahogany says this, an NYPD policeman with a capillary-crisscrossed face like in an anatomy illustration enters Mahogany's office, drops a white envelope on Mahogany's desk, says in English, "Mahogany, that's for you," and walks away like an extra in some conventional movie.

"You pay him?" asks Johnny.

"Yes. We split the $2,000, whatever, and he splits his $1,000 with the NYPD. But tell me, Johnny," Mahogany resumes, using the gangster slang for gun. "Do you want a cannon in New York City?"

"I don't need one in Hong Kong."

"But there's muggers in New York City. Muggers, robbers, murderers . . ."

"Maybe some other time," says Johnny politely, and Mahogany (a fox who's biding the right psychological moment) postpones his entrapment plan. He takes Johnny instead to Delancey Street, near Chinatown, to the market where in his disordered stall he sells discounted sneakers ("They're hijacked," reports Mahogany, the *hijacked* in English, and Johnny asks, "What does hijacked mean?") and also sells counterfeit watches. He next takes Johnny to his fourth-floor apartment on West 14th, near the meat market run by the Mafia, to his studio where in artistic frames are the labels for EAGLE, GLOBE, LIONS and 999 heroin ("A friend gave them to me," Mahogany says, concealing that this was a DEA friend) and where on artistic mountings are a dozen vintage guns like a Russian nine-millimeter. He then takes Johnny to Chinatown for duck in salty garlic sauce, and Johnny (not signing with him but sternly saying, "If you ever fuck me, you're dead") appoints him his loyal lieutenant in the United States.

And loyal Mahogany seems to be. He doesn't blow up the American base at Quantico (*patience,* thinks Johnny) but runs Johnny's warehouse in Jersey City and Johnny's showroom in New York City, off Seventh Avenue, the sites of the canine remains that Macy's and Gimbel's call fun fur. When, in 1980, the teenyboppers abandon this fad (the fun fur sheds on their boyfriends)—when fun fur is *déclassé* and Johnny's distributors can't pay him, Mahogany goes to Seventh, unbuttons his bulging jacket, sprawls on the visitor's chairs, displays his .45 cannon, and says, "Let's work this out." One snowy night, he climbs onto Johnny's warehouse, uses a crowbar to pry the asphalt away, lets the snow settle on $500,000 of Johnny's fun fur, and also uses a water hose on that unfashionable merchandise. He then calls Johnny in Hong Kong and says in Shanghai dialect, "Bad news. A blizzard in Jersey City. It blew off the warehouse roof. All the fur got flooded. But," Mahogany laughs, "we're lucky, we're insured."

"I'll come to New York," laughs Johnny.

"Yeah. I'll show you," Mahogany laughs, and it's while they're driving to Jersey City on the West Side Highway, the Hudson outside of the window, the wharves wooden teats, the freighters suckling pigs, it's while they're approaching the Holland Tunnel that Mahogany next attempts his cunning entrapment act. "Hey, Johnny," he says outspokenly. "I need some white powder."

"Heroin? What for?"

"To sell it. You know what a kilo's worth in New York? $100,000. Can you score some for me in Hong Kong?"

"Not that I know of."

"My uncle the Northerner can. Why don't you get some from him? And wrap it in mink and ship it to Jersey City?"

"It's not my business."

"My friends the Italians will buy it. You and I will split the $100,000. You and I and the Northerner."

"I'd rather sell fur," says Johnny, a newcomer to New York who assumes that a kilo of heroin in a shipment eventually meant for Macy's and Gimbel's is normal conversational matter in cars on the West Side Highway. By the time they're dipping into the Holland Tunnel, he's thinking of minks, legitimate minks, and his lieutenant the uninhibited capitalist is thinking of rackets that he might conduct in Johnny's legitimate warehouse. *I've got one,* Mahogany thinks, and one month later when $250,000 of almond-colored, coconut-colored, and coffee-colored minks come to Jersey City, Mahogany rents a U-Haul-It and loads on $150,000 worth, drives through the Holland Tunnel, and sells it on Seventh Avenue. He pockets the $150,000 and doesn't tell Johnny, his "If you fuck me, you're dead" plain-spoken employer.

NEW YORK

"Johnny, I found something out," says Mahogany's friend from the NYPD, the man who dropped the envelope on Mahogany's cluttered desk and said, "Mahogany, that's for you," and also met Johnny that day. A red-faced man—an Irishman—today in Johnny's bright showroom, off Seventh Avenue, his capillaries are ten shades redder than ever and his neck is colored like a thermometer during an August dog day. It's red all the way to 100° as he splutt-splutters to Johnny, "That motherfucker Mahogany! I said when I went into business with him, I told him, 'Don't fuck me,' I told him, 'Don't double-cross me.' You know what he did? Got $2,000 here, got $2,000 there, and," says the Irish policeman, his red attaining a level never recorded outside of Death Valley, his eye whites are red, his ear whorls are red, a psychic would sense a red aura around him, "the motherfucker didn't split with me. He told me, 'I haven't collected yet.' And Johnny," continues the man, who's now well acquainted with Johnny and is now wearing civilian clothes, "he's also stealing from *you.*"

"Mahogany stealing from *me?*"

"He's stealing your fur in Jersey City."

"No, I got five thousand mink."

"According to Mahogany."

"He lying to me?"

"Go ask your inventory people," says the Irish policeman, the cop who learned of Mahogany's swindle God knows how, and Johnny calls up Jersey City and, oh, so casually, lest he arouse suspicion, converses with an employee in Cantonese.

Then he hangs up. "That motherfucker Mahogany," says Johnny, just as the Irish policeman did. "I meet him, he selling sneakers. Best opportunity never has, I give him at Imperial Fur. I tell him, 'Don't fuck me,' I tell him, 'You fuck me, you're dead.' You know what that motherfucker took? Three thousand mink. More than half. I hate him."

"What do we do about him?"

"Go to Hop Koon. And talk."

To any Chinese, few matters are so hush-hush that he can't confer about them at some tempting restaurant like the Hop Koon, in Chinatown, and now the two plotters proceed there in the Irish policeman's Honda. On the south side of Canal Street, the policeman stops at a hydrant, lowers a visor, reveals a POLICE credential, gets out, and gazes voraciously into the Hop Koon's window. On each of a dozen hooks is a roasted duck that if a customer points to, a chef in the window and in a sauce-stained apron takes down. Then, with a sauce-sopped brush, he glazes it like a candied apple until it reflects the sunset outside, then with a gangster's machete chops it into mouth-watering portions. Hurrying in, the policeman (using his fingers) gobbles down most of a duck and Johnny (using his chopsticks) ingests what's left, the policeman tosses a Budweiser down and Johnny drinks Tsingtau. "Delicious," the policeman says, then says, "Now about Mahogany. What do you want me to do?"

"Nothing," says Johnny. No way will Johnny sue his embezzling employee: once in Zurich he sued someone for $150,000, the lawyers' fees were $150,000, the pleas, demurrers, counterdemurrers were like in Jarndyce and Jarndyce, and Johnny lost all $300,000. What Johnny (and maybe you and I) would want to do to Mahogany is gleefully kill him, but Johnny cannot proclaim this to a cop who might testify against him. So Johnny lies to the Irish policeman, "Nothing."

"Well, I want to kill him."

"All right."

"And I want your help."

"All right."

NEW YORK

New Year's Eve (the Chinese one) is the night of a great reception at the Chinese consulate. Under red banners are colorful terraces of tuna, shrimp and caviar crackers, of Chinese hors d'oeuvres that Johnny compiles a dinner of, Johnny and almost no one else. "The guests, where are they?" asks Johnny in Mandarin, and learns that like all of Manhattan they're stuck in their limos, stuck in their taxis, stuck in their buses playing games like

> *I spy*
> *With my little eye,*
> *Something that starts with S,*

they're stuck on First, on Second, on Third, stuck on the bridges, stuck in the tunnels like logjams. Not since China became the People's Republic has there been such a mighty blizzard in Manhattan, and except for a choir of honking horns an eerie silence surrounds the Chinese consulate.

At eight o'clock Johnny, his alibi clear to the consul general, slips out to Twelfth Avenue. The nearest subway stop is on Eighth but Johnny doesn't have skis, and his handmade shoes, worth $1,000, are like old saddlebags by the time he's inside the Port Authority Terminal. He boards the A train downtown. Like bears in a cave, hibernating, are the men sitting near him in wet black overcoats as Johnny speaks telepathically to his father in Shanghai. *I'm sorry, father,* thinks Johnny. *Ninety percent of what you've told me, I've done. But ten percent, I must do my own special way. I hear what you're whispering to me, "Forgive Mahogany." But father, if I forgive him, then everyone else will act like him, and I'll be impoverished and Jonquil and all my children destroyed.* The train comes squealing into the station on West 14th and Johnny steps into Alaska again, then slogs to the narrow apartment house where Mahogany once showed him his Russian Beretta.

Tonight Johnny carries a .22 caliber gift from Mahogany. At the apartment house, the downstairs door is locked, but some adventurer exits and Johnny (tilting his wet umbrella, hiding behind it, a man in a Hitchcock movie) walks in, walks onto the elevator, rides to the fourth floor, walks off, and knocks on Mahogany's door. He hears Mahogany's feet, Mahogany's hippopotamus feet as *clump, clump, clump,* they clomp out an SOS, then hears someone say, "Motherfucker! Keep quiet!" That gruff voice is the Irish policeman's, a man who according to plan arrived many hours ago at Mahogany's snowswept downstairs door. Using his Visa, he jimmied in, rode up the elevator, and hid behind a corridor door till Mahogany came back home from Imperial Fur. Then, pulling his .38, the policeman murmured, "Don't move or I'll kill you," the two hurried into Mahogany's apartment, and it's now the policeman who screws up his eye and squints through the peephole in Mahogany's door.

He lets Johnny in. Johnny, not wearing gloves, uses his embroidered handkerchief to close the door behind him. "Where is he?" Johnny asks, the policeman points and Johnny turns to Mahogany, a fat man creating a sinkhole in his overstuffed sofa, his hands cuffed behind him, his arms contorted like stumps, his sock (like a bubble-gum bubble) stuffed in his mouth, his conversation reduced to "Mmf!" His eyes are like two black marbles as Johnny, his finger aimed straight between them, says in Shanghai dialect, "Mahogany, today you're dead."

"Mmf!" Mahogany answers.

"All right, you can talk," says the policeman, turning the TV on (*The Beast Must Die*), "but if you yell, you're dead right away." And from Mahogany's boar-like head the policeman takes the baked apple.

"Help me," Mahogany says to Johnny in Shanghai dialect.

"Help me? What do you mean about help me?"

"Help me, I did nothing wrong."

"Nothing wrong?"

"Stop!" the policeman cries. He turns up the TV and says, "I don't understand you two," and the two Chinese citizens switch to English, Johnny going first.

"Mahogany, did I trust you?"

"Yes."

"I ever sign contract with you?"

"No."

"I tell you my word like gold?"

"Yes."

"So why you fuck me with my fur?"

"I didn't!"

"Why you sell and not pay me?"

"I not pay you 'cause *I* not paid."

"Oh, fuck you," says Johnny. His characteristic smile is indiscernible, inconceivable, his mouth tonight is an oblong, the mouth of a Mayan god, a hole in a Noh mask, tonight he's the very personification of Wrath. "You remember last time I'm in New York?"

"Yes."

"I asked if you selling any fur?"

"Yes."

"You told me you not selling?"

"Yes."

"But you selling lots, correct?"

"Yes."

"So why you saying not selling?"

"Because! Because I not paid!"

"You liar," says Johnny. His lips are wrinkled as if he were drinking rancid milk. "That day I asked, 'You selling?' I didn't asked, 'You getting paid?'"

Mahogany doesn't answer. Do you know those beds where you put in a quarter and get a one-minute massage? The sofa Mahogany's on could be such a Sonair, for his fat twisted torso shivers convulsively on it.

"My heart very kind," says Johnny. "When I was small, when someone come to our house like this," his palms together, his body bowing, "I always give them rice. My mother say, 'Son, you have very good heart.' Now *you*," he continues, his finger flicking at Mahogany as though he's throwing a Chinese star, stiletto, poisoned dart—"*you* are the benefit of my kind heart. If you not kind-heart with me, I mad."

"I'll pay you, I promise," Mahogany sobs.

"No need," says Johnny, "I just forget it." Magnanimous as this announcement sounds, what it connotes is "I'll cancel your $150,000 debt. You won't have to pay it, because, being dead, you won't be in any position to." "Mahogany," continues Johnny, his lips still sucking an incorporeal lemon. "You also fuck with *him*," tossing his head toward the Irish policeman, "and also with Ng," a Chinese man who Mahogany (as Johnny recently learned from *The New York Times*) had lured to New York, then lured to a Mafia dinner where the Mafia men in their diamond rings were all DEA, then lured to a Holiday Inn where the DEA tapped them and taped them, then lured to a multi-million-dollar heroin deal. "And you also fuck with *me*," Johnny says. "You try to set me up on West Side Highway. You tell me you want white powder. You tell me to ship to Jersey City. You tell me we split the $100,000."

"We'd split it! We'd both make money!" Mahogany says.

"No, motherfucker. You snitching to DEA. They paying you $150,000 reward. And when I'm in fucking jail, you stealing my $250,000 fur."

"No, Johnny, I'm loyalty. My uncle—"

"You uncle another motherfucker like you."

"My uncle the Northerner, he's your good friend."

"Also good friend of Ng. Oh, what sort of people you two? To come to innocent people like us? To tell us, 'Hey, you be drug dealer, please?' And then go and snitch to the DEA. To fuck us the jail and fuck us the $400,000. What sort of people you are? I help your uncle fifteen years. I help you too, Mahogany. I let you run Imperial Fur and pay you $40,000 salary. What am I doing anything wrong? What, Mahogany? What?" For one brief moment no anger surges from Johnny, melancholy like a gray cloud supplants it but Johnny dismisses it before it betrays itself. "I warned you," he says through firmly clamped teeth. "You fuck me and then you die."

"Don't kill me!" Mahogany cries, but the wind outside the window and the TV muffle this reckless yell.

"And if I not kill you? You think I'm stupid? You not telephone police? And tell them—" Then suddenly Johnny stops. He sniffs as if something's burning and says, "You shit? You shit your pants? You coward, Mahogany?" He turns to the Irish policeman, who for ten minutes has hovered here like the Angel of Death, his .38 at Mahogany's temple. "Where is that fucking thing?"

He means the .38 silencer. Even this thunderous night, a *bang bang bang* in Mahogany's brains would rouse Mahogany's neighbors, people who'd surely call the NYPD. "The silencer was too big," the policeman says. "I left it out in the Honda."

"Where?"

"Underneath the driver's seat."

"But where the Honda?"

"Across the street."

"I go get it."

The policeman slips Johnny the car key, Johnny (his handkerchief shielding his fingertips) leaves, and the policeman stuffs the bubble-gum bubble back in Mahogany's mouth ("Don't kill me! Don't kill me! Hic!"). Ten minutes pass, in time they're ten, twenty, thirty, in time they're an agonizing hour and Johnny, the key to the Honda, and the indispensable silencer aren't back in Mahogany's apartment. *That damn Chinaman. What's keeping him?* the policeman wonders as *tick, tick, tick,* as slow as a sun-dial shadow the hands of his Casio make their imperceptible arcs. One hour, two hours, three hours—god! it's well after midnight now, and Johnny in his striped suit is a dim recollection, hallucination, someone who for some sinister reason could be on Pan Am and halfway to China now. It occurs to the Irish policeman that *he* is the man really trapped under EAGLE and GLOBE amidst the smell of Mahogany's stool. A silencer, a silencer, the policeman's world for a .38 silencer! As the one, two, three, four, five's of the morning drip on his brow like Chinese water torture and as Johnny remains in the realms of Judge Parker, the policeman sits cracking his knuckles to frighten off Morpheus, but Mahogany's snores (Mahogany still on the sofa, cuffed and stuffed) soon have his captor yawning too.

Cut now to Johnny Kon. Eight hours ago, Johnny got the car key but tsk! not the key to the downstairs door, then plunged out into the Klondike, the snow almost up to his overcoat, his legs like snow shovels, and in front of the bolted doors of the Church of Saint Bernard got into the Honda. The silencer (an 18-inch silver pipe) was under the driver's seat, and picking it up he sat immobile, wondering what to do next. He couldn't re-enter the building, since no one was exiting it, since every tenant but Mahogany was in front throwing snowballs, shouting, "I gotcha!" For one hour Johnny sat shivering, then left the Honda for coffee (three coffees) at Dunkin' Donuts on Eighth, then warmed himself at a flame-crackling garbage can (the street people standing like Druids, flames on their faces, snow on their caps), then got in the Honda again, the snow-shrouded windows concealing him. The snowball fight went on and on like the Seven Years War. *Another hour here and I'll die,* Johnny thought, and he got out and, clipping the car key under the windshield wiper, went to the subway stop on Eighth and took the A and F trains to his quarters (a friend's house) on Coney Island. But the tracks were so deep in drifting snow that the F train couldn't make it and, backing up, abandoned him at the subway stop in Greenwich Village. He took the next train to Coney and back to the Village, then the next train to Coney and back to the Village, his strategy being that of his fellow commuters, all of them street people keeping warm. Next he took the E train to West 53rd, on the corner of Seventh, got off, and went outdoors. His shoes like Dutch sabots, socks like ice, he walked to the first hotel he'd patronized in New York: the Americana, now the Sheraton Center, and called up Jonquil in Hong Kong to help establish an alibi and to reassure her in Shanghai dialect, "It's stormy but I'm okay." At the Sheraton's Café Colombia, he sat down under a totem of a Colombian god and hour after hour drank coffee, the god glaring at him indignantly as though it were the protective god of Colombian coffee beans. Perhaps there's a moral here: if you set out to murder someone, don't be too sanguine where you'll end up.

At seven the sun comes up. It doesn't light up the Café but tints the snow on its picture window platinum gray. Downing another blood-warming coffee, Johnny takes the E train back to West 14th and trudges back to the Honda, discovering the Irish policeman jiggling the car key and paying five dollars apiece to four young boys to shovel the car out. "I sorry," says Johnny, "but I no have downstairs key."

"I finally figured that out," the policeman says, and the two partners get in the Honda, which doesn't start till the shovelers roll it east on West

14th and the policeman catches first gear. He turns south to Chinatown and says, "I killed him."

"How you do?" Johnny asks.

"My knife," the policeman says, and from his overcoat pocket he pulls a six-inch switchblade and says, "I cut his stomach first. That way he had no strength. Then I cut his jugular vein, then his whole throat, then I cut a triangle onto his stomach like all the Triads do." In fact the Triads don't, but if (Johnny thinks) the policeman and all his NYPD believe that an equilateral triangle cut in Mahogany's stomach means he was killed by a Chinese secret society, killed by inscrutable aliens, fine. "If anyone asks you," says the policeman, "you and me were together, stuck in the goddam subway."

"*Gong xi,*" says Johnny in Cantonese.

"What?"

"Happy New Year," says Johnny in English, for now they're in Chinatown and on its snow-white streets are the dancing dragons, red, black and gold, squirming like sidewinder rattlesnakes from one to another merchant to feed on his $100 bills and, in exchange, to grant him good luck for the coming year. And *bang! bang! bang!* like a .38 without any silencer go the firecrackers the Chinese invented 1,500 years ago for joyous occasions like this, and Johnny repeats, "*Gong xi!* Good luck for us!"

"*Gong xi!*" the policeman attempts. And with a happy high-five, the murderers go for dim sum at a crowded restaurant on East Broadway.

NEW YORK

The body's discovered, and Johnny's interrogated about Manhattan's latest lurid murder. It isn't that Johnny's a suspect, for in the past several days he was seen by a number of men being vividly palsy-walsy with Mahogany. It's just that Johnny was Mahogany's boss, and in their chaotic office on West 20th the detectives think, *Well, maybe,* maybe Mahogany once told Johnny about prospective assassins.

"You were Mahogany's employer?"

"Yes. Mahogany sell fur for me."

"Did you know he was murdered?"

"Yes. Saw newspaper story." The story that Johnny refers to ran in the *New York Post,* for among other callings the victim snitched for the DEA and his grim punishment was one of the *Post*'s sensations that day. "Nice guy," says Johnny nostalgically.

"Why would anyone kill him?"

"You not know? He police." In fact the *Post* identified him as a DEA informer, but Johnny learned to act ignorant when he was eight years old and selling his fighting crickets in Shanghai. "I've got a better cricket," a boy in Shanghai would brag in Shanghai dialect, and Johnny in his gown would answer, "Yeah. It looks better than mine." "You want to fight crickets?" the boy would ask, and Johnny would answer, "Okay, but if I lose I'll give you one cent, and if you lose you'll give me five." "How someone can kill him?" Johnny now asks the disoriented detectives. "Mahogany police. Always carry gun."

"Um," the detectives ask Johnny. "Do you know who'd try?"

"I'm thinking. Oh, maybe a month ago Mahogany tell me . . ."

"Yes?" The detectives are scribbling on wide-lined pads.

"I'm thinking. Mahogany tell me something about . . ."

"Yes yes?"

"Oh!" says Johnny, snapping his fingers. "Was Singapore!"

"Singapore!"

"Mahogany tell me: Someone in heroin business ask him for help him in Singapore. Is maybe those people kill him? Those people in Singapore?"

"We'll find out," the detectives say.

"I'm more than happy to help you."

HONG KONG

By now Johnny's forty years old. A furrier in Kowloon, his scheme to avenge his massacred children and to destroy the United States is the same half-awake dream he had in his armchair under the Dippers five years ago. With nobody's help, Johnny could carry some stones from the mountain known as the U.S.A., but without his own terrorist organization, without his own ten thousand dauntless men, the mountain would squat on the planet forever like an enormous warted toad. As a White Paper Fan, Johnny can call out the fifty thousand brothers in or linked to the Gang of Tranquil Happiness, but in the approximate words of Hotspur will they come when Johnny calls? Will they give up their quest of money, coveted money, to consecrate themselves to a cause across the Pacific, a cause that no matter how glorious won't earn them a plastic nickel? Will they desert capitalism to defect to unselfish idealism?

No, my friends, the brothers won't. Not only that, but if they even aspired to, the brothers don't have the derring-do to blow up a building, say, in New York City or Oklahoma City and thereby confront the army, navy, marines, you name it, and the half million police of the Big-Nose Nation. Nor does the Green Gang, nor does the Red Gang—the Gang of Loyal Tranquillity, the Gang of Righteous Tranquillity—nor does any of Kowloon's cautious secret societies, champions of the status quo. Nor does anyone except, perhaps, a gang that's newly arrived from China, a gang that's not a traditional secret society, is not—by 290 years—three hundred years old, and is not partial to rituals where it queues up in its underpants saying, "I'll honor my father and mother." Not long ago in China, its members were in the Red Guard, a militia established by Mao to enforce the Great Cultural Revolution and (somewhat like the Nazis) expanded to men who beat, abused, and murdered everyone who Mao didn't appreciate. When, three years later, Mao called the Revolution off, the Guards often swam to Kowloon (or were cheerfully eaten by great white sharks) to continue their magisterial ways without any British bureaucratic endorsement. From their armbands (red armbands) in China, they called themselves the Big Circle, and much to the mortification of all the secret societies they started seizing the streets of Kowloon and the headlines in Kowloon's fifty daily papers.

Imagine it. Imagine that every several days on Fifth Avenue, or Michigan Avenue, or Wilshire Boulevard you and hundreds of other civilians crouch in the gutters as gangsters battle the NYPD or Chicago PD or LAPD, the guns banging, bullets whirring, chips of concrete flying from off the sidewalk, stinging your neck. That happens now in Kowloon whenever the hooligans of the Big Circle are spotted robbing a watch store, a ring, bracelet and necklace store, or (as happened once) a Chinese medicine store with $300,000 of antler velvet, abalone, ginseng, and curative birds nests. "Stop! Or we'll shoot!" cry the Royal Police in Cantonese, but heedless of constituted authority the Big Circle not only doesn't stop but shoots at the flabbergasted police. Its loot and its .38s in its tightened fists, the Big Circle runs recklessly from the watch store, whatever, bumps into the startled pedestrians—it bumped into Johnny on two occasions—ignores the supersonic traffic, the meteoric double-decker buses, the red lights depicting pedestrians standing stock-still, it lunatically ignores them but runs across boulevards and (the hats still shouting, "Stop! Or we'll shoot!") disappears into Kowloon's alleys. Now *those* are the sort of desperadoes that Johnny will need if, as he day-dreams, he'll ruin the United States.

And slowly Johnny sees it. He sees that he, Johnny Kon, the bon vivant, the owner of Imperial Fur, the father of Isabel's three children and Jonquil's two, the buyer of children's toys like Artoo Detoo, of *Star Wars*—that Johnny must somehow take command of the gangsters of the Big Circle and must relocate them to the United States. But how?

P a r t T w o

9
Big Brother

HONG KONG

It's teatime, and Johnny is waiting in suit and tie for one of the rough, tough, unpredictable bosses of the Big Circle. The meeting, arranged by a gangster-gambler-interior-decorator in New York, is not about to occur in a grocery but in full view of humanity at one of Kowloon's most glamorous spots, the atrium of the New Miramar Hotel. It will be as if Donald Trump and John Gotti, Senior, have chosen to rendezvous under the clock at the Biltmore, in New York City, for the atrium of the Miramar is three floors high and on each marble balcony the guests, the teatimers, and (for all Johnny knows) the plainclothes policemen hang like ivy and stare at the circular table where Johnny now sits. Johnny has chosen this public place for its proximity to Imperial Fur, and the man he's meeting in the Big Circle, a man whose nickname is Fat Ass, has chosen it for its fat-ass-inflating delicious desserts. Epicures all, the Chinese are different from John Gotti, Senior.

At five o'clock Fat Ass enters. At 180 pounds, he isn't fat like Fatty, the vat-shaped wanted man in the Golden Triangle, but he's solid, sturdy, built like a granite statue, and he's strutting across the Miramar rocking from side to side as if each foot were being planted by a construction derrick. He's wearing a $200 silk shirt and the acknowledged badge of a Chinese gangster: a Rolex, one that was doubtless heisted at one of his recent robberies at Geneva Watches, Mercury Watches, Oriental Watches, or Sun Sun Jewellers. He's five years younger than Johnny, and though etiquette doesn't require it, Johnny stands up, shakes hands, says in Cantonese, "I'm pleased to meet you," and sits down elegantly as his partner drops like a sledgehammer onto another chair and as his four scowling bodyguards take a table at point-blank range. To their rear in a giant crockery bowl are bird-of-paradise flowers.

"My name is Moy," says Fat Ass to Johnny in Cantonese. He puts his left ankle on his right knee as if he's announcing, "My office today is the Miramar," and from a table vessel he pulls a toothpick, sticks it between two naked molars, and, while reciting his résumé, chews on the toothpick like on a celery stick. "People call me Fatty," he says rather euphemistically. "I'm from Canton. I was Red Guard, then I was one of the Thirteen Tigers," a gang of infamous robbers eventually killed by Chinese firing squads or mistreated (like Fat Ass) in Chinese labor camps. "A few years ago I escaped and swam to Kowloon. The sharks didn't mess with me." His toothpick becoming limp, he flips it onto the Miramar's marble floor, pulls out a firmer toothpick (which, in time, he'll flip to the floor until there are two dozen there, lying like sawdust) and says with pride, "And now I'm Big Circle. What about you?"

"I'm like you," says Johnny. "A boss of the Gang of Tranquil Happiness."

"A boss of that secret society. Hm," says Fat Ass, his toothpick tilting up.

"So what are you doing now?" says Johnny. "I've heard that it's robberies."

"Yeah," says Fat Ass. And taking his toothpick from its interproximal area, he replaces it with a Kent even before the flaccid toothpick hits the Miramar's littered floor. His lighter goes *bong* as he opens it, and he says with undiminished pride, "I like that sound. I've got the best lighter there is, DuPont. Yeah, I'm doing robberies."

"The items you get, are you selling any?"

"Yeah, pretty soon. I'll get you a menu."

"Menu?"

"A catalog. Or I'll get your requisition."

"My—?"

"Your requisition," says Fat Ass, his head rolling cockily as if his incessant subtext is "If you don't know something, I do." "You yourself go to the watch store, see? You see the watch or watches you'll want. You tell me and I'll get them for you. Your requisition."

"No, thanks. The menu is all I'll need."

"I'll get you one," says Fat Ass. He takes his Kent and taps the fragile span of ashes onto the Miramar's soiled floor, but a still, small voice (or Johnny's split-second glance) disconcerts him, and he uses a shoe to pulverize the unsightly ashes into a rather stylish streak in the marble.

A waiter comes by. Johnny orders coffee for himself and, rather gallantly, for the four dour bodyguards, and Fat Ass like some detective in search of incriminating evidence inspects the laden dessert tray. The caramel custard is a Vesuvius whose lava is strawberries, blueberries, kiwis. The cherry and kiwi gelatin stripes on the honeydew-melon pudding create a fairyland flag, while the kiwi slices and tangerine wedges on the Japanese ube pudding, whose color is livid violet, guarantee that the ube (whatever it is) is also emphatically palatable. Eschewing them all, Fat Ass selects an American cheesecake, an American edifice topped by a cherry, a pineapple slice, and a whipped-cream lather. He pounces like a predator onto the cherry, pops it between his teeth, snaps out the cherry-colored stem, flips it onto the Miramar floor, chews the cherry conspicuously, says to Johnny, "It's good," spits the pit to the trashcan floor, and (the still, small voice that he may have acquired in kindergarten admonishing him) mightily tries to grind it in, the pit remaining resilient to his firmly wiggling shoe. On his lip is whipped cream that he wipes his napkin across, wipes it fast and firmly as though he's pulling a zipper, and in his ashtray, half-smoked, is a Kent he improvidently ignores. Instead, with a sonorous *bong* he now lights another one, inhales, coughs, spits on the much-abused marble floor, sees that Johnny looks shocked—that Johnny is pulling his head back—and awkwardly grinds the inelegance in. It's then that Johnny strikes.

"Do you have some tissues?" asks Johnny.

"Uh, no."

"You can use some of mine," says Johnny.

"Thanks."

"Next time don't forget tissues," says Johnny.

"I won't." One-upped by the older (hence senior) man, Fat Ass stabs his dessert fork into his cheesecake as if he's killing a squawking chicken, does this to demonstrate to Johnny that he's still a gangster king. "Next time I'll bring a menu too," says Fat Ass.

"Good, we'll do business," says Johnny.

HONG KONG

It's nighttime, it's twenty past ten in the tourist part of Kowloon: no theater, no concerts, no Chinese opera: no bookstores but one as diminutive as an ancient-history alcove at a Barnes & Noble: no gyms, no joggers, no shuffleboard players: nothing but ten thousand tourists who at this almost eleventh hour shop till they drop for gold, silver, diamonds, emeralds, jade, and watches that now run to $500,000. Into the glitter of Lily Jewellery, on Peking Road, come three Chinese men with red-white-and-blue-striped shopping bags, also with guns and gasoline that one of them sloshes onto a jewelry counter. He holds up his cigarette lighter and says in Cantonese, "Don't anyone move. Or I'll set this place afire."

Easy money this isn't. For weeks these men (all Big Circle) have checked out Lily Jewellery, its cases, counters, windows, where are the Piaget watches? where are the Patek Phillippes? where are the bracelets of undappled jade, the $15,000 ones? and when is the store almost empty? when do the robot police pass by? when *to the second* are traffic lights green? The men have mothers, and in their hearts they feel it's improper to try to make money without doing *work* for it. One late afternoon in Kowloon, two of these gunmen heard an old woman cry, "Thief!" and saw a man running toward them with the old woman's purse—at once they kung-fued him, kicked him, told him in Cantonese, "You want to rob someone? Don't rob a defenseless old lady! Rob a respectable jewelry store! The lady," they told him, their feet treating him like a soccer ball, "doesn't have money, the jeweler does! She doesn't have guns, the jeweler does! Now scram!" the gunmen concluded, then like the knights of the Middle Ages or like people in the secret societies gallantly gave the old lady her purse. For their sortie tonight, they have drawn careful maps of Lily and (like American coaches) a vector for every offensive player, and in inch-by-inch accordance one of them holds up his lighter now and says in Cantonese, "Don't move. Or I'll set this place afire."

"Put your hands where I'll see them," another says.

"Open that window right now," the third man says, his .38 at the head of the tall trim-mustached manager.

"Easy, easy," the manager says, unlocking the sliding glass to a window full of his best rings, earrings, bracelets, necklaces. He hands these trays to the gunman, who dumps them irreverently into his red-white-and-blue striped bag as, like jackpots, his partners dump the diamond-dazzling watches into theirs. The ten salespeople at Lily press their hands to the counters, fingers apart to show there's no .38s between them.

Four little minutes: that's what the timetable called for, then one of the gunmen says, "We're going. Don't follow us," and, hurrying out, bumping into the startled pedestrians, all three run in their sneakers through the all-green traffic lights. By now they don't carry incriminatory red-white-and-blue-striped shopping bags, for the bags are now in the manicured hands of "the startled pedestrians," of women who casually carry them into the subway, down the long escalators, onto the whirring trains, carry them to the Kowloon apartment of a Kent-smoking, ash-dropping, floor-scuffing boss.

HONG KONG

At his marble-topped desk at Imperial Fur sits Johnny. Beneath its mahogany base is a kangaroo rug he bought (along with some dingo dogs) in Melbourne, Australia, and beneath that is a camel-colored carpeted dais. Johnny now swivels right to study a TV monitor where every two-thirds of a second there flashes a scene from his factory: from the dyeing, drying, cutting, stitching, lining or labeling rooms or his own reception room, a room that by tapping a button he now stops the TV monitor at. In center screen is a red-and-green ceramic statue of Kuan Kung, the God of Loyalty, the god who Johnny and his grade-school gangsters prayed to in Shanghai long ago as instructed by a Chinese comic book. On this ceramic statue, the god (who once was a real mortal, born in A.D. 162 and promoted to god by an emperor 1,400 years later) has two fiercely slanted eyebrows that like on a Kabuki actor seem to proclaim that he isn't pleased, isn't pleased at all. He once was a Chinese general (he's also the God of War and strangely of Literature) and in his right hand is a lance with a blade like a lobster claw, doubtless a fearsome weapon if it's descending upon your neck. Also in the reception room and on the monitor is Fat Ass, the graceless boss from the Big Circle, and Johnny sees with satisfaction that Fat Ass has paused at the bronze-armored statue to put his palms together and (although there's no audio) to presumably murmur in Cantonese, "I pray I'll be loyal like you, Kuan Kung." Then switching the monitor off, Johnny phones his receptionist, saying, "Send in Mr. Moy."

Gallantly, Johnny steps off his dais to welcome him. "Make yourself comfortable," Johnny says on orchestra level, and Fat Ass crashes onto an L-shaped sofa, crossing his knees but showing respect for Johnny by letting his ankle dangle, unlike in his insolent posture at the New Miramar Hotel. He reaches into a back pants pocket, extracts a few folded papers, shakes them open as though they're stuck with Elmer's Glue, and hands them to Johnny. The papers are in Chinese handwriting and say something like

> 6 *diamond rings* @ $7,500
> 8 *diamond rings* @ $5,500
> 2 *diamond bracelets* @ . . .

the grand total (including watches) coming to $2,000,000, meaning American dollars.

"The menu," says Fat Ass.

"Yes, I understand that."

"My friends hit a store."

"I know about that," says Johnny, who read it this morning on the front page of the Hong Kong *Sing Tao*. The hit was the biggest in history by any branch of the Big Circle.

"It's all or nothing," says Fat Ass.

"You mean I buy everything . . ."

"Or you buy nothing at all. I don't want multiple customers. A customer is a potential traitor. Mind if I smoke?"

"I don't mind, but I'll want to peruse this list," says Johnny, and, his Kent still unlit, Fat Ass leaves Johnny's opulent office and Johnny's omniscient monitor, but at Johnny's telephoned invitation (and with five glowering bodyguards) he comes back the following evening. He falls like a wrecking ball onto the L-shaped sofa, slaps a black briefcase onto the marble coffee table, opens it and upends it as though it's a wastepaper basket and the table a Dempsey dumpster. A few hundred watches come tumbling out.

"I got Rolexes here," says Fat Ass. "I got Piagets and Christian Diors—"

"Diors," says Johnny immediately. "They aren't easy to sell anywhere."

"I know. But I got Patek Phillipes and Vacheron Consa—Vacheron Conta—I don't know how to pronounce that one."

"Constantin," Johnny says. "Help me check them against the menu."

"Mind if I smoke while I do?"

"Not at all," Johnny says, and with an orotund *bong* his visitor lights up a Kent, painstakingly tapping the ashes into a crystal ashtray. The loot and the menu matching, he then dumps onto the coffee table a shopping bag so bloated by rings, earrings, bracelets, necklaces, by gold, silver, diamonds, emeralds, jade, that Johnny hasn't the leisure to double-check them. "I'll take your word," Johnny says. "I'll give you ten percent for it all. That's $200,000."

"I never get less than fifteen percent."

"I'll give you fifteen for the Rolexes only."

"The Rolexes? They would be thirty-five."

"No, I get just twenty selling a Rolex."

"Anyway, it's all or nothing," says Fat Ass.

"At ten percent. I should have said eight."

"Please," says Fat Ass, a word that's a no-no in any negotiation (he should have stood up and said, "No deal," and Johnny would have said, "Then eleven percent")—"please, can you give me more than ten?"

"You're lucky with ten. You can't sell this whole mountain. You can't even give your girlfriend one ring. But me," says Johnny, jabbing his thumb on his chest, "I'll take it. A lot of it's junk but I'll take it. I'll have to hold it another year," Johnny exaggerates, "then I'll have to ship it. And pay for the shipping. And what if it's seized? I'll lose my $200,000 but you will lose nothing at all. And," says Johnny, standing up, walking to his dais, then to his desk, taking two fat manila envelopes off it as Fat Ass, entranced, lets a stack of his cigarette ashes settle onto the camel-colored carpet, "I'm not paying installment plan, I'm paying right now. The ashtray is right over there."

"I'm sorry," says Fat Ass. His handkerchief coming out, he sweeps the ashes into a wastepaper basket as Johnny descends from the rostrum, returns to the coffee table, and as slow as a man dissecting a snail uncoils the little red string from the little brown button on one of the manila envelopes. Onto the table he shakes out its contents, $100,000: six rubber-banded packets, in each packet ten folded wads, in each wad ten local bills, each bill worth about $166: bills that Johnny shrewdly withdrew yesterday (along with $100,000 for his other billowing envelope) from his box at the Hang Seng Bank. And just like in *Treasure Island,* Fat Ass has suddenly shining eyes. He sets his Kent on the ashtray lest one impertinent cinder queer this imminent deal.

"You can try someone else," Johnny says. "Maybe he'll offer fifteen percent, but if he does be careful he's not the police."

"If I take the ten percent," says Fat Ass, "can I get fifteen another time?"

"Of course. Even twenty," Johnny exaggerates. "Every deal's different."

"Umm . . ."

"Your people can't wait," Johnny guesses correctly. "If they get 200,000 tonight, tonight they'll go gambling and get themselves girls. Go ask them. Get their approval."

"No!" says Fat Ass, slapping the coffee table, the pile of jewels going *tinkle.* "I don't need their approval! I'm boss!" and, just as Johnny shrewdly intended, the deal is done, the jewels remain on the marble table, and the two fat manila envelopes exit with Fat Ass.

The next day, Johnny hands the swag to his longtime courier, a Eurasian, a multitalented man who speaks American English, Mandarin, Cantonese, Taiwanese, and Johnny's own Shanghai dialect, a man who carries passports from the United States, China, Thailand, Japan, France, Switzerland, Brazil, Bolivia, Colombia, Costa Rica, the Dominican Repub-

lic, and Saudi Arabia and who can pass as a citizen of any of those twelve
countries whenever he smuggles something to places like Tokyo. The
courier and his associates put the rings, earrings, bracelets, necklaces,
watches into their money belts, wrap these belts around their waists,
carry their bulging bellies to Tokyo, and sell everything to Japanese gangsters: to Yakuza, who sell it to Ginza bar-girls, who sell it to tourists like
you. The profit for Johnny is $250,000.

HONG KONG

In no time he's the permanent fence for Fat Ass, who starts hitting
jewelry stores (one day, two simultaneously) as though he's the local
sales rep for Tiffany's. Nor is Johnny just wide receiver, often he's the
quarterback, too, the man who asks Fat Ass in Cantonese, "Your men.
Are they wearing gloves?"

"No. Why should they?" asks Fat Ass.

"So they don't leave any fingerprints."

"In gloves the guns wouldn't be wieldy."

"How about fingernail polish, then?"

"On their fingernails?"

"On their *tips*," Johnny says, Johnny who also procures some guns for
Fat Ass but tells him, "Don't shoot them. Just scare people with them."

"Do you mean shoot at the walls?"

"No. What if a bullet ricochets? What if it hits some salesgirl? What if
she's also pregnant? You'll kill two innocent people. That isn't right," says
Johnny, Johnny who's thinking of a disquieting evening long ago in
Vungtau, Vietnam. He was at the Pacific Bar, outside the window were
Vietnamese, and a GI with Johnny asked him, "Do you know who the
civilians are?" "Yeah, everyone is," Johnny answered. "No," said the GI,
"some of them may be VC. And maybe they'll try to kill us. And they'll
open fire, and we'll open fire, and we'll kill the civilians, too," the GI
explaining over his Bud why ninety percent of the people that he and
his compatriots kill are Vietnamese civilians. "No, don't kill them," Johnny
moaned, and now he often tells Fat Ass, "We don't want to hurt poor
people. We want to hurt rich sonofabitches. That is the Triads' tradition."

Nor are criminal tactics the only counsel that this Solon, this Nestor, this White Paper Fan gives Fat Ass at five-star restaurants and at Johnny's new apartment on Homantin Hill Road. "You want money, don't you?" Johnny asks Fat Ass in Cantonese. "You tell yourself, *And then I'll have confidence.* You're wrong," Johnny says like an "est" instructor who for $250 per person teaches exactly this at vast meetings in the United States. "No, you need confidence first, then the money comes naturally. You," Johnny also counsels as Fat Ass puts cigarettes, toothpicks, even the stem of a cherry into his unappeasable mouth, "are like a baby, you're always needing a nipple."

"Aw, I smoke just a pack a day."

"You aren't counting. It's two."

"And every cigarette, I only smoke two-thirds. The last third I leave in the ashtray. The last third, that's where the nicotine accumulates. The first two-thirds, that's good for you. The last third's bad."

"Oh, bullshit," says Johnny in Cantonese slang. But also Johnny gives Fat Ass a crocodile cigarette case, and he tries to clothe this wolf in other gentlemanly accessories. "The way you dress, if I were police I'd watch you," says Johnny. "Why do you always wear sneakers?"

"So I can run away faster."

"And the police know it. You've got to dress better. You've got to look like a corporate executive," says Johnny, and he sends the still-spitting commoner out for $800 shoes and $800 suits. He says this and does this for all the rough, tough, often quarrelsome men who Fat Ass is introducing him to: the bosses (there is no overall boss) of one dozen families of the Big Circle. And soon (like Johnny when he dined on crab, shrimp, chicken, goose and duck with the Dragonhead) the bosses automatically call him Big Brother.

HONG KONG

How does someone become the *capo di capi* of the Big Circle? It's not by being its meanest man, the tyrant of everyone's flesh, the absentee in everyone's heart: it's not by being its Genghis Khan. In the Chi-

nese Mafia, as against the Italian one or the white establishment one, a
CEO has pride of place because of his integrity, because his subordinates
trust him. His staff, remember, are criminals, are liars, cheaters, double-
dealers, men without rectitude, are men who can't trust their partners in
crime even as these earnest partners promise, "I promise." What happens
when a tough criminal says, "For the stickup at Lily Jewellery you owe
me $100,000," and the other tough criminal answers, "No, I owe you
$33,333"? Who shall decide when dacoits disagree? Excluded from all the
civil courts, a criminal's dire necessity is a set of good dueling pistols or
a benevolent despot, an unappealable arbitrator, a leader of unimpeach-
able integrity: an Aristedes, a Kenesaw Mountain Landis, a Johnny Kon.

One night to Johnny and Jonquil's apartment come all the Big Circle
bosses. In the foyer (across from the goldfish, angelfish, platyfish tank)
is a red-faced statue of Kuan Kung, the God of Loyalty, his beard, mustache and sideburns hanging down like hippie-hair, the five strands con-
verging at his mesosternum, where (to maneuver his lobster-clawed
lance) his left hand draws them aside. In front of this busy statue stops
Fat Ass. From nearby he takes three sandalwood incense sticks, lights
them, clasps them in his two hands like a suitor's flower stems, bows to
the god three times, murmurs in Cantonese, "I pray I'll be loyal like you,
Kuan Kung," and leaves the burning incense in a ceramic tray like his
Kents. Most other bosses (some fatties, some leanies, most in their thir-
ties but one in his twenties) do these obeisances till the ceramic tray is
like the flame beneath the Arc de Triomphe, then Johnny comments in
Cantonese, "For thirty years I've prayed to Kuan Kung." His maid serves
everyone tea, then Fat Ass comes bowing to Johnny: bowing just mod-
erately and not horizontally like a Japanese. "Big Brother," says Fat Ass in
Cantonese. "We like you. You're honest. Your words are like gold. You're
smart and, unlike the rest of us, you've had experience overseas. You're
kind to us. You can help us." His hands free of toothpicks, cigarettes,
cheesecakes, he turns up his palms as if he's holding a bowl of exquisite
fruits, and he offers this hypothetical feast to Johnny. "Big Brother?" he
asks to Johnny's complete unsurprise. "Will you be our leader?"

"Are you all for it?"

"Yes, we all are."

"Then I accept," says Johnny. He squeezes both hands of Fat Ass and says, "We are brothers now." He does this with each other boss, then says, "You are family now. You aren't factions anymore. You don't have to show each other you're tough. As long as I'm boss I know you're tough, and it's enough if I know it. Just look at *me:* I'm tough when I need to be, but I'm polite until then. Spies, terrorists, contract killers, they're always polite. And you, little brothers, you shouldn't go around acting tough but go around acting cowardly. That way the hats will ignore you. That way you'll do greater things. That way," says Johnny, raising his hands, clapping them loudly, the goldfish darting away—"that way you'll make money!" Not yet entirely honest, he doesn't tell the Big Circle, "And you'll somehow destroy the United States."

HONG KONG

"Big Brother," says one of the bosses other than Fat Ass. It's six months later and Johnny's gang, the Big Circle, has robbed dozens of jewelry stores, has gun-battled with the Royal Police, has shot three dozen rounds one day, has killed some constables, cops, and has also been killed, has been tortured (arms, legs and necks have been broken) in windowless rooms of the Royal Police, has smuggled its rings, earrings, bracelets, necklaces, watches to Tokyo and Taipei, has sold one that you might be wearing right now, has made more than $1,000,000 for Johnny. It's now almost midnight, and to Johnny and Jonquil's plushy apartment comes a far-from-fat-assed boss, a tall, thin, anorexic, and Modigliani-faced boss, a man who drops on the coffee table a half-dozen books by Mao like *On the People's Democratic Dictatorship*. The boss is a Mao enthusiast, Mao groupie, someone who's constantly quoting the Chairman or, just tapping one of Mao's books, peremptorily saying, "The answer's here." In the sixties you and I were driven silly by people like this, but Chinese expatriates like Johnny (who at age ten wrote a letter to Mao and lo, Mao answered him) and the other bosses tolerate him. "Big Brother," the man commences in Cantonese in Johnny's terraced living room. "Do you know what I want in Hong Kong?"

"No, what?"

"It isn't money. It isn't jewels. It isn't watches," the boss continues, and, as though knocking on someone's locked door, his knuckles rap *On the People's Democratic Dictatorship.* "What I want is a Revolution."

His big eyes blaze with I'm-not-kidding conviction. So sobersided, so wanting in risibility, so brimming with "I'm talking business," so professorial is this boss, whose surname is Chan, that he's commonly called the Professor. Born under Mao, raised under Mao, he was a teenager when in the 1960s he became a Red Guard in Canton. Not that that was exceptional, but the Professor killed a man and fled on a train to Kowloon, fled in a vegetable freight car, his carcass crated among many tons of bok choy, cores of lettuce, and winter melons, melons the Chinese boil with mushrooms for a delicious shrimp sauce. Safe in Kowloon he extricated himself, formed his own family of Big Circle, but (still in his early twenties) tried to look venerable by wearing glasses he didn't optometrically need, the frame gold wire, the "lenses" panes, the two round windows tinted on top and less and less tinted below it. He wears these bogus glasses tonight, sitting in a soft armchair in front of his little library of Mao.

"A Revolution?" asks Johnny, bewildered. "What sort of Revolution?"

"Well, Chairman Mao," the Professor says, opening one of Mao's lighter books, *Quotations from Chairman Mao,* "says this. He says, 'A revolution isn't a dinner party. It isn't writing an essay, it isn't painting a picture, it isn't doing embroidery. A revolution,' says Chairman Mao, 'is a violent act.' Big Brother," the Professor continues as Johnny thinks, *What is he trying to tell me?* "You're very rich. Most people aren't. That isn't equitable."

"I agree absolutely," says Johnny sincerely.

"Their blood, their landlords suck it."

"They're bloodsuckers, yes."

"Chairman Mao," the Professor continues, opening Mao's *Analysis of the Classes in Chinese Society,* "says this, 'The landlords' existence is incompatible with the objectives of the Chinese Revolution.' The landlords," the Professor says unassisted, "don't grow rice. The *farmers* grow rice but the landlords snap up three-fourths of it. How can the farmers live like you, Big Brother? How can they live like that without a Revolution in Hong Kong?"

"But there are no farmers in Hong Kong."

"But poor people here are like farmers."

"I agree absolutely. When I arrived twenty years ago," says Johnny, comfortable with this intelligible topic, "I saw whole hillsides of matchbox houses. With paper walls, with plastic roofs. And without water. The people walked down to the fire hydrant and," says Johnny, his arms at his shoulders, his arms with an incorporeal pole, his neck bent like in Gongjalu, "carried the water up to their paper houses. That wasn't equitable."

"Chairman Mao," the Professor says, flipping to *The Reactionaries Must Be Punished,* "asks the question, asks, 'Then who should we punish?' He answers, 'We should punish,' oh, you should read this, Big Brother—'we should punish reactionaries.' We need a Revolution in Hong Kong."

Johnny still doesn't get it. "Do you want to be Governor?"

"No."

"Do you want to throw out Sir Edward? And replace him?"

"No," the Professor repeats. "Chairman Mao says, and I'm quoting him, 'The only effective way to suppress reactionaries is to execute at least those of them whose wrongdoings are the most serious.'"

"And those reactionaries are—?" *And what is he driving at?* thinks Johnny.

Up until now the Professor has been soft-spoken, icicle-worded, precise, but now he succumbs to an almost paroxysmal passion. "The hats! The hats!" the Professor practically bellows. "The worst reactionaries are the Royal Police!" He clenches both fists, and he jiggles them up and down dyskinesiacally like Alex van Halen drumming out *Dance the Night Away.* "I want to get guns, grenades, machine guns, want to get mortars, rockets, recoilless rifles, want to get armored cars, even tanks, want to hit every precinct there is! I want," the Professor continues, *dance, dance, dance,* "to kill every hat in Hong Kong! 'Policemen,' says Chairman Mao, 'will tremble when they see the farmers' spears,' and I say let's kill them all! Big Brother? Do you approve?"

Slowly, Johnny stands up. It's one o'clock now, and for more than an hour he has been listening motionlessly. He puts his palms on his ilia and arches his back like in yoga, *ahhh*. He clasps his palms behind him and stretches them up, up, up, his pects extending, becoming kinetic again. He stares at the plaster ceiling, considering what to tell the eggheaded gangster sitting in one of his ecru armchairs. No doubts are in Johnny's mind that the Professor's in deadly earnest, for the Professor's always in earnest and it's almost always deadly. As for the egghead himself, he stands up, walks determinedly past the wide-eyed goldfish, and in the kitchen brews up some jasmine tea, the maid and Jonquil being asleep. His fists still quivering, he carries this tea to the living room, then sits down again with Johnny.

"All right, I'll tell you," Johnny commences. "Twenty years ago when I came to Hong Kong, I was riding a bus and I saw a Chinese man and a Chinese woman. The two were running and, as they were, were pushing carts full of oranges, apples, pears. I asked the man riding beside me, 'Why are those people running?' and the man said, 'They're running from the Ghosts.' I told him, 'I don't understand,' and the man said, 'Did you just arrive in Hong Kong? They're running from the Royal Police.' I twisted around and saw they were being chased by a British police supervisor, a British white ghost. He caught them and put them inside a van for selling unauthorized oranges, apples, pears. I told the man beside me, 'But these are Chinese! Our own Chinese people! The white ghost humiliated them!' The man said, 'Yes, you just arrived in Hong Kong. The bigwigs here are the British.' I said, 'Well, fuck them,' and now I've said that for twenty years, *ta ma di*. My brother, I am like you," Johnny tells the Professor, who's phagocytizing every word. "I too hate the Royal Police: the British pigs and the Chinese dogs. You want a Revolution against them? You want to get guns, grenades, whatever? You want to hit their despotic precincts? Very well, I approve."

Now, Johnny honestly isn't fond of the tan-hatted swaggerers the Royal Police. He watched twenty years ago as they helped themselves to the oranges, apples, pears of the Chinese man and Chinese woman they put in the Black Maria. He learned since then that if Chinese pilfer a Coke bottle, say, the hats will report that they pilfered emeralds, and if Chinese (like Johnny's own "little brothers") die at a precinct, the hats will report that they killed themselves in some strange black-bruising way. He also accepted the Chinese concept that the army, navy, police protected the Emperor but the secret societies (like the Green Gang in Shanghai, whose fungus-eared leader supported a number of schools, orphanages, hospitals, and two hundred needy households) protected the Chinese people. But it's not Johnny's priority to slaughter the 24,000 oafish officers (many of them in the secret societies) in the Royal Police, no, Johnny's priority is the extermination of all the super-super police in the Big-Nosed, Round-Eyed, Mutton-Smelling Nation. So why didn't he tell the Professor tonight, "Maybe you're overreaching," or "Maybe you're overoptimistic," or "Maybe you're completely nuts"? For one reason only: Johnny had stared at the plaster ceiling, stared at that whiteness unwritten upon, and had decided, *Well, I'll scratch the Professor's back, and the Professor will scratch mine.* Johnny would aid the Revolution against the Royal Police, and the Professor would aid the revenge against the United States. Tit for tat.

"I approve," says Johnny.

"Thank you, Big Brother."

"One small caveat, though."

"What is it, Big Brother?"

"Many police are our brothers too. Many are in the secret societies like the Gang of Tranquil Happiness. We must telephone them on the eve of the Revolution and ask, 'Are you working tomorrow?' They'll understand."

"Of course, Big Brother."

"I'll get you the weapons."

"Thank you, Big Brother. Chairman Mao," the Professor continues inevitably, "says that like weights on the Chinese people are two enormous mountains. One, says Chairman Mao, is called feudalism, meaning in Hong Kong the British, meaning the Royal Police."

"The other mountain," says Johnny, himself a Mao bibliolater, "is called imperialism, meaning the United States. According to Mao, the people must end the aggression-oppression of U.S. imperialism."

"I've read this, Big Brother."

"Let me tell you about the United States," continues Johnny, "and about their war in Vietnam, Cambodia, Laos. Once, I had two little kids . . ."

HONG KONG

It's three in the morning when the Professor departs, taking with him his Mao collection, but Johnny remains in his own ecru armchair. *Hmm,* Johnny thinks. He's pondering how to afford the guns, grenades, and who can say? the $45,000,000 fighter-bombers that the Professor will need for his Revolution and Johnny will need for his revenge against the Kid-Killing Nation. It's true that Johnny's a millionaire, but (like them all) he became one by his adherence to three great entrepreneurial principles, one, *I make money,* two, *I don't spend it,* three, *I surely don't spend it on items that, if I use them, there's nothing left.* How, thinks Johnny, can he get the capital to compete realistically with the $250,000,000 annual budget for the Royal Police and the $200,000,000,000 one for the American military-industrial complex? Certainly not by selling hot earrings in Tokyo and Taipei, and certainly not by legitimate means like an IPO. For one hour Johnny sits cogitating, slowly a scheme assembling itself, a wild, woolly, improbable—*no,* thinks Johnny, *impossible*— scheme, its elements (like a house of cards) falling together, falling apart, falling first this way, that, when lo! at four in the morning the phone in his living room inexplicably rings.

MONTCLAIR

Synchronicity. Four in the morning in Hong Kong is four in the afternoon at 244 Midland Avenue in Montclair, New Jersey, the cozy wooden home of Jonathan James Ruotolo. A policeman for eighteen years with the NYPD, Ruotolo at first patrolled the black part of Brooklyn ("You pig," the people who passed him said), then the "silk stocking" part of Manhattan ("Good morning," the people said), then he was a vice-squad sergeant in Times Square, and then a taxi hit him and he retired to Montclair. But even with part-time employment as a bugger, debugger, and private eye, his $27,000 pension and $13,000 social security doesn't pay for his mortgage in Montclair, his pad in Manhattan in Stuyvesant Town, his three daughters' educations, his wife's impeccable tastes in Chinese coats and in Tabriz rugs with tableaus of Persians hunting for boars, his coin collection, his gun collection, and his mistress in Stuyvesant Town and her troublesome son. Retired, the Sergeant needs money desperately.

He has just reminded himself of Johnny. Like the Irish policeman, the Sergeant was introduced to Johnny by the man with an iron in everyone's fire—by Mahogany. He bought a $4,000 mink from Johnny ("For you it's $900") and soon became one of Johnny's trusted buddies. And now he has phoned him in Hong Kong and, having heard him say "*Wei*," the Cantonese for "Hello," the Sergeant says, "Johnny, it's Jon! How are you? You're good? Myself, I'll tell you. I'm broke and I'm thinking: Do you have some work for me in the States?"

"Yes!" the Sergeant hears.

"Great, Johnny. What is it?"

"Fly here and I'll explain."

"Johnny, I can't afford it."

"No problem, I reimburse."

"When will you want me?"

"Now!" the Sergeant hears.

HONG KONG

It's just after four in the morning in Johnny's dark living room in Kowloon, the GHQ for his intended adventure against the United States. Hanging the phone up, Johnny blurts out an English word he learned at a church in Brooklyn one Sunday evening. The word, which isn't from the Old or New Testament, is "Bingo!"

10
Dragonhead

Hong Kong

The next night, Johnny summons both Fat Ass and the Professor to his apartment on Homantin Hill. The two men are friends ("My best friend," said Fat Ass on first introducing him to Johnny under the skylights of the Coffee Garden at the Kowloon Shangri-La)—are friends though they run two factions of the Big Circle and are as dissimilar as Macbeth and Macheath. "Did you hear the joke about . . . ," laughs Fat Ass in Cantonese at every meeting of all the bosses, but the Professor interrupts and says, "No joking now. We're serious now." It's evidence of the attraction of opposites that the two bosses aren't always at each other's throats.

The fat one and thin one sit down on Johnny's soft sofa. The maid (a Filipino) brings in a pot of green tea, and Johnny pours it into three delicate pink-and-green-flowered white cups. Then Johnny says in Cantonese, "Money. We need weapons, and to afford them we need money. How," he continues, knowing the answer precisely but, like Socrates, artfully withholding it to let his guests stumble onto it—"how do we get more money?"

"How about this?" the Professor asks. "We rob another jewelry store. There's one at the corner of Cornwall, Minden and Mody. We can escape four ways."

"Good idea," says Fat Ass. In his lips is a Kent, in his ashtray two.

"No, I don't think so," says Johnny. "The money there isn't enough."

"Then how about this?" the Professor asks. "We rob a bank, instead. At the same corner there's a branch of the Dai Sing Bank."

"Another good idea," says the Kent-shuffling Fat Ass.

"No," says Johnny. "A teller just has $10,000."

"Then how about this? We rob a bank vault. That's $100,000,000."

"*Another* good idea," says Fat Ass.

"No, that'll take hours," says Johnny. "By then there'll be hundreds of hats outside. Ah Tung," says Johnny, using a more respectful nickname for the Professor. "If you get $100,000,000, if you can't escape you got $0."

"Then how about this? We stall a car at one end of Mody Road. At the other end, we stall another car, and, in between, we rob the Securicor car that's bringing the $100,000,000 to the Shanghai Commercial Bank."

"Good idea," says Fat Ass. In his tray is a Kent museum.

"Your guns," says Johnny. "Are you going to use them?"

"Only to scare the Securicor guards," says the Professor.

"What if the guards start shooting?"

"Well, then we'll shoot them back."

"What if you hit civilians? The bullets don't have eyes, Ah Tung, and I don't want bullets hitting civilians. I don't want guns, period."

"How do we rob anything without guns?" asks Fat Ass.

"We—" begins the Professor, then becomes speechless.

Johnny just sighs. Oh for a Plato tonight! Productive as Socrates was in Athens, his method collapses in an agora peopled by such obsessive robbers as Fat Ass and the Professor. "I've got another idea," Johnny announces. "It's safer both to civilians and us. The one time I did it, I didn't accept money for it. But there's lots of money in it."

"What is it, Big Brother?" ask Fat Ass and the Professor.

"For years I've gone to New York," Johnny says, "and I've seen papers and TV news there. They're flinging billions into the white-powder market." Now, what Johnny saw in the *Times* and on ABC, NBC and CBS was, the Mafia in America ran the heroin business but had a hellish time of it. Ten years ago, the Turks burnt the Turkish poppies and the French uncoupled the French connection, and now the Mafia's raw material—opium—comes from backwater ports like Basra, Bushire, Bandar Abbas and Karachi, is distilled in inadequate laboratories in Sicily, and is (as the *Times* and the TV will soon learn) inelegantly distributed in pizza parlors across the United States. The product is not outstandingly white, the profit is not spectacular, and Johnny continues to Fat Ass and the Professor, "We should enter the white-powder market in New York."

"White powder?" asks Fat Ass. "That's heroin?"

"Yes."

"Heroin looks like powder?" asks the Professor.

"Yes. During transportation it looks like bricks."

"Well, either way it's bad," contends Fat Ass.

"Bad?"

"If I deal in it I'll lose face. I'll lose respect."

"You run some whorehouses, don't you?"

"Two. One on Kimberly, one on Austin."

"Do you think people respect you for it?"

"No," broods Fat Ass. "People don't."

"Is heroin any worse than whores?"

"No," broods Fat Ass. "Heroin isn't."

"Where do we rob it?" asks the Professor.

"We don't. We buy it in Bangkok."

"Then what?" asks the Professor, perplexed.

"We fly it by courier to New York."

"And then?"

"A friend in New Jersey, I'll have him sell it."

Fat Ass and the Professor look lost. The two are professional robbers, are men who don't know white powder from Bromo-Seltzer, men who Johnny could tell with equal success that in the United States, "They're flinging billions into NASDAQ." "We buy the powder in Bangkok and sell it in New York," the Professor says. "How do we make money from that?"

"Consider this cup," says Johnny, and raises his pink-and-green-flowered teacup as though he's toasting his porthole-spectacled inquirer. "In Bangkok I can fill this with powder for $1,500. I can then ship it to New York and sell it for $20,000. The profit practically overnight is a thousand percent. One night," says Johnny, "in Quantico, U.S.A., I saw our Chinese book *The Art of War*. It tells us to forage, forage, to use the enemy's weapons against the enemy, and now we'll use America's money against America and against the Royal Police."

"One teacup?" asks the Professor.

"Yes."

"Twenty thousand American dollars?"

"Yes."

"My god," the Professor gasps. "I'll do it! So will Fat Ass, I'm sure! Our soldiers, they'll do it! When do we start it?"

"My friend in New Jersey, he's already flying to Hong Kong."

HONG KONG

Fat, full-jowled, full-bellied, his collar button opened, his shirt buttons opening autonomously, his pants button opened, his stomach slopping out like the crust of a cheese soufflé, the Sergeant walks out of Kai Tak International Airport. It's hot out, his silver hair like silver wires reflecting the sun and his brow creating a delta of trickling sweat. "How was your trip?" asks Johnny in English, supernaturally cool in his gray silk suit and his pink-and-gray silk tie.

"It was long," the Sergeant pants.

"You will enjoy in Hong Kong."

By limo they drive by enormous murals for Marlboros, Salems, Kents, by friezes on one whole building for Mild Sevens, a British brand, by limo they drive to a grand hotel called the Royal Garden. Nowhere in Brooklyn or Manhattan has the former flatfoot seen its like. Inside is an atrium whose waterfalls above river rock, whose pools under marble bridges, whose forests of Kentia palms conjure up paintings of paradise for the Catholic Sergeant, and the sounds of its tinkling fountains could be the harpsichord section of Gabriel's symphony orchestra. As though in a Christlike ascension, the Sergeant (escorted by Johnny) soars in a glass-sided elevator up to another atrium and its lofty twelfth floor. In this upper atrium, enormous enough for a thousand angels or for the *Hindenburg,* the sound is of *Yesterday* as played on a baby grand on a birch-

wood island in a celestial blue pool, a baby grand that the pianist presumably swims to in his tuxedo prior to every sonorous set. On all four
atrium walls, in back of pothos-railed balconies, are the four hundred
guest rooms, and the Sergeant (with Johnny) goes to his own peach-
carpeted one, adorned with a bowl of bananas, oranges, grapes and a
vase of yellow carnations and red bird-of-paradise flowers.

The breathtaking view is of Hong Kong Harbor and Hong Kong
Island, but the Sergeant draws all the curtains: the sheer one, the buttercup-colored one, and the louvered sliding doors, and he turns on the
crimson ceramic lamp. He asks Johnny in English, "Could I have a Coke?"
and when Johnny gets one (and gets himself orange juice) says, "Am I
tired. Johnny," the Sergeant continues, the two sitting down at a circular
rosewood table. "I'm broke. I need money bad. Remember my Dodge
St. Regis? It's six years old and the door comes off, but I still drive it. You
said I could work for you in the States. What work?"

"All sorts. On telephone I couldn't say."

"I figured."

"One, I got jewelry. Can you move it?"

"Sure, Johnny. Where did you get it?"

"From jewelry store. I got it for free."

"For free?"

"My guy with gun, he got it for free."

"A stickup!" the Sergeant laughs. A moment ago his jet lag was cured
by Johnny's word *jewelry,* and now he's in vigorous health again. His
eyes shine as if they're implanted with some of Johnny's hot diamonds.
"Yeah, I got Italian connections, I can move jewelry."

"Two, I got this," says Johnny, pulling his sleeve up and showing his
Rolex Oyster. "Day, date, diamonds, can you move them?"

"Sure, I can move 'em. Anything else?"

"Three, I got counterfeit traveler's checks."

"Can move 'em, can move 'em. Anything else?"

"How about greenbacks? Counterfeit $100s?"

"Can move 'em, but better are $10s and $20s."

"Why? In transportation they're heavy."

"$100s, Americans look at carefully."

"All right, I'll order some twenties."

"Anything else?" the Sergeant appeals.

"Number five—no, five isn't right."

"What is it?"

"I don't think you can handle it."

"I can handle *anything!* What is it?"

"Is drugs."

"What kind?"

"Is heroin."

The former policeman hesitates. A cloud passes over his shining eyes. He knows what the drastic penalty is for heroin importation: a thimbleful could be fifteen years. "Heroin," the Sergeant muses. "That's the best drug to deal in, but I don't know the wholesale price. Well, I'll find out. And get back."

"If you can' move, I get someone else."

"No, Johnny, I can handle it!" the Sergeant protests, the Sergeant's professionalism impugned exactly as Johnny intended. "I'm a retired policeman. My house in Montclair, no one'll guess there's heroin there. No one'll search my Dodge, either, a Dodge with a siren and flashing lights. No one'll stop me if I'm delivering."

"No one will stop you? Why?"

"No one'll *be* there to stop me. I know who the plainclothesmen are. I'll drive around and if I see one, I won't deliver."

"You are good man."

"I can move heroin, Johnny."

"You are now part of Big Circle."

HONG KONG

It's noon, but the Sergeant's circadian rhythms tell him, *It's midnight*. He falls asleep in his peach-colored bed as Johnny tiptoes out. At 7:30 Johnny returns, and the two descend in the see-through elevator, walk by the tinkling waterfall, exit the Royal Garden, cross Mody Road ("Careful in Hong Kong," says Johnny. "Don't look left, look right") and take a glistening escalator up to the Rich River Restaurant. At one round table with a magnificent view of millions of mountainside lights on Hong Kong Island are Fat Ass, the Professor, the other heterogenous bosses of the Big Circle, a Chinese policeman from Interpol, and a Chinese sergeant from the Royal Police. It's scandalous, but all the important sergeants in the Triad bureau of the Royal Police are and always have been in the Triads, amassing enormous sums (like $600,000,000, amassed by a sergeant renowned as "the $600,000,000 man") by switching their hats in sync with opportunity's oscillations. It is to one of these versatile sergeants that Johnny now introduces his American visitor. "He my best friend," says Johnny in English. "He sergeant for New York Police."

"You and I," the Sergeant laughs. "We both work for the government."

"What what?" says a boss in Cantonese. "This man's an American hat?"

"Yes, just like the Chinese one," says Johnny in Cantonese.

The food (twelve courses) comes on plates that a clothespin is always clipped to, a clothespin bearing the number of Johnny's restaurant table, a clothespin of avocado green that the waiter tastefully removes prior to serving the Peking duck, whatever. The soup is shark's fin, the Sergeant sipping a porcelain spoonful and *oww!* and spraying the tableclothed table as Johnny says tardily, "Is hot." The salad is lobster with AA battery eyes that the Sergeant praises, saying, "It's beautiful," and one main course is chicken with nuts that, unlike in Montclair, aren't voluminous walnuts but little ellipsoid cashews that with the plastic chopsticks the Sergeant can't get a purchase on. Three consecutive times, a cashew slips from the Sergeant's sticks as the spellbound bosses (most of whom haven't eaten with an American) watch. On each of their faces is a politely suppressed dismay. "On television," says one of the bosses in Cantonese, "the white ghosts utilize forks. Not chopsticks."

"He's practicing," says another boss.

"A few more times and he'll get it."

"No, he never will. They never do."

"Shouldn't we get him a fork, then?"

"Help him, Big Brother," says Fat Ass.

"Jon," says Johnny in English. "Don't worry chopsticks," and Johnny offers him a porcelain soupspoon, instead.

"One more time," the Sergeant insists, but, like a minnow, the cashew skitters away from his plastic wands. And using one like a croquet mallet, saying, "I'm sorry," the Sergeant knocks the recalcitrant cashew onto the soupspoon, swallowing it. After dinner, everyone goes to the Fortuna Club, the Sergeant chooses a $500 slit-skirted girl ("I hope she's clean, or my wife'll kill me") and, after a memorable week of restaurants, nightclubs, slit-and-short-skirted girls, the Sergeant boards a plane to Newark with $50,000 of for-free jewelry, $500 of sample counterfeit traveler's checks, $500 of sample counterfeit money, and his new Rolex Oyster, a diamond-studded memento from Johnny. But heroin he doesn't board with, not yet.

HONG KONG

Because. Because the crotchety bosses (except for Fat Ass and the Professor) still haven't heard that Johnny will transfer them to the heroin export-import game. Nor, thinks Johnny, will they be happy to hear it, for Johnny has hesitations himself. To push white powder on impotent addicts, even on imperialistic ones, is this concordant with his Buddhist philosophy? Is it conceptually ethical? One night on Homantin Hill, Johnny doesn't pray to Kuan Kung, the God of Loyalty, or to Jonquil's favorite god, Khun Ying Mo, the Goddess of Good Fortune, but (God being everywhere) lies on his bed, hands under his head, eyes on his plaster ceiling, lies and sees Buddha and says, "I'm sorry, Buddha." The mural transforms itself into Johnny's virtuous father, and Johnny repeats, "I'm sorry, father. You told me don't gamble, and I didn't. You told me don't smoke, don't drink, don't use any drugs, and I didn't. But something I know you'll deplore, I must do: I must sell drugs, and I must use the income to wreak havoc upon the United States. If the United States has done it to tranquil countries like Vietnam, Cambodia, Laos, why can't I do it to the United States? I am not balanced, father, and not till I get revenge for my murdered children will I be. My drug business I'll keep secret. I'll put it," Johnny continues, picturing a little jewelry box, a box lined in quiet black velvet, locked with an intricate key, "in some little box, and I'll never tell my brothers, my sisters, or Jonquil. I'm sorry, father," says Johnny and, sitting up, picking the phone up, summons his often recalcitrant bosses to Homantin Hill.

They come that night, seating themselves in Johnny's big living room. At once Johnny tells them in Cantonese, "From now on, we must deal drugs." All their shocked objections, he has anticipated. The bosses don't know about drugs? "You don't know about picking pockets, either," Johnny tells them. "But if you wanted to, you could learn it." The bosses, if caught, don't want to serve lengthy sentences? "The sentence in Hong Kong," Johnny tells them, "is twenty years for robbing watches and is twenty years for smuggling drugs." The bosses object that the sentence is death in Singapore? "You won't operate in Singapore," Johnny tells them. But just like Johnny's, the most intense objections are the ethical ones, the ones like "Drugs are bad," and "Drugs are evil," and "Drug dealers are scum." "And robbers aren't?" asks Johnny. "Now, I'm not saying robbery's wrong, but if you rob and you shoot civilians, that's wrong. If you kill a Pakistani, a man with three little children, as happened in August across from the Hyatt, that's wrong. You all know the Golden Rule. What you don't want done to yourself, don't do it to someone else. If someone isn't shooting at you but you're shooting at him, that's wrong. What isn't wrong is if someone mistreats you and you, in return, mistreat him. What isn't wrong is 'Do unto others what they have done unto you.' How many people," asks Johnny, scanning the somewhat shamefaced men on his sofas, armchairs, chairs, "know about the Opium War?"

"We all know," says someone.

"From school," someone else.

"Good," says Johnny. "You know that in 1839 opium wasn't legal in China. We had sort of a DEA, a Drug Enforcement Administration, and when the British started importing opium, the Commissioner wrote to the Queen reminding her of the Golden Rule. He wrote her," Johnny continues, Johnny who has been boning up, has been reading history books, "'The Way of Heaven doesn't permit us to hurt other people to help ourselves.' He wrote her, 'All people are like this. We all cherish life, and we all hate what endangers life,' and he wrote her, 'The Way of Heaven prevails for the British, too.' He then wrote the Queen, 'We ban opium forever in China,' then he had twenty thousand chests of British opium thrown into the China Sea. And what did the British do? They sent their army and navy, their infantry and artillery, to Shanghai. To defend ourselves, all we had were swords and wickerwork shields, spears and medieval halberds, bows and feathered arrows, and muskets set off by kitchen matches. In three days the British took Shanghai." Dramatically, Johnny jabs his index finger against his temple and says, "The white ghosts held their guns to our heads and said, 'You will buy our opium.'"

"'And you will give us Hong Kong,'" says someone resentfully.

"'And for the opium chests you'll pay us $21,000,000.' And," says Johnny, "the white ghosts sent us their opium till World War I. And sent us what's worse, their tobacco. A cigarette," says Johnny correctly, "is ten times more addictive than opium, morphine, heroin—all of them, they're related—but the white ghosts of America sent us Pirate and Pinhead, Rooster and Ruby, cigarettes. We boycotted them. We sang about them,

> *You're down and out,*
> *American cigarette,*
> *Our love affair*
> *Is over.*

And what did America do? Its President sent its Secretary of War to China, and," says Johnny correctly (the President was Theodore Roosevelt and the Secretary of War was William Howard Taft), "and the boycott collapsed. Then in China the Americans put up millions of cigarette posters. The scenes were from Chinese operas and *Twenty-Four Stories of Filial Piety,* but the captions were Pirate, Pinhead, Rooster and Ruby. The ads profaned our ancient walls, our lunar calendars, our vegetable carts, our rickshaw rugs, our movie screens. By World War I, the Americans sent us six billion cigarettes every year. And yet they wouldn't pay the cigarette tax," says Johnny correctly. "They threatened to call in sixteen thousand soldiers instead."

"Chairman Mao," says the Professor, "wrote about that in *The Cigarette Tax*. He said if our foreign masters fart, it's fragrant perfume to us Chinese."

"And even now, Americans aren't paying the tax," says Johnny correctly. "Most of the Marlboros, Winstons, Camels and Kents in China are smuggled in. The average adult in China, how many cigarettes do you suppose he smokes every year? It's 1,500," says Johnny as, *flick,* into an ashtray goes two-thirds of Fat Ass's Kent. "And how many people living right now in China will die of American cigarettes? Ten thousand? One hundred thousand? No," answers Johnny correctly. "One hundred million Chinese people will die."

"Chairman Mao," says the Professor, "wrote about that in *People of the World, Unite*. He said that American imperialism is riding roughshod everywhere."

"And he's right," says Johnny. "If the white ghosts sell us cigarettes, it's ethical if we sell them heroin. Are we behaving like the British in the Opium War? Do we hold guns to Americans' heads and say, 'You buy or we'll kill you?' Are we acting like the Americans nowadays? Do we put murals on American walls, murals of young people hiking, murals of young people paddling kayaks, murals that say, 'Buy Big Circle Heroin'? Do we put murals there of the Big Circle Man?" asks Johnny, referring to the lariat-swinging, fence-vaulting, bronco-busting cowboy that a man looking down from Mars might think is China's tutelary god. "No, the Americans come to *us*. Even the oafish officer comes to *us*. They tell us, 'We want your white powder, please.' In China," continues Johnny, "the years go in twelve-year cycles. The year of the Opium War," that's 1839, "was the Year of the Pig, and now," it's now 1983, "it's the Year of the Pig again. For twelve twelve-year cycles, America has dealt drugs to China—well, now we'll deal to America. I tell you, my little brothers. Don't agonize about it. It's ethical."

Sold! One man who's sitting on Johnny's floor, someone who smuggles angora wool from China to Japan but who's afraid to smuggle drugs to America, says, "No, I'm too busy," and Johnny tells him, "You don't have to if you don't want to." But all the other bosses say yes.

HONG KONG

One more ethical obstacle faces Johnny. A cycle ago, he stripped to his Jockeys for his initiation into the Gang of Tranquil Happiness. In both hands he held a lit incense stick (the lit end pointed down) and said, "I won't sell heroin. If I do, may I be hanged," then he dashed out the red-hot stick to symbolize how *he'd* be snuffed out if he flouted that stringent oath. In conscience, he now cannot export-import until he has dispensation from the elders of Tranquil Happiness, and one afternoon he escorts these men to his conference room at Imperial Fur, his Muzak-suffused, triple-spotlighted, air-conditioned conference room. The walls are mirrors, are mirrored doors that, as Johnny opens them, disclose a hoard of minks, lynxes, and silver foxes that the principal elder of Tranquil Happiness (not the Dragonhead, who typically hasn't come, but the small, skinny, white-haired man who once told Johnny, "I hope you'll open branches in the United States")—the principal elder says of in Cantonese, "They're beautiful." With wrinkled fingers the elder starts petting them, saying, "They're soft."

"Big Brother," says Johnny, "I'll give you one."

"Oh, no," says the incorruptible elder. His nickname is Uncle Wo, for in the Cantonese language the Gang of Tranquil Happiness is the Wo On Lok, and with forty smaller gangs (forty smaller secret societies) it's the Wo Chi Tau, the Wo Organization.

"As you wish, Big Brother," says Johnny. He gestures respectfully, and the ten elders take their seats around his teak conference table, its top yellow marble, its trim yellow gold, an obeisant receptionist serving them tea and Coca-Cola. Sitting down too, Johnny turns to Uncle Wo and says, "Big Brother. You've heard about the Big Circle. For one year I have hung out with it. Its men are good, honest, brave, and I want to relocate them to the United States. I want to use them for a particular purpose. I want—"

Johnny stops. Already he's noticed an ominous frown on Uncle Wo, who isn't looking at Johnny or, in the glistening mirrors, at his own wrinkled reflection but at the inconsequential parquet ceiling. For several seconds he frowns silently, then says in Cantonese, "No." His voice so low that it's almost imperceptible, he says to Johnny, "No. I know about the people in the Big Circle. I'm sure they're nice, but," he continues, his manicured fingers (on his ring finger imperial jade, glittering in the bright spotlights) tapping the table emphatically, "they're like a gang of high-school adolescents. They're running here. They're running there. They aren't dependable. What do I do if I have trouble with them? What if I ask them, 'Who's your boss? Who's responsible for you?' What if I ask them, 'Who do I talk to?' They cannot tell me."

"You talk to *me*," Johnny answers.

"You speak for all the Big Circle?"

"No, maybe half."

"You speak for how many bosses?"

"Well, maybe ten."

"But there are ten other bosses," says Uncle Wo. "And next month maybe there's twenty more. Are they all speaking with you?"

"No," says Johnny candidly.

"How can you control them, then? How can you speak for the Big Circle if half the Big Circle isn't speaking with *you?*"

"Big Brother," says Johnny. As deferential as Johnny is (for the much older man is Uncle Wo) he isn't obsequious. His own home ground is this conference room, and he has seated himself at the head of this teak-gold-marble conference table, his left-hand man his "Big Brother." What's more, he's executed a subtle one-up on this sweltering afternoon by dressing in a white shirt, a $100 chamoline tie, and a $2,000 champagne suit, even as the unfastidious elders (who didn't anticipate air conditioning) dress in short sleeves and no jackets at all. As always, Johnny's supremely polite, but not like the servile receptionist with the tea-toting silver tray, no, he's polite like the Prince of Wales, is so inherently confident that he needn't stoop to shouting/screaming. Already he's seen that the elders don't care if he profanes his sacred oath and if he sells heroin, hemlock or arsenic to the United States, the elders don't care as long as *control* remains in the Gang of Tranquil Happiness. "Big Brother," says Johnny. "My ten bosses are the most powerful in the Big Circle."

"But what about the other ten?"

"My ten will influence them."

"But they won't *control* them."

"In some ways they will. The Big Circle is structured like General Motors. If I own fifty percent of General Motors, then I own all of it."

His argument fails. Once again Uncle Wo says, "No. It's not traditional. It's not how we've done this for three hundred years. We aren't a bunch of kids playing tag. We have an undisputed leader, the Dragonhead. He issues orders to me, a Double Flower White Paper Fan, and I issue orders to you, a White Paper Fan. If you want underlings, you get yourself some number four nines. We will initiate them into the Gang of Tranquil Happiness, and you'll issue orders to them forever. That's the traditional way."

"All right," says Johnny, settling back in his high-backed, rattan-backed chair. "Then that's the way we'll do it."

HONG KONG

Naked except for Jockeys are ten incomparable bosses (and forty assorted soldiers) of the Big Circle. On some the Jockeys lie loosely, as if they were scrubbed on a scrubbing board every day for the past seven years, but on others they're bloated by volumes of functionless fat, are four-gallon garbage bags. The flesh of some men is crisscrossed by scars, mementos of ancient machete wars, but the flesh of several black-belters is smooth as on newborn infants. And now these felons (armed robbers, occasional murderers, nemeses-to-be of the U.S.A.) participate in the great ceremony: the sword, the blanket, the hoop, the pot, *I'm floating, on calmer, water,* the ribbon, the chicken, the pinprick—no, there is no pinprick, this is the age of AIDS—and the fire-tipped sandalwood incense. The georgic poems, the gangsters recite, and they take the thirty-six oaths like "I won't sell heroin. If I do, may I be hanged," an oath countermanded by their oath to obey their leader, who's Johnny, and "If I don't, may I be poisoned."

Then everyone leaves (they've been in a villa outside of Kowloon) for shrimp, scallops, etcetera, at a Chinese seafood restaurant. "Our tree is now blooming," beams Uncle Wo. "We have branches in Europe, and now we'll have one in America. And you, Ah Kon," a friendly nickname for Johnny, "are now the Dragonhead for North and South America, you now are the Dragonhead for the United States."

II

Ash Carrier I

Hong Kong

Heroin. Horse. The Big H. Harry, Hairy and Henry. China White. In the 1830s when the British were pushing opium into China, they called it cotton, called it chintz, and nowadays heroin is called the *goods* in Johnny's organization. In the far-away 2000s when the Americans will smuggle cigarettes into Europe (sixty percent of the Winstons in Spain will be smuggled in) the Americans will call them *merchandise,* consumers will call them cancer canes, and the addicts to China's heroin will call it dirt, dreck, dogfood, call it DOA. Will call it red chicken, red eagle, and (in right-to-left spelling) red rum.

For starters, Johnny will export fifteen pounds of this multinominal item from Bangkok to New York City. His courier won't be his longtime one the Eurasian, the man with passports from the United States, China, Thailand, Japan, France, Switzerland, Brazil, Bolivia, Colombia, Costa Rica, the Dominican Republic, and Saudi Arabia, a man who can coast through customs like a frolicsome tourist in a T-shirt saying, "I♥NY," a man who unfortunately isn't Big Circle. Instead, Johnny's courier will be another incomparable boss, a thin man who always, *always,* dresses in impeccable suits like a business executive and who is deferentially known as the Four-Star General, a close approximation to his real name in Shanghai dialect. One night at Johnny's apartment on Homantin Hill, the other bosses in short-sleeved shirts in the living room, drinking, and Jonquil in a pink-flowered white gown in the kitchen, cooking, her body adorned with $200,000 of jade rings, bracelets, earrings and brooches (all trimmed with glittering diamonds) that Johnny has pressed upon her to distract her from her Cambodian babies, Johnny who hasn't told her "I robbed these from Sun Sun Jewellers"—one night the General and Johnny conspire in the master bedroom to send red rum to America. Also present is Fat Ass, the Kent-intemperate boss who, in the absence of armchairs, crashes like under a hail of bullets onto the butter-colored carpet, his back against the bedstead, his legs out straight. On the carpet also sits Johnny, his knees up, ankles crossed, arms embracing his legs, right hand holding his left, body locked like in hatha yoga, the Sukhasana posture. As for the General, he tidily takes off his silk suit jacket, folds it as though it's a wedding gift, lays it primly and even prissily over the footboard, loosens his $100 red yellow-bamboo-patterned tie. Like a real general, inspecting, he brushes his fingers on Johnny's carpet, lifts them up to his gold-rimmed glasses, checks them for any unwelcome dust as Johnny thinks, *Why? No one walks here but Jonquil and me.* The carpet having passed muster, the General pinches his knees, pulls up his trousers, gingerly settles down, and softly, slowly, meticulously says in Cantonese, "I'll buy the goods in Bangkok."

"Not the goods. The *bads,*" laughs Fat Ass. Or something like that in Cantonese.

"I'll put the goods," the General continues unwaveringly, "in a soft canvas bag."

"Why soft?" asks Johnny. "You're carrying bricks. The hats will feel them."

"They won't feel them, Big Brother. I'll first pulverize them."

"You'll pulverize bricks? Or pulverize hats?" laughs Fat Ass. Still guffawing, he pulls out his Kents, but the General glares at him frigidly, meaning *You dolt. We're in the Dragonhead's bedroom,* and Fat Ass quickly repockets the inappropriate coffin nails.

"The bricks, you'll crush them?" asks Johnny.

"Yes," the General says. "From Bangkok, I'll drive south to Kuala Lumpur."

"They have the death penalty in Malaysia."

"I know. They'll never suspect me. From there I'll drive south to Singapore."

"They have the death penalty there, too."

"He already died in Malaysia," laughs Fat Ass, but the General ignores him.

"I know, Big Brother," the General says. He takes off his glasses, takes out his handkerchief, wipes the already immaculate glasses, puts them on. If he were sitting at some elliptical conference table and not on Johnny's modest carpet, the General could be an IBM senior executive. "From Singapore I'll fly to Toronto. Since I'll be coming from Singapore, the hats in Toronto won't suspect me. That's why I'm coming from Singapore."

"You're sure this will work?" asks Johnny.

"Yes. Your man in New Jersey, I'll meet him at the Hilton Hotel in Toronto."

"Which Hilton Hotel? There's several in Toronto."

"I don't know which," the General admits, ashamed of this slight imperfection.

"*I* know," says Fat Ass, and from his back pocket pulls a Hilton brochure.

"Which one, then?" the General grimaces.

"I don't know. The brochure is in English."

"You don't know bullshit," the General says in Cantonese (the bosses are often contentious) and takes the brochure from Fat Ass. He scans it and says, "The Toronto Airport Hilton Hotel."

"All right," says Johnny uncertainly. "But never forget: Be secretive. No one must see you. No one must hear you. No secrecy," says Johnny in one of those pithy phrases like *no pain, no gain,* like *easy come, easy go,* like *first come, first served,* like *monkey see, monkey do,* that we have adopted from the Chinese—"no secrecy, no success." In some crowded corner of Johnny's mind are the gaily chirping cicadas he caught at age ten in his side-buttoned gown in Shanghai. To catch them, Johnny took flour and water, mixed them, kneaded them, squeezed them into a glutenous ball of golf-ball proportions, put the ball on a bamboo pole, went

154

out and, not letting any cicadas see, not letting any cicadas hear, carefully raised it into a sonorous zelkova tree. And lo! as Johnny retracted it, a chirping cicada adhered to it, an insect he sold for a penny to one of his Shanghai schoolmates. "Be secretive," Johnny now tells the General in his bedroom on Homantin Hill. "Assume that anything you say, Americans will analyze it, Americans will unravel it," the recollection in this tenacious cerebral corner being of General Abrams, who told him in Saigon, "We had information. We knew the VC were coming. We *trapped* 'em."

"I won't forget," the General says.

"One wrong word, they'll get you."

"I won't forget, Big Brother." Abiding by the proprieties, the General doesn't say "I won't forget, oh, Dragonhead," just as a Western man doesn't address the Pope with "Good morning, Pope," and (except for Jimmy Durante) doesn't address the Queen of England with "I'm pleased to meet you, Queen." To his associates in the Big Circle, Johnny the big drug smuggler (the *ash carrier* in gangster slang) still is Big Brother.

MONTCLAIR

Be secretive. At his boar-hunter-carpeted home at 244 Midland Avenue, the Sergeant's telephone rings. "How are you?" a voice with a Chinese accent asks.

"Hey, Johnny! I'm fine!"

"You want vacation here?"

"Sure!" says the Sergeant, and after hanging up he books himself onto an 18-hour flight to Hong Kong. It's eighteen hours he'd have saved if Johnny had simply told him to meet the General at the Toronto Airport Hilton Hotel, but Johnny (who phoned from an outdoors booth) couldn't be certain the DEA wasn't listening in.

HONG KONG

Fat and open-buttoned, the Sergeant walks with Johnny out of Kai Tak International Airport and drives with him to a splendid hotel, this time the Holiday Inn Crowne Plaza. He meets the General ("Now you met. You won't forget," says Johnny in English) and dines at the Great Shanghai, his hips overflowing his wooden chair, his chair flaunting mother-of-pearl flowers, his fingers gripping his coral-colored shears, his shears cutting claws off his Shanghai crab, his crab disgorging the ghastly green crab's eggs that the Sergeant eschews.

"Is the best part!" cries Johnny.

"No, you Chinese are different from us Americans," the Sergeant says.

"Cost fortune!" cries Johnny.

"No, it's not for me," the Sergeant says, then he flies eighteen hours home.

BANGKOK

For $40,000, the General buys fifteen pounds of heroin in the configuration of white-colored bricks. With a mallet and rolling pin he pulverizes these, with a soupspoon he fills up Ziploc bags. He puts these not in his soft canvas bag—not yet, anyway—but in his gas tank and starts driving south in his summer suit along the Isthmus of Kra. Alas, in Bangkok the General didn't do what every respectful courier must: he didn't stop at the southeast corner of Ratchadamri Road and Phloenchit Road to pray for divine assistance from the incense-intoxicated idol who sits in a lotus position inside the Temple of the Four-Faced Buddha. He didn't tell it, "The hats, make them unaware of me."

KOTA BHARU

His suit spotless, the General enters Malaysia at the Beach of Passionate Love, a beach the color of wet cement that got its inviting name from the Tourism Promotion Board. At the border, the hats don't assume that a man wouldn't come to Malaysia with a warrant for his own execution inside his gasoline tank, no, the hats have found heroin in honeydew melons, soy-sauce bottles, surfboards, and (all knotted in condoms) a tourist's stomach. Four years ago, a woman crossed to Malaysia with a sleeping child who, the hats discovered, had been kidnapped, murdered, eviscerated, stuffed full of H, and rushed to the border before it turned white. But today the hats don't siphon the General's gasoline tank to detect the General's heroin, and the General continues south.

SINGAPORE

The death penalty doesn't deter all the tourists to Singapore, either. So many tourists import drugs that by the 2000s there will be giant posters on every immaculate avenue, posted there by the Partnership For a Drug-Free Singapore. A frowzy brown, the posters will depict dirty toilets and say,

> *Your anus blisters with open sores. Toilet tissue feels like broken glass. Heroin is living hell,*

but in his respectable suit the General enters Singapore easily. At his hotel, he dries off the Ziploc bags, sews them into the sides of his soft canvas bag, calls up Johnny in Hong Kong and says in Shanghai dialect, "Tomorrow I'll fly to Toronto. Tell your man in New Jersey." Alas, the General didn't do what every cautious courier must: he didn't phone from a telephone booth, he phoned from his hotel room, and Johnny's telephone number will be on the General's bill. A few days from now in Hong Kong, Johnny will be brought in by the Royal Police, who'll ask him in Cantonese, "Do you know a Mr. Kwok?" "No." "Do you know why he phoned you from Singapore?" "No. Unless," Johnny will say, and the police will believe him, the pin-striped man, the commendable citizen— "unless he got the wrong number."

TORONTO

His suit still spotless, his passport obviously phony, the General flies into Pearson International Airport and into the black-gloved hands of the Royal Canadian Mounted Police. "In his bag they found eight pounds of heroin," a half-accurate reporter says on the TV set in the

Sergeant's room at the Holiday Inn Crowne Plaza, and the Sergeant hurries down to the wood-pillared lobby, then to an outdoors booth, then calls up Hong Kong. "Hey, Johnny, your friend's on TV," he says nonchalantly.

"Oh, yeah? How about this," says Johnny. "Go home."

"I'll leave now," the Sergeant says unconcernedly.

HONG KONG

A smog of melancholia surrounds all of Johnny's brothers. They're in his ecru-carpeted home but, to look at, could be sitting around a coffin instead of a glass coffee table. Johnny himself thinks, *I'm to blame. I didn't tell the General clearly enough, Be secretive.* "We need $25,000 for a Toronto lawyer," Johnny says now in Cantonese. "Where do we get it?"

"I know," says the Professor, sipping tea. "We rob another jewelry store."

"And lose another brother?" asks Fat Ass. "A better idea is, We squeeze."

"We squeeze who?" asks Johnny.

"I know this antiques dealer on Hong Kong Island," says Fat Ass.

"Have we any right to squeeze him?"

"He bought some antique paintings from my friend in Canton. My friend sent him ten paintings, but the antiques dealer paid for just nine. He said he didn't receive the tenth, that's $65,000."

"But maybe he *didn't* receive it."

"He got the others. Why not this?"

"Maybe your friend didn't send it."

"He sent the others. Why not this? Well," continues Fat Ass. "Maybe my friend sent it, maybe he didn't. The antiques dealer, maybe he got it, maybe he didn't. That isn't our concern, that is the antiques dealer's. I say let's squeeze him."

"All right. Go squeeze him," says Johnny, who's thinking, *Well, I'm a gangster, aren't I?* and Fat Ass and two other grim-visaged bosses drive to the antiques dealer's on Hong Kong Island. In the man's office, where

the pagodas of papers on perpendicular spindles mirror the red pagodas
on antique paintings (all of them smuggled from Canton) and where the
old antiques dealer mirrors the grandfather who, on one green water-
color, is chatting with an empathic tortoise, the bosses say in Cantonese,
"Our friend wants his $65,000."

"No, I don't owe him," the dealer says.

"Then come with us," the bosses suggest, none of them saying please
but one of them holding a Bowie knife to the dealer's throat to under-
score his invitation. "If you yell, we'll kill you," the bosses add, then drive
him to Johnny's split-level office at Imperial Fur, Johnny on his dais to
welcome him.

"How are you?" says Johnny in Cantonese genially, for today he's playing the White Face or, as Americans call him, the Good Cop. "I'm sorry
these people mistreated you."

"No!" cries the boss who's playing the Red Face. "We told him nicely!
He wouldn't pay us! Let's throw him out the window!" the tilting window
in Johnny's office, thirteen stories high. The view of one hundred
rooftops and, beyond them, of Hong Kong Harbor is unnerving enough,
but for extra emphasis the Red Face cries, "Let's throw him off the thirteenth floor!"

"No, I know him," says Johnny. "We're friends."

"No, he thinks we're kidding!" the Red Face.

"We aren't kidding!" cries Fat Ass. "We are Big Circle! I'm known as
Fatty! Go ask about me! I—"

"Please please! You people shut up!" Johnny shouts. "My friend," he
says to the shaken antiques dealer. "They say you owe $65,000. Let's set-
tle this for, oh—for $35,000."

"What?" cries the Red Face, slamming Johnny's desk.

"I don't have the $35,000," the dealer apologizes.

"*What?*" cries the Red Face, who's standing behind him.

"What?" echoes Johnny. The sides of his mouth drop down, drop to
an angle iron's shape as Johnny tells the stingy dealer, "I save you
$30,000? And you say no? All right, I'll just forget it. You can deal with
these people instead."

"No, I'll deal with you! But can you come down?"

"I'll say one word," Johnny says, "and I'll say nothing after that. Not one penny more or one penny less. You pay $25,000."

"What?" cries the Red Face. "No more than $25,000?"

"You heard me!" cries Johnny. "Not one penny more!"

"If he doesn't pay it, I'll throw him out the window!"

"I'll pay the $25,000! I'll pay the $25,000!" the dealer promises, he isn't defenestrated and Johnny has his chauffeur return him to Hong Kong Island.

HONG KONG

But the man doesn't pay. He runs whining to a great secret society, the Gang of Tranquil Victory, and offers it $6,500 to flatten out the Big Circle and its extortionist bosses like Johnny. Seizing up its machetes, the ones that whack watermelons apart, the Gang gives notice to Johnny to rendezvous with it, combat-ready, in the spacious lobby at 64 Mody Road.

The site of this imminent mayhem won't be the New Miramar Hotel but (the Chinese are different from you and me) an even more gorgeous grand hotel, the Kowloon Shangri-La. The lobby is dominated by an enormous fountain, a birdbath that's spilling into a bigger birdbath that's spilling into a *bigger* one, all three octagonal birdbaths chiseled of glistening marble. On one wall, large as a Gobelin, is an artist's conception of the tranquil land the hotel is named for: the sun, sun-tinted clouds, great guardian mountains like guardian giants, and in the leafy lowlands a red pagoda whose residents all are birds, are finches, cardinals, crossbills, in vests, embroidered jackets, robes, in the quietude of a philosopher's life: a sparrow scanning an ancient scroll, a parrot thoughtfully holding it, a parrot doing tai chi. Over this Eden egrets fly, and at the painting's edges a hummingbird and an envious kingfisher watch. To this idyllic lobby, full of tourists in tailored suits and of women tourists in dresses, kimonos and saris, at eight o'clock in Levis and T-shirts come one hundred men from the Gang of Tranquil Victory, in their front lines their brawny leader—their Red Pole—a man about thirty years old who parades a machete scar on his right temple as vainly as any duelist at Heidelberg, a man whose nickname is Cat Kid. "Take some tables. Order some tea," he commands, and his one hundred soldiers do. The trio (it's saxophone, flute and double bass) takes an unscheduled break, and the customers prudently pay and walk out till only the slow-witted tourists, almost all Americans, are left in the white-marbled, dragon's-blood-granited, quadruple-chandeliered lobby.

The air's on edge. The bellboys are all wax statues. Nearby in the Lobby Lounge, Cat Kid sits down in an armchair with a Navaho cinnamon-colored design, sits down under a painting of a Picasso harlequin, a man who's juggling red, pink, yellow and purple balls as, in the picture windows to his right and left, there juggle the million lights of Hong Kong Island. A minute later, Johnny, his own hundred soldiers behind him, comes in in his suit and tie to attempt to avert armageddon by sitting down with Cat Kid. But politic Johnny isn't. "I'm angry," says Johnny in Cantonese, his finger tap-tapping the table as though it's a telegraph key. "This little antiques dealer. Why must you and I sit down about him?"

"He's our friend," says Cat Kid. "He says you're milking him."

"He owes $65,000 to Canton. We're collecting part of it."

"No. He owes nothing. He never got the painting."

"For this little thing there'll be civil war?" asks Johnny, hinting he's in a secret society and not just in the Big Circle. Only his dignity stops him from saying, "Hey, Cat Kid, I'm your cousin—I'm in the Gang of Tranquil Happiness," or, like the Northerner, from setting his teapot out and his teacup behind it, or from asking Cat Kid, "Where are you from?" and waiting for Cat Kid's fraternal answer "I'm from the East." Or from submitting to Cat Kid's sphinxian Q&A, "Where were you born?" "Beneath a peach tree." "When were you born?" "On the twenty-fifth day of the seventh month." "Where do you live?" "On Five-Finger Mountain." "Haven't you died?" "I have died once." "Three times eight is—?" "Twenty-one." Or from abdicating all majesty by saying in sign language, "I am the Dragonhead," his left fist over his heart, his thumb pointed up, his pinkie down: a dragon's two dreadful horns. Not stooping to this self-promotion, he tells an attendant boss to quietly clue in Cat Kid, and the tall, dark-skinned, handsome boss says, "Cat Kid, let's you and I talk."

They walk to a neutral corner. The boss is another of Johnny's incomparables, someone born in Canton, raised under Mao, admitted to the Red Guard, smuggled to Hong Kong, and now addicted to all-night discos, where he spends his ill-gotten gains dancing to Michael Jackson, to spirited lyrics like

> *I wanna rock with you,*
> *I wanna groove with you,*

and where to his great delight he's known by the English name Michael Jackson. Off the dance floor he's quiet, conciliatory, and now he starts patting on Cat Kid's arm like someone who's tamping out some smoldering ashes. "Cat Kid, Cat Kid," says Michael Jackson in Cantonese emolliently. "You're with the Gang of Tranquil Victory. I'm with the Gang of Tranquil Happiness. You and I, we're kith and kin. That clown there," meaning the antiques dealer. "Is he one of us?"

"No. He's our friend," answers Cat Kid.

"He's just your friend. Do you see Johnny Kon? He's our top man," says Michael Jackson. Not saying "Dragonhead," he whispers the euphemism as though it's the secret it certainly is and continues to pat his cousin-in-crime as though he's reminding him, "This strictly is *entre nous.*" "That clown there. How much money did he offer you?"

"$6,500," says Cat Kid.

"You risk your life for $6,500. The clown does nothing for $18,500. Listen," says Michael Jackson, still patting soothingly. "You and I don't want war. Not for this silly antiques man. You and I, let's split the $6,500. And tell him to pay us the $25,000." As if it's plain that the answer's yes, his arm arches overhead like an Indian's saying *"How,"* his signal to his one hundred men to accord safe conduct out of the lobby to Cat Kid.

A soft answer turns away wrath. His arm massaged, his pride untarnished, the scar-templed boss of the Gang of T.V. pats Michael Jackson and, with his one hundred soldiers, leaves the Shangri-La, a Sikh like a stevedore heaving a two-foot handle, opening a ponderous front door. From behind their rampart (the lacquered bar) the waiters and waitresses emerge as gaunt as a gunman's hostages, and the trio (the saxophone, flute, and double bass) play *All I Ask of You* from *The Phantom of the Opera*. The next day, Johnny collects the $25,000 that, as an ethical entrepreneur, he wants to share with the man who was or wasn't cheated in Canton, but Fat Ass has his own ethics and tells Johnny, "No! The money is all for the General! We must liberate him!"

TORONTO

To the General's jail comes a Chinese man who gets by the barbed wires, the yellow brick walls, by taking a business card that says, "Solicitor," from a $2,000 black crocodile attaché case. The man, whose shirt is white, whose tie and handkerchief are the same paisley pattern, whose glasses, cufflinks and Rolex are gold, whose hairs almost follow a blueprint—the dandified man is no lawyer but the messenger for Johnny's gang. A potpourri of cologne refreshes the visitor's room as he sits with the General (wearing green slacks, green shirt, pinching his green knees primly) and says, "Your father sent me," and not "The Dragonhead sent me." "Do not talk. Do not admit anything. Do not cooperate with the hats," the messenger continues. "Our firm will take care of you, your father and mother, your wife and kids." His implication is, "If you inform on Johnny, we will take care of your father and mother, your wife and kids, in a less benevolent way."

"Thank you," the General says. Never will Johnny's name pass the General's lips. His case will cost $100,000, and he'll serve in Canadian prisons, and all because (the General thinks) he neglected to ask for God's saving grace in Bangkok, at the Temple of the Four-Faced Buddha.

12

Ash Carrier II

BANGKOK

If at first you don't succeed, try, try . . .

Johnny is in Bangkok, the temple-topped city, the tiles orange, green and blue, the spires impaling all evil spirits that fall from the sky like Beelzebub. Johnny is in the Dusit Thani ("Palace of Paradise") Hotel, it's midafternoon and Johnny is in its orchid-exuberant restaurant, the Pavilion, his lap between an orchid-upholstered chair and an orchid-colored napkin. Of the dozen exotic fruits at the Pavilion (the red and green-thistled rambutan like a dead armadillo, the red and green-warted mangosteen like Arcimboldo's *Allegory of Summer,* the pea-green durian like a thorny honeydew melon that, if you cut and don't eat in a minute, deteriorates to an odorous slop)—of these disconcerting fruits he has chosen a lowly orange, and the Chinese man sitting with him has chosen a lowly mango. The man, who blinks persistently, as if there's a gnat that inhabits his eye, is a courier from Fatty, the heroin-happy wanted man in the Golden Triangle. In suit, shirt and tie like Johnny, the courier carries a $500 black leather briefcase that no other diner would guess has $45,000 worth (in Bangkok) or $600,000 worth (in New York) of heroin in hard white bricks inside it. Johnny gives him his key, and the courier rides up the elevator, takes the briefcase to Johnny's room, sets it on Johnny's teakwood desk, brings the key back to Johnny, departs.

Then Johnny goes to the Library 1918, the period coffeehouse of the
Dusit Thani. On the walls are old sepia photographs of Bangkok sixty-
five years ago, its streets full of leisurely carriages, open-topped automobiles, trolleys, its riverbanks full of the same spectacular temples as in
Bangkok today. On the walls, too, are latter-day bottles of Amaretto,
Creme de Cacao, and Irish Cream to add extra pick-me-up to Brazilian,
Colombian and mocca coffees, to English, Darjeeling, and passion-fruit
teas that Johnny comfortably chooses among. He sits sipping coffee-and-
cream as into the Library someone with an incredible physical presence
comes. A man in his forties, he's neither Caucasian nor Asian: his skin
isn't perfectly white but his nose isn't perfectly flat, his hair isn't blond,
brown or black but red, and his eyes (are they slanted? straight? *mezzo
mezzo?*) are totally veiled by his Ray Bans. His clothes are white: white
leather loafers, white socks, white slacks, white belt, though the buckle
is gold, white T-shirt inscribed "I♥NY," white blazer, white linen handkerchief. At his side is a white leather shoulder bag that he sets on
Johnny's glass table, sits down, and says in Shanghai dialect, "The Ori-
oles won the Series."

"Are you sure you can handle this?" Johnny asks.

"I can handle *everything,*" says the fabulous man, his palms down, his
hands apart as if to cover the whole broad field of human accomplish-
ments. He is, of course, the Eurasian who isn't in the Big Circle but who's
Johnny's old courier, the one with passports from the United States,
China, Thailand, Japan, France, Switzerland, Brazil, Bolivia, Colombia,
Costa Rica, the Dominican Republic, and Saudi Arabia, his age on these
papers sometimes thirty, sometimes sixty. In fact he was born in Shanghai in World War II, his mother an Asian, his father an American marine:
that or the other way round or possibly both, the courier cannot remember. His birth name was Yin unless that, too, was an alias that, once having put on a passport, he slowly got to believe in and didn't believe he
came from somewhere like Saudi Arabia ("*Salaam aleikum,*" a customs
inspector said one day, and the courier answered in English, "I don't
speak Arabic. I was born in Switzerland"). Confused by his many iden-
tities, his acquaintances seize on his off-white skin and call him the
Ghost.

"This time you'll follow orders?" Johnny asks him.

"I will, Big Brother."

"If I say do one, two, three, you won't do three, two, one?"

"I won't, Big Brother."

"I can work with a dummy as long as the dummy follows orders."

"I'm aware, Big Brother."

"Then here's $5,000." Along with these American bills, Johnny hands him the key, and the Ghost leaves the Library striding, strutting, his arms and his shoulder bag swinging as though he's accepting an Oscar. For five minutes, Johnny sits alone, thinking, *The dummy's not him, it's me,* watching the splashing waterfall beyond the frangipani tree until the Ghost returns with the $500 black leather briefcase full of hard heroin bricks. "Now, don't disappear on me," Johnny orders in Shanghai dialect.

"I won't. I'll go at once to New York."

"Phone me as soon as you get there."

"I will," says the Ghost and departs from the Dusit Thani. In his hotel room, he leaves the black leather briefcase unopened, then goes to a loud karaoke club in the midst of one hundred others on Silom Road. He uses some of his $5,000 to buy himself and the B-girls drinks. Then laughing, laughing, talking like an auctioneer, he sets down a counterfeit 50-baht bill, sets a whiskey on top of it, tells a silver-toothed girl in English, "Pull out the bill! But don't spill the drink! Or you've got to drink it!" He makes a plumeria-colored lei of counterfeit bahts, with it he lassos the singer onstage, wiggles his fingers as if he's blowing a trumpet, sings,

> *Well, my friends, the time has come*
> *To raise the roof and have some fun,*

with the silk-dressed singer in Mandarin. By now totally blotto, he picks up three girls for $60 and takes them to his hotel, where he has sex with each serially while, with the other intertwined girls, he has foreplay simultaneously. He then passes out, and all week he's in this disordered and quite disorderly room as *ring!* on the phone there's a ring, ring, ring and, finding the phone among the bed sheets, blankets, bedspreads and towels, the Graces tell Johnny in Hong Kong, "No, we don't know the Ghost." Pity poor Johnny. Running a gangster gang isn't easy. By definition, no one inside it is an honest man.

BANGKOK

One week later, his $5,000 almost gone, the Ghost sobers up and dismisses his three-woman room-service staff. He opens the black leather briefcase, takes out the ten almost-concrete bricks, then *wham!* then *wham!* then hammers them with a hammer he bought in a Bangkok hardware store. The bricks become pebbles that (like someone making tortillas) the Ghost then rolls with a bottle until they're white powder, powder he spoons into Ziploc bags. Then, stepping outside, he takes a 50-cent taxi to the traffic-clanking, construction-clanking corner of Ratchadamri Road and Phloenchit Road to observe the religious rituals that the General, to his regret, neglected.

He enters the Temple of the Four-Faced Buddha. No temple at all but a roadside shrine like one to the Virgin Mary—and the Buddha really is Brahma, the Hindu god—it's crowded with supplicants, their hands in prayer position, their knees on cobblestones, hips on their heels, sandals pulling away. Taking his white leather shoes off, the Ghost kneels on a marble slab at the Buddha's northwest face. "Oh, Buddha," he half-thinks, half-says in Shanghai dialect. "I'm going to New York City. My trip, make it safe and successful. The hats, make them unaware of me." His auditor, a golden idol, its height that of a ten-year-old, its posture a lotus position, gazes at him benevolently, its left hand holding an orb, its right hand holding a rod. "If you grant this, oh, Buddha," the Ghost continues, "I'll come back and I'll bring flowers," then, rising, the Ghost walks clockwise to the Buddha's north side, the Buddha's three-quarters faces. At the railing, strung into leis, are numerous jasmines and marigolds, and the Ghost drapes some of his own sweet-smelling and melon-smelling flowers (bought from a busy vendor) on the luxuriant railing. At its base is a garden of sri sai flora incense sticks that the Ghost adds some of his own glowing incense to, but, as he plants it, the incense that is already there singes his arm and the smoke scratches his eyes, there being a wind up Ratchadamri Road. Crying, sniffling, his membranes burning, a man who's been practically pepper-sprayed, *help,* the Ghost moves clockwise to the Buddha's northeast face (the Buddha's *left* hand now has the rod, and its right has a finger cymbal) and says, "Oh, Buddha," etcetera, and "If you grant this, Buddha, I'll come back and I'll bring oranges, coconuts, pineapples." At the Buddha's southeast face by a man who's patting a bamboo drum, another who's playing a xylophone, and eight gorgeous girls in gold-embroidered pants, gold-spangled jackets, and gold-steepled headdresses who (with their fingers, mostly) are dancing liquescently, the Ghost says, "If you grant this, Buddha, I'll come back and I'll bring barbecued pig," and when, at the southwest face, he appeals for a safe, successful and hat-exempt trip to New York, he raises the ante to "Buddha, I'll come back and I'll pay these girls to dance naked," an entertainment the Buddha allegedly relishes. His prayers said, the Ghost takes a hard white lotus, a flower seemingly carved from soap, dips it into holy water, and spatters his head with it before returning to his hotel and his Ziploc bags.

He tapes them (well, ten of them, there isn't room for all forty) to his waist, stomach, thighs and legs, dresses in white, chooses his Swiss passport today, rides to Don Muang International Airport, and takes off on Thai International. Beneath him are the quilted paddies, then the China Sea.

TAIPEI

Itching, suffering, squirming, the Ghost is 30,000 feet over the Taiwanese capital. He waddles back to the lavatory, locks the door securely, drops his white slacks, peeks under the Ziploc bags. *Oh no,* thinks the Ghost. His skin looks as though the bags hold boiling water. His skin is red-meat red, its hairs have come out and are swimming in sweat, sautéing as though they're in melted butter, some of the heroin having osmosed through the Ziploc. *Help me, Buddha,* he thinks, but he can't remove the bags or even scratch underneath them. He pulls up his slacks, and he returns to his iron maiden, his purple business-class seat.

TOKYO

He lands at Narita International Airport to switch to another passport and to Northwest Airlines. His skin aflame but his shirt jauntily saying "I♥NY," his watch a Rolex, his camera a Minolta, he rides the garrulous monorail ("The doors will close. We are about to arrive. The doors will open") to another terminal, then walks through the metal detector, his ten plastic bags of heroin (well worth their weight in gold) not at all tripping it, then, *oh, help me, Buddha,* he finds himself facing a Japanese hat, a Japanese cop in a slate-colored, black-visored, gold-banded hat, a Japanese cop who's frisking everyone, one and all. "Please raise your arms," the Japanese says in English, and, when the Ghost does, the Japanese in his white cotton gloves starts patting his shoulders, moving on down, patting his arms, moving on down, patting his chest, sides, waist . . .

HONG KONG

It's been one week since Johnny said, "Don't disappear on me," at the Dusit Thani, in Bangkok, and all week he's phoned over Asia for his incomparable courier, phoned and not found him. *The hats caught him,* Johnny worries. *They questioned him. They threatened him. He squealed on me. They're setting me up.* All week Johnny has sworn off the heroin business, better (he tells himself) if he exported-imported furs, even jade apples, bananas and grapes, then Johnny's phone rings and it's the Ghost. "Where *are* you?" asks Johnny in Shanghai dialect.

"I'm in New York."

"Where in New York?"

"At the Hilton. Do you have a pen with you? Write down these letters. M-I-M-I," says the Ghost, says that or some other mysterious word.

"M-I-M-I," says Johnny. He writes down these letters, hoping the Ghost is in no one's clutches but his own irresponsible own.

MONTCLAIR

The phone at the Sergeant's cozy home rings. On the line is Johnny, who says in English, "Write this down. M-I-M-I," and the Sergeant does. He learned this cipher one day at a castle of Viennese pastry, the Café Vienna in Kowloon, learned it amidst the German cheesecakes, strawberry fruitcakes, raspberry tarts, pear custard tarts, apple strudels, grape strudels, orange-and-Cointreau mousses, crème de Grand Marnier mousses, mango puddings, and rum raisin puddings roofed by chocolate sugared slabs. At the Café Vienna, the Sergeant fattened himself with a sachertorte (the chocolate heated to 225°, poured onto a marble table next to a statue of Jo Kuan, the God of Cooking, and brushed and brushed with a spatula as the Viennese chef cried in Cantonese, "Shinier! Shinier!") as Johnny told him in English, "You take name Imperial Fur. You number letters,

$$I = 1$$
$$M = 2$$
$$P = 3$$
$$E = 4$$
$$R = 5$$

you leave out I, you already used it,

$$A = 6$$
$$L = 7$$
$$F = 8$$
$$U = 9$$

you leave out R, you already used it,

$$C = 0$$

C meaning Company," Johnny explained. "M-I-M-I," says Johnny now, and the Sergeant transcribes it, hangs up, walks to his Dodge, drives

170

through the Holland Tunnel, drives to West 54th, parks at the New York Hilton—the plan was always the Hilton—and on the house telephone calls up the Ghost under one of his countless aliases in Hilton room M-I-M-I, in Hilton room 2121. "I'll come down," the Ghost says in English.

Hong Kong

It's later that week, and Johnny and his heterogenous bosses wait, wait, in Johnny's apartment for the Ghost's well-scheduled return. On the L-shaped sofa, Fat Ass is drinking a San Miguel and nervously joking with Michael Jackson as the Professor sits looking displeased, looking as though he might suddenly yell, "This isn't a laughing matter!" The doorbell announces the Ghost, a man too wound up to do his normal obeisances: to take three sandalwood incense sticks, light them, bow to Johnny's red-faced statue of Kuan Kung, the God of Loyalty, and set the sticks in Johnny's ceramic bowl. As always, the Ghost is wearing white, but his hair isn't red tonight, it's blue, green and violet and Johnny cries in Cantonese, "Ronny," the Ghost's most common nickname. "Your hair, it's like peacock feathers!"

"I dyed it," the Ghost explains.

"But the dye. From here," says Johnny, circling around him, "it's blue. But from *here* it's green. What fucking dye is it?"

"A new one," the Ghost explains.

"It's iridescent," laughs Fat Ass. "But what is the purpose of it? Do you have a yen for peahens?"

"No, it's to look like a tourist."

"Like wearing I Love New York?"

"Yeah," the Ghost laughs.

"Do you really love it?"

"Of *course* he loves it," laughs Johnny, his left hand flinging itself to the winds as if to toss away every doubt. "He made $150,000 there."

"$175,000, Big Brother," the Ghost laughs. He drops on the coffee table a big black canvas bag, unzips it and lo! the bosses are oval-eyed clones of Long John Silver as $10s, $20s, $50s and $100s, all rubber-banded in $10,000 bundles and one $5,000 bundle, tumble out. "It wasn't easy, Big Brother," the Ghost continues in Cantonese. "No one could do it but me. Do you know what happened in Tokyo? A hat in white gloves told me, 'Come this way.' I'd been through the metal detector, and now I couldn't turn back," the Ghost continues, swiveling like a quarterback in a T-formation, invisibly sacked. "The hat started frisking me. Started frisking my shoulders, chest, waist. Did you see *Midnight Express*, Big Brother? I felt like the man in *Midnight Express*. I had the goods on me," the Ghost continues, gesturing, feigning hysteria, clapping his hands to his temples like someone moaning, *"Vay ist mir,"* if he had a microphone stand he'd be Rodney Dangerfield. "I had ten plastic bags on me. Three on my waist, three on my stomach, four on my legs. All right, Big Brother. What did I do?"

"I don't know," laughs Johnny.

"Brothers? So what did I do?"

"I don't know," laughs one.

"Then guess."

"The hat," laughs Michael Jackson, "may have searched the Chinese people—"

"But you," laughs Fat Ass, "look like an American—"

"So he may not have searched you."

"He *searched* me," the Ghost guffaws.

"How could he search you and miss the ten plastic bags?" asks another boss.

"Guess! What did I do?"

"I give up," laughs Johnny.

"Tell us," Michael Jackson.

"I'll only tell if you pay me!"

"I'll pay you," laughs Johnny.

"All right," the Ghost continues, laughing until he's red. "I stood there. My arms were like this," like a T. "In one hand I had my white leather bag. In the other I had my Minolta camera. The hat touched my waist, and I acted as if he had tickled me. *Ooh,"* the Ghost giggles, "and I dropped the Minolta."

Someone says, "What?"

"I dropped the Minolta camera. It hit the floor and the lens broke. The hat was just mortified. He kept saying, 'I'm sorry,'" the Ghost says amid growing laughter. "I squatted down, and I started picking the pieces up. The people behind me were waiting for me. The hat said, 'I'm sorry, I'm sorry, move on,' and I did. I went with the ten plastic bags to New York."

"You're really good," laughs Fat Ass.

"You're number one," Michael Jackson.

"Big Brother?" the Ghost concludes. "The camera was $500. Will you please pay me for it?"

"I'll pay you, I'll pay you," laughs Johnny.

The maid brings the dinner in. It's garlic chicken and cauliflower. As everyone eats it, toasts the Ghost, and pictures him shuttling across the Pacific with $500,000 a week for the Big, Bigger, Biggest Circle, the one man who isn't even grinning is the Professor. "Ronny," that solemn boss says. "Did this really happen?"

"It happened. I swear it."

"You didn't make it up?"

"I swear on my mother."

BANGKOK

Then back to the Four-Faced Buddha goes the Ghost gratefully. With him he brings some leis, oranges, coconuts, pineapples, barbecued pigs, then pays the grass-fingered gorgeous girls $2,000. The girls strip down to their lipstick (on some girls it's pink, on others it's Valentine red) and, unencumbered by sweat-sopping silks, do their lithe finger-dancing and sing in Thai,

> *Beautiful blossoms*
> *Buzzing with butterflies*
> *Like blushing maidens*
> *In their first bloom,*

their fingers all curved into "okay" signs,

No flower is, Brahma,
As precious as You.

Unluckily for the Ghost (though not for the Four-Faced Buddha, who allegedly has Superman eyes) the girls do this behind a thick curtain and the Ghost cannot ogle them. But that night in his rumpled room, he rounds up his room-service girls to play ring-around-the-rosie with him, to play it all week to Johnny's consternation, then he gathers ten Ziploc bags, puts five in each of his white leather boots, rides to Don Muang International Airport, and takes off for ♥-Land. Again completely successfully.

13

Ash Carrier III

HONG KONG

The trouble is, the users, pushers, dealers, and the Sergeant keep asking for more, for more, but $175,000 of Ziploc merchandise is all the Ghost can carry on any transoceanic trip. A trunk, a GI duffel bag, a Gucci suitcase—Johnny could fill it and sell it in New York City if the Ghost could slip it past the nosy parkers at John F. Kennedy International Airport. Where, thinks Johnny, can the Ghost hide white powder except on his own narrow body? What weighs a hundred pounds yet is too innocuous to arouse suspicion at Kennedy? Nothing that Johnny knows about, until one day in his kangaroo-carpeted office he puts his question to an old gangster from Bangkok, a man known as Old Fox, a man who then seats himself at Johnny's coffee table, lights up a 555, leans back his head, blows a wan smoke ring, observes it as though in its whorls is the answer in Chinese characters, and says in Cantonese superfluously, "Let me think."

He's like this, Old Fox. In life he proceeds deliberately, as if the course of the planets depend on his every choice. Ask him something simple like "What'll we eat?" and he'll light up a 555, lean back, blow a ring, watch it like someone at Delphi, and say, "Let me think." "How about shark's-fin soup?" Johnny (for instance) will ask him, and Old Fox will study the vorticose smoke for thirty, sixty, ninety seconds and then say,

"No . . ." "How about soy-sauce goose?" Johnny will ask him, and Old Fox will ponder the consequences of a "Yes . . ." and a "No . . ." as intently as if the question were "How about ellipses? Should we ordain ellipses for Mercury, Venus and Earth?" And today, asked where the heroin could go, Old Fox is halfway through his 555 before saying slowly in Cantonese, "I know a man in Bangkok."

"Yes? What about him?" asks Johnny keenly, but Old Fox sits smoking, blowing his whirling tori, till the 555 almost burns his brown-stained fingers. He puts the 555 out and lights up another one.

"Let me think," says Old Fox. And one minute later, "Well, I must speak with him."

"About?"

"Let me think." He blows another ectoplasmic doughnut and, as it eats itself leisurely, slowly says, "He makes vases."

"Vases?"

"Engraved aluminum vases. You must have seen them in Bangkok. They're—they're—*lovely,*" says Old Fox. "Yes, I must speak with him."

"Like flower vases?" asks Johnny. He looks at the white carnations in the narrow ceramic vase on his marble coffee table. A vase? To put heroin in? Suppose the customs inspectors look in it? Or turn it upside down?

BANGKOK

It's three weeks later, and Johnny is at Old Fox's (a great estate, two women opening its wrought-iron gate) to see one of these incomprehensible vases. At midnight he's sitting at a teak coffee table, a troop of monkeys carved into it, a sheet of glass over them, he's eating the mangos and mangosteens (but not the malodorous durians) brought in a bamboo basket by Mrs. Old Fox. She then brings a tall and red-flowered can of chiu chao tea that Old Fox prepares like an alchemist concocting the secret elixir of life. The tea leaves, he first shakes into a ceramic pot engraved with a mountainside scene. The water (which started as rain, which fell on his roof, then went to a pipe, a ceramic barrel, a bottle, and an aluminum pot, then the old gangster boiled it over kerosene on his monkey-troop table)—the water he pours on the waiting leaves. At once he pours it off again, explaining to Johnny in Cantonese, "The first batch of water isn't strong," then he pours a second dose that, a while later, he pours with a flourish into Johnny's pink-flowered cup. The tea's almost black, like Turkish coffee.

"It's wonderful tea," says Johnny appropriately.

His ritual over, his wife bowing out, Old Fox brings Johnny what somewhat resembles a tall umbrella stand. An aluminum vase, it's carved with fearsome dragons like on the King and Queen's barges on the Chao Phraya River. "It's made-to-order," says Old Fox in Cantonese. "Inside there's space for one and one half bricks. One vase, in other words, carries half as much white powder as the Ghost's whole body. One trip with twenty vases is equal to ten without them."

"I don't understand," says Johnny, who has been peering into the vase like into a telescope, has even upended it, shaken it, all but shattered it. "Where does the white powder go?"

"The vase is hollow," says Old Fox. He screws off the base, and lo! between the inside and outside walls like in a magician's trick is a quarter-inch gap, indeed enough for the powder from one and one half bricks.

"Wonderful, wonderful," says Johnny. "The vases cost what?"

"$200 apiece."

"I'll buy fifty."

"No problem," says Old Fox. "I'll have them next month."

"*What?*" exclaims Johnny. "I'm not a Sunday shopper! I am in business here! Work the workers overnight! Pay the workers overtime! I'll buy fifty every week!"

BANGKOK

And *tap, tap,* all night long go the artisans' tools. By the scores, the vases go to an old wooden frosted-window house in back of a man-high concrete wall at 18 Soi Sukhumvit Twenty-Three, next door to the Wanakarm Restaurant in Bangkok's sort of the Bronx. In the house the brothers use hammers and rolling pins (labeled with black-tied, black-jacketed, white-smiling black men, for the brand name is Black Man) to crumble the heroin bricks, then they use spoons to shovel it into a vase's false wall, then they use rebars to wad it. The heroin drifts into the air and sticks to the brothers' sweating arms, engendering blisters—that, or it settles onto the brothers' lips, it burns and the brothers lick it. They vomit and go to emergency rooms just as the people who'll buy these goods a week from now in America will. The vase, the brothers put AA glue in its threads before screwing the bottom on, then wash it in Kiwi Bitotex Concentrated Liquid Laundry Detergent. As the glue hardens, they spray everything with Glade Autumn Flowers or Haze Alpine Meadow and drive downtown for a couple of well-earned hours off at a movie or disco, at the Mona Lisa Massage Parlor or the Lipstick Bar, a bar whose billboards advertise,

> *Pussy shoot banana*
> *Pussy shoot balloon*
> *Pussy open bottle,*

etcetera, a bar whose tin-trumpet music is pussy-generated, sometimes. In this way the brothers go about raising funds for the Revolution against the Royal Police and the revenge against the United States.

BANGKOK

Seven vases. Ten white bricks. $600,000 in New York. The courier won't be the Ghost or, as the brothers now call him, the Tardy Ghost, who Johnny is having nightmares about (the Ghost gets caught and tattles on Johnny) but someone who once was a naughty boy, for his parents nicknamed him Dead Man. While tough, he isn't as tough as he often pretends, sitting, slapping his leg, slamming his thumb against his chest, talking (for instance) about a shoot-out in Kowloon, saying in Cantonese, "I stayed there! I stayed there! No one but me! Everyone fled but me! Me alone!" And now this braggart puts the aluminum vases into a black canvas traveling bag and takes them aboard an airplane at Don Muang International Airport. His cover is, he's a salesman carrying samples.

TOKYO

Dead Man is now at Narita, sitting on a lilac-colored seat, watching the wrestling on TV, the wrestlers whales, their flesh blubber, their buttocks full of harpoon wounds, full of red splotches, sores, the wrestlers scrimmaging—*hike,* and in one second one of them shoves the other out of the circular ring. But now an American-Born Chinese (an ABC in gangster slang) sits down by Dead Man and whispers in Fractured Cantonese, "How many vases have you?"

"Seven."

"Whoo! That's $600,000 in New York."

"$10,000 for you and me. All the rest for Big Brother."

"Yeah. He gets the lion's share."

"You and I should smuggle too."

"Maybe we should," says the ABC, who picks up the black canvas bag and boards a Mexico-bound plane.

MEXICO CITY

"What's this?" asks the customs inspector in English.

"Samples," says the ABC at the International Airport.

"What price are they?"

"$25 each."

"Can I keep one?"

"Next time," says the ABC, and slips him $100.

"No duty," says the Mexican customs inspector.

NUEVO LAREDO

Zzz! And off comes a dragon's snorting head. Just south of the Rio, the ABC uses a hacksaw to dissect the once-lovely vases, then dumps the heroin into some Ziploc bags. "Why all this money for Big Brother? Why not some money for *us?*" he says in English to an ABC who's driven down from New York. The second man, big and burly, is wearing hand-carved cowboy boots, designer jeans, and a belt buckle big as a brand-

ing iron. On his head pointing backwards, announcing he's a noncon-
formist, is a blue and silver cap for the Dallas Cowboys.

"We could keep one bag," says this ABC.

"And sell it. And use the $60,000—"

"To buy more in Bangkok—"

"And then sell *that.*"

"Let's do it," the Cowboy says, succumbing to that great capitalist
imperative: the more you've got, the more you want. Then, stashing the
Ziploc bags in their door frame, the ABCs drive across Lincoln Bridge to
the old Republic of the Rio Grande, now the State of Texas.

LAREDO

"What were you in Mexico for?" asks an American customs inspector.

"For vacation," the ABC with the Cowboys cap answers, but two Chinese from Chinatown dancing to a mariachi band in Nuevo Laredo, Mexico, seem incongruous to the white customs inspector, and he dispatches
the highway patrol to follow them up Interstate 35. "Take out the
Ziplocs," the ABC with the Cowboys cap tells the other one. "Put them
in the black canvas bag. I'll slow down at that turn ahead. Jump out with
the bag, and I'll see you in Chinatown." And stars over Texas silver the
mesquites and prickly pears as ABC number one does a stuntman's leap,
eludes the law, walks through the brush, returns to Laredo, and takes a
Hertz or an Avis north.

NEW YORK

Like most ABCs, the two Chinese speak sort of a Pidgin Cantonese, a language compounded of Cantonese beans and American peppers like "Okay?" "All right?" and "You know?" "We got all the vases,
okay?" the ABC with the Cowboys cap phones from a Chinatown telephone booth in Cantonese/English, phones to Johnny in Hong Kong.
"But you know? We lost two pounds in Mexico."

"How did you lose them?" asks Johnny.

"They stuck. They wouldn't come out."

"Don't worry about it," says Johnny.

"Okay."

"Deduct it from the money you owe."

"Okay," the ABC says, and smiles to ABC number one. He means they're on their way to a $1,000,000 deal.

HONG KONG

Johnny has made this call from the pier for the British cruise ships. He hangs up and, in Cantonese, tells the boss who's with him, "Chinatown got the white powder. But," he continues as the two start walking by the rocking sightseeing boats ("11:15. Noonday Gun") in Hong Kong Harbor, "it's two pounds short. It stuck to the vases in Mexico."

"No way!" says the boss who's walking with him.

"The white powder doesn't stick?" Johnny asks.

"Not one grain! Chinatown is getting greedy!"

But being ripped off of $80,000 is no great annoyance to Johnny. $80,000 could buy a whole lot of Uzis for the Revolution against the Royal Police and the revenge against the United States, but though the Professor needs them, Johnny doesn't. He's seen that white powder itself is more than enough exquisite revenge. He's seen on TV what heroin does to America. Walking along the wharf, he peers across the Pacific toward New York City, picturing City Hall, Penn Station, Columbus Circle, the Plaza Hotel, picturing people lining up as if to buy football tickets but, in fact, buying his heroin, picturing them in the stupor that he once joked about with skinny lieutenant in Saigon, picturing all of America stumbling stupidly. Take that, Uncle Sam! Take that for what you did to my adorable babies and did in Vietnam, Cambodia, Laos! Yeah, there are good profits in heroin, the $80,000 could buy a Mercedes or two but Johnny doesn't care if the $80,000 goes to the Chinatown people, not him. Already at crabmeat dinners at the Great Shanghai, in Kowloon, he's telling competitive gangsters from the Gang of Loyal Tranquillity, the Gang of Righteous Tranquillity, "Sell drugs! You can make triple money in the United States. They've broken the French Connection. They've broken the Pizza Connection. All five Mafia bosses are in court, and we Chinese can take over. One hundred years ago, the white ghosts sold us their opium, but are we Chinese immoral like them? Do we hold guns to Americans' heads? Do we say, 'Buy or we'll kill you?' No, the Americans come to *us*. They tell us, 'We want white powder.' So let's sell them white powder. If you can't afford it, I'll finance you."

At age forty-one, fulfillment has come to Johnny, who tells the boss he's walking with to fly to Bangkok immediately and to start sending the hollow-walled vases out, by dozens and dozens and dozens.

14

Poisonous Vulture

NEW YORK

It's one month later, it's June 1984. On some waste-ridden street
in Alphabet City, on Avenue A, B, C or D or (it happens, sometimes) on
Park Avenue a man lies unconscious, a needle in his black-and-blue-
blotted arm. He wears stained sneakers or (it happens, sometimes)
shined shoes, he wears stained jeans or expensively tailored slacks. As
wet as a fresh-caught fish is his face, for it has been splashed many
times by his friends, splashed by their glasses of water amidst ineffective
cries of "Wake up!" And now, its siren sounding, there comes to this
unconscious *shpos* (a word among paramedics: a *subhuman piece of
shit*) an ambulance that two paramedics climb out of. They shake the
man, slap him, ask him, "Can you hear me?" They take their pens, press
them on the man's thumbnails, press them with all their might, wait for
his *"Get the fuck off me!"* The curse doesn't come, and one paramedic
takes a laryngoscope, depresses the man's limp tongue, passes an endo-
tracheal tube into the man's windpipe, blows a balloon up to hold it in
place, extracts a crooked stylette, and, like a bagpipe player, pumps a
black plastic "ambu" bag to do the man's breathing for him. The other
paramedic, meanwhile, picks up a small vial of narcan, an anti-heroin
medicine, snaps off the top, and fills an 18-gauge needle with it. "I don't
have access," he mutters as, for another minute, he hunts for a vein that

isn't scarred by too many prior incursions. At last discovering one, he shoots up the narcan, takes out the needle, waits for the fast withdrawal: the moaning, groaning, vomiting, the *"Man! You're taking my high away!"* He waits for the belligerence: the spitting, the biting, the swinging fists, the guaranteed cry of *"I got rights!"* Of all who overdose on the east side, west side, all around town, ninety-nine in a hundred announce they're alive with a fulmination like this, but no words of wrath or of thanks emanate from this man in Manhattan tonight. He's had respiratory arrest. He's had cardiac arrest. He's dead, and the paramedics call for the coroner, saying, "Another *wafwot*," another *what-a-fucking-waste-of-time*.

And waste of a God-given life. How long was the man addicted? How long only marginally alive? How much misery rended his heart before it suffered standstill? How many American men are like him? How many American women? How many are Vietnam veterans? The coroner doesn't know, nor do the coroners in Boston, Providence, Philadelphia, Baltimore and three dozen other cities, they only know that in these cities 757 people died of heroin last year. By New Year's Eve, the coroners will know that this year 1,072 people (three hundred more than last year) will die, that many of them won't be *wafwots,* many of them won't be *shposes,* that by the tombstones for Janis Joplin, Jim Morrison, Elvis Presley and John Belushi a new one will be planted this year, the tombstone of Truman Capote, the author of *In Cold Blood.*

NEW YORK

And the preeminent pusher (*poisonous vulture* in gangster slang) is Johnny. It would astonish the DEA, but one-fourth of the heroin here (three years ago it was three percent, three years from now will be seventy percent) arrives from Asia via the Chinese secret societies like Johnny's. His vases, fifty or sixty or seventy at a time, worth up to $6,000,000, come straight to Kennedy International Airport, the "samples" of one busy courier, a man with thick oval glasses whose nickname is Four Eyes. Johnny has no more talented partner than this tall, thin, well-dressed man, his M.O. being one of exquisite courtesy. "I have some sample vases," he tells an American customs inspector in English. "I want to pay the tax."

"How much are the vases?"

"$15 apiece."

"How many vases you got?"

"Let me look," says Four Eyes and patiently takes off his glasses, breathes on the lenses, wipes them, *tick tick,* this man isn't anxious at all, he could be in line at Safeway, he puts the owlish glasses back on, takes out his counterfeit invoices, adds up the Kmarts and Wal-Marts, and says, perhaps, "Fifty. That's $750."

"No tax," says the customs inspector.

And waves him through. In the parking lot, Four Eyes passes the vases to his U.S. connection, the Sergeant, who takes them (his car equipped with a siren, flashing lights, and NYPD credentials) to his girlfriend's apartment in Stuyvesant Town. In the bathroom he cuts them open, throws them away, and passes the heroin to Johnny's branch manager for the Big Apple. The soft-spoken manager is Johnny's own Michael Jackson, who now is known simply as Michael, for the Professor has shown an unforeseen facet to his personality by asking to be "Michael Jackson" too, and Johnny has avoided discord by naming one man "Michael" and the other man "Jackson." Months ago, Michael (well, let's call him Michael Jackson) flew from Hong Kong to Toronto and paid a Chinese criminal $3,000 to smuggle him past Niagara Falls into the United States. Oh, the stress and strain of it! The man laid Michael Jackson in his automobile tire compartment, tamping him down like sod, telling him in Cantonese, "Squeeze," and screwing the cover on, and Michael Jackson lay for the next thirty minutes like a fetus enduring contractions. When, somewhere east of Buffalo, the man unscrewed him and Michael Jackson was metaphorically born, he did indeed feel like crying *waa.* His arms and legs were of rusted iron and, as he moved them, they creaked like an old barn door on its chipping hinges. They still were stiff in Chinatown as Michael Jackson had shark's-fin soup to celebrate the grand opening of Johnny's branch office.

The office isn't in Chinatown. Chinatown is tong territory, a tong being sort of a Chamber of Commerce peculiar to America: an association of all the shops, restaurants, ice-cream-and-sprinkles parlors, etcetera in a two-block to four-block area. A tong is not particularly criminal except that in back of some doors whose small paper labels say *in operation* in Chinese characters it runs the poker, pai-gow and fan-tan dens the Chinese don't consider inherently evil. Even an Occidental who visits these crowded cellars is apt to consider, say, fan-tan (two dozen beans, cover some beans with a bowl, bet on how many beans there are) as something less than criminal or, for that matter, particularly fun, but the Chinese are natural gamblers who bet their entire fortunes on how many orange seeds exist in an unopened orange, and Chinatown's one dozen poker, pai-gow and fan-tan dens make $500,000 every night. The tong in the south half of Chinatown (south of Bayard Street) is run by a man who emigrated from Harbin right after World War I and worked in a Chinese laundry for thirty cents per day, and the tong in the north half of Chinatown (north of Bayard Street) is run by a retired sergeant from the Triad bureau of the Royal Police who emigrated from Hong Kong in the 70s, who was already a multi-multi-millionaire, and who was the prototype (down to his business: a funeral parlor) for the Chinese criminal in *The Year of the Dragon*. Like Rotary Clubs, the tongs are no threat to Michael Jackson, but both tongs associate with neighborhood gangs—in the south the Flying Dragons, in the north the Ghost Shadows—with teenagers who are robbers, extortionists, muggers, mayhem-makers and murderers and who Michael Jackson is disposed to steer clear of. And disposed to steer clear of any informers among them.

So he hasn't opened an office in the Borough of Manhattan but in a lower-middle-class home on Austin Street, in Rego Park, in Queens, near the site of the 1969 and 1973 World Series. His twenty employees (and employees they are, for Michael Jackson pays them $1,000 per month, plus profit shares of $1,000 per vase, plus room, board, transportation, medical and dental care) sell the heroin to the Mafia and, increasingly, to Mexican, Dominican and black middlemen in New York and to distant importers in London, Amsterdam, Brussels and Paris. What becomes of these ill-gotten gains? Far from investing them in Fidelity, at night the brothers exhaust them on girls and gambling, the girls on their arms and the pai-gow tiles in their fingers, making their exhilarating clicks. But one night the brothers go with great expectations to a new movie from Hong Kong.

NEW YORK

The movie, called *The Big Circle,* is about the very men who are sitting enchanted at this theater in Chinatown. It isn't about their lives as heroin dealers in America but about their antecedent ones as armed robbers in Hong Kong. At some swank store like Geneva Watches, Mercury Watches, Oriental Watches, or Sun Sun Jewellers, an American actor sits at a shining counter, saying in Texas-accented English, "$20,000! That's a lot of money!"

An actress playing a saleswoman nods.

"Can you give me a better price? Some kind of discount?"

The actress says, "$18,000."

"$18,000! That's still a lot of money! I mean— You know—"

"No, George," an American actress says. "It's really rather cute."

"My friend came here," the American actor persists. "You gave him a forty percent discount. His name was Stan Kaufman. Y'all remember Stan Kaufman? Nobody? Uh," the actor says, then into the high-priced store comes what's meant to be the Big Circle. Four young actors whose names in *The Big Circle* are Chubby, Rooster, Blockhead and Bull's Eye, they pull out their guns and in Cantonese say, "Stickup! Don't move! Get down!" To the brothers in Chinatown, the movie is practically cinema verité as the actors wield axes on counters, then dump the Piagets and Patek Phillippes into shopping bags, the bags emblazoned in red, white and blue like the Union Jack. But art expands upon life and the brothers need to suspend disbelief as *bang!* the actors shoot at the ceiling, the TV monitors, and the Sikh security guard, melodramatically dropping him. "You've killed him. Let's split," says Chubby, the actor playing the Big Circle boss—says, doesn't shout, in Cantonese, for the actor's emotional range is *un* to *un* and, no matter what happens in *The Big Circle* (next, Chubby seizes a chair, smashes a window, escapes to a hilltop, stomps an informer, battles with British soldiers, battles their friggin' *helicopters,* tosses grenades, gets napalmed, doesn't lose his shopping bag, changes to surgeon's scrubs, extracts a bullet from Blockhead, watches as Blockhead dies, takes a hostage, gets shot)—no matter what happens, his oily round face is as bland as Buddha's. Hollywood wouldn't have cast him as an inveterate gangster, since even while holding a pistol to some other actor's head (a store manager's, a fat policeman's, another gangster's) he looks like a callow clapper boy holding a black-and-white clapper stick. Without emoting, Chubby eventually dies in an attic, his blood dripping passively through the floor and onto the Royal Police.

The end. At the credits (Bo Ho Films) the real brothers leave the Chinatown theater acting as if they're celebrities, though no other moviegoers seem to know they're the real-life characters of *The Big Circle* or know they're responsible for America's two million heroin-heads and the first lady's importunations of "Just say no."

HONG KONG

Guess what? The baby-faced actor, Chubby, who wouldn't get the part in Hollywood, has more than done research on it, he's actually one of Johnny's incomparable bosses. Off-stage he runs some two-bit rackets: picking pockets, prostitution, shaking shopkeepers down for $500 a month and, if he doesn't get it, slashing their tires, smashing their windows, beating them up. His name is Muy, but he's gotten so cocky about his new status as movie star that his new nickname is Movie Star. He fancies that he's his character, and in his tailored jacket and his Italian shoes he meets with Johnny tonight not at the Miramar, not at the Shangri-La, but at the city's (and one of the planet's) grandest hotels, the Peninsula, the choice through the twentieth century of Clark Gable, Cary Grant, Charlie Chaplin, Elizabeth Taylor and recently of Presidents Nixon, Carter and Reagan. On the capitals of its gilded columns, plaster busts of Bacchus and Venus (or some such classical couple) look down on the pink-and-plum carpet, the burgundy-fleur-de-lised chairs, and the black-granite brass-rimmed tables. On the right side or the "right" side of this magnificent lobby (the "wrong" side in the 1930s was for the British prostitutes) the Star and Johnny sit down amidst the crumpet-nibbling beautiful people. They order coffees and finger sandwiches but not any scones with

Devonshire clotted cream, and, as the string quartet in the balcony plays
A Ghost of a Chance,

> *I need your love so badly,*
> *I love you, oh, so madly,*
> > *But I don't stand*
> > *A ghost of a chance —*

they plan the Crime of the Century, worth $20,000,000, plan it in Cantonese.

"We followed him," says the Star.

"He didn't spot you?" asks Johnny.

"No. We found his routine out."

"And now you'll kidnap him?"

"And hold him for ransom. This bloodsucker," says the Star, his countenance void of frowns, scowls, glowers, grimaces, *lines,* his voice made of sweet cotton candy, the string quartet playing,

> *If you'd surrender just for a tender*
> > *Kiss or two,*
> *You might discover that I'm the lover*
> > *Meant for you,*
> > *And I'd be true,*

"he owns almost half the real estate in Hong Kong. He drinks the blood and eats the bones of poor people like you and me. Father," says the Star super-respectfully, "this isn't just."

"I agree absolutely," says Johnny.

"We must act like in *Robin Hood.*"

"Or like in *Water Margin,*" says Johnny, citing a Chinese classic dear to the Triads. "We must rob the rich and pay the poor. I agree absolutely."

"That's why we'll kidnap him."

"But what will the ransom be?"

"Big, big money. $20,000,000."

"Once he pays it, what'll we do?"

"What'll we do? Release him."

"Hmm," says Johnny, nibbling a finger sandwich, pouring coffee out of his silver pitcher. In his heart he believes that the Star has half the brains of a hare tonight. It isn't that kidnapping hasn't a place in a secret society's repertory, even (as happened in May 1923) kidnapping all three hundred passengers on the Blue Express, the train from Shanghai to Beijing. In the 1920s in Shanghai, the Green Gang often "plucked mulberry leaves" by kidnapping girls and it often "moved rocks" by kidnapping boys, the girls then going to brothels and the boys to Buddhist monasteries, and it once kidnapped the wife of President Chiang Kai-Shek ("We found her," said Big Ear, "in her Rolls-Royce in the dangerous streets of Shanghai. We're safeguarding her")—an act equivalent today to the Mafia kidnapping Jacqueline Kennedy. But that, Johnny knows, was Shanghai, and this is Hong Kong. The man who the Star would seize (like the man Johnny's grandfather kidnapped, ransomed, and was shot for in Shanghai)—the man he'd shanghai is a VIP, the local equivalent of Donald Trump, on TV they'd play it at one hundred decibels, on the fifty front pages in commies-are-coming fonts, the hats would put a battalion on it, *slap! slam!* the brothers would all be tortured till one of them blubbered who did it, no, believes Johnny, one might as well stand in this aristocratic lobby and cry, "I smuggle drugs to America! Try and catch me!" "Release him, you say?" says Johnny, acting ignorant, acting like the cricket vendor he was thirty years ago in Shanghai. "And let him suck blood again? And let him gnaw bones again? No, we should *kill* him," says Johnny, then pauses, then as the string quartet plays,

> *What's the use of scheming?*
> *I know I must be dreaming,*
> *For I don't stand*
> *A ghost of a chance—*

says, "No. If we kill him, we'll have the heat on us."

"For months, I suspect."

"Hmm . . . ," says Johnny.

And one hour later the Star is telling his men, "I saw Father tonight. He's all for the kidnapping, but we must postpone it."

HONG KONG

One day into Johnny's office storms the Professor, the boss with the Modigliani face, the one who can't forgo quoting from Mao. His eyes flashing, his teeth grinding, his fists jiggling up and down as though he's steering on a rutted road, he acts like someone who Mao would denounce as a lumpen-proletarian putschist. He's learned that in China-town, the two ABCs stole $80,000 of heroin from the dragon-emblazoned vases. He's learned that the ABCs sent the $80,000 to Dead Man, in Bangkok, the chest-thumping brother, the one who bragged, "I stayed there! I stayed there! No one but me!" the courier from Bangkok to Tokyo. He's learned that Dead Man has bought enough heroin in Bangkok to sell in New York for $1,000,000, and now the Professor seethes to Johnny in Cantonese, "Those three aren't loyal! If others emu-late them, then you and I are fucked! Do you know what Mao would say? Mao would say *kill* them!"

Well, maybe Mao wouldn't, but the Professor at least understands the Kantian imperative. In any gang, individual business is a serious no-no, but to the Professor this isn't simply a gang but a political party he calls the Flaming Eagles and needs for his Revolution against the Royal Police. He's written an oath for it in Cantonese,

> *I hereby join the Flaming Eagles. I will accept its glories and its ordeals. I will follow its rules and obey its orders. No matter what difficulty comes, I will cast my lot with the Flaming Eagles. If I betray this oath, I will accept death with-out complaint,*

a sacred oath that the brothers, including himself and Johnny, have taken. Nor is the Professor frivolous when he says *kill*, for at all events and occasions his way with maleficent elements has been to threaten to murder them. Let someone who owes him $1,000 not pay him, and the

Professor will pull his Beretta, slam it on the man's knee and say, "Motherfucker, pay up!" or the Professor will pull his Bowie and, his fist curled around it, hit the man's shoulder and say, "Motherfucker, pay *up!*" Just like us Americans in Vietnam (or on America's own Death Rows) the Professor has one antidote for all mischief-makers, which in gangster slang is to "Let him go," or "Send him west," or "Invite him to dinner," or *"Lon him."* "Chairman Mao," the Professor tells Johnny today, "writes about this in *On the Correct Handling of Contradictions among the People.* He writes that if someone violates discipline, we must allay the people's anger by killing him, we must educate the people by killing him." And now the Professor treads to and fro on Johnny's camel-colored carpet saying death to the Chinatown Two and death to Dead Man.

"Hmm," says Johnny. He has two minds about this. He likes the Professor, the only one of the bosses who, like Johnny himself, thinks of more transcendental things than of dollars, dollars, thinks of such things as social justice, revolution, revenge. "I'm ready to die for my country," said Johnny to the Professor one day, and to his satisfaction the Professor replied, "Me too. I'm ready to die for my country and you." Nor does Johnny suppose the Professor's oath ("I will accept death without complaint") is so much rodomontade. All humanity signs a social contract, said Rousseau, but only the brothers *truly* do, truly put a pen in their fingers and sign their names to a document, a Mephisthophelean deal: in their lives will be money, tailored clothes, polished cars, will be gambling and girls, but if they renege on their contract they die. To send the three renegades west to where the sun sets, to let them *go* is no more reprehensible than to be Mephistopheles and say, "I've come for you, Dr. Faust." Without the will to enforce it, a contract like the Professor's is not worth the paper it's xeroxed on. Without that will, a brother isn't under the rule of law but of his own egocentric whims, and Johnny would gladly *lon* the three double-dealers if the heroin business didn't depend on the Chinatown ABCs, the connection to the Mafia, Mexicans, Dominicans and blacks in New York. "We need those two," says Johnny to the Professor in Cantonese.

"No, we don't need traitors! Wang Ching-Wei," the Professor cites, "was a traitor in 1939, and Mao said we must demand that he die."

"Then send a warning to Chinatown," says Johnny. "Don't kill the two traitors in Chinatown but, to educate them, kill Dead Man."

"I'll kill him, Big Brother," the Professor says, and, rushing out of the well-appointed office, he boards the next plane to Bangkok.

BANGKOK

Dead Man, who isn't yet, is with other brothers at Johnny's secret handgun range, training for the Revolution. "We can train outside of Kowloon," the Professor once told Johnny. "People will think we're shooting pigeons," but Johnny said, "No. If we're shooting pigeons we're going *bang,* but if we're shooting targets we're going *bang bang bang,*" and Bangkok became the staging area for the Revolution. Today, their rounds expended, their targets in shreds, the men at the rifle range go to the Shangri-La (the one on the river in Bangkok) for the daiquiris in the Lobby Lounge. Just like at the Shangri-La in Kowloon, on the lobby's south wall is a giant painting of the utopia that the hotel is named for. But unlike in Kowloon, this fairyland isn't at the rainbow's end but in this very neighborhood, for the painting is of the nearby temple known as Arunratchawaram or Temple of Dawn, and around it are one or two hundred merry-makers like in a Bruegel: are people walking, running, riding on frolicsome elephants, smashing cymbals, beating drums, eating, feeding chickens, romping with dogs, and, on the river, fishing, rowing, and riding in gondolas (riding downstream to the Shangri-La) while tickling one another's chins or puffing one-foot opium pipes, entirely blissed out—hey, we're in Siam, we're *already* in Shangri-La. At their orchid-decorated table in the Lobby Lounge, some brothers from the rifle range spot a Chinese in a white short-sleeved shirt, a rose-white-and-blue-striped tie, and a pair of round glasses tinted on top and less and less tinted below it. "This is Mr. Chan from the Philippines," the brothers tell Dead Man in Cantonese. "He deals drugs like us."

"Yes, and I need some now," Chan says.

"No problem," says Dead Man in his I-stayed-I-stayed-yes-I-can-accomplish-anything braggadocio mode. "We can supply you."

"Where can you and I talk?" Chan asks.

"I've got a Honda," one brother puts in.

"Fine. Let's use it," Chan says, Chan who *shh!* is actually the Professor in his usual pseudo-spectacles and his 20/20 porthole lenses, and the Professor, the Honda driver, and Dead Man exit the Lobby Lounge. They pass two wooden elephants (poinsettia-colored elephants, their halters flowers, their tusks gilded wood) and pass through the see-through doors to their silver car in front of the Shangri-La. In the driver's seat sits the "I've got a Honda" man, in the passenger seat sits Dead Man, and in the rear seat, just behind him, sits the Professor as they cruise the ninety per-cent of Bangkok that never makes it onto picture postcards. To look at the battered buildings there, the Mongols have just passed through. On the cracked plaster are spider webs of languid electric wires, of wires in jump-rope geometry, of hazards to all combustible flesh. In the traffic, where nothing moves but the deafening motorcycles, boys at the han-dlebars, girls at their backs, the smog is like something at Auschwitz, and for their protection the police are in white masks, white helmets, look-ing like surgeons at a disaster zone. In these awful environs, the Honda drives aimlessly north on Charoenkrung Road, east on Silom Road, north on Ratchadamri Road, and east on Phetchaburi Road, it drives past the tatty franchises for KFC, Sizzler's, Pizza Hut, McDonald's and Dunkin' Donuts as Dead Man twists around in the passenger seat and asks the Professor in Cantonese, "How many units will you buy?" A unit is one standard brick.

"I want at least fifty," the Professor says.

"No problem. We can supply you," says Dead Man, his thumb driving an incorporeal nail into his swelling chest.

"How much will the fifty cost?"

"The market price. $3,400 each."

"Fine. I'll pay that tomorrow."

"I'll have the fifty next week."

"Fine. Tonight I'll treat you to dinner at the Restaurant of Grandfather Rain."

"Thank you. I like that place."

So saying, Dead Man turns forward again, and the Honda turns south on Witthayu Road. A wider, quieter, tree-shaded road, it's Bangkok's answer to Massachusetts Avenue in Washington, D.C., it's home to the Vietnamese, Taiwanese, British, Norwegian, Swiss and Spanish embassies. In front of these gated places, the guards sit at homemade checkerboards playing checkers with Pepsi bottle caps, a cap that's rightside-up meaning red and one that's upside-down meaning black. As the Honda passes the embassy of New Zealand, the driver turns up the radio, the rock-and-roll music resounds, and in the back seat the Professor reaches into his shoulder bag, withdraws a .25 pistol, and sets it against the thick black hair of Dead Man. Not even pausing to educate him and tell him, "You have betrayed us," the Professor fires twice, *bang bang,* but as Dead Man jerks forward, as blood bespatters the Professor's shirt, and as the Honda driver employs his left hand (in Bangkok the cars have right-hand drives) to prop up Dead Man, to pull up his seat's reclining lever, and to let him go plopping into the Professor's lap, the Professor announces instructively, "He deserved it." He doesn't quote from Mao, from *Strive to Learn from Each Other,* he just puts his .25 into a Ziploc bag and imperturbably wipes his hands (but not his blood-splattered shirt) on a car-window-cleaning rag. Outside the Honda some Thai police, Thai blue-beret soldiers, Wackenhut men, and even a U.S. marine appear, but the Professor knows they're not an antimurder patrol but the guards at the U.S. embassy.

The Honda turns east on Sarasin Road, north on Soi Ruam Rudi, and east on Sukhumvit Road, and it continues into the monkey-infested, mosquito-infested jungle outside of Bangkok. There the Professor, the driver, and one other brother dig a one-fathom hole (six feet, so the dogs, wolves and monkeys do not disturb it) and lay the truly dead man inside it, lay him face down so he doesn't rise up and return as a ghost, floating a foot above ground, turning the candle flames green, prowling the planet till *ark!* the cock crows, spooking the brothers, seeking revenge. As further insurance, the Professor throws in a sort of Monopoly money, saying in Cantonese, "I brought this for you, Dead Man. Buy some nice clothes in—*ow,*" the Professor interjects, slapping a needle-mouthed mosquito, "in heaven, and don't come and haunt us."

"You shouldn't haunt us," the driver says, throwing in Monopoly money, Monopoly money with golden insets. "You shouldn't harass us. You broke your oath and, *ow,* you deserved to die."

"Ow," the third brother says, throwing more make-believe money in. "You said you'd be loyal to us. You said you'd never betray us. But *ow,"* says the brother, who's sweating, who's undisguisedly scared, "betray us you did. You knew what the consequences would be. So don't come and haunt us, Dead Man. Don't try to take revenge against us. Don't. Please don't. You don't have authority to. You and I aren't enemies. I've got nothing against you. *Ow!"*

Then the three mourners shovel the dirt back into the head-deep hole, then *stamp!* then *stamp!* like Indians doing a warpath dance, they pack the dirt down hard, very hard, lest the dogs, wolves and monkeys dig up Dead Man or, of its own malicious accord, his ghost comes soaring out.

BANGKOK

But tsk. The brothers didn't stamp on the dirt enough, for the ghost comes that very night. It comes to the home of the man who was scared, the one who beseeched it, "Don't. Please don't." Another incomparable boss, a Cantonese known as Tiger, he was raised on a lettuce, cabbage and bok choy farm where at age seven he pulled up the weeds, pulled off the silkworms, rolled the worms in the weeds, and made a precious by-product, silk. At eighteen he climbed at midnight into a narrow canoe, and, as a man with a rice bowl bailed the icy water out, he paddled to the bright lights of Macao, then motorboated to Hong Kong. There, Tiger worked from six to six, from morning to evening, mopping, bussing, and waiting in restaurants where signs in the kitchen in Chinese characters said, "You must work," "If you don't you're fired," and "You mustn't steal food." For lunch he was served the brown outer leaves of bok choy: he almost starved, but if he pilfered just one little dumpling, the fat, sedentary, slothful restaurant owner would seize it and *charge* him for it, taking some dimes from his $1 daily salary (the owner also took Tiger's tips). At thirty Tiger became assistant manager of a restaurant called the Pretty Palace, a restaurant patronized by the late-night mahjong-clicking-and-clacking bosses of the Big Circle. By then he'd concluded that men we call capitalists (like restaurant owners with Daimlers, Mercedeses, Lincolns) are nothing but state-sanctioned robbers, and in furtherance of his own equal opportunity he joined the Big Circle and did his own robbing without the official endorsement of Sir Edward Youde, the Governor of Hong Kong. "Society isn't fair to us," Tiger told other bosses in Cantonese. "It robs us although we're poor, but *we* rob well-insured millionaires. Which of us is the more unjust, society or us?" Tiger asked, Tiger who'd gladly rob Geneva Watches, Mercury Watches, Oriental Watches, or Sun Sun Jewellers, rob the supercilious men who charge up to $100,000 for pebbles the poor people find in South Africa, but Tiger who wouldn't rob $1 from some poor prostitute and, in fact, interceded for one when her creditors hounded her ("She and I are friends," he told some unnerved creditors at a "sitdown" at Tin Tin Restaurant). Tiger soon was a boss, but at bottom he still was a farmer's son (a nickname for him was Country Boy), a man with a bronze, stubbled, buck-toothed face, a face that slanted to its own left as though from the forceps of some clumsy obstetrician, a Leaning Tower of Pisa face. His shoes were black but his socks were white. His pants were slacks and his jackets windbreakers. His shirts came straight from the dryer without the rigorous intervention of a Chinese laundryman's iron. And though in self-defense (or in defense of his ethical principles) he had killed several men, he couldn't surmount the conviction that one of their ghosts might someday turn in his grave face up, then rise up and take revenge.

As chance would have it, this superstitious boss is the one the ghost visits tonight. Unlike an American ghost (but like Dickens's Marley) it isn't clad in white like a Ku Klux Klansman but in the same white shirt, blue tie, that its progenitor was buried in with ceremony tonight: the same blood-splattered shirt and tie. At about two a.m., it comes to Tiger's tropical villa, built of exquisite slender bricks near the Argentine Embassy. Matter being no obstacle for a dexterous ghost, it *whoo!* with a wind-in-the-willows sound it floats through the bedroom window, saying to Tiger in Cantonese, "I've come for revenge." It grabs Tiger's throat, Tiger who was asleep but who now, stricken with terror, wakes up.

"Get out!" Tiger cries, fighting back.

"You killed me, and I'll take revenge."

"You have no right to! You deserved it!"

"What's happening, husband?" cries Tiger's wife, who was asleep with him. "Why are you shouting? Why are you sweating?"

At those words, Tiger really wakes up. In the moonlight the sweat really glistens on his skewed countenance. "I dreamt I saw someone's ghost," he says, in no way consoled to know that the ghost didn't come to his real-world rented apartment but to the dreamland that he can never vacate. The ghost, in fact, keeps coming every night, coming at two o'clock, three o'clock, four, coming until the cock crows (or rather till *gobble,* the turkey outside of the window calls), till one day Tiger drives to the Temple of the Four-Faced Buddha. "The ghost of Dead Man is hounding me, Buddha," he says in Cantonese at each face of the incense-intoxicated god. "Don't let him do it. He is the one who wronged *me.* If he seeks revenge, he must seek it against himself, not *me."* Tiger offers the Buddha some jasmines and marigolds, some apples and oranges, and he pays $40 to the gold-panted, gold-jacketed, gold-hatted girls to walk clockwise with him, to move their fingers fluidly and to sing in Thai,

> *Oh, revered Brahma,*
> *With Thy four faces,*
> *May Thy eight hands,*
> *Protect this man,*

their fingers curved into "okay" signs. But sadly for Tiger, it isn't okay with the Buddha, for every night after that the ghost comes trespassing into Tiger's dreams, floating through Tiger's window, dripping gore onto Tiger's carpet, curling its ectoplasmic thumbs onto Tiger's throat, moaning to Tiger, "I'll take revenge," and to escape its unwelcome presence he and his wife fly to Tokyo.

TOKYO

Bad idea. Dead Man, if you remember, himself was in Tokyo, he sat at Narita with seven vases, watching the whalelike wrestlers on TV, watching the Japanese watching as no Americans watch, their faces as dead as during commercials, telling one of the ABCs, "You and I should smuggle too." His flesh having been to Tokyo, his ghost has credentials for Tokyo too, and that night it comes to the Hilton to Tiger's pink-bedspreaded room, still clad in its out-out-damned-spot bloody shirt and tie. No less mysteriously, it comes through the door, not the window, it doesn't tell Tiger, "I'll take revenge," but it descends on him quiet as a glider and it starts choking him.

"Get out!" Tiger cries in Cantonese, throwing the vicious presence off. His will is again indomitable, for the ghost floats out of the room, exiting through the rice-paper window and its solid steel crossbars, then Tiger throws off his colorful bedspread: his bedspread with six pink mountain ranges and with interposed cumulus clouds. He tells his wife, "I saw the same ghost," then goes to the bathroom, runs the hot water, fills up the bathtub, pours the green bath salt in: it turns to white bubbles, and *aah!* he settles into the tub to stare at the flower-fired tiles and ask, *What's happening here? Is the ghost really invading my dreams or am I just dreaming it?* The question is one that doesn't yield to intellectual processes, least of all to a Cantonese country boy's, and Tiger doesn't cry out *"Eureka"* in his hot bubble bath. His muscles relaxed, his mind-muscles taut, he climbs from his tub and, drying himself, into his pink-mountain-topped bed, but he can't sleep and by morning is hollow-eyed, sunken-cheeked, pale.

What to do? A *ghost* and a *devil* are the same words in Cantonese, and Tiger has Lucifer chasing him over the Orient. Tiger's advantage is, Johnny is also vacationing at the Hilton, Johnny who comes down to Tiger's room, sees his drained countenance, and asks him in Cantonese, "What's wrong?"

"Do you believe there're ghosts?"

"No, I don't. Why are you asking?"

"The ghost of Dead Man is after me."

"Little brother," says Johnny compassionately. "When I was small I believed there were ghosts. My grandmother told me, 'If you aren't good, the ghosts will get you,' and I believed her. But then," says Johnny, sitting on one of the two pink armchairs, patting his reassuring fingers on Tiger's knee—"then I lived in the morgue of the Heaven Eternal Cemetery. The gravedigger laughed when I said that ghosts scare me. He told me, 'When someone dies, he's dead.' One morning he dug up a woman whose children and grandchildren wanted to bury her in Sinkiang. He called to me, 'Hey, Kon! Come look!' I was afraid to, but I was also curious, and I did. The woman lay in her coffin in a red blanket with a gold dragon embroidered on it. The blanket had rotted but she herself hadn't. 'She's about ten years dead,' the gravedigger told me. 'Her nails are still growing, though. Just look!' I looked and *brr,* " says Johnny, recalling the woman's candle face, her paper skin, and her letter-opener fingernails. "I asked him, 'How can her nails still grow?' and the gravedigger said, 'I don't know.' He wrapped her up in a sheet, then put her over his shoulder, then took her by passenger train to Shanghai. He took her to a crematorium, then sent her ashes to Sinkiang, then came back to the Heaven Eternal Cemetery. And then he got her coffin, planed it, painted it, oiled it, and sold it to someone else. I asked him, 'How *could* you? How *could* you? How could you sell her secondhand coffin? Won't her ghost haunt you now?' He told me, 'No, when she's dead, she's dead.' Little brother," says Johnny to Tiger. "Don't dream anymore of Dead Man. His light has gone out."

"Thank you, Big Brother. I'm much relieved."

Oh, yeah? The two men go by elevator to the Sakura Coffee Shop, the Cherry Blossom Coffee Shop, and Tiger renews himself at a breakfast of cherries, pineapple slices, and mandarin orange wedges. *I was just dreaming it,* Tiger convinces himself. But for the next three years the unwavering ghost, its shirt unlaundered, its blood unstanched, its quest of revenge unquelled, will come into Tiger's nightlife in every capital city it has a visa for: in Bangkok, Hong Kong and Tokyo.

J
o
h
n

S
a
c
k

15

Piece of Meat

MONTCLAIR

What is it with people? Why when they're making money do they covet more, more, more? The next man in Johnny's gang to succumb to inordinate greed is the fat, sweaty, silver-haired retiree from the NYPD, the Sergeant, the man who called up Johnny last year and told him, "I'm broke. Do you have some work for me?" In his girlfriend's apartment in Stuyvesant Town is $1,100,000 of heroin that's meant for Michael Jackson, Johnny's soft-spoken manager in New York, but whenever the Sergeant sees it he suffers the Silver syndrome, the wide eyes of Long John Silver that Johnny once saw in a Chinese edition of *Treasure Island.* *Why,* the Sergeant wonders, *should the Chinaman get the $1,100,000? Why not me?* and one night in Montclair, New Jersey, the Sergeant chooses to look after number one. He walks to Budget and rents a Lincoln Continental. He drives east to Jersey City and the Holland Motor Lodge, a beige-bricked motel by the long line of cars approaching the Holland Tunnel. He meets with the ABC with the cowboy's boots and the Cowboys cap, the ABC who months ago sent $80,000 to Dead Man and, not having heard from him, has become staunchly loyal to Johnny, his one honest business partner. "I'm going to Hong Kong," the Sergeant tells the ABC. "I'll take these with me," and he puts two black traveling bags into the Lincoln's trunk, then he queues up at the toll booths beneath the big brown HOLLAND TUNNEL sign. In each of the bags is $200,000 cash.

NEW YORK

Money, money, the Sergeant thinks, and he drops off the bags at his girlfriend's apartment, now like an Inca palace. The lovers (he's fifty, she's half that: a pretty brunette about five foot two) then drive out to drinks and dinner, then to more drinks at the Mirage Bar of the New York Hilton, on the Avenue of the Americas between 53rd and 54th. They sit on a wine-colored loveseat. Near them are two enigmatic statues, two stone sphinxes with lion claws, milk-cow breasts, human curly hair, and, on their backs, copper saddles, as if some sheik of Egypt might hop on at any moment and cry "Giddiup." On one sphinx's lips is a "What's gonna happen?" look, and on the other one's is "Whatever happens, I don't think I'll like it." Between the two sphinxes, a woman in black plays a baby grand piano almost inaudibly.

At midnight something happens. Into the bar in his "I♥NY" white T-shirt, white blazer, white linen handkerchief comes the Ghost, that incomparable courier, who under the plausible alias of Antonio Vargas of Bolivia has just checked into the Hilton with $3,600,000 of Johnny's dragon-embellished vases. At the Mirage he sits down with the Sergeant and the Sergeant's squeeze, but, not knowing who she is, he keeps his conversation confined to innocuous topics like the Baltimore Orioles. They're about a dozen games behind the Tigers.

"The merchandise, where is it?" the Sergeant suddenly asks.

"It's— It's upstairs in my room," says the Ghost, surprised.

"Bring it to 54th Street. I'll bring the car around," the Sergeant says. He and his girlfriend leave, get the Lincoln from the Hilton garage, bring it past the movie marquee for *The Karate Kid,* and park it by the Hilton's side door. Into the trunk the men put two vase-weighty suitcases, then, with his girlfriend beside him, the Sergeant drives to her apartment, augments her Inca storeroom, celebrates by having sex with her, his hundreds of pounds bearing down on her, returns to the Lincoln alone, drives it to a Bronx side street, leaves it, and takes a cab to the precinct he recently sergeanted at, on West 35th near Times Square. "My car was carjacked," he tells a sergeant, signs a complaint report, and takes a cab through the Lincoln Tunnel to those industrial wastelands: to Wee-hawken, Secaucus, the Hackensack River, and his own home in Mont-clair.

MONTCLAIR

"Johnny," he says at his cozy home, calling up Hong Kong. "The fur you sent me, I picked it up."

"You got all the fur?"

"I got it. By the way," he says casually, lest he's being telephone-tapped, "I had some trouble."

"What sort trouble?"

"I'll tell you in Hong Kong."

"Is serious trouble?"

"I'll tell you in Hong Kong. My wife," the Sergeant says, "and my daughter get there tomorrow," the subtext to this announcement being "You mustn't kill me in Hong Kong, Johnny, for I'll have witnesses there," the flaw to this same announcement being that Johnny, his dupe, his pigeon, his *piece of meat* in Cantonese gangster slang, might also kill *them.* "Myself, I'll be there the day after that," the Sergeant concludes. The next day, he says goodbye to his wife and his twelve-year-old, has more sex in Stuyvesant Town, and availing himself of his eighteen years with the NYPD, thinks up a diabolical lie that the ABC and the Ghost won't dispute and Johnny (he's certain) will fall for, the story of How I Lost Your $4,000,000.

HONG KONG

His body shredded by jet lag, his brain by Johnny's probable ques-tions, the Sergeant arrives at ten in the morning like a wildly wobbling top. He gets into Johnny's Mercedes, Johnny in his usual climate-defiant suit and tie, Johnny saying, "Welcome to Hong Kong."

"It's good being back. How's my wife?"

"She waiting at Holiday Inn. She fine."

"And how is my little girl?"

"She fine. She also waiting for you."

"My brother in the States says hello," the Sergeant continues. "I told him I'll be seeing you," the subtext to this irrelevance being "You mustn't kill me in Hong Kong, Johnny, for I have witnesses in the United States."

"I thank him. What trouble you have?"

"Real trouble," the Sergeant sighs as the driver pulls out of Kai Tak and past the enormous murals for Marlboros, Salems, Kents, the friezes for Mild Sevens. "I was robbed."

"You were *what?*"

"I was fuckin' robbed. They took everything there was."

"They took *what?*"

"The $400,000 cash and Ronny's," the Ghost's, "white powder."

A rash of blackheads seems to appear on Johnny's face. He pulls his head back, an act that accords him a wide-angle view of the Sergeant and, at the same time, distances himself from him. "Jonathan Ruotolo," says Johnny. "You lose $4,000,000?"

"Yeah, I was robbed," the Sergeant explains dispiritedly.

"This is big fuck-up, is biggest fuck-up there is."

"Yeah, Johnny, I know it."

"The drug there, the man is there," says Johnny. "The drug gone, the man is gone," meaning dead. "I take you to your hotel now. You sleep. You shower. You shave. Then this afternoon—"

The driver pulls up at the Holiday Inn Golden Crowne, a hotel close to Kowloon's shops, a hotel specifically chosen for the Sergeant's wife. She's waiting in the elegant lobby with the Sergeant's daughter, a pretty little girl in a red-flowered dress and, in her hair, a red ribbon.

"Hello, little girl," says Johnny, smiling. "You enjoy in Hong Kong?"

"Yes!"

"This afternoon I pick you up," says Johnny to the Sergeant, smiling.

HONG KONG

Where are they taking me? the Sergeant thinks. It's afternoon, and the Mercedes (a gray-upholstered, gray-tinted-windowed, no-one-can-see-who's-in-it Mercedes) is moving at half a mile a minute away from the safe embrace of the Holiday Inn. It's moving on one-way streets where above it the signs with incomprehensible characters reach for the Sergeant's eyes like a witch's fingers, then on wide boulevards where the Chinese walk on arching overpasses, then on a road that twists left, then right, a superhighway so serpentine that (like the Sergeant) it seems severely disoriented, lost. Flashing past like Kodachromes are a firehouse, an ocher-bricked university, a red-roofed, cross-crowned and Russian-suggestive church, a building whose purple walls say United Artists, an American baseball diamond—*Where the hell are they taking me?* the Sergeant thinks, and he squirms around in the passenger seat to keep an eye on the scowling brother behind him: the Professor. Sitting with that recent murderer is Johnny, and the Sergeant attempts to make small talk with him, "Hey, Johnny? Where we going?"

"You will find out."

And *arrr!* A clue is the roar of a passenger plane that the Sergeant is dive-bombed by in the course of its standard landing at Kai Tak International Airport. In this nerve-racking neighborhood, the Mercedes slows down at a shop where men without shoes are squatting and making wood cartons, caskets or coffins, then stops at the dark back door of the Regal Airport Hotel. A giant clinic for jet lag, the Regal has guests from Europe whose biological clocks are saying wake up for coffee, croissants, and it has guests from America whose clocks are saying good night—the Regal has legions of groggy guests who now are in bed, convalescing, and aren't at this back door hailing cabs to the Tai Wong Temple. The only observer here as the Sergeant is hustled inside is a doorman in white pants, white jacket, and white pillbox hat, a man with an occupational illness, a 20/2000 vision. He doesn't descry the anxious hostage in the firm custody of two members of the Gang of Tranquil Happiness.

The three take the elevator up. As queasy as the Sergeant feels, he glows with a glorious tan in the brass plaque proclaiming a $600 fine for smoking on elevators like this. At the penthouse floor, the men go through delicately frosted doors down a sweet-smelling garden path: a corridor drenched in Diversey deodorant. "Quite a few guys," says Johnny, knocking on a door that's tagged with a DO NOT DISTURB, "want to see you," the peephole opens, the door then opens, and lo! in front of the Sergeant's darting eyes is a virtual dormitory for the Big Circle, for Fat Ass and Michael Jackson, for Four Eyes and Tiger, for the messenger and a half-dozen more. The bed, the desk, the orchid-carpeted baggage stand—everything in this dangerous room is a perch for one or more brothers, everything but a lilac-upholstered armchair that, at a gesture from Johnny, the Sergeant settles into and a pale-pink-upholstered stool that Johnny rolls up. The curtain is already closed, and the light of a table lamp is pleating the thick cigarette smoke. "Jonathan Ruotolo," says Johnny in English with all the formality of a judge who's convening court. "What happen?"

A thousand times in New York, a suspect has squirmed in a hot seat under the almost palpable pressure from the Sergeant's eyes, eyes that inflicted the sort of duress the Bill of Rights doesn't disallow. So why is the Sergeant, who's wise to this tactic, as nervous as any juvenile in a room at the Fourteenth Precinct? "Well, I've been thinking about it," the Sergeant begins. "Maybe when I saw Eddie," the ABC in the Cowboys cap, the Sergeant's jacket off, his red-and-white necktie loose, his finger prying it off his mucilaginous neck, "maybe Eddie had somebody follow me. And maybe—"

"Jonathan Ruotolo. Begin at begin," says Johnny. He knows that to heckle, hector, interrupt is how to break up a practiced actor, and, rolling his stool closer, he flourishes his diamond-studded pen as though it's a dentist's drill, as though he'll drill out the Sergeant's brains neuron by neuron.

"All right," the Sergeant says, commencing another part of his obstinate script. "Eddie told me to meet him in Jersey City, the Holland Motor Lodge. I went there, I parked the car, the car was a Lincoln, a rental, and Eddie gave me two traveling bags, two black traveling bags, and—"

"You give any merchandise to Eddie?"

"What? No, I didn't."

"Why didn't? You had $1,100,000 worth."

"I was going to Hong Kong. Vacation."

"So?"

"If I gave some to Eddie, then when Eddie got paid I'd be in Hong Kong and Eddie couldn't pay *me*. What if I got back from Hong Kong and Eddie was robbed?"

"Then," says Johnny coolly, "Eddie has the responsible to us. You not have the responsible for it. Excuse me. I translate," says Johnny, and talks in Cantonese to brothers whose eyes send curare-tipped spears at the Sergeant. In each brother's fist as stiff as a scepter is a Coca-Cola, Pepsi-Cola or, for Johnny, orange juice, Johnny who now says in English, "You can keep going."

"The traveling bags," says the Sergeant, his face like a half-flat inner tube, "I put them into the trunk, then I drove through the Holland Tunnel to New Yor—"

"Why not you drive back home?"

"Cause I was meeting with Ronny."

"Jonathan Ruotolo," says Johnny again. A foot from the Sergeant's face, the nib of his dentist's drill is practically going *whirr.* "You can meet Ronny midnight. One o'clock, two o'clock, Ronny not going anywhere away. You carrying $400,000. Why you not going home? And putting the money safely?"

"My home, it's too far away."

"Why you don't careful? Not afraid people steal your car?"

"No, I wasn't worried," the Sergeant says, an assertion so contradicted by the sweat that's swamping his armpits that Tiger whispers to the Professor in Cantonese, "He's lying."

"I translate," says Johnny. He does, then asks, "Any questions?"

"How far," asks Michael Jackson, "from the motel to his house?"

"Two hours."

"Just two?"

"Round trip."

"That's *all?*"

"Ask him," says the messenger, "why he wasn't worried."

"Why you don't worry for?" asks Johnny in English.

"I didn't worry. I didn't think anyone'd steal the car."

"I translate," says Johnny. He does, and from every chair, table and bed there comes a cacophony of Cantonese monosyllables. "Bullshit!" "Bullshit!" "We don't believe him," cry the brothers, who'd no sooner trust a Lincoln in a den of thieves like New York as trust a Wells Fargo Wagon on some dark alley of Dodge. "They don't believe story," says Johnny in English. His subtext is "Open wider! *Whirrr!*"

"But it's true!"

"Then you can keep going."

"In New York," the Sergeant says, his handkerchief out, his hand scraping it on his sodden cheeks, the handkerchief turning glaucous gray, "I went to a bar, had dinner, then went to the bar at the Hilton and—"

"You drink two bars?"

"Yeah."

"You drink a lot today. You drink a lotter than anyone."

"That's cause I met this girl."

"This *girl?*" cries Johnny. "What in this picture this fucking *girl?*" He translates this into Cantonese—he elicits another cacophony and says, "They ask where this *girl* come from."

"Some other city. Real pretty girl. She was staying at the Hilton," the Sergeant says, the Sergeant an actor seeking safety in a script that he's practiced, practiced, across the Pacific, "and she was at the next table alone and I asked her to sit have a drink with me. Well, Ronny came down and I told him I'd drive the Lincoln to the side door on 54th Street. 'I'll meet you,' said Ronny, 'on 54th.' So the bar bill, I paid it and went with the girl to the parking level and me and her—"

One brother gasps. He's Four Eyes, the talented courier, who understands all this English, and the others look at Johnny inquisitively. Johnny translates the Sergeant's words into Cantonese, and at once there's another uproar, the brothers all spitting out Cantonese syllables.

"What are they *saying?*" the Sergeant asks, alarmed. Behind his lilac electric chair and the lilac closed curtain is a window he cannot escape

through, for two feet beyond it another window softens the sounds of
the planes coming in (at window level) at Kai Tak.

"They say," says Johnny, "you meet this girl one hour, right?"

"Yes."

"So why you let her to go to the car and go to the drug deal?"

"Johnny, I liked her. A real sweet girl. I wanted to drive her to a motel
have sex with her."

"He wanted to fuck her," says Johnny in an incredulous tone in Cantonese.

"He's lying! I don't believe him!" cries Four Eyes in Cantonese.

"*Kkk!*" cries Fat Ass, tossing his shoulders dismissively.

"He thinks we're stupid!" cries the Professor.

"If we were kids," cries Tiger, "then he could hand us candy balls and
tell us, 'This candy's for you!' He thinks we're kids? And we'll swallow
this?"

"I don't want to listen!" cries the Professor. A gun in his belt, he would
willingly turn the music on, turn the TV on, let the old refrigerator continue to chug like a washing machine, wait for a passenger plane from
LA or London to strafe them, then *bang,* then let the last little bubbles
out of the Sergeant's inner tube. Without any guilt the Professor would
bury him in the double window, embalm him in water, and let him float
in that giant aquarium like a big blowfish, belly up, a "sight" for the
unappeasable tourists.

"Let the man talk," says Johnny in Cantonese, meaning "Let him convict himself. You can keep going," says Johnny in English, his dentist's
drill whirring again.

"All right. I drove around to the side door and Ronny came out—"

"The girl. She with you?"

"Yes. Ronny and me, we put the two suitcases into the trunk—"

"You got two bags there. You can put four?"

"Yes, this was a Lincoln. Then—"

"Why not you give the $400,000 to Ronny? He was the courier."

"I was flying to Hong Kong, Johnny. I figured I'd bring it myself."

"Keep going."

"Then this girl and me, we drove to an all-night motel had sex—"

"How long?"

"An hour."

"I translate," says Johnny. He's thinking, *Why drive to an all-night motel? You said she's staying at the Hilton,* but he doesn't ask this, why bother, clearly the Sergeant is lying and why should a busy judge/jury like Johnny elicit another contemptuous lie? Johnny just translates, and in the explosive uproar the loudest voice is Tiger's, "This man! He's not rich! In his car are millions of dollars more than he's ever seen! And he'll park? And make out? With somebody he's just met? This man knows New York! He's a cop!" While all Tiger's words are in Cantonese, they come with an air-gun impetus that the Sergeant can understand without a Berlitz dictionary. His skin is so red it seems inside out.

"I left the motel and—"

"You left with girl?"

"She stayed there."

"She live motel?"

"Yes. Well, now it was one o'clock, two o'clock, and I drove to the Lincoln Tunnel and stopped at, Johnny? do you remember the Market Diner? on Eleventh Avenue? opposite UPS?"

"Yes."

"I bought a coupla coffees to go and," the Sergeant continues, coming to his climactic scene, the *pièce de résistance* of all his rehearsals, "went back to the car, and there was a car parked next to it, and two guys came out and they pointed guns at me and they pushed me into my car, the Lincoln, into the Lincoln back seat. I thought they were cops and—"

"They search you?"

"Yes."

"You have a gun?"

"Uh, no."

"Why you not have?

"I was with Eddie and Ronny that day. I was with our own people."

"They handcuff you?"

"Yes. I mean no," the Sergeant says, thinking, *They know I'm lying. But now I'm stuck with this story.* "Well, they drove around, and in the dark they stopped and I thought they'd kill me. But fortunately—"

"Yes, fortunately. If they killed you," says Johnny coolly, "then you not here today. But fortunately you are."

"Yes. All they did was push me out."

"I translate," says Johnny, and does, then he appends a personal note in Cantonese, "He's bullshitting us. Why would these people kidnap him if they weren't going to kill him? Why," asks Johnny in English now— "why they didn't kill you?"

"They must've known I had money, known I had drugs. They must've wanted that, not me."

"Very good answer," says Johnny, but his unspoken thoughts are *All the more reason to kill you, or you'd be a witness against them.* "Keep going."

"I went to the precinct house—"

"Why?"

"To tell them the car was stolen—"

"Why?"

"It was stolen. I had to report it."

"Very good answer," says Johnny, but in his cerebrum's corner is *What if they found your car? And found your money? And found your drugs?*

"I've got the report with me. You want it?"

"No, Jonathan Ruotolo. I trust you."

"From there I went home."

"How you get home?"

"Took a taxi."

"I translate," says Johnny. He does, then asks, "Any questions?"

No questions. What sort of question could there be? "Do you want extreme unction?" "Do you want a Catholic burial?" Like someone crushing a cockroach, the Professor snubs out his cigarette, saying in Cantonese, "We must *lon* him. 'We must object. We must protest,' said Chairman Mao in *The Reactionaries Must Be Punished.* 'We must kill traitors. It's only natural.' Dismiss him, Big Brother, so we can discuss him." To the bathroom goes the Professor, to the phone (for his beeper is beeping) goes Michael Jackson, to a wickerwork basket goes Fat Ass and scrounges up M&Ms, Mars Bars, and Männer *haselnusscremeschnitten,* and Johnny says, "So, Jonathan Ruotolo," standing up, pulling his jacket on, adjusting his Windsor knot, "you and I go Holiday Inn. Tonight with wife, little girl, we go best seafood restaurant in Kowloon." A look on his sweat-wetted face of *Is he putting me on?* the Sergeant almost uses a spatula to scrape himself off the armchair, then, with Johnny, he stumbles down the deodorized corridor, down the golden elevator where in the gilded mirrors a row of his well-tanned reflections fades toward eternity, down past the cataractous doorman, down into Johnny's dim Mercedes, off toward the Holiday Inn.

HONG KONG

In the room at the Regal Airport Hotel it's like at a Superbowl party. Everyone's yelling—yelling in Cantonese, "He lied!" "He lied!" "Do we do it tonight?" "Yes, he's on his way tonight!" "He's taking a tour tonight," a one-way tour of the China Sea on one of the picturesque fishing boats that by day are the focus of sightseers' cameras at Hong Kong Harbor. The item on the agenda where unanimity falters is, Who is this tour for? The traitorous cop, well, sure, it's for him, but for the potential witnesses, too? For the two women who'd tell the Royal Police, "We saw him with Johnny Kon"? The tour of the China Sea, is this for the Sergeant's wife and the Sergeant's red-ribboned twelve-year-old? "Of course!" the Professor announces.

Kill. The lesson the Professor has taken from Mao (and not just from Mao: from doctors who kill with antibiotics, farmers who kill with insecticides: from most of the people around him) is, If something offends you, kill it. Last month the Professor killed Dead Man, last year (with Johnny's approval again) he tracked down a Jewish woman from Frankfurt, a furrier who owed Johnny $100,000, and he found her at the Regent, a top-notch hotel by Hong Kong Harbor. His plan was to tie her, gag her, crate her, and export her by fishing boat to coordinates in the China Sea—his *plan* was this, but the woman checked out to China. And now the Professor selects *kill, kill* as his final solution to the Sergeant's improbity. From this orchid-carpeted room at the Regal Airport Hotel, he phones one of his people (one of his soldiers, number four nines) and says, "I need some rope," phones another and says, "I need some gags," phones another (a manager of a Macao casino) and says, "I need some slot machines." He phones another and says, "I need your van," and phones another (a fisherman, captain of the *Victory*) and says, "I need your float," in Cantonese gangster slang your boat. He then phones the Mercedes as it pulls up at the Holiday Inn. "At five o'clock," the Professor asks Johnny, "can you meet us at the Fortuna Restaurant?"

"I can," says Johnny in Cantonese. "I come seven o'clock," he tells the Sergeant in English, "and you, wife, daughter and I go seafood." Then Johnny goes to the Fortuna and finds the Professor, Fat Ass and Michael Jackson, Four Eyes and Tiger, the messenger man and the fisherman already at a circular table, their eyes afire. "Oh, you're here too?" says Johnny in Cantonese to the short-haired, silver-haired, sun-tanned fisherman.

"They need my float, they told me."

"Why?"

"To feed the sharks, they told me."

"What?"

"Here's what we'll do," the Professor commences. He spits out the words like watermelon seeds. "You pick up the Ruotolos, Big Brother. You drive them out Mody Road. At one point there'll be a van that's stalled and a man who's waving *I need your help*. You stop for him. I jump from the van. I hold a gun on those motherfuckers. *Oh,*" the Professor fumes. He's so upset that he takes off his bogus glasses and he inserts them into his jacket pocket, where they won't break. "No one must fuck with us!"

"Shh. There's people around," Johnny says.

"We tie them. We gag them. We put them onto the *Victory,*" the Professor continues. "We take them fifty miles out. We tie them to the old slot machines. We stab them (that's so the sharks will smell them) and we toss them overboard. Do they want a seafood restaurant? We'll give them the whole Pacific. Do they want to eat seafood? Well, I want their food to eat *them.*"

Everyone, including Johnny, laughs. He has no qualms about using the Sergeant as shark-bait, *I myself could chop him up,* Johnny thinks, but he's reminded of General Cushman of the marines in Vietnam, Cushman who told him, "My hands are tied." Johnny hasn't the heart to kill the Sergeant's innocent daughter, presumptively innocent wife, but if he doesn't kill them how can he kill the Sergeant? How can he show him the China Sea and Davy Jones' Locker if he doesn't also kill the Sergeant's brother? the man somewhere in the States who the Sergeant told, "I'm going to Hong Kong, and I'm seeing Johnny Kon"? and who the Sergeant may have told, "Johnny and I sell heroin"? And what of the $1,100,000 of that precious substance in the apartment in Stuyvesant Town or—as the Sergeant told Johnny and Johnny believes—in the Sergeant's two-car garage in Montclair? How can Johnny recover it if the Sergeant (and his wife? daughter? brother?) is the subject of a missing-persons investigation? How can Johnny? How can Johnny not? Round and round go the electrons in Johnny's cerebrum until he convinces himself, *Yes, I'm like General Cushman. My hands are tied.* He has some hot dim sum and asks the Professor rhetorically, "How about Ruotolo's hotel room?"

"No problem. It's in my name, not his. I'll just check out."

"How about Ruotolo's luggage?"

"No problem. I know some busboys. They'll take it out."

"How about Ruotolo's garage? What if he's missing, and the police investigate, and they see his garage, and they find heroin there, and . . ."

HONG KONG

Two hours later, Johnny, Jonquil, the Sergeant, and his wife and red-ribboned daughter are at a seafood restaurant in Kowloon, making merry. On their table is steamed grouper, steamed scallops, and lobster with ginger and onions—also barbecued pigeon, the Sergeant's daughter asking, "What's that?"

"Johnny, Johnny," says the Sergeant's wife, meaning "Don't tell her."

"Is baby chicken," Johnny laughs. "Be careful, little girl, because hot."

"We three women," says Jonquil, "are going shopping tomorrow."

"My wife," laughs the Sergeant, "wants to bring this whole city back."

"I'm already overweight," laughs the Sergeant's overweight-baggage wife.

"And me, I'm already broke," laughs the Sergeant meaningfully.

"Now and then everyone broken," laughs Johnny. He dips his fingers into a bowl of warm water and of red tea leaves, and he tells the Sergeant quietly, "I'm serious, Jon." To stab, to shove, to let the sharks swallow him, to end his curriculum vitae as bouillabaisse is a course of immediate action that the Sergeant hasn't a clue was proposed, considered, and, with misgivings, rejected by the Big Circle so as to safeguard the $1,100,000 hoard in (it believes) the Sergeant's garage in Montclair. "Listen to me, Jon," says Johnny. "Everything in your garage, you got to return to us."

"I will when I'm home. I guarantee it," the Sergeant laughs.

NEW YORK

Do not believe it. Once he's in Stuyvesant Town, the Sergeant sells the $3,600,000 stash *and* the $1,100,000 stash, sells them to some black middlemen (who, as justice will have it, will never pay him) who operate on his old beat in Brooklyn, and he launders the $400,000 cash. He then calls up Johnny in Hong Kong and says, "You know those guys at the Market Diner? The ones who pulled their guns on me? They took my car keys and my garage key, too. And when I got home from Hong Kong, I saw that they stole all my fur."

BANGKOK

Traitors, traitors, is there no end of traitors in the Big Circle? Apparently not, and the next to disgrace himself is Old Fox, the man who makes fifty vases a week for Johnny and $50,000 a week for himself but who still yearns for the Big Bucks. He buys three heroin bricks, packs them into two of Johnny's dragon-embellished vases, gives the vases to his own courier—an Italian diplomat—to smuggle into Italy. His scheme doesn't work. He soon reads in the Bangkok papers that the Italian and his two teeming vases were seized at Kennedy International Airport, in New York.

HONG KONG

"The vases at Kennedy. Do you think they're like ours?" asks Johnny in Cantonese, Johnny who's also abreast of the Bangkok papers. He and Old Fox are having lunch (sweet-and-sour soup, duck feet with celery, tripe, and Peking duck: the duck, scallions and sauce rolled in crêpes) at the Peking Restaurant in Kowloon.

"Oh no!" says Old Fox. "There are all kinds of vases in Bangkok! No no! There are so many kinds! On every street in Bangkok there're vases! No!"

He's lying, knows Johnny, for he's seen the photograph in one of the Bangkok papers. "Good," says Johnny in Cantonese, and "Cheers," says Johnny in English, raising his San Miguel. Oh, what a greedy world he's in—having ordered a hit on the Sergeant, he now orders one on Old Fox.

BANGKOK

No longer does Johnny's heroin go into hollow vases, now it goes into hollow buckets, buckets ostensibly meant for ice. Nor are the buckets dragon-embellished, now they're embellished with flying flowers, their lids with 16-pointed rosettes as if they were compasses. One thing that's still the same is the talented courier, who's Four Eyes, and who today has sixty buckets worth $3,600,000.

"We want to inspect them," say the police in English at Don Muang International Airport.

"I'm sorry, I'm rushed," says Four Eyes in English, and pole-vaults onto the next plane out.

HONG KONG

It takes him to Hong Kong, it takes him out of the frying pan into the fire, for the customs inspectors in Hong Kong are watching for travelers from Asia's heroin capital. But *voilà!* when Four Eyes comes into Kai Tak International Airport, his ticket says that he's come from Singapore. On board he made use of some of the tools of his trade: his timetable, airplane tickets, airplane ticket tabs, pen: his own little jiffy ticket kit.

"The ice buckets," says the customs inspector. "Where did you get them?"

"Singapore," says Four Eyes, showing his counterfeit ticket.

"Go on through," says the customs inspector.

NEW YORK

One last hurdle is customs at Kennedy Airport. "I have some sample buckets," says Four Eyes to an American customs inspector. "I want to pay the tax."

"How much are the buckets?"

"$5 apiece."

"How many buckets you got?"

"Sixty."

"Let me see one," says the customs inspector, and he takes off an ice-bucket lid, a north, north-northeast, etcetera, lid, and peers inside suspiciously.

"I also have this," says Four Eyes, and like Houdini he distracts the customs inspector by snapping a pair of ice tongs, *snap, snap, snap,* eight inches from his inquisitive nose. "It's twenty-five cents. It's twenty-five cents," says Four Eyes.

"No tax," says the customs inspector, practically hypnotized.

And motions him through. "Thank you," says Four Eyes.

Up on the terminal balcony is Johnny, thinking, *Bingo.*

16
Iron Carrier

HONG KONG

And how goes the Revolution, the one against the Royal Police? Splendidly, says the Professor—he now has an armory near China, and proudly he shows it to Johnny. To look at, the concrete house is one of a hundred white-collar-class ones in this little suburb of Kowloon, but as the Professor unlocks it he says to Johnny in Cantonese, "The mat that I'm standing on. It's flashing alarms to a house across the way. A brother there is watching us with binoculars." Then the Professor steps inside, touches one of the windows, and says, "Now the window is flashing alarms. The brother knows that I'm touching it." Then the Professor steps into the bedroom, pulls some shoes from under the bed, pushes the bed aside, pulls up a square of linoleum, pulls up a square trap door like the one Johnny saw in the Vietnamese hut (the replica, rather) in Saigon, and climbs down into a cellar smaller than a one-man jail cell. "Chairman Mao," the Professor says, quoting from *Problems of War,* "says that only with guns can the workers defeat the bourgeoisie, only with guns can the masses transform the world."

The hitch, as Johnny discovers, is that in this secret cellar there aren't guns. The pistols, silencers, and 2,750 rounds the Professor has bought in Bangkok to use when assaulting the precincts aren't here, they're still in Bangkok waiting to be spirited into Kowloon. The hand grenades the

Professor bought in Bangkok aren't here, nor are the rockets to use when the precincts send in reinforcements in Challenger tanks. Nor are the Uzis that Johnny bought in Miami, hid in refrigerators, converted to full automatic and "silenced" in Santa Cruz, Bolivia, the Uzis that sound like champagne corks now, *pop, pop,* the Uzis that Johnny will send across the Pacific for $100,000 via Bolivian diplomatic pouch. Nor are the twenty bulletproof vests that Johnny bought totally lawfully in New York to protect his courageous soldiers from the responses of the Royal Police. Nor, nor, nor, for the awful truth is that nothing exists in this armory except, at present, the Professor himself, a man in a manhole looking up at Johnny. "Are you getting wet?" asks Johnny in Cantonese solicitously, kneeling on the linoleum where the bed was.

"No, it's all concrete down here," says the Professor, playing his flashlight around.

"Beautiful," says Johnny. "No one else could construct this. You're like my son."

"Big Brother," says the Professor, climbing out. He knows that according to Mao, power won't flow from the shelves of an empty underground armory. "When will I have some guns?"

"This month."

"Thank you, Big Brother," says the Professor, who knows that Johnny's word is a contract, a signet in sealing wax. And soon Johnny boards a Bangkok-bound plane.

PATTAYA

A beach east of Bangkok on the Gulf of Siam. The screech of seagulls, the stink of seagull-eviscerated fish. The beach isn't sand but mud, and walking along it in $1,000 leather shoes is Johnny, and with him isn't the sun-tanned fisherman (the man in Kowloon appointed to feed the sharks)—isn't the captain of the *Victory* but his massive navigator, a man with an eye condition: a right eye that always looks up at the smokestack, the union jack, the sky. It looks today at the circling gulls as the navigator and Johnny walk to a fisherman's boat, *walk,* for the boat's on the mud like a big beached whale, its smokestack slanted, its bottom barnacle-covered, its propeller clawing the air. "Can this boat *move?*" asks Johnny, no nautical man, in Cantonese, asks the Thai fisherman.

"Yes, when the tide comes in."

"Then what speed will it go?"

"Twelve knots."

"Can it get to Hong Kong?"

"No, only to Vietnam."

"Our own boat the *Victory* is in Hong Kong. Let's meet near Vietnam," says Johnny, and the sky-eyed navigator pulls out a chart of the China Sea. Like on a treasure map, he draws an X on a rock in the Paracel Islands, two hundred miles off Danang.

"The iron carrier," the navigator says, meaning the man who's running guns for the Revolution, "from Pattaya to the Paracels will be you," the Thai fisherman. "From the Paracels on, the iron carrier will be us."

"We'll meet at the X," says the Thai.

HONG KONG

But first the captain, navigator, engineer, cook and crew, and the boss who'll be on the *Victory* must pray to Tin Hau, the Goddess of the Sea. The boss on the *Victory* will be another incomparable one, a man whose head is a grid of crisses and crosses like on a butcher's block—which, in fact, his head often was, for he's the chief machete-wielder in the Big Circle. For ten years he's led (he's *led,* like an ancient king) his men into wars in the streets of Kowloon, succumbing to other people's chops until he looked like the Man on Mars, the man whose head is latticed with Mars's canals. His name is Lum, and, though he's bulky, he moves so much like a panther that he's known as Fat Cat. With the captain, crew, of the *Victory,* he strides today to a temple containing a pink-cheeked statue of Tin Hau, a mortal born in 1098 who rescued her drowning father and was with justice promoted to Goddess of the Sea. He brings along a roasted pig and says in Cantonese, "We're sailing to the Paracel Islands, Tin Hau. We'll bring another pig if you bring us back safely to Hong Kong."

An unanswered prayer. As soon as the *Victory*'s on the China Sea, Fat Cat has oatmeal inside his throat, stomach, bowels: he becomes seasick (so does the boss on the Thailand boat) and he becomes sicker and sicker as the clouds become black, the southerly winds pick up, the waves become hills, and the *Victory* rolls up and down them like a wild roller coaster. As nauseated as he is, he still cries like Columbus, "Sail on!"

"We can't! We have a typhoon ahead!" says the sky-eyed navigator.

"I said sail on!" cries Fat Cat (and the boss on the Thailand boat).

"The radio says it's dangerous! If we sail on, we'll die!"

"How much farther are the Paracels?"

"A day away!"

"I am the man responsible! We've come this far," cries Fat Cat, "and we'll sail on!" His voice, which is normally loud, now is a foghorn that, like the roaring wind, seems part of nature itself, and he provides exclamation points by slamming his fist against his knee as forcefully as a man driving dowels. But now the waves are Godzilla high. The boat is at times horizontal, the lines slide around the deck like snakes, the chairs in the pilothouse like at a poltergeist party. At the wheel, the captain is a man who's fighting a one-ton marlin. But long live the Revolution: as boards break, as water enters, as everyone bails, even then does Fat Cat (and the boss on the Thailand boat, who pulls out his gun) cry, "Sail on!"

Not till an engine fails and the philosophical captain says, "If the other engine fails, we're dead," does Fat Cat (and the boss on the Thailand boat) consent to limp back to Hong Kong (and to Pattaya).

HONG KONG

For three weeks and $15,000 the boat's repaired in Kowloon. It sets out in better weather, meets the Thailand boat at the rock in the Paracels, takes on the pistols, silencers, 2,750 rounds, stores them in the engine room in the toolbox, turns to the north-northeast again, heads up to Hong Kong. All alongside are the flying fishes that *bang!* that *bang!* that Fat Cat uses for targets against the day his shot would be heard round the world, his .38 aimed at the Royal Police. He prudently hides it as customs inspectors climb onto the *Victory* at the approaches to Hong Kong Harbor. The harbor is the world's third largest (the largest isn't New York but Rotterdam) and one hundred ships as well as thousands of ocher-sailed junks come and go every day, and the customs inspectors just have a minute on the *Victory*. They come upon nothing suspicious. It's eighty feet, its hull is red, its pilothouse green, its figurehead is of Tin Hau, the Goddess of the Sea, who's pacifying the parting waves like on most other trawlers. It smells of a thousand—*fish,* think the customs inspectors, *where are the fish?* for surely a boat whose log says it's been at sea for a week and a half would have some. This boat hasn't any, not even sardines, and in their stead the customs inspectors discover those pistols and (oh, yes) and $7,000,000 of heroin, too.

They arrest the sun-tanned captain, the sky-eyed navigator, the rest of the mortified crew, and Fat Cat. They take them ashore to deliver them to those sworn counterrevolutionaries, the Royal Police. Tied, beaten, tortured, telephone books on their stomachs, sledgehammers slamming the telephone books, the captain and crew behave like Chinese: they don't tattle, neither does Fat Cat, but the sky-eyed navigator caves in: he tells the amazed detectives that the chief of the iron carriers is the respected owner of Imperial Fur, is Johnny. "He and I went to Pattaya," the navigator informs them, and the police rush to Johnny's apartment, finding a chart with a pen line leading from Pattaya to the Paracels and with another line from the Paracels to Hong Kong Harbor. Johnny at once is number one on the Royal Police Most Wanted List.

SAN DIEGO

Where's Johnny? He's here in California, sitting on a black naugahyde chair at San Diego International Airport: at Lindbergh Field. Two hours late, his bag from Kennedy tumbles onto the carousel, it starts moving counterclockwise but as Johnny grasps it, two sports-jacketed men say, "We're DEA," they're from the Drug Enforcement Administration. They flash their eagle-surmounted badges and say, "We want to inspect your bag." They take Johnny and Johnny's bag to their office and lo! inside it are one and a half cubic feet of American bills, of $1 bills, a hundred bills to a pile, a thick rubber band on each pile, more than a hundred piles in all, a boodle of more than $10,000. "What is this money for?" ask the DEA agents.

"I can't have money?" Johnny asks.

"You can, but why have it in $1 bills?"

"I am in retail business," Johnny begins.

"What sort of retail business?"

"Imperial Fur in Hong Kong. All this money petty cash. Is $1 here, is $1 there, is I collect maybe five years. I thinking, *Is too much money,* and I bring to United States."

"What will you do with it?"

"My children, I give them for Christmas."

"$13,000?" asks a DEA man who has counted it.

"Is $13,000? I never count. Officer," Johnny says, doing his I-am-an-ignorant-cricket-vendor routine, "in my Hong Kong, they never mind if I carry $1,000,000. Why you worry for $13,000?"

"We're worried you're buying drugs here."

"Oh, they produce drugs in San Diego?"

"No, the drugs come from Mexico."

"Oh, what sort drugs?"

"Cocaine."

"No, I just businessman," Johnny laughs. "You come to Hong Kong," he continues, handing the DEA men his business card, "and I give discount. This money for my two children for Christmas. For candy."

At his dusty computer, one DEA man has been punching in "Kon." "It says here you're clean," says the DEA man, for the Royal Police have learned that Johnny isn't in Hong Kong and, not wanting to warn him, have held their tongues about the Buddha-fronted boat, the sixteen pistols, the 120 heroin bricks, and the chart of the China Sea, and they haven't sent out an all-nations alert. What aroused the DEA was nothing but Johnny's especially heavy bag.

"I'm always clean. Can I leaving now?"

"We're sorry we've bothered you. Yes," say the men, and Johnny takes a taxi to a two-story hillside home and—*surprise*—to his eight-year-old and his four-year-old by Jonquil and to Jonquil's baby-sitter mother. The $13,000 in $1 bills (which truly is petty cash, from drugs) is truly a Christmas present.

SAN DIEGO

The two adults and two children go to Sea World. In wonder they look at the catfish: a "glass" one whose heart they see, an "upside-down" one that swims belly up, an "electric" one with 350 volts. A mola-mola, six feet across, looks like a stone-carved face of an Aztec god, a four-eyed fish looks like Eddie Cantor and Johnny's children are bug-eyed too. A mudskipper climbs from the water like a museum exhibit about the Ascent of Man, it climbs over mud, climbs up the mangrove roots, then *aiiii,* then leaps on an unaware insect like Batman. *"Water,"* cry Johnny's two children, shielding themselves as a tail-wagging dolphin splashes them, then, like a boat with a figurehead, swims by with a wet-suited, rein-holding, standing-up, barefoot rider. Cheers from the children, and squid, smelt and herring from the figurehead, are the dolphin's emoluments, and Johnny exclaims in English, "Look! They feed them fish! They catch with mouse!" meaning mouth. A pilot whale (its lower jaw white, its upper jaw black) is the next creature to splash them, squirt them, stand on its tail, flap its flippers at them, meaning *hello,* and be the surfboard for an attractive rider, then Johnny and the children go to the dreadful shark tank. The four-year-old touches the inch-thick glass, the shark swims up to see if the flesh-colored finger is edible, and Johnny cries in English, "He coming! He coming!"

"Daddy! Big teeth!" says the boy, and pulls his finger away.

"No, he don't bite you. Don't worry," Johnny assures him.

"Daddy!" continues the boy, his fist bangs the glass and the shark swims away. "He's scared of me!"

"Right. He scared of you and he go," Johnny says.

At night they stop at a Vietnamese restaurant for Vietnamese finger-width spring rolls, soup, and shrimp that's mashed like mashed potatoes and wrapped with sugar-cane strips. Next door is a Vietnamese souvenir shop, and Jonquil's mother buys a bronze elephant on whose tusks rests a telephone, an appliance that jogs Johnny's memory. In his pocket are several rolls of American quarters, and at a phone booth he drops a fist-ful into a slot and dials 011852 and a telephone number in Hong Kong. "Any news?" he asks in Cantonese, meaning "Any news of the *Victory?* The fishing float with the pistols, silencers, and 2,750 rounds?"

"No news," says the Professor.

"Any news from Prayerland?" asks Johnny, meaning "Any news of the float that returned to Pattaya?" In phone conversations, the code word for Thailand is Prayerland and the code words for some other countries are Sunland, Philland, Braland, Guayland, Boland, Canland (aka Maple Leaf) and Flower Flag for the United States.

"No news," says the Professor.

"I'll call you again tomorrow."

ANAHEIM

The next day, the four go to Disneyland. A horse-drawn streetcar carries them up Main Street, U.S.A., a street populated by Mickey and Min-nie and other four-fingered creatures. A train with a red locomotive takes them by a noisy landslide, and a Jeep takes them by the rats, bats, ravels of venomous snakes at the Temple of the Forbidden Eye, in India. In the Congo, a riverboat takes them by a yawning hippopotamus, in the Caribbean a dinghy takes them by raping, pillaging, plundering, and madly guffawing pirates, on the Mississippi a raft takes them to the cave of Injun Joe and a paddlewheeler to the vivacious carnival in New Orleans. Dumbo, the flying elephant, takes them in circles, a teacup at Alice's party takes them in dizzying epicycles, and a bobsled takes them down the Matterhorn and past an Abominable Snowman on vacation in Switzerland. The scariest ride is a "doom buggy" rattling through the Haunted Mansion, for Johnny was told over coffee once at the Holiday Inn in Kowloon that some of the ghosts in the Mansion are real. "No, they're imitation," said Johnny in Cantonese, but his friend in Kowloon said, "Some are real. At night they creep into the Mansion and hide with the imitation ghosts. I know a Chinese watchman at Disneyland. At night he hears ghosts having conversations inside the Mansion. He himself told me." *Oh, god, maybe it's true,* thought Johnny in spite of his earthly experiences at the Heaven Eternal Cemetery, in Gongjalu, and outside the Mansion ten minutes ago he told his two children in English, "We don't go in. You will see," and Johnny switched to Cantonese, meaning ghosts—"you will see *kwai.* You maybe scared." But the children insisted, telling him, "Daddy! We want to see *kwai!*"

So be it. In the cobweb-curtained living room of the Mansion, a see-through organist plays the *Grim Grinning Ghost Waltz* as eight see-through revelers in frayed tuxedos, tumbledown gowns, and hideous smiles waltz to it. "Daddy! They're ghosts!" says the four-year-old, burrowing into Johnny's chest.

"No, they not real," says Johnny. "You see? The ghosts have legs. They dance with legs. Real ghosts," Johnny continues, Johnny who's versed in Chinese demonology and Johnny who's reassuring *himself,* "not have legs. They float."

"Daddy! I want to get out of this house!"

"We finish soon. Don't scare."

"Daddy! Daddy!"

The children escape from the Mansion. They have strawberry frozen yogurt. They hug Mickey, Minnie, and Donald Duck. The four-year-old disappears, and for ten minutes his daddy asks other human beings but not Mickey, Minnie or Donald, who are aphonic, "You see Chinese boy?" The four-year-old reappears, his face full of streaming tears, at the lost-and-found-children's room. At nine at night (at noon in Hong Kong) Johnny says, "Wait, I make phone call," and on the Disneyland map the four-year-old finds the nearest phone. Johnny puts towers of quarters in, dials 011852 and eight more numbers, and asks in Cantonese, "Any news?"

"No news," says the Professor.

"Any news from Prayerland?"

"Yes. They're already back."

"I'll call you again tomorrow."

ESCONDIDO

The next day, Johnny, his spellbound sons, an African spoonbill, a Madagascan hammerkop, and an Ethiopian go-away bird make various raucous squawks (like *"Go away. Go away"*) in a bird cage enormous enough for a gaggle of pterodactyls, a tree-pillared, moss-pillowed, waterfall-rippling cage that is the lush entryway to the Wild Animal Park. In the park itself, the family without feathers boards an open monorail that, with a world-of-the-future *hummm,* departs on a great grand tour: in fifteen minutes all Asia and Africa.

At once a real lion crawls from the brush around them. "Son!" cries Johnny in English as, with catlike indifference, the lion licks one of its paws, then wipes its face. "Did you see the lion lip his hand? Did you see him wet his face?"

"Yes, daddy."

"Did you ever see the cat do the same?"

"Yes, daddy."

"The lion and the cat the same family!"

"Daddy?"

"But one was big and the other was small!" *Oh, goodness,* never has Johnny seen such wide eyes as those of his wonderstruck children now, no, not even when the bosses stared at the $10s, $20s, $50s and $100s—the $175,000 that tumbled out of the Ghost's canvas bag in Kowloon, no, never has the magic of daily life, of life that unrolls every moment in every beige-carpeted bedroom, overwhelmed him like now. "Yes!" says Johnny joyously. "The lion and the cat cousins! They use *hou soi,"* he continues, not knowing *saliva* in English and saying it in Cantonese, "to clean their face. But you and I," laughs Johnny, "use faucet!"

"Yes, daddy!"

And *hum,* the monorail moves to a veldt full of African elephants with ears like old maps of Africa, ears slowly flapping, tails slowly wagging, trunks picking up the dusty turf to splash it like talcum powder on their sun-baked backs. "You see the big white things?" cries Johnny, not knowing *tusks* in English or Cantonese but spreading his fingers into a V and launching the V from his nose. "Is where ivory come from. To get this ivory," says Johnny suddenly joylessly, "the people shoot rifles. And kill this beautiful elephant. And pull from elephant's mouse. And why they do it? To make more money. Daddy," says Johnny sadly, "don't like it," thinking of the brown ivory god that he himself brought as a bribe to Vietnam, thinking of Vietnam, thinking of the rifle-slinging soldiers who shot human beings in Vietnam, thinking of his children in Cambodia—

"*Ohh!*" A cry from everyone else on the monorail takes Johnny out of his retrospection to the here and now: to a small white rhinoceros, a rhinoceros small as a farmer's pig: a baby born three months ago to a mother who's now standing over it as proudly as if she's entering it in a baby beautiful pageant. "Son?" cries Johnny. "You see? The baby under the mother stomach. The mother protect it."

"But what if she steps on it?"

"She never step. She know the baby under her. She never lie down, neither, because she love little baby so. All animal love their baby. Just like men," says Johnny, scooping up his eight-year-old and propping him onto his lap. "Some people shoot the rhinoceros, too. They pull the horn from rhinoceros head. But what about the rhinoceros baby? Who care for the rhinoceros baby? No one," continues Johnny, hugging his eight-year-old and reaching out for his four-year-old, who has been sullenly sidling away. "You not happy? You jealous?" asks Johnny.

"*No,*" says the four-year-old, pouting.

"Don't jealous with him," says Johnny, boosting him onto his lap. "I love you and I love your brother. I love you both," but Johnny's still thinking, relentlessly thinking, of hunters who for a pai-gow chip, an alleged aphrodisiac, or a silver star on a shoulder will kill a peace-loving elephant, a peace-loving rhinoceros, or his own peace-loving progeny in Cambodia.

He tries to forget it. He concentrates on his awesome environment. On his left are Omani oryxes whose slender horns, from Johnny's perspective, merge into one, one fabulous horn like a unicorn's on a Chinese scroll. On his right lie Persian gazelles, lie on the grass facing east, lie as though praying to Mecca, lie like porcelain ornaments until they wiggle their squat black tails. In this golf-course-like park, the sand traps gullies, the water hazards morasses, the water itself an absinthe-colored sludge, are Congolese okapis licking their eyeballs and Turkomen markhoors climbing trees and Kenyan impalas that, if they tried, could vault over the cyclone fences into Johnny's populous lap. After ten minutes, he and his family come to a boulder that's full of gorillas, some rolling, some wrestling, some looking for God knows what in each other's anus, some playing: ascending their Mini-Matterhorn. "Did you know," asks Johnny, "that monkeys have king?"

"They do?"

"Monkeys have boss," Johnny says, pointing to the biggest and grimmest gorilla. "One boss. Not two."

"Why not?"

"If two, the two fighting. Is same human beings. In the United States," says Johnny parentally, "there is one president, not two. Monkey, president and *you* got to fight for survive. You got to go to school, and you got to study hard. You got to smart if you want success. If you want to be," says Johnny, "like daddy."

The monorail slows. It slides to an imperceptible stop. *No, not like daddy,* Johnny thinks as he and his chattering children get off. *No, not like myself,* he thinks as they achieve intimacy with the discrepant species that land in their hair in the lorikeet cage and the owl-eyed butterfly cage. Not like the only animal in this vast habitat who doesn't retaliate against his children's assassins, his peace-loving kids in Cambodia. *I'm wrong, I must take more revenge,* Johnny thinks as he and his two replacement children return to the cage with the bird that screeches unsociably, *"Go away!"* He drives from the Park daydreaming about the $7,000,000 of heroin on the *Victory,* and at a roadside telephone he calls up Hong Kong and asks in Cantonese, "Any news?"

"No news. It's three days late."

"It maybe has engine trouble?"

"I don't know."

"I'll fly tomorrow to Hong Kong."

HONOLULU

Thirty thousand feet above the Pacific, Johnny's on Northwest Airlines and reminiscing about his Christmas vacation in Flower Flag. He's proud of his children, he is. One day the four-year-old had a copy of *Batman Comics* and, pointing to Batman and Joker, precociously said, "He's the good guy. And *he's* the bad guy." Another day the eight-year-old bit a pretzel: he loosened an upper molar, it bled on the leftover pretzel, he bravely let Jonquil's mother pull it, and under his pillow the tooth fairy left him $20, all in $1 bills. Around the lit Christmas tree, accompanied by a Christmas cassette from J.C. Penney, the children taught Johnny that after they sang,

> *Jingle bells, jingle bells,*
> *Jingle all the waa . . . ay,*
> *Oh, what fun it is to ride*
> *On a one-horse open sleigh,*

that Johnny should heartily call out, *"Hey!" Ah, those were magical days,* thinks Johnny above the Pacific. *They were the best days of my life.*

TOKYO

He transfers to Cathay Pacific. As he takes off, he's reading the Hong Kong *Sing Tao,* its Chinese characters saying— Oh no! saying, "Saturday Night Gang War." In the story he sees that some gangsters were dining out in Kowloon when, with flailing machetes, some men in another gang rushed in, whacked at their heads, necks, shoulders and arms, sliced one head in two red halves like a watermelon, and, not tipping the waiter, exited fast. *Oh no,* Johnny thinks, for the man most likely to act that way (to act like a Hollywood gangster) is the man called the Movie Star, the baby-faced boss in the cinema verité movie about the Big Circle. As Johnny knows, the Star has a grudge against the other gangsters, who once ran the countless houses of prostitution (*girls, girls, girls,* say the red-lettered signs in Chinese) north of the chirping bird market in Kowloon. This year the Star has run them, but, to acquire them, he had to fight with the other gang, and the *casus belli* on Saturday night was, the Star lost money while waging this war and, as reparations, asked the gang for $5,000, but the gang offered him $2,500 down, $2,500 later. "Now, don't go to war *again,*" Johnny ordered the Star, but on Saturday night the man went to war regardless, or so Johnny judged from the melodramatic story in *Sing Tao.*

HONG KONG

Johnny judged right. "Big Brother," the bosses tell him in Cantonese as, looking worried, his eyebrows together, his skin in ripples between them, he enters the red-chaired passenger lounge at Kai Tak International Airport. "There was a war on Saturday night, and Muy," the Star, "killed one man and wounded more."

"How are Muy and his men?" Johnny asks.

"Muy's fine. Two men are wounded."

"Where are they staying now?"

"They're hiding."

"Muy," Johnny declares, "has made much trouble for us. Not that we didn't have trouble already. Is there any news of the *Victory?*"

"No, Big Brother. It's five days late."

"It isn't just engine trouble," Johnny declares, but not till he and the bosses go to his office building do they apprehend what the trouble is. In the lobby, they're waiting for the elevator when *beep,* Johnny's pager beeps, and on the pager there flashes the telephone number of a Chinese friend in the Royal Police. Not going up, he uses a lobby telephone to call this policeman and ask him in Cantonese, "What is it?"

"Big Brother! Where were you?"

"In the United States."

"Do you know a trawler captain?"

"Yes."

"I'll simply tell you. There's trouble."

"When?"

"It happened five days ago."

"Thank you for telling me."

"Goodbye."

No amplification needed. The Chinese policeman hangs up, and Johnny turns to the bosses saying, "They seized the *Victory*. They seized the crew and Fat Cat. They seized the white powder, the sixteen pistols, the 2,750 rounds. But worst of all," says Johnny, "they seized the three silencers—*silencers*, a watch robber doesn't need them, a watch robber wants to scare people, wants to shoot at the ceiling loudly, but an assassin needs them. The hats know about the Revolution, and they know I'm behind it."

"That couldn't be!" cries one of the bosses: the Revolution's passionate leader, the Professor. "If the hats seized the *Victory*, the story would be in *Sing Tao!*"

"The hats didn't announce it," Johnny declares. "They knew if I learned about it, I wouldn't return to Hong Kong." The implications of what he's just said flash on Johnny, and, with the worried bosses, he jumps back into his limousine, rides back to Kai Tak International Airport, and hurries to China Airlines. "Everyone else," says Johnny, "go to Tokyo, go to Seoul, the people already in Bangkok stay in Bangkok. But don't stay in Hong Kong," says Johnny, then takes the last seat on the next plane out. Ten minutes later the engines roar, and Johnny, age forty-two, a fugitive from the Royal Police, a fugitive too from Interpol, is eastward bound to Taipei.

Part Three

17
Runner

TAIPEI

Flat on their backs on a buttercup-colored bedspread at the Howard Plaza Hotel are Johnny and Jonquil, his guileless wife, who Johnny has just invited to follow him to the Republic (not the People's Republic) of China. A pattern of tropical leaves adorns the bedspread beneath them. The pillows are two tiers deep, the headboard is rosewood fit for an emperor's palace, the tables and chairs are rosewood too, and the scene between the buttercup-colored drapes (if Johnny and Jonquil had the occasion to enjoy it) is an enormous atrium and a waterfall three stories high. On the bed, Johnny, his shoes off, his socks on, his pajamas on, his arm festooned by Jonquil's black hair, is staring at the ceiling, thinking, *What should I tell her?* Guns, drugs, Revolution, revenge—Jonquil knows nothing about them, never was told.

"Husband? What are you thinking about?" asks Jonquil in Shanghai dialect, Jonquil who's also wearing pajamas and who has half-rolled to Johnny, her elbow beneath her, the back of her hand resting tranquilly on Johnny's stomach.

"I am in trouble, sweetheart."

"What trouble?"

"Did you see the TV news last night?"

"A little of it."

"Did you see about the *Victory*?"

"What about it?"

"It was seized by the Royal Police. They found some drugs, some guns. My brother was smuggling them into Hong Kong."

"What brother?"

"Chiefly Ah Tung," the Professor.

"Au Tung was smuggling drugs?"

"Yes."

"And also was smuggling guns?"

"Yes. He was the brother behind it."

"But *you're* the one who has run to Taipei."

"I'm worried. What if the police suspect me?"

"*Should* the police suspect you, Johnny?"

"Of course not. I was in San Diego."

"Why was your brother smuggling?"

"I don't know. I must ask him."

Jonquil reflects. She's often seen the Professor with Johnny, his face like a Modigliani, eyes behind tinted lenses, lips saying, "Yes, Big Brother," and citing corroboration from Chairman Mao. She rises onto her elbow, peering into Johnny's eyes like into a crystal ball. "Husband," she asks him. "Why did you tell him to smuggle those things?"

"Please don't ask. That's just for men."

"Why can't I ask you, if I'm your wife?"

"The rule is we mustn't tell women."

"But I'm not women, I'm your wife."

"Especially wives, we mustn't tell."

"But I'm not *wives,* I'm your *wife.*"

"You are," says Johnny, hugging her, drawing her nearer, smelling her perfumed hair, "and you always will be. But some things I mustn't tell you. Some things I must put in a velvet-lined box and keep the key. My father, brothers, sisters must never see them."

"That's them. But I'm your—"

"—wife, and if the police suspect me, I don't want them suspecting *you.* I want you to honestly tell them, 'My husband didn't tell me. He told

me this wasn't for women—women, he told me, must simply care for
their sons.' Sweetheart," says Johnny. "I promised that when I married
you I'd never hurt you. If you don't know about smuggling, then smuggling can't hurt you. Please understand me. Please forgive me."

Her head settles down on Johnny's arm, her hair ripples out to
Johnny's cheek, the ceiling engages her moistened eyes. It's Jonquil's
flaw, remember, that no one can tell her something *once,* once isn't
nearly enough, can't stick to Jonquil's cerebrum, must be re-re-reapplied
like a durable lacquer. "I'm your wife. You must tell me," Jonquil says.
"Do you still smuggle things?"

"No," lies Johnny protectively.

"Do you ever intend to?"

"No," lies Johnny.

"Promise me you'll never do it."

"I promise."

"Look at me, Johnny. Promise."

"I promise," lies Johnny, rising onto his elbow, looking into Jonquil's
moist eyes, "that I'll never smuggle." In fact Johnny knows that this very
day, Four Eyes, his talented courier, the one who says disingenuously,
"I'll pay the tax," has smuggled $6,000,000 of heroin into Kennedy Inter-
national Airport, knows that $5,000,000 more is queued up at the old
wooden frosted-window house by the Wanakarm Restaurant, in Bangkok, but knows that if (God forbid) someone should ever ask Jonquil
about it, Jonquil can honestly answer, "I didn't know."

"Smugglers. Promise you'll shun them."

"I promise," lies Johnny. In fact Johnny knows that he can't abandon
his brothers, that he must provide for the lawyers, wives, kids of the captain, cook, crew who are still being tortured by the Royal Police, of them
and of Fat Cat, too, must even provide for the Star, wherever he's lurk-
ing nowadays, and for the Star's machete-wielding associates.

"Thank you," says Jonquil. "You have enough money already, and I
don't need money at all. What have I always said I need? Just rice," says
Jonquil, "and I need *you.* But now the police suspect you. What happens
now?"

"I can't go to Hong Kong," says Johnny. "I can't use my passport, either. I've gotten myself a Taiwanese one. Tomorrow I'll go to Bangkok, a few days later to Singapore, a few days later to—I don't know, but I'll keep moving. I've got to."

"When will I see you in Hong Kong?"

"As soon as this typhoon blows by."

"When will that be?"

"A month, sweetheart," lies Johnny.

BANGKOK

His passport Taiwanese, the name on the passport this one: Mario William Yian, he arrives on Thai Airways International. Do not imagine that Johnny, a fugitive, a *runner* in Chinese gangster slang, but a man with $20,000,000, will hole up in some secluded shack in the Golden Triangle. No, Johnny checks into the Dusit Thani ("Palace of Paradise") Hotel, the one with waterfalls, with rambutans and mangosteens, with Amarettos and Creme de Cacaos. He steps out to get another passport and, a day later, departs.

SINGAPORE

On the seventieth (yes, seventieth) floor of the world's tallest hotel, the Westin Stamford, Johnny has grilled goose liver in a cream sauce of butternut pumpkin roesti, this at the Compass Rose Restaurant. With him is a Filipino who tells him that in Manila are seven casinos run by the brother of President Aquino. "It's scandalous," says the Filipino in English. "The casinos are in the newspapers every day, and the Aquinos must drop them. If you pay the Aquinos $8,000,000, you can run them yourself."

Johnny considers. A man in a zeppelin, he gazes down seventy stories to the rippling river and the Sir Stamford Raffles Landing Site. He knows that two sorts of people are on the move constantly, fugitives are number one and businessmen number two, and he sees in adversity opportunity: he can be both number one and two while investing (very well, laundering) his $20,000,000. "We go to Manila," says Johnny.

MANILA

At the Casino Filipino, he wears a black hairpiece and a black mustache held on by smelly spirit glue, a lifelike disguise that he got from a Taipei motion-picture studio. His nose full of caustic fumes, he watches the Filipinos in their outside-of-their-pants white shirts surrender their pesos to the Aquinos at the whirling roulette wheels, the craps, blackjack, baccarat and pai-gow tables. The gross is hundreds of millions but the net is hundreds of thousands, and Johnny says in English, "Not little business. Why little money?"

"We're skimming," a Filipino says.

"What if Aquino government fall?"

"We bribe whoever replaces them."

"Another $8,000,000," says Johnny. "Thank you but I not invest. I offered another casino in Atlantic City."

SÃO PAULO

From automobile exhaust pipes come 5,000 tons of carbon monoxide every day. A tarpaulin of carbon monoxide sprawls on Brazil's biggest city (and Earth's second biggest) and throat-clutching pigeons fall to the sidewalk, slit-eyed, dead. What this almost treeless metropolis needs is not another chemical plant (the river is already sludge from 1,000 tons every day of polysyllabic compounds, frothing detergent, excrement) but Johnny invests $1,000,000 in another chemical plant. For two years he's been obsessed by Ziploc bags, vases, buckets, drugs, by Bowie knives, machetes, guns, by what the civilized world calls vice.

> *Vice is a monster of so frightful mien*
> *As, to be hated, needs but to be seen;*
> *Yet seen too oft, familiar with her face,*
> *We first endure, then pity, then embrace,*

wrote Pope in *An Essay on Man,* and now the faintest aroma of vice clings to all of Johnny's investments. His chemical plant in the suburbs (cooler by fifty degrees, sometimes) will be for bulletproof plastic.

He also gets what a man on the lam cannot have a surplus of: a Brazilian passport.

ASUNCIÓN

Seven hundred miles long, Paraguay is the footprint of President Stroessner. To impede him is to be beaten, tortured, have your testicles wired, to simply stare at his palace is to be shot immediately by the khaki-suited police. A war against crime isn't one of Stroessner's priorities, and on the sidewalks the Indians sell yellow water in bottles whose labels say Arpege, rhinestones whose labels say Tiffany's. In this permissive city Johnny invests $1,000,000 to build an assembly line for Seiko counterfeit watches, Citizen counterfeit watches, and his own brand of Champion watches that he will smuggle from Paraguay, and to balk *banditos* he bribes a Paraguayan general to station a squad of *caña*-quaffing soldiers there. He also gets (you guessed it) a Paraguayan *pasaporte.*

LA PAZ

The capital of Bolivia is at ten thousand feet, and on the sky-high sidewalks the Indians in their black bowler hats sell, no, not oxygen canisters (though the concierge does at Johnny's hotel) but the source of the demon cocaine: coca, a scrawny green leaf that Johnny sprinkles into his tea to cure his *soroche:* his oxygen-deficient viscera. He invests $100,000 in a Bolivian gold mine and, a paragon of civic-mindedness, invests $100,000 in President Banzer—$100,000 for Banzer balloons, Banzer ballpoint pens, and Banzer bumper stickers *("Vota Banzer")* in the Bolivian colors of red, yellow and green, outsourcing the printing to Taipei. He cautiously asks a Bolivian friend in English, "We put all eggs in one basket?"

"Yes. This basket will win," the Bolivian says, and Johnny throws in a Mercedes.

"If Banzer wins, he keeps the Mercedes," Johnny laughs, but Banzer wins a plurality, not a majority, and the Chamber of Deputies elects someone else. A Bolivian passport, Johnny gets.

QUITO

Unlike the Bolivians in their bowler hats, the Indians in Ecuador sell their beads on the sidewalk (illegally) in hill-shaped hats like Chico Marx's. Like spring are the mornings here, like summer the afternoons, like autumn the evenings, like winter the nights outside of Johnny's plushy suite. He doesn't invest here, but like a mad stamp collector (or like the Ghost, who has twelve) he gets an Ecuadorian passport.

BOGOTÁ

A fugitive's life is one without friends, family, wife. In his Colombian hotel, Johnny hits on a Colombian girl, and in his room he pinches his shirt, wiggles the pinched part, tells her in English, "Take off." Their clothes coming off, the two making love, Johnny then says in English, "You very nice."

"You like me?" she says in English.

"*Sí,*" says Johnny in Spanish.

PANAMA CITY

For the first time since coming to Latin America, Johnny takes off his thick toupee and his pungent mustache to fly in a wind-riven helicopter past the ships lined up like gray circus elephants outside the Panama Canal. His pilot is an aide to President Noriega (the helicopter also is Noriega's)—a man who over the headphones asks Johnny in English, "What business you do?"

"I'm real estate," Johnny tells him.

"Maybe," the Panamanian laughs. "Maybe you also do drugs."

"You think I'm look like drug dealer?" Johnny asks.

"I can smell. Look your watch. Over $50,000."

"No, I'm just real estate," Johnny says.

"I do drugs myself. I fly from Colombia for President Noriega. You want to do drugs in Panama? I can arrange for you. But you must pay $4,000 per kilo."

"I'm real estate," Johnny says. His silk suit ripples like water in the onrushing wind. Just underneath him are eighty-five acres of Panama farmland that, back on terra firma, he buys for $1,000,000, then from an architect gets a plan for a 900-home development. On every acre, ten little ticky-tack homes.

LOS ANGELES

Chinatown. In the old days two Chinese actors slashed at each other with knives whenever the big-nosed tourists came by. At the car-ridden, carbon-monoxide-ridden union of two great freeways, the cars roaring by, the rubber against the road going *hum,* Johnny now leases a $200,000 motion-picture theater.

SAN FRANCISCO

Chinatown. In the old days 22.5 percent of the people here were prostitutes, who the secret societies sold at loud auction houses. Some roads running uphill, some running downhill, some made from tire-traction brick, the signs in English saying,

CURB WHEELS

PARK IN GEAR

SET BRAKE,

Johnny now buys a $3,000,000 motion-picture theater.

TORONTO

Chinatown. In the old days the *Star* and the *Spectator* had head-lines like "CHING CHANG CHINAMEN" and "THE YELLOW PERIL." A sort of space needle looming above it, a UFO restaurant revolving above it, a table of aliens talking in Pleiades language above it, Johnny now buys a $650,000 motion-picture theater.

NEW YORK

Chinatown. In the old days, the 1860s, just one Chinese man (the local tobacconist) lived here. No one does now but Chinese, and Johnny now buys a $4,000,000 motion-picture theater for Chinese movies. And yes, and Johnny builds a $20,000,000 twenty-story building on one of the chewing-gum-sticking streets. And yes, and Johnny buys a $2,000,000 one-acre supermarket and shopping center in Queens. And yes . . .

And this year (while still a fugitive, changing hotels, at dawn checking out, driving to side streets, parking, raising binoculars, *the DEA, are they following me?* driving to faraway phone booths, phoning just once, then scramming)—this year Johnny does business in Albany, Albuquerque, Atlanta, Baltimore, Boston, Charleston, Charlotte, Chicago, Cleveland, Dallas, Denver, we're up to the H's, Houston, Jacksonville, Jersey City, Kansas City, Las Vegas, Miami, Minneapolis, Newark, it's downhill from the P's, Philadelphia, Phoenix, Pittsburgh, Portland, St. Paul, San Antonio, Seattle, Tampa, Trenton, Tucson and, now the checkered flag, and Washington, D.C.

NEW YORK

And all Johnny's capital comes from H. Today he's in his lower-middle-class office/home on Austin Street, in Rego Park, in Queens, he's doing some manual labor here, his French-cuffed sleeves rolled up. The house, like the hundreds around it, all six feet apart, has cheap-looking vinyl sides, a wooden front door, four brick steps leading up, and along the walkway marigolds. A paradox is, the less the house resembles the houses around it (it has, for instance, brick-looking vinyl: the houses around it have pine-looking vinyl, stone-looking vinyl, vinyl-looking vinyl) the more it *exactly* resembles the houses around it. Venetian blinds in the windows foil all inquisitive neighbors, but all the windows on

Austin have these venetian blinds (or shades, drapes, or gray plastic lamina) to foil inquisitive neighbors. To walk open-eyed down Austin is to see well-kept gardens of marigolds, geraniums, impatiens, azaleas but to see nothing inside the houses except, perhaps, a rose in a vase on a windowsill. In front of the brick-vinyled house that Johnny is in, as (from time to time) in front of the houses around it, a girl skips rope as two girls swing it and in their high-pitched voices chant,

Teddy bear, teddy bear, turn around,

the rope-skipper facing about,

Teddy bear, teddy bear, touch the ground,
Teddy bear, teddy bear, tie your shoe,
Teddy bear, teddy bear, how old are you?

the rope-skipper doing eight skips.

In the brick-vinyled house, a brother with a .22 squints through the first-floor venetian blinds as, in the messy cellar, full of old greasy automobile parts, some soldiers, couriers, bosses and Johnny unload the ninety-nine buckets loaded a day ago next door to the Wanakarm Restaurant, in Bangkok. The director of this unloading is another incomparable boss, a man whose name is Fa and who because he's intelligent and not because he's a fathead is known as Buddhahead. Five foot five, he's built like a fire hydrant. Alone among the Big Circle, and almost alone among all Chinese, he goes to a gym every morning, sits at the chromium machines, flexes his big biceps, triceps, infiniticeps, lifts ten to twenty ten-pound bars of anvil-colored steel, does all this pumping and five hundred push-ups, too. In the grease-smelly cellar now, Buddhahead, his ceps distending his T-shirt, uses a spike to bust each bucket, then uses shears to slice it, and Johnny in silk suit trousers though not a silk suit jacket uses a hammer to whack every little heroin mote onto the New York *Sing Taos* on top of the cardboard on top of the grease-stained cellar bench. The man who scoops all the heroin ($6,000,000 worth, looking like quicklime worth about $18) into the Ziploc bags, the one-pound *exactly* bags, is that fabulous courier, that half-Asian, half-American who every month moves like a ghost past the gullible customs inspectors: the Ghost, his T-shirt today imprinted with the Statue of Liberty, his hair imperial-purple-tipped. "Today," says the Ghost in Cantonese, zipping another expensive bag—"today I'll get rich."

"And tomorrow you'll spend it," says Johnny, "on B-girls."

"No, Big Brother. This time I won't. This time I'll save it."

The air is heavy with heroin mist. It drifts like sawdust into everyone's nose. Becoming woozy, the Ghost excuses himself, climbs up the indistinct cellar stairs, sits down in a blurred red armchair, moans. His only thought is *I'm sick, I'm sick,* until in around ten seconds—*bang,* his attention is quickly diverted to a .22 bullet whizzing by his whirling head. *"Ai!"* cries the Ghost, as running upstairs from the cellar come Johnny, carrying a U.S. army rifle, and Buddhahead, carrying an Israeli Uzi.

"What's happening?" shouts Johnny in Cantonese.

"This stupid idiot," says the Ghost, pointing to the brother who once was squinting through the opaque venetian blinds but now is kneeling in front of the Ghost, sobbing, sputtering, hands in a prayer posture, the Chinese aren't safety-aware, "was playing games with his .22!"

"I'm sorry!" sputters the brother. "I took out the magazine first!"

"The round was still in the chamber!" says the Ghost.

"I didn't know!"

"You idiot, you almost killed me!" says the Ghost, as pale as a real ghost, his eyes black cutouts, his slumping head just an inch below a big splintered bullet hole in the wall behind him.

"Quiet!" Johnny commands. "Did the neighbors hear it?" He squints through the venetian blinds at the *"teddy bear, teddy bear"* girls, the marigold-sprinkling grown-ups, the NYPD screeching up in its blue-and-white car—no, there is no NYPD. For twenty minutes Johnny watches, the Ghost getting nauseated, going to the toilet, vomiting, the .22 gunman repeating, "I didn't mean it," and Buddhahead (heroin-unaffected, for in the clouded cellar he wore a doctor's mask that he had packed with wet Kleenex) stretches his tired muscles by raising his big clenched fists to his ears and pumping his bulging biceps up, *mmf! mmf!* his T-shirt stretching, his trunk twisting left, his trunk twisting right, his eyes staring into a closet mirror, admiring his Schwarzenegger physique. In his white doctor's mask, he goes downstairs to do more incisions, but Johnny doesn't accompany him: for Johnny has become woozy too, and, after twenty minutes, the NYPD not appearing, he falls supine on a wine-colored couch.

Oh, god, Johnny thinks. He closes his eyes, but on the insides of his eyelids a Roman candle explodes, the red-hot ashes falling on his reti-nas, igniting fires. He gets to his feet, goes to the toilet, vomits, stumbles back to the wine-colored couch, closes his eyes again, but on the insides of his eyelids it's Chinese New Year's in Chinatown, the fireworks blan-keting out the February constellations. *That's enough, waiter,* his stom-ach is stuffed, it's full of pork dumplings that he must vomit three more times, then he collapses onto the wine-colored gurney. His eyes burn like someone's who's chopping onions. His nostrils run, and his breaths are like someone's on Everest. In his ears Johnny hears *beep, beep, beep,* on a pager are lucky numbers like 33, 88, 99, the codes of the anxious brothers in all five boroughs attempting to get to Buddhahead to ask him, "Where are the fishes?" "Where are the shrimps?" or "Where are the lob-sters?" the codes for "Where are the goods that all Americans crave?" *They're crazy,* Johnny thinks dizzily. *They're calling to ask us, "When do we get it?" But why do they want it? Why, when it makes them sick like me? Why do I even export it? It's poison!*

No, this sagging gurney is no proper place for a businessman, an investor in mines, casinos, airlines, factories, farms, twenty-story build-ings, supermarkets, shopping centers, motion-picture theaters, and Boli-vian presidents, a jet-setting executive, an entrepreneur whose red-headed pins would pepper a map of North and South America and Asia, a cap-italist in a tailored silk suit. Through clouded eyes, Johnny looks down at the $1,000 black crocodile shoes that he bought (along with gray, brown, burgundy and white crocodile shoes, with lizard shoes, ostrich shoes, leather shoes) on a shopping trip with his natty messenger man in Rome, his dandy messenger man who didn't want to seem better dressed than the Dragonhead, his chichi messenger man who pleaded with him, "You mustn't look like a country boy, Big Brother," and who then guided him on a one-week extravaganza on the Via Condotti, Via

Boca di Leone, Via Borgogna, and Via Barberini, the air in all the stores golden, the air just misted with gold dust, the consequence of lights in brass fixtures, of lights in Tiffany lampshades, red, orange, yellow lampshades, of copper walls, of bright brass railings, of gold-plated doorknobs, shoehorns, shoetrees, of golden statues of Indian girls fingering golden flutes, charming golden cobras. In these great Roman palazzos, the $1,000 black crocodile shoes (and the $100,000 of suits, jackets, cashmere overcoats, the salesmen at every front door saying, *"Avanti!* Come in!" and the prodigal messenger saying after every sale, "Big Brother! You look much younger!")—the $1,000 black shoes seemed burnished with gold, the shoes that today on the wine-colored couch seem old, *old,* the clogs of some homeless man on Queens Boulevard. *No, I don't belong here,* Johnny thinks, *I don't belong in the heroin hustle. I don't—* The beeper goes beep. On it appears number 33, and Johnny slogs to the cellar stairs to call down to Mr. Universe, to call down to Buddhahead in Cantonese, "33, 88 and 99 called."

"Not again! Turn off the beeper. I'm not ready yet," says Buddhahead. "How are you, Big Brother?"

"Still sick," Johnny says.

"The new people always are," says Buddhahead. "They don't wear doctor's masks. They don't put wet Kleenex in."

"Next time I'll know," Johnny says.

Next time! His throat full of oatmeal, he falls on the couch again, thinking, *Next time will never happen. Never again will I handle heroin.* Red rum, murder spelled backwards, that's just for the Americans, let the Americans vomit, groan, overdose, die (and this year 1,315 of our writers, rockers-and-rollers and bums, two hundred more than last year, will die of Johnny's commodity)—let the Americans get extravagant habits, steal, rob, get arrested, go to our bloated prisons, come out as habitual criminals, that is God's punishment for the Hairy-Armed Nation, for its offenses in Vietnam, Cambodia, Laos, its wanton murder of Johnny's innocent babies. *But me,* Johnny thinks, *no, I'll never handle heroin. I'll handle factories, theaters, tracts. I'll attend to legitimate businesses. Who'll handle heroin for me? My brothers.* His bosses like Buddhahead, couriers like the Ghost, soldiers like "Gee, the gun was loaded," these are the people who'll export-import the DOA as Johnny invests the profits around the civilized world in something other than B-girls and Chinese poker. His mind made up, he falls asleep on the couch, arising from time to time to vomit into the woebegone toilet. All the next day he lies sleeping, eating nothing, the day after that he has orange juice, vomits again. By now he's decided which of his brothers will run the round-the-world heroin trade, become the new CEO.

NEW YORK

At eight p.m. one night in Queens, Johnny, in burgundy leather shoes, also in black mustache and wig, and four incomparable bosses meet in a rear-windowed room at the Pan American Motor Inn, at 7900 Queens Boulevard, across from McDonald's and Burger King. All the men carry pistols because it's after dark in New York. As they enter the fifth-floor room, they look in the closets, the creaking armoires, the brass-handled dresser drawers, they look (like frightened children) under the chairs, the tables, the bed, they look (like Hamlet) behind the folds of the undulatory curtains, they look for the little steel beetles that may be DEA bugs, DEA taps, they don't find any but, in case they missed them, they turn on the sink, the shower, the TV's thunderous movie. Outside the wall-to-wall window there are no DEA vantage points except for the two big red-and-white cylinders that we often hear about on AM 880 and AM 1010, "Traffic on the Long Island Expressway is backed up to the Elmhurst Tanks." The window itself is a one-way one: the silver inside is cracked, is stained the color of drying glue, but if a DEA agent were perched on a red-and-white cylinder, he couldn't look into the bedroom, all he'd see was his own dim reflection. No matter: the brothers close the wrinkled curtain, then sit on the bed and the chairs around the circular coffee table.

The table lamp's on. Johnny removes his caustic mustache and wig but not his suit jacket and tie. "We're here," he commences in Cantonese, "to talk about the Big Circle. Our white-powder operation is doing phenomenally. So far we've netted $20,000,000 in American dollars that's now in accounts in Chinatown and Switzerland. But white powder isn't a stable business, it's an unsteady one. Last year in America five thousand people went to federal prison for it. We ourselves could be caught, as we were in Toronto and Hong Kong Harbor. We could be betrayed, as we were in New York, Hong Kong, and Bangkok. What then should the Big Circle do? My answer is, We should grow. We should enter legitimate businesses. We should diversify."

In short-sleeved shirts, the bosses say nothing. Some of them don't even know what diversify means. All of them (also Johnny) are smoking cigarettes, saturating the room with murky smoke, dropping the ashes into trays with PA, for Pan American, on engraved heraldic shields. All of them (also Johnny) are drinking coffee or Coca-Cola.

"With $20,000,000," Johnny continues, "I've borrowed $40,000,000 from banks. And with it I've bought property (naturally in other people's names) in New York, Toronto, San Francisco, and Los Angeles."

"Good move, Big Brother," says Buddhahead, the biceps curler, who's one of the four alert bosses here.

"Nowadays property's cheap," agrees the Professor, the Mao man, who has been smuggled into New York.

"Next," Johnny continues, "I've bought property in Panama. You may not know it, but there's a canal in Panama."

"I know it, Big Brother," says Four Eyes, the talented courier, the "I'll pay the tax" man, his hand shooting up.

"I too know about it," says the Professor. "In the old days, a lot of Chinese helped build it."

"They did," Johnny says. "And now there's a free port in Panama City. Hundreds of freighters come every day. We can use freighters instead of freight airplanes to transport our products, whatever they are. Next, I bought a gold mine in Bolivia."

"I've been to Bolivia," says Four Eyes. "It's hard to breathe in Bolivia."

"I get dizzy there," Johnny says. "One block and I'm panting, *huh, huh.*"

"I'm that way in Bolivia too," says Four Eyes.

"I don't understand. Why is it hard to breathe in Bolivia?" asks Michael Jackson, the boss who was smuggled curled like a fetus into the United States and now runs Johnny's office in New York.

"You don't know?" Johnny asks. "The capital city is ten thousand feet. A man can't breathe enough oxygen there. A *foreign* man can't, but I have a lovely villa there, and I've seen my twenty maids playing soccer outside it. Next, I'm building a watch factory in Paraguay. Not in the capital city, Asunción," pronouncing it *A-sun-shun,* "but two hundred miles east in the Port of President Stroessner. And last, I'm building a plastics factory in Brazil. I went to Brazil at Carnival time. I didn't sleep. I drank, danced, and ran in the streets just like in a Revolution."

"Maybe next time I'll go," says the Professor somberly.

"All these legitimate businesses," Johnny continues, "I myself will run. From now on I won't have time to run the white-powder business. You four brothers and Tiger," the branch manager in Bangkok, the man who's still being haunted, who's still being told, "I'll take revenge," "will be the committee who'll run the white-powder business. If there's dissension, phone me and I'll decide for you, but otherwise you and Tiger will be the control committee, and the committee chairman will be Ah Tung," the Professor, the man who, like Johnny, cares about right and wrong and not just about "What's for *me?*" the man who's closest to Johnny's heart. "It's like," says Johnny, thinking of the hierarchy among the American Green Berets in the Vietnam War in the port of Nhatrang—"it's like there'll be four lieutenant colonels and one full bird-shouldered colonel, who'll be Ah Tung."

"Good. That's what I want," says the Professor, smiling his seldom-seen smile.

"I want that too," says Buddhahead, the Professor's housemate in Queens.

"Big Brother," says Four Eyes, "I don't care about rank. What will I be, a full colonel? I don't care. Or will I be a lieutenant colonel? I don't care. I just care about this: that I accomplish whatever you tell me to. You tell me, 'Do one,' and I'll do one. You tell me, 'Do two,' and I'll do two. But from now on, Big Brother, who do I listen to? You or Ah Tung?"

"You listen to Ah Tung," says Johnny. "If he tells you, 'Do one,' you do one. But you aren't doing this for him. You're still doing this for me. Any questions?"

"No questions," says Four Eyes, all four eyes (to Johnny's perception) looking glum.

"Well, I have some questions," says Michael Jackson, a boss who, like most of this sudden committee, is older than the Professor. "I'm worried about Ah Tung. I'm not saying he's not good. We all know he's good, but he has a certain proclivity whenever a brother botches things. And that proclivity is to ruthlessly kill him. If he's a colonel and I'm a lieutenant colonel, what if I somehow screw up? What if he says some ambiguous thing that I misinterpret? He'll ruthlessly kill me."

"No, Michael," says the Professor. "You and I are good friends. We are the two halves of Michael Jackson, you are Michael and I am Jackson. I won't kill you."

"But what if I do something wrong? What if you simply think, *Oh, Michael did something wrong.* You'll ruthlessly kill me, won't you, Ah Tung?"

"No, Michael," says the Professor. "If any brother, including me, does anything wrong, it's the *committee* that kills him. Not just me."

"Listen, everyone," Johnny commands. The cigarette that he has puffed just once, he now extinguishes in the PA-engraved tray. "No one kills anyone casually. If all five committeemen say, 'We should kill this man,' then fine, they can kill him. If just one committeeman says, 'No, we shouldn't kill him,' then the committee refers it to me, and I'll tell you yes or no. I'm still the Big Brother, and I still run the Big Circle. I'm not the man carrying ashes now, but I'm the man behind it. Do you understand me, Ah Tung? You aren't the Dragonhead?"

"I understand you, Big Brother."

"Michael? Do you understand?"

"I understand too, Big Brother."

"Buddhahead? Four Eyes?"

"We both understand."

"I wish you all well," says Johnny. It's two in the morning now, and the four bosses leave the room surreptitiously, several minutes between them. The last who's about to go is Ah Tung, the Professor, his round-windowed glasses on, his eyes well-framed, his smile well-entrenched, but Johnny asks him to linger awhile. "My little brother," says Johnny. "You know I like you. I feel you're my son. You're ambitious like me. Ambitious, ambitious, that's what a leader must be. But if I say something, forgive me. You haven't enough social skills. You mustn't issue orders, boom, boom. You mustn't say, 'Do it, I order you to.' You must be nicer than that. You must be respectful, gentle, polite. You must say, 'Brothers, I need your advice,' and, 'Brothers, I need your decision.' You need the committee with you, or you won't last as committee chairman. I myself, I need the Big Circle. If it's against me, I'm out as the Dragonhead. Do you understand this, Ah Tung?"

"I understand it," says the Professor, but all his assumptions about an effective chain of command come from Mao.

BANGKOK

And not understanding at all, the Professor takes over in Bangkok, assumes command of the ice-bucket business in Bangkok. A gun, said Mao, is what power flows from, and the Professor comports himself like someone with a Kalashnikov. He tells every heroin wholesaler, heroin hammerer, heroin bucket-packer, heroin courier in Bangkok, "I'm running things now. Do what I say or you're out." He tells Fat Ass, the man who first introduced him to Johnny, calling him "My best friend," "Do what I say or you're going to South America. You'll watch the water behind the dam," the expression in Cantonese for "You'll watch the grass grow." He tells Four Eyes, a central committeeman, "Are you with me or Big Brother? I am the colonel now, and you're taking orders from *me.*"

But more than that. The $5,000,000 here, the $5,000,000 there, that in his six months in New York the Professor has raptly gazed at have acted quite like the blinding sun, have burned the Professor's retinas out. No longer visualizing his Revolution, he sees only visions of money, of money for *him.* To men who don't gamble, the thrill of winning $5,000 at poker, pai-gow or fan-tan if they're making $5,000 a month would appear to be homologous to the thrill of winning $5,000,000 if they're making $5,000,000, but the Professor (like most other brothers) somehow derives a "high" from those supererogatory zeroes when he's at a poker, pai-gow and fan-tan den in Bangkok, and, like a heroin addict, he can't walk away from it. Like most millionaires in America, what $5,000,000 brings him is not particularly happiness but a score, a statistic, an algorismic ornament that's more than $500,000, much more than $50,000, and much, much more than $5,000, but that's totally unconnected to good food, good clothes, good homes, totally unconnected to the Good Life. Behold! From outer space (or from poker, pai-gow and fan-tan tables, or from white-powder transactions) there falls the sum of $5,000,000, but it's just glittering digits on a clattering pinball machine to the Professor's glassy eyes. A pure Pythagorean, that's what he's become.

And feeling this way, the Professor takes over in Bangkok. And within days, the bosses in Bangkok abominate him.

18
Ash Carrier IV

HONG KONG

We last saw Muy, the Movie Star, at a turbulent restaurant in Kowloon, his fist curling, his sharp machete chopping up human watermelons. All his opponents dismembered, he fled on a ferry to Hong Kong Island, to an unobtrusive apartment near the old kindergarten where Johnny had once cleaned the toilet bowls with Comet. Slyly the Star had the newspapers delivered every day, but he let them accumulate outside his modest apartment door. His stratagem was, his neighbors would surely recognize him as the Buddha-bland star of the action-adventure movie about the Big Circle and would report him to the Royal Police, but those oafish officers would—and did—see the *Sing Tao*s on his welcome mat and, not kicking down his apartment door, would and did say in Cantonese, "Oh, there's no one inside." On the telephone now, the Star calls up Johnny, the international businessman, the man who's presently buying a $150,000 air-cargo airline in Panama City, and tells him in Cantonese, "Father. The hats are looking for me."

"Of course they are," says Johnny. "Didn't I order you, No more wars?"

"The hats will catch me, Father, if I don't escape from Hong Kong."

"Why didn't you know that," says Johnny, "if I did intuitively?"

"Father, please save me. Me and my one dozen soldiers."

"If you'd listened to me," says Johnny, "you and your soldiers wouldn't need me. But you're my little brothers, you're loyal toward me and I am toward you, and I'll save you. I'll buy another fishing float, and I'll send you all to Prayerland."

"Thank you, Father," the Star concludes, then Johnny buys a $100,000 boat with a captain, navigator, cook and crew, and one night in Hong Kong Harbor the Star and his cutthroats stealthily board it. It's negligent, but the Star (the one boss who never pauses to pray at a white-bearded, white-mustached, white-sideburned statue of Kuan Kung, the God of Loyalty) has failed to propitiate the Goddess of the Sea, Tin Hau, at her golden temple near Kowloon. In the Gulf of Siam, the engine goes out, the second engine goes out, the boat drifts indolently over a barracuda rock, it gnashes a gash on the starboard side like on the *Titanic,* the Gulf of Siam starts spouting in, and (how discontent can the Goddess be?) the water pump goes out too. The captain, navigator, cook and crew, the Star and his soldiers don't use the kitchen sink but do use the pots, pans and ladles to try to bail out the fishing float, but it starts sinking determinedly. Around it there circle pearly-toothed sharks, and one ironical brother says in Cantonese, "We ate too much shark's fin in Hong Kong. Now the sharks will eat *us.*"

"I don't think that's funny," another brother says.

"I see land!" another brother cries, a man who isn't bailing but is sitting on top of the pilothouse, peering west, pointing like in a heroic painting to a small sandy point about a mile away. The boat drifts nearer the sand, then, slowly sinking, some gunwales submerging, the deck dipping into the sea, the sea like a tide creeping up, up, up, the boat drifts farther away. "We'll never be nearer than this," the man on the tilted pilothouse cries.

"If we don't swim, we'll die," the Star says without emotion. "If we swim, some of us may not die. So we must swim."

"Do you know how to?" the half-awash captain asks.

"Yes," the Star and his soldiers say, men who a decade earlier swam past the saber-toothed sharks from China to Hong Kong to found this sect of Big Circle. Now they slide down the sloping deck into the China Sea and commence to Australian crawl, right, left, the salt water burning their lips, the sharks retiring as though they're outmanned, the men swimming till their tenacity and the easterly current carry them and the sailors to the Isthmus of Kra. On the sand they fall asleep, then wake up, walk across mountains, descend through jungles, meet a Thai army patrol. "You're illegal immigrants," the Thais say in Thai. "You're under arrest," but the Star takes off the Rolex the water didn't corrode, and he bribes the Thais to let them onto the tumbledown bus to Bangkok. Their great adventure, costing them a $100,000 trawler and a $20,000 wrist watch, doesn't quite end as the Star and his soldiers stagger into the old wooden frosted-window house next door to the Wanakarm Restaurant.

There the Colonel, aka the Professor, aka something unprintable, grants the Star an imperious audience, saying in Cantonese, "I'm running things now. Do what I say or you're out."

BANGKOK

Another boss the Professor provokes is Tiger, the farmer's son, the man with erratic buck teeth and a Leaning Tower of Pisa face, the one with the bath salts who, in the tub in Tokyo, thought, *Is the ghost invading my dreams or am I dreaming it?* The titular boss in Bangkok, Tiger by now has spooned $18,000,000 of heroin into the flying-flower buckets bound for New York. His next shipment is $2,500,000 in forty buckets bound for Chicago, then New York, but the Professor (who's ambitious, ambitious and who wants money, money) feels that Tiger is thinking small, is still thinking lettuce, cabbage and bok choy raised on a Chinese tenant farm. Why only forty buckets? the Professor feels. Why not forty buckets times *two* and why not forty buckets times *three?* Is he, the Professor, the committee chairman, the eagle-shouldered one—is he an incomparable kingpin or a co-partner in Mom and Pop's white-powder store? "No, not just forty," the Professor tells Tiger in Cantonese at the frosted-window house. "What is in Bangkok? How much white powder? How many bucketfuls?"

"130-something," says Tiger warily.

"Ship them all," the Professor says.

"No, Ah Tung," argues Tiger, not even coming close to calling him Big Brother. "All those buckets, they'll be a gigantic shipment."

"Ship them all, I'm ordering it."

"That many buckets, the customs inspectors will be suspicious at Don Muang and O'Hare Airports."

"Also ship them tomorrow."

"No, that's wrong, Ah Tung. The ones we've already filled, even on those forty buckets the glue hasn't dried. The bottoms will open. The powder will leak. The dogs will smell it."

"The glue will dry in another hour."

"It will still smell like glue. The dogs won't react, but the customs inspectors will. The glue's got to dry several days."

"I know what I'm doing, Tiger."

"And then we've got to wash every bucket with Kiwi Laundry Detergent. Or *still* it will smell like glue."

"I am the boss now, Tiger."

"No, the whole committee is."

"And I'm the committee chairman. I've almost always been lucky. I'm counting on being lucky tomorrow."

"And what if you're not?" asks Tiger, who has played mahjong with the Professor and knows just how lucky he is: fifty-fifty, like everyone else. The fifty times the Professor wins, he slams his bams, cracks or dots on the table heavy-handedly, shouting in Cantonese, "I win!" and the fifty times the Professor loses he gets sullen and says, "I'm not playing anymore. I'm going dancing." "If you aren't lucky tomorrow," says Tiger, "you will lose $8,000,000. Why don't you *think* before you act? If you just *think*, you won't need luck."

"Listen!" shouts the Professor, pointing his half-inch-long little manicured fingernail ("I like it," he has curtly explained) like a stiletto at Tiger. "I'm the one running things! Do what I tell you to! 'The lower level,' says Chairman Mao, 'is subordinate to the upper level.' You are the lower level, little brother! I am the upper one!"

"I'm on the control committee!" shouts Tiger.

"And I'm the committee chairman! If," the Professor shouts—"if you won't obey my orders, get out!"

"Get out of this room?"

"No, get out of Bangkok!"

"Get out I will!" Tiger shouts. "And you, Ah Tung! If you want to ship those 130-whatever buckets, do it! If you want to ship them tomorrow, do it! But any tragic consequences will be on your shoulders! Not mine!"

"Get out!" the Professor shouts, and Tiger (his hand on his holster) exits the frosted-window house, drives through the gate in the high concrete wall, continues to Don Muang International Airport, and boards the next plane to Taipei.

BANGKOK

The next day to this same airport come 138 buckets, reeking of AA glue, haphazardly washed, bubble-wrapped—eighteen buckets in one cardboard carton, twenty in each of another six cardboard cartons, the cartons bigger than Bekins boxes. The cargo belt is too narrow for these monsters, each of which must be dragged along by two brawny men. "What's inside them?" asks one, probably thinking cast-iron stoves.

"Samples," the courier blandly explains.

The courier today isn't Four Eyes, the "I'll pay the tax" sophisticate, but his most promising student, whose name is Chen and whose nickname is Tommy. Young, light-skinned, well-dressed, well-bred, a man of exquisite courtesy, he looks like a student at Chulalongkorn University, the Stanford of Bangkok. On trip after trip, he has been trained by Four Eyes, has prayed for safe passages at the Temple of the Four-Faced Buddha, has said, "If you grant this, Buddha, I'll pay the girls to dance naked for you," has stood behind his veteran mentor next to American customs inspectors, young and old, men and women, amenable and mistrustful. "The little bird," said Four Eyes to the Professor recently, "can now fly alone." On this solo trip, though, the bird won't be quite alone: a "watcher," an old professional, is right behind him in Bangkok and will be right behind him in Tokyo, Chicago and New York to watch him like one of the watchbirds in the books by Munro Leaf. Bound to each other by virtual chains, the bird known as Tommy and Tommy's watchbird board the 138-bucket-burdened airplane bound for Tokyo.

TOKYO

Coincidence. As the plane lands at Narita, the paddies, paddies, runway beneath it, the bounce of the rubber wheels, a *boom* resounds in a passenger lounge, there is a bomb explosion there, the Sikhs of India did it. The air is black from the jagged shrapnel, billowing smoke, it smells like the Fourth of July and people lie on the carpet screaming, bleeding, dying, and people on the periphery run through various doors like the little green round-headed men on the luminous exit signs. Amidst pandemonium, Tommy and Tommy's watchbird go to another passenger lounge to get patted down, to learn that the flight to Chicago won't happen, to check the seven cast-iron stoves in a storeroom, and to sleep overnight in sight of planes landing, taxiing, taking off. *Bad luck,* thinks Tommy's watchbird, for jade is said to bring good luck and, without apparent causation, his jade ring suddenly cracks in half and two jade semicircles fall to the floor like little green worms. *Is this Buddha's warning?* thinks Tommy's watchbird. *Probably not.*

The next day, the flight to Chicago's full, and Tommy and Tommy's ringless watchbird board a flight to Seattle, though Johnny has often told them, "Stay away from Seattle, the customs inspectors are too meticulous there."

SEATTLE

On the walls of a whimsical corridor at Sea-Tac International Airport are pink, purple, yellow silhouettes of tourists with pink, purple, yellow suitcases, of businessmen with pink, purple, yellow attaché cases, of children with no pink, purple, yellow cases at all, all striding to U.S. customs. Striding with them in three dimensions and in dress slacks, open-collared dress shirt, and brass-buttoned blazer is Tommy, tailed by his ubiquitous raven. At the carousel for U.S. customs, Tommy puts the seven cardboard cartons in supermarket carts, then rolls them to the meekest-looking inspector, a motherly gray-haired forty-year-old in a blue open-collared blouse and a gold INSPECTOR badge.

But meek she's not. She looks at Tommy's passport (a Bolivian one: *suspicious*, the gray-haired inspector thinks) and sees two entry stamps for Thailand, two days apart. "What were those trips for?" the motherly woman asks.

"It was just business," says Tommy.

"What business?"

"The electronics business," Tommy.

"What are those cardboard cartons?"

"Ice-bucket samples," says Tommy. His hand shakes slightly as he produces a counterfeit invoice for all 138. "I'll sell them to restaurants in Chicago and New York."

"What restaurants?"

"Oh, various restaurants."

"How much are the buckets worth?"

"It's on the invoice. $1,200."

"Are they electronic, somehow?"

"No," says Tommy nervously. "The profit from them, I'll open an electronics business in the United States."

The woman looks at Tommy curiously. An electronic business for $1,200? She walks back to a bearded, mustached, long-haired man, an I'm-still-a-hippie forty-year-old in a blue open-collared shirt and a gold INSPECTOR badge, a man who walks to Tommy and says, "You made two trips to Bangkok. What were they for?"

"It was just business," says Tommy.

"Can you please elaborate for me?"

"It was just business," says Tommy.

"Well," the hippie inspector says, "I'd like to see one of those buckets, please." He couldn't have had a more savage reaction if he'd said to Tommy, "I'd like to search you. Drop your drawers, please."

"*Why?*" Tommy shouts, forgetting the imperturbable manners that Four Eyes has taught him at international airports from California to Florida and backsliding to his Chinese criminal self. His eyes turn round, his face turns red, his voice is an active volcano as Tommy continues, "Why must you see one? What must you see one for? Do I owe you money? Do I owe you taxes? If so," Tommy shouts, pulling his wallet out, pulling out $200 or $300, waving it like at an auctioneer—"if so, I'll pay it!"

"Well," says the hippie inspector politely, "I'm a customs inspector, see. What I do for a living is, I look at ice buckets, things like that." He takes out a buck knife, cuts the straps on a cardboard carton, takes out one of the fabled buckets, carries it to an x-ray machine, looks at the x-ray monitor. He then opens a toolbox, takes out a $\frac{9}{64}$-inch drill, drills into one of the flying flowers. The watchbird, who has been leaning stoically on a chromium railing, says to Tommy in Mandarin, "I'm leaving. You're staying here. When they ask you, the cartons belong to me. You know nothing about them." With those words, the watchbird walks to the men's room, takes off his jacket, takes off his $2,000 wig, and, his scalp shining like a one-ball—as a child he had alopecia—walks out of U.S. customs. As he does, a squad of gold-badged inspectors descends like the Seahawks' defensive team onto Tommy, seizes him, and in great consternation asks him, "Where did the other guy go?"

"The guy with these cartons? He said to the men's room."

Some manic inspectors (manic, for the $8,000,000 or, on the street, the $80,000,000 catch is the most white powder in American history and the first white powder from Asia instead of Basra, Bushire, Bandar Abbas or Karachi, from Chinese instead of Italians)—some manic inspectors run to the empty men's room, *damn, he's gone,* some others take Tommy and run with him to an eight-foot-wide, eight-foot-long, eight-foot-high cubic room. In yellow on a steel table are two silhouettes: two human hands, the fingers spread, and an inspector puts Tommy's hands against these as another inspector frisks him. In front of Tommy's moist eyes is a red-white-and-blue-bordered poster that says,

> *Whoever forcibly assaults, resists, opposes, impedes, intimidates, or interferes with a customs officer shall be . . . Whoever uses a deadly or dangerous weapon shall be . . .*

Seeing no weapon on Tommy, the customs inspectors handcuff him and exit the cell-like concrete room, locking the door behind them. For one hour Tommy sits in a corner on a triangular bench, then a couple of suited civilians enter and say, "We're with the Drug Enforcement Administration. It seems," says one, a DEA man who hates heroin, a boy he played baseball with at age ten, eleven, twelve became an addict and died in Alphabet City, a second addict stabbing him and robbing his $10 bag—"it seems," he says, almost shouting, "that in the buckets there is a large amount of heroin, a large amount of pure heroin, and you can be charged with heroin importation and heroin possession. For starters you're looking at twenty years."

"I don't know anything about it," Tommy cries, really cries, the tears running down. "The guy and I, we met in Bolivia. We played mahjong in Bolivia. The buckets belonged to him, not me. How could I know what's inside them? If I knew it's heroin, why did I wait to get caught? Why didn't I walk away like *him?*"

"I don't believe you!" shouts the DEA agent.

"Do you have a wife?" shouts the other one.

"Yes," Tommy cries.

"Do you have kids?"

"Yes," Tommy cries.

"You won't see them for twenty years!"

"How can I see them?" Tommy cries.

"By leveling with us. By cooperating with us. By telling us all you know about this. We'll relay that to the U.S. attorney. He or she can ask the judge to reduce your time. Now, Tommy. You *knew* there was heroin in those buckets, didn't you?"

"No," Tommy cries.

"In that case we're done!" shouts a DEA agent.

"We don't want to talk to you if you won't cooperate with us!"

"I want to see my wife again! I want to see my kid again!" Tommy sobs, truly sobs, his throat gasping, his shoulders shaking. "Of *course* I'll cooperate with you!"

"The other guy. Where was he headed to?"

"Chicago," Tommy sobs.

"Whereabouts in Chicago?"

"The Airport Hilton," Tommy.

"What would he do at the Hilton?"

"Deliver the buckets to someone there."

"Will you come with us to Chicago?"

"Of course I will," Tommy sobs.

CHICAGO

In an eighth-floor room at the Hilton Chicago O'Hare is Tommy, sitting in a purple armchair, waiting (or so he's said) for the ice-bucket connection. The door to his room is chain-locked and two of the chain-links are handcuffed together, the chain-lock is rigid and Tommy cannot unlock it. Even so, two DEA men are sitting in this same room, keeping their eyes on Tommy lest he crawl into the heating duct, jump out the eighth-floor sliding window, do something melodramatic like that, and in the adjoining room are a number of other armed agents. Now one agent in Tommy's room crosses into the adjoining room, the other agent in Tommy's room goes to the bathroom, and Tommy, for one minute alone, does indeed open the eighth-floor window and scramble onto the sill. Below him the taxi traffic is like little model cars. To his left, running straight to the ground, is a thin architectural element: a strip of aluminum a half-inch thick, and Tommy seizes it between his thumb and his index finger. In his other hand is his attaché case, but, this handicap notwith-standing, he pinches the half-inch-thick steel strip with this hand, too, and hand over hand starts slowly descending like Spiderman.

Out from the bathroom comes the DEA agent. Not seeing Tommy, he crosses into the adjoining room and asks, "Where is he?"

"Tommy? He's still with you."

"He's not," says the DEA agent.

"Come on. You're putting us on."

"Go and see," says the DEA agent.

The agents, their breath suspended, for they have already forfeited the wig-wearing man in Seattle, rush into Tommy's room, look in the closet, look in the dresser, look under the purple-bedspreaded bed, but not even a brass-buttoned blazer attests to Tommy's recollected existence. *A practical joke,* an agent thinks, then he hears the windy-city wind and sees the open sliding window: leaning out, he sees a crowd in front of the Hilton staring up. *He's escaping,* the agent thinks, and he runs down eight flights of stairs, down that silo of stairs into the crowd in front of the Hilton. And still there's no sign of Tommy: not on the half-inch-thick aluminum strip, not on the Hilton's aluminum wall, not in the Hilton's murmuring crowd. The crowd tells the DEA agent, "He took a taxi."

In time, what happened reveals itself to the DEA. Tommy did his Spiderman act for a couple of feet, then couldn't hold on and slid eight stories onto the Hilton's asphalt canopy. His hands bleeding, his leg broken, his spine broken, his side paralyzed, he put his scattered papers into the attaché case he had understandably dropped, jumped off the Hilton's canopy, told a Chicago cop, "Two black people mugged me," hobbled into a waiting taxi and, at times passing out from the pain, went to West Harrison Street and the Greyhound station, where an hour from now the DEA will perseveringly find him. For three months Tommy will lie in the hospital while the well-dressed messenger reminds him, "We hired a lawyer for you. We're taking care of your wife and kid. Don't tell anyone anything."

Like the General in Toronto (though not like the Navigator in Hong Kong) Tommy will never tell, never reveal that the Chinese kingpin is Johnny. The hippie customs inspector will fly to Chicago, New York, Miami and San Francisco to tell everyone to beware of Asians bearing buckets, beware of white powder (which the chemists in Bangkok have subtly adulterated until it's like the white powder coming from Sicily)—white powder coming from Asia. From what particular person, the customs inspector doesn't know, but Tommy will be tried, convicted, and sentenced to twenty years.

BANGKOK

No more vases. No more buckets. No more consignments of white powder to the land of Flower Flag. The worst development is, no more multi-million-dollar loot. No more gambling, no more girls, slam your fist on the table, *bam!* and blame it on the Professor, the man who shouted at Tiger, "I'm counting on being lucky!" the man who sent seven cartons and a gross of glue-reeking buckets to the canny customs inspectors in the United States. Yes, blame the insolent two-birded colonel, that's how the bosses in Bangkok feel, and the bitterest of all is Fat Ass, the Kent-addicted man, the man who first came to Johnny and, as it happened, introduced him to the Professor, calling him "My best friend." No longer. Robbery, drug-running, kidnapping, murder—at Johnny's orders, Fat Ass has done it, Fat Ass has even gone straight at Johnny's orders ("Close down your prostitution house." "But the girls want to do it." "But *you* shouldn't want to." "Why shouldn't I?" "A real man doesn't pander"). But staging a Revolution? Running guns into Hong Kong? Shouting, "Up, brothers, and at 'em"? Throwing grenades like custard pies at the Royal Police? Seizing their precincts? Using bazookas to hold off Challenger tanks? Telling the Governor, "You're not in charge, now it's *us*"? "No, the Professor's crazy," Fat Ass told Johnny in Cantonese one day. "Politics aren't for me, Big Brother," and with a modest bow he resigned from the Flaming Eagles, the Professor's clandestine political party. Deeply disappointed in Fat Ass (*If it isn't money, money,* thought Johnny, *if it's just altruistic, he has no heart for it*), Johnny didn't promote him to the five-man committee, even to advisory status, and his once-best friend the Professor told him, "You'll go to South America. You'll watch the water behind the dam."

The loss of white powder worth $8,000,000 was the last straw for Fat Ass. In his bedroom on Pattalung Street he picks up a pad about the size of a business envelope, four by ten inches, tears off the top piece of paper, lays it on his bedroom table, and, in pencil, carefully draws a diagram of the Professor's nearby home. The living room, bedroom, bathroom, kitchen—like a draftsman he draws them all and labels the neighborhood streets in Thai as if this were an invitation to the Professor's outdoors barbecue. "What's this?" asks Tiger, walking in, asks Tiger in Cantonese, Tiger who's titular boss in Bangkok and has just flown from Taipei with a "Well, did I tell you or did I tell you?" self-satisfied look.

"A map," says Fat Ass.

"Of what?" asks Tiger.

"His home. The Professor's. I was the one who originally brought him to Big Brother. And now he tells me to watch the water behind the dam. He's fucking with me."

"Who is the map for?"

"Golo. Golo the hit man."

"Golo will kill the Professor?"

"Golo or one of his soldiers will."

"But why would they want to?"

"I'm paying them $15,000."

"Did you ask Big Brother?"

"No, and I don't intend to. You too, Tiger, you mustn't tell Big Brother. He likes the Professor. If he hears that Golo will kill him, he'll tell Golo not to. And always we'll have the Professor around. 'Do what I say, little brother, do it or get out of Bangkok.' Instead," continues Fat Ass, and Tiger doesn't remonstrate with him, "I'm taking this map to Golo today." And folding it, sliding it into his Levi's back pocket, he stomps from his bedroom, drives through Bangkok's sort of the Bronx, narrow streets, two-story houses, stops at a redolent coffee house, passes the map (the pin-the-tail-on-the-Professor map) to Golo, a skull-headed man from Canton, and passes the $15,000, too. "He dies tonight," says Golo in Cantonese, then Fat Ass and many other incomparable bosses from Bangkok, Hong Kong, Manila, Tokyo, La Paz, Asunción, São Paulo, and New York fly to Tokyo, where Johnny has summoned them to an emergency meeting on the topic of After Seattle, What?

19

Hand-Tied Man

TOKYO

Sitting in chairs and on tables, dressers, desks and beds in a twin-bedded room at the Hilton are a dozen of Johnny's incomparable bosses. Between the pink-mountain-bed-spreaded beds is the room's entertainment center: a Princess telephone, a switch for Toshiba color TV, a radio, a music channel, a classical music channel, and an all-English channel reporting the Dow, dropping today to 1,351 points. On the wall in a golden frame is a glorious *obi,* a belt for a woman's kimono, woven of golden silken threads, embroidered in pink and purple flowers. Outside the window is Tokyo's version of Century City: is Shinjuku, all gray, black and glassy skyscrapers without so much as a noodle counter among them, but it could be Fujiyama for all the bosses know, for the rice-paper windows are closed lest the Royal Police or the DEA read people's lips from a perch in the nearest building, a black granite cylinder blocks away. The rice paper practically curls from the hot cigarette smoke as, on the door, there's a knock and Johnny walks in in his mustache, wig, and brown lizard shoes from Rome, and with something else from Rome: a black ostrich attaché case, its sides all sicklied with blackheads where the ostrich feathers once sprouted. The bosses stand up and in Cantonese say, "Big Brother."

"So," says Johnny, dropping his plucked attaché case, dropping his thick black mustache and wig, keeping his small-scaled lizard shoes, sitting in the corner armchair, "in Seattle we've had a problem, huh?"

"Mm," a couple of bosses agree.

"Tommy's in Chicago now. He's in the prison hospital. I've informed Ah Tung," says Johnny, then looks around for the Professor and says, "Now where is Ah Tung?"

The bosses turn to each other as though the other might know or, by some miracle, might *be* the Professor in his graded tinted shades like a gallant fighter-bomber pilot. At last it's Four Eyes, in his mid-thirties the oldest committeeman, who tells Johnny, "He said he'd come."

"Fat Ass," continues Johnny. "You came from Bangkok, why didn't he come with you?" The other bosses nod at Fat Ass on his pink-mountain-topped bed, his Kent in his fist, his ashes dusting the rose-colored carpet, nod as though they're entreating him, "You tell him, Fat Ass."

"He isn't coming, Big Brother," says Fat Ass.

"Why not?" asks Johnny. "What's wrong?"

"He acted like the Dragonhead," says Fat Ass.

"He made trouble for us," "He made problems for us," "He couldn't get along with us," a half-dozen bosses interrupt.

"Quiet, quiet," says Fat Ass, his palms down, his hands apart, his arms pushing all the hullabaloo back into people's throats. "I'll explain to Big Brother. Big Brother," continues Fat Ass, "I don't know why, but suddenly he's a full colonel."

"You don't know why?" asks Johnny. "Because we're an army now. We have four lieutenant colonels," pointing around the room, pointing overhead to New York, "and one full colonel, who is the Professor."

"So now he's a colonel. So what am I?" asks Fat Ass.

"The same as you've always been. A boss under me."

"No, now I'm under the Professor. You know what he told me? He'd send me to South America. To watch the water behind the dam. To make sure the water stays there."

"He told me," says Four Eyes, "'You're taking orders from *me.*'"

"He told me," says Tiger simultaneously, "'Send out 138 buckets.'"

"Slow down, everyone," says Johnny. "One man after another."

"One man after another we'll die," a boss on the far bed says.

"What?" Johnny gasps.

"He has too much ambition," says Fat Ass, his arms surrounding an invisible medicine ball, symbolizing the Professor's ambition. "He's been recruiting in China. He'll have his own personal army. He'll outnumber the rest of us. He told me to watch the water in South America. He really meant he'll kill me."

"How can he kill you?" asks Johnny.

"Because he's colonel now," Fat Ass.

"He needs the committee's approval."

"*He* doesn't think so," says Tiger, sitting at the desk as though taking minutes. "He doesn't ask the committee what to do. He *tells* the committee what to do."

"He can't. We agreed in New York—"

"We agreed, Big Brother," says Four Eyes. "But the Professor doesn't do what we agreed to."

"There must be some misunderstanding."

"He just wants power," says Four Eyes.

"He wants to overthrow you," says Tiger.

"No," says Johnny. "There is some misunderstanding. I'll call the Professor in Bangkok tonight. As soon as he's in Tokyo we'll straighten this out. Will he come to Tokyo tomorrow?"

"We don't know," says Fat Ass.

"The day after tomorrow, then?"

"We don't know," says Fat Ass.

"I'm confused," says Johnny. "We can't meet without him. I'll call him tonight." Of course, Johnny cannot call the Professor from the Princess phone by the TV-and-radio switches, for the Professor's number will be on the Hilton's bill, a hot discovery for the Royal Police or (if it's been alerted) the DEA, and Johnny adjourns the meeting *sine die*. He exits the rice-paper-windowed room, then, one by one, a minute between them, the other uncomfortable bosses go, the fat-assed one of them muttering, "I'm not a colonel now, I'm just a major now."

TOKYO

Nor can Johnny call the Professor from the Princess phone in his own suite across the street at the Century Hyatt. His suite is in excellent taste, in fact a half-dozen excellent tastes, a carpet of Caribbean blue, a taffy-colored flower-embossed soft sofa, a circular mahogany coffee table, a couple of Turkish place mats—mats of gold-bordered velvet—a *faux* jade ashtray, a huge mahogany television set, and, above this eclectic decor, a small chandelier refracting the TV colors. On the wall are two Japanese prints, one of some rose-breasted bullfinches, one of some black-throated wagtails. His brown lizard shoes coming off, Johnny lies down on his king-sized bed, his head on his hands, his eyes on the ceiling, thinking, *What's going on? I told him to come to Tokyo. Why didn't he?* Johnny, squeezing his cerebrum, squeezes out one little bead of sweat, it trickles along his furrowed brow as, from the shower, wearing a pink-flowered white silk robe, there comes a girl aged twenty-two, a China doll who isn't Jonquil (who Johnny still loves) but his cat's-away-and-the-mice-will-play new girlfriend, named Dominique, who Johnny recently met on a plane to Shanghai. She lies down beside him, saying in Shanghai dialect, "Are you tired, husband?"

"Yes," says Johnny. "I had a very long meeting."

"What was the meeting about?"

"The Professor. He didn't come to Tokyo," says Johnny, who can confide in Dominique as he cannot in Jonquil, a less worldly woman who, if Johnny is ever arrested, mustn't be aware of anything except how to raise the kids.

"Why didn't he come to Tokyo?" asks Dominique.

"I don't know. The brothers all are against him. He wants to take over, the brothers say. He wants power."

"If he wanted power, then he'd come to Tokyo."

"Exactly what I've been thinking," says Johnny.

"I like him," says Dominique. "He's a good man."

"I like him too. He's like my own son. Oh," Johnny moans, "have I got a splitting headache."

"Do you want some medicine, husband?"

"Please."

"I'll get you a Tylenol," says Dominique. She gets him two, and Johnny, taking them, takes a ten-minute nap. He then stands up in the same tailored suit but, for variety's sake, puts on the burgundy (not the brown) lizard shoes from Rome. He and Dominique, in a silk evening gown from Paris, descend on an outdoor elevator, descend past the Tokyo skyscrapers, descend as if by parachutes into the world's largest city, then into the pestle-shaped-chandeliered lobby of the Century Hyatt. They cross a wide street to the Hilton, pass through the scroll-shaped-chandeliered lobby, all these chandeliers twenty feet high, climb up a copper spiral staircase to the Dynasty Restaurant, a Chinese restaurant where at the circular tables sit two dozen bosses, girlfriends, wives. One dish they're eating is steak, majestically guarded by a tall orange pagoda sculpted from a colossal carrot. Another dish is shrimp, jellyfish, and beef-wrapped asparagus, guarded by a white panda sculpted from a skinned radish, a panda whose eyes, ears and paws are brown bean-paste. Off the edges of one dish (a dish of brown braised shark's fin) fly six sculpted orange birds, birds made of carrot slices, birds whose eyes are tiny green cucumber bits. Should we even mention the sautéed lobster in plum sauce, a cornucopia lobster disgorging its pink innards onto a broccoli bed? While feasting on all these birds, pandas, pagodas, the bosses ask Johnny in Cantonese, "Did you call the Professor?"

"Not yet. I'll call after dinner."

"What if he won't come to Tokyo?"

"Then I'll go to him in Bangkok."

"Oh no, Big Brother!" says someone.

"It's dangerous for you!" another boss.

"He's crazy! He'll kill you!" another.

"Don't go to Bangkok, Big Brother!"

Tokyo

The public phones in Japan are seaweed green, so studded by coin drops, coin returns, credit-card swipes, red digital displays, gray light-emitting diodes, and chirping touch-tone tabs that the instructions (in small type, in Japanese) are like those on the toilet in *2001*. The nearest phone to the Hyatt is by a black granite gazebo, and Johnny (who has had practice) uses a Japanese telephone card to swipe the narrow slide and call the Professor's home in Bangkok. A woman answers in Cantonese, for Mao has said that women hold up half the sky and the Professor has recruited "sisters" like her, a good-looking twenty-year-old.

"Hello," says Johnny.

"It's you, Big Brother."

"Where is Ah Tung?"

"He's here, Big Brother."

"Let me speak with him."

"One moment, Big Brother."

Johnny waits several seconds, surveying the granite gazebo through the gray-glassed telephone booth. Then onto the phone comes the Professor, who is alive—surprise—and who says in Cantonese, "Big Brother."

"Ah Tung! How are you?"

"I'm fine. But have you heard what happened in Bangkok?"

"No. What happened there?"

"I can't say on the phone."

"Then come to Tokyo."

"I can't do that, either, and I can't say why. But I'll send the Jap Man," the Professor's lieutenant, the Professor's man Friday. "He'll see you in Tokyo tomorrow night. Listen to him, the Jap Man, and you'll understand."

"And then you'll come to Tokyo?"

"Yeah, yeah," says the Professor.

"You should. You're boss now."

"Yeah, yeah," says the Professor.

TOKYO

The next night the Jap Man (in World War II, the Japs were known as the Shorties, so a Chinese who's called a Jap Man is less euphemistically a Shorty)—the Jap Man, who's five foot two, and Johnny in burgundy lizard shoes meet in the red granite lobby of the Keio Plaza Hotel and walk to Johnny's Century Hyatt. Uncharacteristically nervous, the Jap Man skitters into the Hyatt like a mouse on a rapid treadmill, in Johnny's heterogenous suite he flinches to see every chair, armchair, sofa as if in its shadows constables lurk. "The bedroom. Is anyone in it?" the Jap Man asks in Cantonese.

"Dominique. And she's asleep," says Johnny.

"I have something important from Ah Tung."

"Let's see it," says Johnny, and, reaching into his left jacket pocket, the Jap Man extracts a golden pack of 555 brand cigarettes. "No thanks, I don't smoke," says Johnny.

"No, this is what's important from Ah Tung."

"What is it? White powder?" frowns Johnny.

"No, look and see," says the Jap Man. He pulls at a corner cigarette, but it's stuck inside like a spike in the Union Pacific. Nervously he shakes all the cigarettes onto Johnny's coffee table and his Turkish place mats. From the ostensibly empty pack he pulls a piece of white paper that he unfolds to business-envelope size. It's full of rough pencil lines.

"It looks like a map," says Johnny.

"It is. It's the home of Ah Tung."

"His home?"

"Someone tried to murder him."

"What?"

"Someone tried to kill him. Whoever it was, he drew this map for Golo, who gave it to one of his hit men and, for the murder, gave him $15,000. But the hit man sold the map instead, sold it for $30,000 to Ah Tung. It's evidence for you, Big Brother. It's yours," the Jap Man says, and gives the exhibit to Johnny.

"Who drew the map for Golo?"

"We don't know yet. Do you?"

"No, why should I know him?"

"No one but one of your bosses could draw it. No one else knows where the home is."

"I myself didn't know it."

"You didn't?" asks the Jap Man. To his ears, Johnny has said, "Well, *I* didn't draw it. I couldn't have, for I didn't know where the home is."

Never having accused him, the Jap Man thinks that Johnny is too much protesting.

"No, I was never there."

"Who drew it? Can you find out?"

"I have to. It's serious stuff," says Johnny.

TOKYO

It seriously is. No laws against attempted murder operate in a Chinese secret society, no juries, judges, bailiffs, correction officers are in reach of policemen's whistles to keep a determined assassin from someone's throat. If Fat Ass one day attempts to kill the Professor, no precinct exists to file an indignant complaint at. All the Professor can do is defensively kill Fat Ass, then Tiger (in fear of his life) can kill the Professor, then the Jap Man (in fear of his life) can kill Tiger, then someone can kill the Jap Man, until by the closing curtain the Big Circle looks like the Danish court at the end of *Hamlet,* bodies on top of bodies like ancient ruins, with Johnny standing mournfully over the massive carnage. It's to avert this catastrophe that Johnny, in white crocodile shoes, white slacks, white belt, and white open-collared shirt, calls a meeting of one dozen bosses the following morning in the rice-paper-windowed room at the Hilton where Fat Ass muttered, "I'm just a major now," and where he confesses today, "I drew that map. I wanted the Professor killed. Or else he'd kill *me.*"

"You don't have evidence," says Johnny.

"He said I'd go to South America."

"But that isn't evidence," says Johnny.

"He said I'd watch the water there."

"That still isn't evidence. But now there's evidence you'd kill *him,*" says Johnny, displaying the 4-inch-by-10-inch map. "What a mess you've gotten into! What a stupid thing you've done! Wasn't it I who made the Professor committee chairman? Would I have done it if he should have died? We swore we'd be brothers forever, but all I foresee is one brother killing another from now on. War, war, war between brothers is all I foresee. I have to prevent this," says Johnny soulfully. "I have to keep fraternity in the Big Circle. And there's just one way to do it," says Johnny, picking up a white match book, lighting the 4-inch-by-10-inch map, holding it in his warm fingers, letting it turn to soot in the crystal ashtray. "And that's to blame it on Golo. To send someone out and kill Golo. If we don't kill Golo, the Professor will capture him, torture him, and learn that the man behind it is Fat Ass. But we'll tell the Professor the man behind it is Golo. And we'll tell him we've killed him for it. Does anyone disagree?"

The bosses agree: there is no smarter, shrewder, wiser, no more ingenious dragonhead than Johnny. They agree to put the quietus on Golo, agree to stop shipping heroin by vase, bucket, or any other manner or means for one half year, agree to invent another clandestine receptacle for it. The summit meeting in Tokyo (for planes, limos, rooms, lobsters, this was a $400,000 meeting) adjourns.

SEOUL

A holiday at a Korean casino, the Walker Hill. Koreans in business suits and Koreans—the women—in high-waisted dresses, the waists an inch below their breasts, like in the 1810s in France. At one of the blackjack tables there's a commotion, and Johnny in nonlizard, noncrocodile, just-cow-leather black shoes walks over to see what's up. In back of stacks of 5,000-won chips like a queen in a counting house is Dominique, his cat's-away girlfriend, giggling at the good luck that's falling on her like won from heaven. Her cards are an iron abacus: if she's holding a ten, jack, queen or king she'll inevitably draw an ace, if she's holding twelve she'll draw a nine, if she's holding thirteen the ineluctable laws of mathematics determine she'll draw an eight, though whether it's hearts, clubs, diamonds or spades seems hopelessly random. The towers in front of her grow like stalagmites till Johnny comes up and Dominique, for once losing, laughs, "Go away, I can't concentrate!"

"How much have you won?" Johnny asks her.

"I haven't counted! Go away!" laughs Dominique.

TOKYO

Changing planes at Narita are Johnny and Dominique, his $60,000-richer friend. All his important calls, Johnny places from airports now: he talks for a minute, then hops on the next plane out, and if somehow the Royal Police (or who knows? the DEA) get his longitude and latitude, as soon as they have zeroed on him he's one thousand miles away. Today at Narita, Johnny now phones the Professor in Bangkok to say they're searching for Golo, the man who would whack him. But having talked to the Jap Man, his right-hand man, the Professor has now concluded that his seeker, his stalker, his secret mapmaker is Johnny, the man who appointed him the tantamount dragonhead and, in just days, in the hole by $8,000,000, must have regretted it. "Ah Tung? Is that you?" asks Johnny in Cantonese on the intricate telephone at Narita.

"No, it's the Jap Man."

"Where is Ah Tung?"

"He moved," says the Jap Man and not very credibly adds, "He didn't say where."

"Will you talk with him?"

"Yeah," says the Jap Man.

"Tell him I must see him."

"Yeah," says the Jap Man.

"Anywhere at all. Anytime."

"Yeah," says the Jap Man.

NEW YORK

The next time that Johnny calls the Professor, dropping in countless quarters at Kennedy International Airport, he learns that the phone's disconnected: there is a siren sound and a recorded message in Thai. The phone's disconnected too at Buddhahead's home in Queens: Buddhahead, the Professor's buddy, who has just vanished with $2,500,000 from Johnny's safe-deposit box at the Golden Pacific Bank in Chinatown. Telephone, telegraph, peremptory knocks in the darkness on Buddhahead's door (and on the Professor's in Bangkok, and on the Jap Man's in Kowloon)—nothing including telepathy reveals the whereabouts of half of Johnny's Big Circle. "I'll check the hotels in New York. You check them in Bangkok," says Johnny in Cantonese, says desperately on the phone to Fat Ass in Bangkok, but Fat Ass says, "If they wanted you to find them, you'd have found them long ago. They have deserted us, Big Brother. They have shelled us of $2,500,000. They have *betrayed* us, Big Brother. Give me one minute," says Fat Ass, and like muffled drums there's an indistinct conversation between him and a few other bosses in Bangkok. "Big Brother," says Fat Ass, returning to Johnny. "We need to meet with you. How soon can you be in Bangkok?"

"I can't. I'll be on vacation in Paris. What if we meet in Frankfurt?"

"Frankfurt it is. We'll all fly to Frankfurt tomorrow," says Fat Ass.

And very soon Johnny is on Lufthansa, first class, his wig and his acrid mustache on, his tournedos on the white chinaware on the white napkin before him. To his left in a wide window seat is Dominique, his confidante, who, as the plane starts across the Atlantic, asks him in Shanghai dialect, "What's happening, husband?"

"The brothers want to kill the Professor," Johnny intuits.

"You and I love him. What will you do?"

"I can't kill someone I love. And yet," Johnny sighs, indifferently eyeing his Burgundy, tournedos, potatoes, "there's nothing else I can do. All of us signed a solemn oath, 'I hereby join the Flaming Eagles.' All of us swore, 'I'll follow its rules, and I'll obey its orders.' All of us stated, 'And if I betray this oath, I'll accept death without complaint.' And now the man who wrote this oath is the very man who betrayed it: the Professor. The brothers will tell me in Frankfurt that he must accept his death without complaint. And I must agree," says Johnny, raising his hand as if voting, raising it very halfheartedly, a flag on a staff on a windless day, a flag that's absolutely draggling, "for I have signed that oath too, and if I sit permissively as my best-loved brother betrays it, then I have betrayed it and I must accept death too. I am now honor bound." His hand drops on Dominique's, and she rests her other hand on Johnny's.

"I love you," says Dominique, says it (as Jonquil consistently says it) in English, for only a child addressing its mother would say it in any dialect of Chinese.

FRANKFURT

Across from the airport is one more great clinic for jet lag, the Sheraton Hotel. In its lobby dozens of aliens on Eastern, Central, Mountain, Pacific and all of Asia's standard times list to their left or right dizzily on bent bamboo chairs, on camel-cushioned chairs, and on old brown leather chairs or, like zombies, float by the souvenirs, float by the cuckoo clocks, float by the pewter-topped porcelain mugs with the paintings of Prussian artillerymen in red-belted blue-colored tunics, float by to try to convince themselves they're in Germany. On the wall dozens of broken bottles, shards of amber jereboams, circle in volatile spirals in an artist's representation of time-altered consciousness. "It's eight a.m.," complains a red-eyed client at the reception desk, in front of him clocks for Rio, Tokyo, New York and Frankfurt, "and my room isn't ready yet." Upstairs in Johnny's room, a drawing of a medieval donjon over the brown-bedspreaded bed is the only suggestion that he isn't, say, in Nairobi, though on his outside doorknob is a BITTE, NICHT STÖREN sign, a DO NOT DISTURB sign in German. A drawing of a bow-tied waiter stands on the phone by the "3" that Johnny, in black leather shoes, taps to order some Diet Cokes, then Johnny tells the jet-lagged bosses in Cantonese, "I still haven't reached the Professor. Have you?"

"No," says the oldest committeeman, who's Four Eyes. "What should we do?" *We should find him and kill him,* he and the other bosses think, that much was incontestable, that was the law of the Medes, the Persians, and the Big Circle, the only question was will Johnny agree? Or must these mobilized bosses kill Johnny, too?

"Somehow," says Johnny, "I should speak with him. I should ask him, 'What do you want to do?' If the Professor wants to leave us, I shouldn't stop him. I shouldn't hold him against his will."

"Father, I don't agree," says the Movie Star, who has dried off (he swam to the Isthmus of Kra, remember) and has joined everyone else in Frankfurt, where he still calls his Big Brother his Father. Six hours behind (or ahead of) his circadian rhythms, no one in Frankfurt has remembered to close the window curtains, and the Star sees planes taking off to all destinations, buses to Sudbahnhof and Sauerbrunn. "All of us," says the

278

Star, staring meaningfully at Johnny, "have sworn an indissoluble oath. If any of us renege, our people in Singapore or in Asunción will too. And then there'll be no Big Circle."

"What would you do?" Johnny asks.

"I'd kill the Professor," says the Star in his sweet cotton-candy voice, the Star who like the Professor (or like himself in the movie about the Big Circle, a movie where he ties someone up, pours gasoline on him, and lights it with a lit cigarette, a movie where he drops someone onto an ice-skating rink to the music of *Jingle Bells,* all the while smiling wishily-washily) believes that *kill kill* is the cure-all for all botherations.

"How can you kill him?" asks Johnny. "We don't know where he is."

"No, now we do," says the Star. "We've learned that he's in Manila."

"Manila," says Johnny, raising his one last shield to protect the Professor—"Manila is an enormous place." The man who once said to Mahogany, "You fuck me and now you die," has no qualms about wasting traitors: he sanctioned the hits on Dead Man and the Jewish woman from Frankfurt, the one who owed him $100,000, he ordered the hits on the Sergeant (who moved discreetly from 244 Midland Avenue in Montclair to 1 Stonebridge Road in Montclair, baffling the Chinese hit men) and on Old Fox and Golo, the hit man who didn't hit the Professor, and he's also ordered a hit on the sky-eyed navigator, the man who blabbed that the principal iron carrier was Johnny, for if the man can't testify against him, then Johnny can stop this exhausting running and go back to Hong Kong. But hit the Professor? The man who Johnny called his son? Who told him he's ready to die for him? Who if he'd only answer his phone like any Tom, Dick or Harry with proper manners wouldn't die at all? "Manila's enormous," says Johnny, making one last try.

"Our brothers saw him in Manila today," says the Star. "He ran a red light and they lost him. If you approve it, Father, they'll find him and kill him."

Sad-eyed, Johnny moves clockwise around the open-orange-curtained room. "Four Eyes," commences Johnny. "What would you do?"

"I'd kill the Professor, Big Brother."

"Wrist Watch," says Johnny to the elegant messenger, using a nickname like the man's real name in Cantonese. "What would you do?"

"I'd kill the Professor, Big Brother."

"Tiger," says Johnny to the black-shoed, white-socked country boy, the man he advised to not think twice about ghosts, they're chimerical, they're unreal, they're people who when they're dead, they're dead: a little advice that Johnny now might be haunted by, for Tiger, who serves as his bodyguard and who, if Johnny continues to stand by the Professor, would *ex officio* be the man appointed to kill him, kill Johnny, would not be constrained by any illusions of Johnny's avenging ghost. It's love of Johnny, not fear, that puts the tremor in Tiger's voice when Johnny asks him, "Tiger. What would you do?"

"I don't like the Professor, Big Brother. But even if I cherished him as you do, I would kill him, Big Brother. Please!"

Man after man, Johnny goes clockwise around the brown-bedspreaded bed, the mirror-topped vanity, and the brass-railed baggage rack, the bosses on all these surfaces telling him, "I'd kill the Professor." "Myself," Johnny tells them in Cantonese, "I don't believe he betrayed us. Why would he want to betray us? He was already committee chairman. He was already colonel, but he ill-advisedly *acted* as if he betrayed us. He disappeared. So did his men like the Jap Man and his friends like Buddhahead. So did our $2,500,000. Now," Johnny says, his eyes moist, "all of you people say kill him. How can I repudiate you? If I did, I'd break up the Big Circle. Business," Johnny concludes, using an old adage in Cantonese, "is business, and I won't oppose you."

"Thank you, Big Brother," says Tiger, relieved.

"I'll telephone to Manila," says the Star and, with the other bosses, leaves the now smoke-filled room.

Johnny, alone in his armchair, drops his head against it and stares at the plaster ceiling. He feels suffused with déjà vu, with the sense he was in this room once before. He zeroes in on the office of General Abrams, in Saigon, the curtains open, the planes taking off to all destinations from the one runway at Tansonhut International Airport. Walking from Abrams' office, thinking *terrible, terrible,* thinking that Abrams slaughters the VC like flies, Johnny imagined the room full of one-star, two-star, three-star generals, pleading with Abrams, "Kill these people in Vietnam," "Kill these people in Cambodia," "Kill these people in Laos," and Abrams gleefully telling them, "I am the greatest, kill them all." Now that Johnny is in Abrams' black leather shoes, he sees that he's no way gleeful, that a general, judge, jury or Dragonhead who can determine who'll live and who'll die has a burden that only a sociopath like the Movie Star (or like the Professor, perhaps) would want. To sanction a hit on his best-loved brother doesn't grant glee to Johnny: it grieves him, and, to rationalize it, all he can tell himself is what another general told him in Vietnam, "My hands are tied."

FRANKFURT

On the phone, a drawing of a knife, fork and spoon stands by the "6" that Johnny doesn't tap. Not lingering in this depressing hotel for its honey-glazed guinea hen, he, Dominique, and all the bosses take the train downtown to dine by a four-foot golden buddha under a golden gable at the Siam Restaurant. *"Sawasdee,"* say the Bangkok bosses, "Greetings," they say in Thai to the golden-gowned waitress, clapping their hands just once like a Buddhist, bowing. On the maize tablecloth, the waitress has set out golden knives, golden forks, golden soupspoons, set out peach-colored candles, cut out rosettes from the peach-colored napkins and, in the golden candlesticks, set the rosettes to catch the peach-colored paraffin. Talking in Thai, the bosses order the spring rolls, shrimp chips, chicken in coconut milk—a soup that's pink like lobster bisque—shrimp in fried noodles, prawns in grated coconut, beef in peanut sauce, beef in oyster sauce, and a tongue-twister in Thai: *kuiti-olukjinnuasod,* beef in spicy green curry, eating them all with wooden chopsticks contrary to Thai tradition. The bosses drink water on cardboard coasters for Henninger beer (*"Das schmeckt!* It tastes!") while talking of everything but the Professor.

After dinner they feed the pigeons, go to the showroom for Mercedeses, go to the local transvestite show, and go to the Red Rose Brothel. "Hello," say the German prostitutes in English, rouged like reddlemen, seated like souvenir salesmen in narrow, gorged, garish stalls, prodded by shameless stares of Asians, Arabians, Americans who prowl the hallways, climb the stairwells.

"Wrist Watch," laughs Johnny in Cantonese, "this one's for you."

"No, I'm just looking," says Johnny's neatly dressed messenger.

"She looks very sexy," laughs Johnny, the *sexy* in English.

"No no, Big Brother," says the fastidious messenger.

Then these gangsters return to the Sheraton, then Johnny and Dominique (and Tiger, their once-again-faithful bodyguard) go on vacation to Rome.

ROME

Your typical tourists, Johnny and Dominique see Vatican City, the Pope at his studio window in Saint Peter's Basilica, the Sistine Chapel, the Catacombs, the House of the Vestal Virgins. At the National Gallery of Ancient Art, in front of a Caravaggio of Judith clutching the hair of Holofernes, Nebuchadnezzar's general, and, with Holofernes's sword, lopping his pop-eyed head off, his blood spurting out of his carotid, three spouts of blood incarnadining his pillow—in front of *Judith and Holofernes,* Johnny in Shanghai dialect says, "That's terrible," and Dominique shudders.

They take a taxi to the Coliseum. Johnny in black leather shoes and Dominique in black leather boots go to the uppermost balcony and, at the iron railing, contemplate the 2,000-year ruins: columns as wobbly-looking as anything in the Canyonlands, some of the well-worn columns supine, lying in unconformable sections, tufts of pale yellow weeds in their clefts. At the Coliseum, Johnny is unusually pensive. "Down there," he says to Dominique mournfully, says in Shanghai dialect, recalling (a bit inexactly) his grade-school history, "the slaves fought lions. And here," in the balcony, "the rich people watched the slaves being killed, being eaten. The rich people then did this," says Johnny, applauding. "The rich people had fun and came back the following day. It was like soccer, like football, like Chinese opera. Unbelievable," says Johnny, shaking his head melancholically.

"It was too cruel," agrees Dominique.

"The Roman Empire," Johnny continues, "was the greatest in human history. It occupied almost all of Europe and part of Russia and Asia, too.

But even the Roman Empire fell. Just like," and Johnny sighs audibly—
"like the Big Circle. Once we were strong. But now we're fighting among
ourselves. Now some brother will kill the Professor, or the Professor will
kill *him*. Well," Johnny rationalizes for his own, not Dominique's, benefit, "sooner or later all people die. All people who are born someday die.
If not today, then tomorrow."

"Husband," says Dominique, aware that Johnny himself is not consoled by his sophistry, "you must renounce the Big Circle."

"How can I? Without me," Johnny laments, scanning the sand-castle
ruins, the grounds eroded, the cells for Christians exposed, the cells
like a Cretan labyrinth, "there will be intramural war. Too many brothers
will die."

"Even with you as Dragonhead, they will die," says Dominique. "Husband, you're older, you're tireder. You haven't time for your children and
Jonquil. Always there is some headache with the Big Circle. You must
retire."

"Maybe you're right," Johnny sighs. "I'll think about it," Johnny says,
and he's still thinking *should I? shouldn't I?* as he and his concerned companion (and Tiger, their faithful bodyguard) go to Milan, Venice, Monaco,
Paris.

PARIS

"Oh! Let's see the new Mercedes," says Jonquil to Johnny in
Shanghai dialect on the Champs d'Elysées near the rue Balzac. It's two
days later, and Johnny isn't with Dominique but with his other ladylove,
his underworld-innocent second wife. She still is a Buddhist, still is con-
tent with rice, still is in diamond earrings only at Johnny's behest, but
she has succumbed to one luxury, one item money alone can buy: Mercedes sports cars. At home in Hong Kong, she drives them like at the
Indianapolis Speedway, her axles slanting, her wheels screeching, her
hair behind her like the wind-whipped scarf of Isadora Duncan, and
now she spies a white *dernier cri* in the Mercedes showroom. "It's
beautiful!" says Jonquil in Shanghai dialect, just like Dominique two
days earlier, and like Dominique she goes inside to caress the white

varnish, white leather. *"C'est beau. Combien?"* she asks a French sales-man.

"Vous êtes française?"

"Non. Nous sommes de Hong Kong."

"Alors, pas de taxe à la valeur ajoutée. C'est cinq cent mille francs."

"What are you two talking about?" asks Johnny in Shanghai dialect.

"He says for us it's 500,000 francs," says Jonquil in Shanghai dialect.

"The money doesn't matter," says Johnny. "It matters that the Mer-cedes's fast. The streets aren't wide in Hong Kong. I'd always worry about you."

"Oh, but I love it, I want it," says Jonquil suppliantly.

"I know you do. You want fast cars, but I don't want people killed. Not now," Johnny tells the salesman in English. "We'll think about it," Johnny says, then with his docile wife he goes and splurges at the Galeries Lafayette, at Guerlain and Valentino instead.

MANILA

At the dim restaurant in Chinatown, the price of the bird-nest soup, etcetera, is in Filipino pesos. In one booth the Professor, his body-guard, and two Chinese girls partake of the many-plated pungent lunch. Not often does the Professor stray from the room-service menu in his obscure hotel, for at a red light several days ago he saw one of the other bosses staring at him and *zoom!* he shot through the light like a Kenyan impala, concluding that Johnny and all his Big Circle were gunning for him in Manila and that he, the Professor, had to gun them down first. "'War,' says Chairman Mao, 'can only be abolished through war,'" the Professor has told his new soldiers, smuggled here from China. But the Professor too is Chinese, he viscerally can't eat at home, easier tell a Frenchman to not dilly-dally at *le café* or an American to forgo potato chips, and he has ventured outside this Sunday and, the fish, shrimp and scallops eaten, the tea imbibed, he now pays the bill from his $40,000 jacket-pocket wad. He, his bodyguard, and the two Chinese girls go walking on Wong Bin Street, go walking by stalls full of lichees, lanzones and santols, full of lottery tickets in rows, lottery tickets in columns, lottery tickets in take-a-card fans, when he hears someone behind him say in Cantonese, "Ah Tung! Today you're dead!" At once the Professor pushes aside the two Chinese girls, grabs from his belt his .38, and spins around to confront another of Johnny's incomparable bosses. A man whose name is Tung and whose nickname is Dawning Hair or, as we'd say in English, is Crew Cut, the man's incomparable in that unlike other bosses he doesn't spit on the floor, doesn't quote from Mao, doesn't prissily pull up his trousers, doesn't dance to

> *I wanna rock with you,*
> *I wanna groove with you,*

doesn't blow smoke rings, doesn't wear "I♥NY" shirts, doesn't wear Cowboys caps backwards, doesn't say "I'll pay the tax," doesn't act in Chinese movies, doesn't dream of vengeful ghosts, doesn't look like a butcher's block, doesn't work out at Gold's, doesn't jump out of the Hilton Chicago O'Hare. A very ordinary man, he does nothing the Chinese around him in Chinatown don't do, nothing but fire an American army rifle into the Professor's chest. Onto the teeming street the Professor falls, dead, his bodyguard also is hit but runs a half block nevertheless, a Chinese girl's hit by a car-scraping ricochet, the Sunday-strolling civilians flee, and the ordinary assassin, who's Crew Cut, returns to the car he was cruising in, jumps in, and tells his driver in Hunanese, "Let's cut." At the post, telephone and telegraph office he calls up Bangkok and tells the soldiers in Cantonese, tells them triumphantly, "We did the job."

PARIS

A few hours later, Johnny in burgundy leather shoes and Jonquil have an American breakfast (croissants, eggs over easy, ham) at the Claridge Champs d'Elysées. The sun out, the weather warm, the people of Paris imperceptible—it's August 1985—they walk to the Rond Pointe and at lunchtime return to the Claridge burdened by suits, dresses, shoes, and a black leather handbag for Jonquil. Most of these spoils they pile on the bed, then walk across the Champs for bouillabaisse (mussels in tomato sauce, too) on the rue Pierre Charron, then walk back across the Champs for espresso and Evian water under the parasols at the Cascades Elysées. At two p.m. Tiger (who's always with them) says in Cantonese, "It's nighttime in Bangkok now," and Johnny excuses himself to walk once again across the Champs to the Poste, Téléphone et Télégraph des Champs Elysées. He calls up Bangkok, saying in Cantonese, "Any news from Manila?"

"Yes, Father," says a soldier of the Star's. "They did the job for two," they killed the Professor and his vigorous bodyguard.

"Oh!" says Johnny, shocked, for he's hoped that in a metropolis with a 1,600,000 population the Professor could elude even the F (for Filipino)—FBI. In his mind he sees the Professor at the gun range in Bangkok, his clothes olive drab, his pants in his boots, his bullets on his belt, his .45 in his two-fisted grip, his lips spitting out, "Big Brother. I'm ready to die for my country and you," for China and Johnny, his tragedy being that a year later he'd die but for neither one. Johnny's heart aches but Johnny's head thinks, *I must congratulate someone,* and he asks the Star's exuberant soldier, "Is Muy," the Star, "there with you?"

"No, he's flying from Frankfurt."

"Is *anyone* there with you?"

"Yes, Father. Baldy," says the Star's soldier, referring to the watchbird who in Seattle said, "I'm leaving," stepped into the men's room, took off his jacket, took off his wig, and walked out of U.S. customs, then went on a "Please hold on to the handrail" shuttle, went up a KEEP OFF THE RED LINES escalator, went in a yellow taxi into Seattle, bought a new suit, toothbrush, passport, but no new wig, and prudently flew back to Bangkok. Now that watchbird gets onto the phone to Paris.

"Big Brother, how's Paris?" asks Baldy.

"The weather's beautiful," Johnny says.

"How's Sister-in-Law?" how's Jonquil?

"She's fine," Johnny says. "How come you're in Bangkok? The hats are looking for you, I'm sure. Go to Djakarta."

"I'll go there tomorrow morning."

"And tell Muy, I'll call him," Johnny says spiritlessly, then Johnny hangs up. He walks across the Champs again to the parasol that Jonquil's under, drinking her Evian water, watching the tourists stroll by. "We need to go to the Thirteenth Arrondissement. To Chinatown," Johnny tells her in Shanghai dialect.

"But it's nicer here. Why must we go?"

"For a Chinese dinner. Also," says Johnny with difficulty, "for a Chinese newspaper."

"Why, what's wrong?" asks Jonquil.

"Someone killed the Professor."

"Someone *killed* him? Who?"

"I don't know. Someone."

"Are *you* behind it?"

"No," says Johnny honestly, then they walk up the Champs to the Metro, the ornate stop at George V, and, changing trains at the Louvre, go to the stop at the Porte d'Choisy, in Paris's Chinatown. At the kiosks, the screaming headlines in the Paris *Sing Tao* say, "Gang War in Manila," and Johnny reads the story aloud to Jonquil, who knows the Cambodian, Vietnamese, French and English alphabets but not Chinese characters. Downcast, scarcely speaking at all, Johnny and Jonquil have beef, pork and shrimp shrouded in rice-flour noodles at a Vietnamese restaurant, then ride the Métro to the Claridge Champs d'Elysees. The boxes of suits, etcetera, that were on top of their king-sized bed, the maid has stacked in a closet conscientiously, and Johnny and Jonquil take off their shoes and lie down on the bed, subdued.

"What will happen with *her?*" asks Jonquil. "With the Professor's wife?"

"She has millions of dollars, honey. She'll be well enough off."

"I heard she's just had a baby, too," says Jonquil.

"A daughter. She's two months old."

"What will happen with *her?*"

"She's taken care of. Buddhahead has $2,500,000 for the Professor's family. Honey, don't worry about it."

For several seconds, Jonquil, lying on her back, nestling on Johnny's arm, observes the rococo ceiling, the plaster animals, foliage, scrolls. Then, rolling toward Johnny, she says, "I also worry about *you.*"

"Honey, don't worry. My time isn't coming yet."

"You must walk away from the Big Circle."

"Maybe you're right," sighs Johnny.

20

Cincinnatus

BANGKOK

War, internecine war, now menaces the Big Circle. In one of its semicircles are the Professor's people: the Jap Man, Buddhahead, and the new recruits from China, even some sisters like the one who went to the morgue in Manila, saw the Professor's body, wept, then disappeared before the Filipinos could question her. In the other semicircle are Johnny, Crew Cut, the other incomparable bosses, and the anxious soldiers at their brick building, brick barracks, at 82 Soi Sukhumvit Thirty-Nine, in Bangkok. On hearing that Crew Cut has killed the Professor, some of these young soldiers, like the one who told Johnny, "They did the job for two," and like Baldy, the one who asked him, "How's Paris?" go out to exult voyeuristically at one of the pussy-shoots-banana bars, but, war being inevitable, most of the soldiers stay in their barracks amidst the mordant odors of powder solvent and gun oil to disassemble, clean and oil, reassemble, and load their .38s and .45s. "I've got two extra magazines" and "I've got four extra magazines," these soldiers announce in Cantonese. Their precautions are not supererogatory, for at midnight the door to the barracks creaks open and, in silhouette against the sky, are two unidentified men. At once waking up, one soldier seizes his Beretta, aims at the two intruders, fires.

The soldier's name is Mu and his nickname is Dopey, from one of the title characters in *Snow White and the Seven Dwarfs*. A man in his twenties, he once was a Red Guard in Canton, climbed across the mountains into Kowloon, became a proficient pickpocket there, and now is a soldier of Tiger's though occasionally, impetuously and insubordinately he gets into fistfights with Tiger that Tiger wins. Dopey, his two buck teeth like a cartoon character's, got his belittling nickname through his abysmal ignorance, since he reads nothing but Chinese comic books with characters like the Three Stooges and knows about nothing but guns or, as he calls them, toys. At the gun range in Bangkok, he often spends $100 to shoot his Beretta all day. He whips it out of its holster as if he's John Wayne and shoots it as if he's Capone, shoots it nonstop as though it's on full automatic, shoots it while hollering in Cantonese, *"Bam-bam-bam-bam-bam-bam-bam-bam-bam-bam-bam-bam-bam-bam-bam-bam!* In just eight seconds! Can anyone beat that? I bet you can't!" Even in the barracks, he twirls the Beretta around his right index finger while the more circumspect soldiers flee or Johnny, inspecting, Johnny who at age sixteen trained with a rifle twenty years old in the Chinese communist army, tells him the Chinese proverb "A gun has a ghost inside. It pulls the trigger even if you yourself don't. Be careful with the Beretta." This wise advice didn't stay with Dopey, who with his Beretta soon killed a local millionaire inadvertently. And tonight, though it was more hazardous, he disassembled, cleaned and oiled, reassembled, and loaded his beloved ordnance in two prestidigitatorial minutes, something he'd also practiced many hours, many days. He depressed the Beretta's magazine release button, grabbed the Beretta's slide serrations, cocked the Beretta's recoil reciprocating slide as his thumb raised the Beretta's slide catch, caught the Beretta's one chambered round. The gun disarmed, he lowered the Beretta's slide catch, lowered and raised the Beretta's safety-decocking lever, recocked the Beretta's recoil reciprocating slide as his index finger depressed the Beretta's disassembling latch release button and his thumb lowered the Beretta's disassembling latch, then took out the Beretta's recoil reciprocating slide, took out the Beretta's recoil spring guide unit—the Beretta's recoil spring and the Beretta's recoil spring guide—and, his index finger on the Beretta's front barrel lug pin, his thumb on the Beretta's rear barrel lug, took out the Beretta's barrel itself. He cleaned the Beretta's parts with Hoppe's Powder Solvent, Number 9, oiled the Beretta with Break Free Gun Oil, then put the Beretta together again by reinserting the barrel into the recoil reciprocating slide, reinserting the recoil spring guide unit into, oh, the hell with it. At about ten seconds short of two minutes, he put another round in the chamber, lowered and raised the safety-decocking lever, depressed the magazine release button, put a sixteenth round in the magazine, reinserted the frazzled magazine, announced in Cantonese, "Two minutes! Can anyone beat that? I bet you can't!" put the Beretta under his feather pillow and, his hands sweating, went beddy-bye. At midnight into the barracks come the two mysterious men, and, thinking, *It's war,* Dopey now grabs his Beretta and fires once, only once. The bullet goes through the stomach of man number one and the heart of man number two, who, having taken his shoes off, has just bent over to put on his slippers, and who dies immediately.

The other soldiers wake up. They turn the barracks lights on. They discover that the two men are the Star's young soldier (the one who told Johnny, "They did the job for two") and Baldy, returning from the pussy-shoots-banana bar. On his bed sitting silently is Dopey, his head down, his arm on his knee, his limp fingers on his Beretta. A moment later, into the barracks straight from Frankfurt comes the Star, who yells at Dopey in Cantonese, "What did you *do?*"

"I didn't think the gun was loaded."

"Then why in God's name did you *fire* it?"

"The men worked for the Professor, I thought."

"But you didn't think the gun was loaded?"

"I didn't think so, no, I didn't think so."

"Then why in God's name did you fire it?"

"The men worked for us. They didn't work for the Professor. What harm could I do if I fired it?" says Dopey, who, it's been mentioned, isn't very intelligent.

"You ignoramus!" yells the Star, for once emotional. "I'm going to kill you!" and with bamboo he starts beating on Dopey as some soldiers load the Star's screaming soldier and Baldy (whose real name was Fang and who, coincidentally, was the man who accidentally shot at the Ghost in Queens) into a car and drive to the very emergency room they went to when, spooning heroin into the buckets, they started itching, blistering, vomiting. At this awful point, another coincidence intervenes. A call comes from Johnny in Paris, and, not being explicit, for the phone could be tapped, the Star says in Cantonese, "Father, I've got bad news. Baldy and Ah Dat," his wounded soldier, "have had an accident."

"How are they?" asks Johnny, startled.

"Baldy's dead. Ah Dat is in critical condition."

"What happened?" asks Johnny, stunned.

"One went off," one bullet went off.

"How did one get two?"

"It went through Ah Dat. It hit the right place in Baldy. Father," the Star says solemnly, "the person responsible is Dopey."

"No!" cries Johnny. *"Don't do it!"*

PARIS

"No!" Johnny cries. *"Don't do it!"* It's midafternoon, and he's in burgundy leather shoes in a telephone booth at the Poste, Téléphone et Télégraph d'Italie in Paris's Chinatown. By now, Johnny and Jonquil have seen the compulsory sights: the Eiffel Tower, Triumphal Arch, and Louvre: the Moulin Rouge, Maxim's, and (with some onstage elephants) the Lido. Paris sewn up, Johnny in fairness wants to show each enticing city to Jonquil that he showed last week to Dominique: Rome, Milan, Venice, not Monaco, for Jonquil isn't a baccarat, blackjack, craps or roulette enthusiast. A minute ago, she ventured into a fresh-fruit store to get some apples, bananas, as Johnny went to the Poste, Téléphone et Télégraph to call up Bangkok, to call up the Movie Star. When the Star told him, "Father, I've got bad news," Johnny thought, *He couldn't mean the Professor.* When the Star told him, "Baldy has had an accident," Johnny thought, *He means that Baldy's been shot. If this were a car accident, the Star would have said, "Baldy has had a car accident."* And when the Star solemnly told him, "The person responsible is Dopey," Johnny immediately thought, *He means that he'll kill Dopey,* and Johnny cried, "No! Don't do it! I'll be in Bangkok shortly! Leave him to me!" Hanging up, Johnny now thinks, *I can't let brothers kill brothers. The dead I can't save from being dead. The living I can save.*

John Sack

292

He goes through an alley to the fresh-fruit store and Jonquil. His moral dilemma is, should he continue his long-awaited vacation with her in Rome, Milan, Venice or should he postpone it on behalf of the dwarf in Bangkok, the most expendable member of the Big Circle? Johnny's fifteen-years wife and Johnny's adopted brother are, in different ways, in Johnny's family, but one would forfeit an Italian vacation, the other would forfeit his life. A no-brainer. "Sweetheart," Johnny tells Jonquil in English, her hands full of apples, bananas, her head full of happy vacation thoughts, then Johnny switches to Shanghai dialect, "I'm sorry. There's been an emergency, and I've got to go to Bangkok," then Johnny (as always with Tiger) takes a cab to the Claridge, another cab to Charles de Gaulle International Airport, and a plane of Thai Airways International, his and Jonquil's vacation adjourned.

DUBAI

The plane stops at Dubai International Airport in this little sheikdom afloat on one hundred billion barrels of oil (some perhaps destined for Thai Airways International) on Arabia's boiling coast. In the air-conditioned passenger lounge are men in white *dishdashas* and, on their heads, in red-and-white checkered *gutras* and, around these, in black *agals,* the ropes that the Arabs use to steady their *gutras* and to fetter their camels, as well as women in black almost everywhere. At one souvenir shop, Johnny buys a sweet-smelling perfume of Araby for Jonquil, who's now flying across the Atlantic to Newark International Airport. He doesn't buy her any picture postcards of Dubai (no sand, just high-rise hotels) because if he mailed one, the Royal Police or (if it's on this case) the DEA could locate him, then Johnny gets back on Thai Airways International.

NEW DELHI

The plane stops at Indira Gandhi International Airport a hundred miles short of the Taj Mahal. It's now the wee hours, and in the passenger lounge are no men in *pyjamas,* no women in saris, no souvenir shops still open, and Johnny doesn't buy any Brahmas, incense, post-cards for Jonquil, who's now at their children's $1,000,000 home at 46 East Hartshorn Drive in Short Hills, New Jersey. But Johnny thinks about Jonquil lovingly, thinks, *I'm sorry I left her, but,* sighing, *once more my hands were tied,* then Johnny gets back on Thai Airways International.

BANGKOK

The plane stops at Don Muang International Airport, and Johnny hurries to a telephone booth to call the Movie Star. A man with all the Professor's ambition—*ambition:* the Star's real impetus, the Star aspires to be Johnny's principal boss—the Star has already taken over in Bangkok. The king is dead, long live the king, the Star has already ordered hits on the Jap Man, Buddhahead, and the Professor's unisexual soldiers though not (at Johnny's insistence, delivered in Frankfurt) on the Professor's pretty wife or the Professor's daughter, just two months old: the Star has ordered these hits lest the Professor's embittered people hit *him.* Already the Star (or someone else: who in these intricate matters actually *knows?*) has thrown one of Johnny's brothers out of an eighth-floor window in Bangkok, murdering him. A soldier named Lee, nick-named Little Lee, to everyone's knowledge he wasn't working for the Professor but for Tiger, but last night he was carousing at his girlfriend's apartment when the Star's people, or the Professor's people, or *(who knows?)* his girlfriend's people threw him out. He grabbed a TV cable alongside the open window, but the cable pulled off the wall and plummeted down with Little Lee, who hit the ground wrapped in TV cable, defenestrated, dead. Alerted by three almost simultaneous casualties—the Star's wounded soldier, Tiger's dead soldier, and Baldy, also dead—late last night the Thai police knocked at the soldiers' brick barracks, the avid police asked questions there, the Star went into hiding again, and the phone is now answered by one of the Star's busy soldiers. "Big Brother! It's not the best time to come to Bangkok," the soldier tells Johnny in Cantonese, explaining why.

"All right, I'll leave," says Johnny from Don Muang International Air-port. "But tell Muy," tell the Star, "to do no mischief to Dopey," then

Johnny hangs up and (as always with Tiger) goes through a golden arch that says, *"Sawasdee.* See You Soon," and gets onto Japan Airlines.

TAIPEI

The plane stops at Chiang Kai-Shek International Airport, and Johnny in the passenger lounge buys a cardboard box of pork-and-beef jerky, reboards, takes off, and sits eating the munchy jerky, watching the billowing cumulus clouds, thinking about the Big Circle. *Jonquil and Dominique were right,* Johnny thinks. *At the Claridge and Coliseum, they were right. Why do I need this aggravation? This running around the world like this? I must retire from the Big Circle.* A stewardess serves him a Japanese noodle lunch, and Johnny thinks, *But if I retire, then what?* Then the Star will kill Dopey. And then (since Dopey is Tiger's soldier) there'll be a war between the Star's people, the Professor's people, and Tiger's people: three sides. A war in Bangkok, Hong Kong, Manila, New York (and not just in Chinatown: in baby-grand places like the Mirage Bar of the New York Hilton, too) and even Asunción. A war of well-armed brothers on streets and sidewalks, in restaurants, casinos and clubs, all scouting for other blood brothers, sisters, *bam-bam-bam,* shooting them dead, as happened with Chinese neighborhood gangs eight years ago at the Golden Dragon in San Francisco and two years ago at the Golden Star in New York. Sixteen people (innocent customers all) were shot in San Francisco and eleven were shot in New York. The headlines said, "IT'S RAINING CORPSES IN CHINATOWN," and the worst dénouement for Johnny would be a lethal long-lasting rain of Big Circle. Oh, the cries of "Today you're dead!" The blood-sodden bodies! The straitened widows! The traumatized orphans! No one but Johnny can stop the slaughter of most of Johnny's devoted wards.

Another no-brainer. His brothers' keeper, Johnny says in Cantonese, "Tiger," to his now vital bodyguard, "when we get to Tokyo, go back to Bangkok immediately. Tell those criminals there that I've taken over. Tell them don't go gunning for the Professor's people. Tell them that you're in charge in Bangkok. Tell them that Crew Cut," the man who shot the Professor, "is in charge in Manila. Tell them that Four Eyes," the committeeman, "is in charge in South America. Tell them that Michael Jackson," the committeeman, "is in charge in New York. Tell them the Star is now in charge in Los Angeles. As well as in San Francisco, Portland, Seattle, all the West Coast. Separate everyone. Send Dopey to South America," *to watch the water behind the dam,* Johnny thinks, "and Fat Ass to New York. Tell them that Wrist Watch," the messenger, "is staying in Hong Kong. Tell them don't obey other criminals anymore. Tell them just obey *me.*"

"I will, Big Brother," says Tiger.

TOKYO

The plane lands at Narita. Oh, for the jet setter's escapades! At once Tiger boards another plane back to Bangkok, and Johnny boards a van to his red-bricked, green-bricked accommodations, the Century Hyatt.

He goes to his chandeliered room. He falls on his rose-embossed couch. In school long ago, Johnny read of a Roman farmer (named Cincinnatus) who, when Rome was menaced by Aequians, Volscians, or its own generals, reluctantly accepted appointment as the dictator of Rome, did the job, and (just sixteen days later, once) went back to his four-acre farm across the Tiber. Like Cincinnatus, Johnny has grudgingly come back as benevolent dictator of the Big Circle. A runner—a world-girdling fugitive—he'll now run the heroin business, its net $25,000,000 each year, in the United States. A man who never does drugs, he's still acting like an addict: he can't tear himself away from them.

BANGKOK

That night (while Johnny's calling up Baldy's wife and Baldy's newborn daughter, while Johnny's saying, "I'll pay the funeral expenses. I'll pay your living expenses, too") Tiger arrives at the infamous barracks in Bangkok. Strung from a ceiling is Dopey, his face black-and-blue, his

neck in a noose, his feet on a stool: is Dopey on whose bloody lips is
"I'm sorry! I'm sorry! If you want to kill me, then kill me! If Baldy's dead,
then he's dead! What can I do?"

"What's happening?" asks Tiger in Cantonese, angry about his own
soldier's mistreatment.

"I've beat him," the Star says, "and now I'll kill him. I've already dug
a grave in the jungle for him."

"What will you tell Big Brother?" Tiger.

"'A life for a life, that's the law,'" the Star.

"Will that be all right with Big Brother?"

"Yes. It will be. I think so."

"In that case," says Tiger, still angry, "you needn't kill Dopey, I'll kill
him for you. In fact I've just come from Big Brother. He says there'll be
no more killing people. He says that he, Big Brother, is now running the
Big Circle. He says I'm in charge in Bangkok. He says you're in charge
in Los Angeles."

"Whatever would I do in Los Angeles?"

"You'd open another market on the West Coast," says Tiger. "You'd run
the white-powder business on the West Coast."

"Hmm," says the Star, intrigued, for LA (compared to Bangkok) is a
much taller platform to launch his ambitions from.

"Now I'll loosen Dopey," says Tiger.

"Sure," says the Star. "No hard feelings."

ROME

A four-acre farm across the Tiber: that's where Johnny would
rather be than in a dictator's mansion in Rome. But second best is the
Coliseum, and, having flown over the Pole, Johnny is back on vacation
track with Jonquil, he's standing with her in the balcony where he and
Dominique stood last week. "Down there," Johnny tells Jonquil, "the
slaves fought lions."

"In this very building?" asks Jonquil, awed.

"Yes," says Johnny. "But it's broken now."

MILAN

In front of the pale mural of *The Last Supper* are Johnny and Jonquil. In front of it Johnny walks to and fro, observing the eyes of the man who's saying, "One of you will betray me," and the horrified eyes of the twelve men around him. The eyes don't follow Johnny as did the eyes of the *Mona Lisa,* by the same artist, as Johnny walked to and fro at the Louvre, in Paris. "Nice picture," Johnny told Jonquil in Shanghai dialect then. "Her eyes always stay with me. Her eyes always look at me. It's like she's alive," but he can't pass the same compliment to the twenty-something eyes in *The Last Supper.*

"Who are those people?" asks Jonquil.

"The center one is Jesus Christ," says Johnny, who learned about this from his Christian first wife. "The others are Jesus's right-hand men. Like me," Johnny laughs, "and the bosses of the Big Circle."

"You should leave them," sighs Jonquil.

VENICE

"O sole mio," the gondolier sings. The bridges pass over Johnny and Jonquil, curved like in China, drifting romantically by. Johnny's silk shirt in the breeze feels sexy, and he guesses that Jonquil's feels sexy too. He cuddles, kisses, tells her in Shanghai dialect, "I think you're beautiful." No question about it, Johnny will keep the promise he made in Saigon, "I'll never leave you. I'll never hurt you. As long as I live I'll care for you."

Then Jonquil flies to the Hong Kong that Johnny can't visit, that Johnny's the man most wanted at, and Johnny (now forty-three) flies to the mother of drug deals: $50,000,000 every month, $1,200,000,000 every two years.

21
Peacemaker

MANILA

Red, orange, yellow meteors crisscross a darkened nightclub on Mabini Street. Overhead is a glittering mirror-moon, and at a large table is Crew Cut, the ordinary-looking boss, the one who said, "Today you're dead!" and killed the Professor with an American army rifle. At the same table are Americans, are air force officers from Clark Field, in Manila, all dining on kneecap soup, vinegar-marinated pork, unripened papaya slices, and, for dessert, *halo-halo,* an ice-cream correlate, the officers drinking the San Miguel Beer and glomming the girlie-girls in G-strings, even less. "That one I like," an American captain says, and Crew Cut (who whispers first with the waiter) tells him in English, "She's yours." For all the American party-hearty officers, Crew Cut gets Filipino girls or Filipino boys, then, the show over, goes home alone, for he lives irreproachably with his Chinese fiancée.

The next day, he picks up Johnny (mustache and wig on) at Ninoy Aquino International Airport and drives him to a resort hotel, a Nautilus, swimming, boating, tennis and golf hotel on Manila Bay: the Westin Philippine Plaza. On the top floor in Johnny's suite, he opens the mini-refrigerator, takes out two pineapple juices, opens the pleated white drapes, steps onto the wide lanai (the orchid-garlanded balcony) and stands there with Johnny, a pool below them, an island inside it, a hut in its center, a place for chi chis, tequilas and daiquiris. "Big Brother," says Crew Cut in a conflation of Mandarin and Cantonese (his native language is Hunanese), "I've got a great opportunity for us. To start with, I'll need two hundred white-powder bricks. What happens will be, my people in Bangkok pick them up. We put them on a Thai fishing float, then in international waters on a Philippine fishing float. We hide them on a distant uninhabited island in the Philippines. For weeks we lie low. Again we put the two hundred bricks on a Philippine fishing float, then take them (we're going island-to-island, so there are no customs inspectors) to the island that you and I are now on. We take them by truck to Manila. We hide them in chairs, armchairs, microwaves, refrigerators. We crate these up and label these crates with an American airman's name, like 'Sergeant Smith.' He's anyone out at Clark Field who has been reassigned to America. We take these crates to the warehouse out at Clark Field. And there I'm in league with an American officer. Do you follow me, Big Brother?"

"Yes yes," says Johnny in Cantonese, absorbed.

"The officer puts the crates onto a cargo plane, a C-130. The plane takes off for Los Angeles," the boss continues as Johnny thinks, *Uh-oh, that's where the Star is.* "It lands in Los Angeles, and the crates go to an air force warehouse where, again, I'm in league with an American officer. He delivers the crates to my people in Los Angeles, who I've already stationed there. If all goes well, every month we send half a ton of white powder there, every year that's $600,000,000. Do you like it, Big Brother?"

"Yes!" says Johnny. "It's nice! It's nice!" it's astronomically more than Johnny (or any Chinese, Italian, Hispanic) has ever sent to America. "Are you sure," says Johnny, "that the American officers aren't with the DEA?"

"I'm sure, Big Brother. I've checked them both out."

"I'm sure too," says Johnny. "In Vietnam I knew some American pilots who flew opium for the CIA."

"I'll need $200,000. For each American officer, $100,000."

"You've got it," says Johnny, standing up, going indoors, going past a ceiling-scraping ficus, going to a louvered rosewood closet, opening a suitcase full of ten-packs of $100 bills, counting out two hundred packs. "One more question. Who are your people in Los Angeles?"

"The main one, his name is Tony. And there's another one."

"I've put the Movie Star in charge of Los Angeles," says Johnny. "Do you suppose there'll be friction between him and Tony, between him and you?"

"Not between *us*. The Star is our brother in the Big Circle."

"Good," says Johnny. "I'll fly to Los Angeles and tell the Star what's happening. We don't want friction," says Johnny, who Crew Cut now escorts down to the Pier Seven Restaurant for lobster, scallops, prawns, for crab with onion, ginger, and red pepper under a glorious sunset over Manila Bay.

MONTEREY PARK

But where the Star is, friction is. In this city of Chinese immigrants east of Los Angeles, its sidewalks walled with Shanghai, Mandarin, Cantonese, Szechwanese, Hunanese and Taiwanese restaurants and with Taiwanese laundries (Taiwanese banks, laundering from $500,000,000 to $750,000,000 each year), the Star and his three soldiers live in a one-story house with Tony and Tony's associate. All the Star's faction speaks Cantonese, but Tony's faction speaks Hunanese. To say the word *we*, the Star's faction says *"Ngo mon,"* but Tony's faction says *"Wo mon."* To eat, the Star's faction cooks mild rice, but Tony's faction crams the red peppers in. At this house divided, the automobile (a *sine qua non* in this sunny sprawl) belongs to Tony, but the Star keeps borrowing it to verse himself in the LEFT LANE and RIGHT LANE chaos of LA's fabled freeways. "No no!" cries Tony, a back-seat driver, in Fractured Cantonese. "Don't take this street!"

"I'm the one driving," says the Star's driver.

"We're on a one-way street!" cries Tony.

"When I'm driving, I know what I'm doing."

"The sign there said DO NOT ENTER!"

"I was the getaway driver in Hong Kong."

"Muy," says Tony imploringly to the Star in the passenger seat. "He's breaking the law! What if the blackfeet," the LA hats, "ever stop him? He doesn't speak English! He doesn't have an American license! What if they trace him to Monterey Park? Soon we're storing white powder there! We're fucked!"

"I'll need the car tomorrow, too," the Star replies.

"You use the car more than I do!" cries Tony.

"We are four people. You are just two."

"You motherfucker!" thinks Tony with silent lips, and no sooner is Johnny in Monterey Park, no sooner is Johnny ensconced at the Lincoln Plaza Hotel than Tony comes to his suite to grouse about the Star's superior airs. *A bunch of babies, that's what they are,* Johnny thinks, but he invites the Star to the usual dinner: shrimp, scallops, clams at a seafood restaurant here in "Little Taipei."

"Muy," asks Johnny. "How much money would satisfy you?"

"Per year? Maybe about $200,000," the Star replies.

"You can make that per day," says Johnny.

"$200,000 per day? Every day?"

"Yes," says Johnny. "If you show respect to Tony. Every month Tony will get (I needn't say how) one half ton of white powder, and you will distribute it."

"$200,000 every single day?"

"Closer to $2,000,000," says Johnny. "If."

"You saved me in Hong Kong, Father," the Star says humbly. "You brought me to Bangkok and now to Los Angeles. I'll do what you say and show respect to Tony."

R, e, s, p, e, c, t. To respect someone isn't the Star's greatest talent, and when Johnny has left Los Angeles, the Star and his soldiers cook a Cantonese dinner and, not inviting in Tony or Tony's associate, sit at the table gaily partaking of it. A man with hair like Crew Cut's, a fast-talking, short-tempered, fist-making man, a Hunanese too—Hunan: a province of hot-blooded soldiers, of Mao—Tony feels totally humiliated. Out through his ears drains intelligence, his brain is an empty coffee kettle, choler rises to fill it. How dare he? thinks Tony. He didn't invite me! He didn't invite us! Losing control, Tony does what the Chinese (though not the Italians) in many gangs would do: he seizes his .38 and, not intending to kill the Star, just intending to chasten him, shoots him in the left thigh-bone. A soldier jumps for the gun, but Tony shoots him in his left thigh-bone too. A whirlpool develops: down on the floor is the .38 and swirling around are the Star's shouting soldiers and Tony's soldier, landing and losing the .38. A siren sounds, and as Tony and Tony's accomplice escape, the blackfeet rush into the blood-spotted house. "Don't move! Don't move! What happened?" cry the cops.

"Two burglars! Two black burglars!" cries one of the Star's quick-witted soldiers. An ambulance arrives, and the Star's taken to the emergency room at Garfield Medical Center. When no one's watching, the Star, not wanting to be interrogated, climbs off the gurney, ties on a bandage, stumbles (much as he did in his movie, stumbling up to an attic, bloodying the attic floor) out of the hospital, into a taxi, out of the taxi at Los Angeles International Airport, and onto a plane to Florida.

ORLANDO

Here in the 'hood of Disney World, the Star has a Chinese doctor friend. Not using an operating room, the doctor operates in his bedroom, takes out the .38 bullet, sets the split thighbone, and has the Star recuperate at a neighbor's home in Orlando, recuperate with a beautiful view (if the curtains were open) of a golf course, tennis court, swimming pool. The next day, the telephone rings and it's Manila, it's Crew Cut, who tells the Star in distress and in Mandarin-Cantonese, "I heard that Tony wounded you. I'm ashamed of Tony, and I apologize for him. If you want," the short-haired boss in Manila *doesn't* say, the Star sits waiting but Crew Cut doesn't say it, "I'll have someone kill Tony."

"Thank you for your apology, brother," the Star replies. "I accept it," the Star continues, the Star who's privately thinking, *He didn't say he'd kill Tony. That means: He ordered Tony to do it. The man behind it is Crew Cut.* "The wound isn't bad. It quickly will heal."

"Still, I apologize."

"Please forget it."

A few days later into Orlando in black leather shoes comes Johnny, and, wooden crutches under his arms, bodyguards bolstering him, the Star greets his "Father" in a tourist-teeming passenger lounge at Orlando International Airport. "You shouldn't have come here," says Johnny in Cantonese, embarrassed. "You should rest."

"If you come, then I must come, Father," the Star replies, smiling his Buddha smile. He escorts Johnny through the great greenhouse airport (the ceiling is skylights, the sunlight stipples the pale green carpets, tiles and trees) into his Cadillac and to his provisional home in the golf, tennis, swimming development. At the front door, the Star's bodyguards remove their shoes and the Star's shoes, too, but "Father, you needn't remove your shoes," the Star tells Johnny, who nevertheless removes them. Into the gun-gorged living room hobbles the Star, then lies on the sofa, head raised onto a pillow, legs raised onto an arm. "The wound isn't bad. It quickly will heal," the Star assures Johnny, patting his aching thighbone.

"Muy," says Johnny urgently as the Star's bodyguards bring tea. "I spoke to Tony. He's sorry he did it. He's young, hotheaded, impetuous. He isn't patient like an old man like me. You too are older, wiser, patient. You can forgive him. You *must* forgive him," says Johnny, "or we'll have intramural war."

"I forgive him," the Star says, smiling.

"If your people kill Tony," continues Johnny as though the Star hasn't spoken at all, "it won't be the end of it. Your people will be killed by Crew Cut's, who then will be killed by yours (if anyone's left) and on and on. The war will never end."

"My people won't kill Tony," the Star says, smiling his irremovable smile, his Noh-mask sculptured smile, his would-I-be-smiling-if-I-were-lying smile. "I've forgiven him."

"You came to America, Muy," continues Johnny as though the Star's words haven't reached him, *What what? Did you say something? I must have missed it,* "to make some money. You still don't have money, but you can make half a billion dollars each year. If you keep peace with Crew Cut."

"I'll keep peace. So tell me, Father. How is Crew Cut?"

"He's fine," says Johnny. From a jacket pocket he pulls three hundred-packs of $100 bills, that's $30,000 that he then hands the Star. "It's for your doctor," says Johnny. "If you need more, call me. Crew Cut," continues Johnny, "asked me to tell you he's very sorry. He's setting up the half-billion dollar deal now in Manila, soon in Los Angeles. He asked me to tell you he'll apologize personally when he's in Los Angeles."

"The blackfeet are looking for me in Los Angeles."

"Then where should I reassign you?"

"New York."

"Then that's where I'll reassign you," says Johnny obligingly, Johnny who's wise to the Star's little ploy—to use his thighbone to get his foot in America's fattest market, New York—but Johnny who'd rather let the Star quarrel with Fat Ass, the other egotist in New York, then let him quarrel with Crew Cut, the one-half-billionaire boy in Los Angeles. "I'll tell Crew Cut he should apologize in New York."

"Tell him I send best regards."

"I will," says Johnny.

"Tell him he's my best friend."

NEW YORK

His thigh healed, the Star now lives behind vinyl sides in a house by the Elmhurst Tanks, the red-and-white cylinders that the traffic on the Long Island Expressway is often backed up to on AM 880 and AM 1010. While waiting (like Fat Ass, like Michael Jackson) for the white powder from Manila, the Star makes acquaintances with the leaders of Chinatown's neighborhood gangs, the Flying Dragons and Ghost Shadows, with kids who recognize him from *The Big Circle* and will now gain prestige—gain face—by distributing heroin for him and slowly dislodging the Mafia. But one day he walks to Queens Boulevard to meet his "Father" in his gray crocodile shoes in front of Alexander's department store.

With Johnny, the Star and some brothers walk by a dirty subway stairway (for the G train to Manhattan) and into the Sizzler's near it. The air in Sizzler's is fraught with the smell of A-1 Sauce, the fans on the ceiling wafting it into the beige-and-brown booth that, with Johnny, the Star sits down in. A waitress in brown slacks, brown shirt, like a UPS uniform (except that her shirt pocket sports a golden bull) writes down the vegetarian order: coffee for two, she walks off and Johnny tells the Star in Cantonese, "I've got good news. The goods," dropping his voice, for behind him are Jews, African-Americans, Russians and Chinese lined up for Sizzler Steaks, are Americans asking their kids in a half-dozen languages, "What do you want, well, what?"—"The goods are ready in Bangkok. This month they'll be in Manila, then in Los Angeles, then in New York."

"Good," says the Star. "I want to make money."

"Crew Cut," says Johnny, "is in Paraguay now."

"Yes, he's at my villa near your watch factory."

"Crew Cut is staying at your villa in Paraguay?"

"A goodwill gesture," says the Star, smiling.

"Good," says Johnny. "You know, then, he's waiting for an American visa. Then he'll fly to Los Angeles and then to New York. Muy," says Johnny earnestly, "with Crew Cut we can make more money than Lee Ka-Sheng," a real-estate man in Hong Kong as rich as Croesus. "We mustn't have war," says Johnny as though he didn't belabor this in Orlando, as though he didn't hammer this in in Orlando, *wham, wham,* with a sledgehammer, practically, driving a spike in a railroad bed in Orlando.

"Don't worry. You told me that in Orlando."

"We must have peace," concludes Johnny. The waitress from UPS delivers the coffee, then Johnny talks when-where-whats with the Star, then Johnny embraces him. A brother drives Johnny by the Unisphere, an enormous globe, its continents steel, its oceans emptiness, and by the Mets' baseball stadium to LaGuardia Airport, and the Star walks back to his vinyl-sided house by the Elmhurst Tanks. He calls up his villa in Paraguay, talks to his haughty girlfriend there, then talks to Crew Cut in Cantonese.

"I'm coming to New York," says Crew Cut.

"Yes, I've heard. What are you doing now?"

"Playing mahjong."

"You winning or losing?"

"Sometimes I win, sometimes lose."

"Heh heh. Please get me the Snakes," says the Star, smiling his Buddha smile. He talks to his soldiers in Paraguay, two wily people called the Snakes—the White Snake and the Green Snake—and tells them, "Take care of Crew Cut."

PORT OF PRESIDENT STROESSNER

At the earth's edge is a cliff, and the ocean is pouring off it. It's pouring at many places, nearly three hundred, and to the disoriented eye it's pouring at different rates in defiance of Galileo's laws. The narrowest waterfalls seem to rush like water-fraught rivers in April, but the widest seem to go slowly, *slowly,* like old rusty water wheels, seem to pause at the crest of the cliff like a man having second thoughts on a diving board, a diving board thirty stories high. Then slowly, or so it seems, it settles until it crashes (*roar,* the roar usurps every part of your thoughts, *Where am I? I am in Roar! What time is it? It is Roar! Who am I? I am Roarrrrr!*)—crashes on the opal-glistening rocks of the Iguaçu River. Nowhere else on this planet can you or I see such perpetual power. Whales rising, elephants mating, volcanoes erupting, after a time they stop, repose, they may be prudently petted, but not the Iguaçu River, in Indian language the Big Water River. Higher than Niagara, wider than Niagara, two thousand tons of Iguaçu are falling every second, raising spray-clouds, creating rainbows, solidifying as red-necked cranes, orange-billed toucans, yellow-winged butterflies, falling as though all God's creation, all fluttering things, all moving things, all the raw nature in South America is being drawn irresistibly into this roaring vortex, into Iguaçu Falls.

A half-hour from this world's wonder is Paraguay, are the filthy streets and the rickety stalls full of counterfeit watches in a city christened the Port of President Stroessner. It's here that Johnny's factory for Champion watches (and Seiko and Citizen counterfeit watches) and the Star's white villa are, and it's at this villa that Crew Cut, the mahjong game over, goes to bed at one a.m. in the Star's flower-filled guest room. A farmer's son from Hunan, he's like a forty-niner now, his mind overrun by reveries of clothes, houses, cars, his pickax a couple of inches away from the glittering mother lode. Like other forty-niners, he has *striven* to get where he is: at night in Manila he's wined and dined, smoked and joked, pimped and pandered for the American air force officers though he preferred to be home with his Chinese fiancée, his Chinese pregnant fiancée, he's done this until he's dug up two officers willing to risk twenty years apiece behind the brick walls of Leavenworth for $100,000 monthly bribes. Just yesterday he got an American visa in his Philippine counterfeit passport, and at daybreak the Snakes will wake him to drive him two hundred rugged miles to Asunción, to President Stroessner International Airport. By Varig he'll fly to Johnny, who's in Panama City, then to the air force officer in Los Angeles, then to the Star in New York to personally say, "I apologize." Then the pickax will strike—*eureka,* it will unearth a $600,000,000 trove every year. Ding ding! Three cherries lined up! A fabulous jackpot for the Big Circle!

He falls asleep. At five a.m. the Snakes enter Crew Cut's room. Not waking him, they take care of him in the manner the Star intended, the Star who required revenge for his wounded thighbone: the Snakes put a .38 to his head and fire it. The blood splatters the guest-room wall, with a rag the Snakes wipe it off and, pulling the bed and the dead man away, paint the wall white again. His papers, the Snakes then put in a pot-bellied stove in the kitchen, strike a match, start a fire—his body they wrap in the bed sheets, carry to the car, and dump in the trunk. They lock up the Star's pretty villa. They drive to the squawking jungle, then, with the body, walk by canjerana, canelapreta, canafistula trees, by tabulla trees whose leaves are for diabetes and by timbauva trees whose trunks are for rustic canoes. The dew still dampens the dirt as they begin digging it up. Six feet deep they bury the body lest the long-snouted coatis disturb it, and face down they bury it lest it return as a ghost, floating through windows, saying in Hunanese, "I'll take revenge." The tires dirty, the hubs dirty, the chassis dirty, dirty, they drive back to the Port of President Stroessner and the factory for Champion watches, telling everyone there, "We took him to Varig."

"Your car's dirty. We'll wash it," the brothers at the Champion factory say.

"Not now," say the Snakes, not wanting to open the bloody trunk. They drive over Friendship Bridge to their newly rented room in Foz do Iguaçu ("Mouth of Iguaçu") in Brazil, closer to the primordial roar of Iguaçu Falls.

That night the telephone rings at the Champion factory. On the line is Johnny, in Panama City, who says in Cantonese, "Where's Crew Cut? He wasn't on Varig." Arming themselves, the brothers drive to the Star's white villa, discover it's locked, kick the door open, discover no sign (except for a jam-packed suitcase: *strange*) of their benefactor-to-be, of Crew Cut. On the guest-room wall is fresh white paint, and by chipping it off the brothers discover bloodstains behind it. The fire in the pot-bellied stove is out, but in the ashes the brothers discover a vest-pocket telephone book with Chinese names, addresses and numbers in Crew Cut's calligraphy. The brothers drive back to the factory, call up Johnny in Panama City, and say in Cantonese, "Big Brother. We know about Crew Cut. He was probably killed."

PANAMA CITY

Yes, the brothers said *killed,* on the phone the brothers didn't say "He's probably gone," or "He's probably west," or any such circumspect phrase. By now the Big Circle is very high tech, for Johnny has spent $8,000 apiece for scramblers-unscramblers for his branch offices in Bangkok, Hong Kong, Tokyo, New York, and the Port of President Stroessner and for his new home office in Panama City. Twice every month, on lined white paper he writes twelve-digit codes (none of the digits is *4,* which also means *death* in Cantonese) and couriers them to the eastern and western, northern and southern, hemispheres, and in his long-distance calls he no longer alludes to Panama as Maland, to Paraguay as Guayland, to the United States as Flower Flag. What the brothers just told him ("We know about Crew Cut. He was probably killed") is absolute jabberwocky to any meddlesome telephone-tapper from the Royal Police or the DEA.

The new home office for the Big Circle, Incorporated, is Johnny's splendid estate on a hillside near the estate of President Noriega. Johnny, still wanted in Hong Kong, has bought it for $1,200,000 from Noriega's chatty helicopter pilot ("You want to do drugs in Panama? You must pay") and, to deflect the bad *feng shui* from an L-shaped estate nearby, has put an octagonal mirror on its massive front door. On the grounds are palm, mango, papaya trees that Johnny can see through his all-glass living-room walls, and in his magnificent office, fit for the title character of *The Godfather,* are ancient paintings of mandarins, black-lacquered screens inlaid with mother-of-pearl, chinaware vases, and an enormous chestnut desk that Johnny, like Marlon Brando, is now sitting behind, listening to the scrambled-unscrambled call from the Port of President Stroessner. "You're right about Crew Cut," says Johnny in Cantonese, stunned, his left hand at his forehead, sloping like a visor over his eyes. "He was probably killed. Hold on to his telephone book. It's evidence."

Johnny hangs up and, his hand still shielding him, calls up the Movie Star in New York and half-candidly tells him, "Crew Cut didn't come to Panama City. He's missing."

"He is?" says the Star, apparently unalarmed by the $600,000,000 loss.

"He may have gone straight to New York. Did he?"

"Not that I know of."

"Maybe," proposes Johnny, "his magazine wasn't good." This call isn't scrambled, and his *magazine* is his counterfeit passport.

"Maybe," agrees the Star, still apparently unappalled. "If he went via São Paulo, the inspectors are tough in São Paulo."

"Yes. If he ever calls you, tell me."

"Sure," says the Star, still la-di-da.

Johnny in his Godfather's office hangs up. He needn't extort a written confession to know the Star ordered this hit. He thinks, *Unbelievable!* To bite the hand that's handing you the treasures of Fort Knox! To live underneath the Elmhurst Tanks and put revenge, revenge, ahead of a mansion in Oyster Bay, a yacht on Long Island Sound! And yet, Johnny realizes, the Star is his real soulmate, isn't it Johnny whose mission (come to think of it) is not making money, is getting revenge against the United States? Incredulous, infuriated as Johnny is, he doesn't order a hit on the Star.

He calls up Manila, the soldiers of Crew Cut, and—this call isn't scrambled—tells them with Cantonese circumlocution, "He's gone."

MANILA

"He's gone, Big Brother? The man who did it's the Star," the soldiers say furiously. "We can't work with the Star anymore. Why should we send these goods to the Star? Why should *he* make money from them? He did this to our beloved brother."

"The money's for all of us," Johnny says.

"It's not, Big Brother. The two American officers trusted Crew Cut. They never trusted anyone else in Manila. If they can't work with Crew Cut, then they won't work with anyone else."

"Tell them Crew Cut is busy in China."

"They'll say when he's out of China, call."

"The deal's dead, then?" asks Johnny.

"It's dead, Big Brother." Dejected, the soldiers hang up. Still loyal to their dear-departed boss, they call up the brothers at the Champion factory, in the Port of President Stroessner, and tell them, "Take care of the Star's assassins," take care of the Snakes. But that week another member of this accursed cast of characters presents himself—correction, herself—as someone the soldiers in Manila must ungently take care of. Sad to say, the requisite victim is Crew Cut's pregnant Chinese fiancée. For days she's sat at their home in Manila, a cross on her breast, a cross on her wall, waiting for her daily telephone call from her bridegroom-to-be, her call that unaccountably doesn't come. She's asked Crew Cut's soldiers in Cantonese, "What happened to him?" and the soldiers equivocated, telling her, "We just know he's in Paraguay." A week goes by, her phone doesn't ring, it squats by her bedside like a black statue, inanimate, mute, and she becomes hysterical. "What *happened* to him?" she asks these soldiers. "Tell me, or I'll call the Philippine police! I'll tell them he's missing! I'll tell them he's dealing drugs!"

Heavy-hearted, the soldiers call up Johnny in Panama City and say in Cantonese, "Big Brother. It's something serious."

PANAMA CITY

"Excuse me," says Johnny in Cantonese to the half-dozen guests in his glass-walled living room. "It's something important," and he goes to his mandarin-painted office to continue this call. "What is it?" Johnny asks the Manila soldiers.

"It's his fiancée. She's asking us, Where is Crew Cut? She's getting noisy about it. We have to remove her."

"No, don't!" cries Johnny, horrified.

"What should we do, Big Brother?"

"Let her alone! She carries his child!"

"Then what should we *do* about her?"

"I don't know, tell her some story!"

"A story like what, Big Brother?"

"Tell her he's dead! He died," says Johnny, his mind in wild overdrive, "in a car accident in Paraguay. No, don't! I'm crazy!" cries Johnny. "My mind isn't working today! She'll ask you, When will the funeral be? When can I see him?" Murder, murder—what a bad business drugs are, thinks Johnny. He's already heard from Paraguay that one of the Snakes (the White one) has been tied, gagged, beaten to death with a hammer, buried in the coati-teeming jungle. And now this innocent girl? And her innocent unborn child? No!

"What story should we tell her?"

"Tell her— Tell her—" Johnny endeavors, then he devises a plot to keep the girl from squealing but to keep her phenomenally alive, a plot that's unprecedented in two thousand years of literature on love and loss, loyalty and betrayal.

MANILA

"We're here to tell you," the soldiers say in Cantonese, simulating anger, the soldiers who have just come to Crew Cut's home, to Crew Cut's fiancée's home. "We hate that man. If he ever comes to Manila, we'll kill him. He lied to us and lied to you, his supposed fiancée. He has a wife in China. Has he ever told you?"

"No," says the fiancée tremulously.

"He's back with his wife in China."

"Why doesn't he himself tell me?"

"He's too ashamed to. Listen," the soldiers say, and hand her $50,000 of Johnny's money. "He's a bad man, but you're a nice girl. Go find a man you deserve," then, as the girl sits sobbing (*sobbing:* a sign that she's still alive and, as things turn out, will bear the fatherless daughter, marry a Chinese man in Manila, and not know the truth till this book comes out)—then, their hearts aching, the soldiers call up Johnny in Panama City and say in Cantonese, "Big Brother. We did it."

PANAMA CITY

"You did it. Thank you," says Johnny, his heart aching too. He hangs up and returns to his living room and his half-dozen summer guests. In addition to Jonquil they're Jonquil's two sons (the avatars of the ones who died in Cambodia) and the two sons, one daughter, of Johnny's first wife: all Johnny's children, together for the first time in Johnny's eventful life. His business done, Johnny, Jonquil, and the children (the youngest six, the oldest twenty-one) sit at the long glass dinner table, sit at the woven reed mats, eat the garlic chicken and the mangos fresh from the visible mango tree. "I'm so happy," Johnny tells them in Cantonese. "All my life, I've waited for this."

After dessert, the kids jump straight from the dinner table into the swimming pool, sauna, Jacuzzi. In the ensuing days, Johnny conducts them to the jungle—macaws, that's what they see—the duty-free stores in Colon, the brunch at the American officers club, the Panama Canal at Miraflores. At the enormous locks, the doors seven stories high, the doors slowly opening, closing, with all the finality of "The moving finger," Johnny makes a staircase gesture to show everyone how the boats descend to the Pacific Ocean. "Step by step," he explains in Cantonese, "they come here from the Atlantic. A lot of Chinese helped build this. They caught a disease called," and Johnny switches to English, "malaria. They took a medicine called," and Johnny switches to English again, "quinine. But many Chinese died." A few days later, it's one son's birthday: he's ten, and Johnny throws him a party at the Ginza Restaurant, a teriyaki restaurant in Panama City. And what a phenomenal party it is! One magician! Two red-cheeked clowns! Red, yellow, blue paper hats on the children's heads, paper horns in the children's mouths! Balloons! Everyone sings in English, "Happy birthday, dear Jerry," and Jerry blows the ten candles out! *If only,* Johnny thinks! If only each day of his life were like this rhapsodic one! If only he weren't compelled to take revenge against the United States!

22
Coke Carrier

PANAMA CITY

One day to Johnny's splendid estate there comes a Bolivian businessman. The two met last year, when Johnny the jet-setter took a detour to South America while flying from New York to Frankfurt for his "I'd kill the Professor" meeting. At Johnny's two-story villa in Asunción, 200-foot-high trees around it, wickerwork baskets inside it, plastic mangos, plastic grapes, and plastic flowers spilling out, Johnny (in gray crocodile shoes) and the Bolivian businessman (in black leather shoes) met and started off in Spanish. *"¿Como esta?"* said Johnny.

"¿Como esta, Señor Yian?" said the Bolivian, for south of the Rio, Johnny was and still is known as Mario William Yian.

"Yeah, how are you?" said Johnny in English and, sitting down at a coffee table under a 17th-century painting of Guarani indians, loincloths around them, spears in their hands, jaguars on the ends of their spears, he got down to business in English. "I sell America, heroin," said Johnny. "Business good, but Americans more and more want cocaine, and I want cocaine for Americans. I buy from you."

"I can get *tons,*" the Bolivian, whose name was Juan, guaranteed. Short, skinny, curly-haired, his hair parted twice—once on the left, once on the right—he'd driven since the 1970s to some of Bolivia's one hundred thousand coca-plant growers and, at rock-bottom prices, from $200

315

to $2,000 per ton, had bought their coca, a perfectly legal thing to do in Bolivia. Converting it to cocaine, he'd smuggled it to Colombia, whose cartels then sold it to American tourists—"mules"—who hid it in soccer balls, rolling pins, statues of Jesus, etcetera, and (don't attempt this) in backpacks to smuggle into the United States. No one in the 1970s smuggled *tons,* but a ton in the States would have sold for $50,000,000 or, if leavened with as much sugar, aspirin or borax, for $100,000,000, and by the 1980s tons and tons of Juan's product were on the freighters from Cali and private planes from Medellín. Then last year, a penchant for violence not to Juan's liking hit the Cali and Medellín cartels. The Calis, like Pharaohs, murdered the men who built their homes, men who knew where their hidey-holes were, and the Medellíns murdered the judges (*plomo o plata,* lead or silver, the judges were told) and the justices, attorney generals, governors, and presidential candidates of Colombia. To add to injury, insult, the Medellíns soon sent Juan a $100,000 monthly bill, a "tax" for its antijudge, antijustice, antiestablishment campaign, a "tax" he could either pay or be murdered himself, him and his wife, children, tropical fish. No wonder he'd sooner deal with Johnny, deal with a Triad! "I can get *tons,*" said Juan last year. "I sell to you in Asunción for $8,000,000 per ton. You can sell in Miami for $24,000,000 per ton or in New York for $32,000,000 per ton."

"The profit," Johnny computed, "is two hundred percent in Miami, three hundred percent in New York. A deal," said Johnny, then they discussed logistics, then Johnny flew to São Paulo, over Dakar, and into Frankfurt to tell the Big Circle, "All of you say kill the Professor. How can I repudiate you?" And now, one year later in Panama City, with Johnny's heroin practically dusting us (and this year 1,549 people will die, two hundred more than last year)—now Johnny diversifies into toot, snort, blow, snow, into Coke, Coca, Cola, California Cornflakes, into Carrie, Candy, Carrie Nation, Henry VIII, into Gutter Glitter. When the Bolivian comes, Johnny introduces him to Jonquil and his unsuspecting children (*"¿Como esta?"*) and serves him tea. Then, excusing himself, stepping into his vase-adorned office, opening a chestnut drawer, taking out a manila envelope, returning to the living room, he hands the envelope and its down payment of $500,000 cash (just withdrawn from his Swiss bank) to his Bolivian connection, Juan. For that man it's total bonanza, since when he consigns cocaine to the Calis or Medellíns he isn't paid beforehand and, in fact, pays *them* $3,200,000 as shipping insurance, like with Lloyd's of London.

"Do you like here in Panama?" asks Juan.

"Yes, sir," says Johnny's youngest son.

"Did you see the Canal?"

"Yes, sir."

"You come to Bolivia sometime. Mario," says Juan to Johnny, "next month I see you there," and, with the unopened envelope, leaves the warm family hearth.

SANTA CRUZ

"*¿Gusta saboriar?*" a vendor at a small sidewalk stall asks Johnny in Spanish. Although the woman (who's wearing an ample satin skirt, a baby-packing alpaca shawl, and a shuffle-off-to-Buffalo bowler hat) sells mandarin oranges, too, she's reaching into a plastic bag as big as a plastic garbage bag and scooping up coca leaves, chewing them with a chaser that looks like Crayola paste, offering them to Johnny. "Do you want to taste it?" she asks him in Spanish so casually that, like Fatty, his former mentor, she could be offering him the drug in a secret shack in the Golden Triangle and not underneath the colonial arches on the Plaza de 24 Septiembre in Bolivia's second city.

"What is it?" asks Johnny in English, asks the Bolivian businessman.

"Coca. From this they make cocaine."

"They sell it? The police not stop it?"

"Sell in Bolivia five thousand years."

"Five thousand years!" says Johnny. He buys some mandarin oranges as men in double-breasted brown suits buy the coca leaves, looking like bay leaves, smelling like spinach. A ton of cocaine is the product of ninety tons of these leaves, eight hundred pounds of quicklime, two hundred gallons of kerosene, and twenty gallons of sulfuric acid, all of these unpalatable ingredients mixed by *pisacocas,* by coca-stompers, by boys who for fifty cents an hour stomp on them barefoot (their feet getting ulcerated, at times getting amputated) as they drink moonshine, smoke cocaine, and listen to American rock and Bolivian rock like

> *I grow little coca plants*
> *And stomp them down,*

at fifty factories outside of Santa Cruz. To blow up these factories, the Pentagon recently sent a half-dozen helicopters with 160 American soldiers to Viru Viru International Airport, the airport that Johnny landed at in Santa Cruz. The mission, commemorated in *Clear and Present Danger* ("Mother of God!" a kingpin cries as a factory explodes like Dresden)— the mission eliminated one lone factory and no kingpin at all.

Our own kingpin is not deterred by the American soldiers somewhere nearby. At night, Johnny, in a white silk suit, white shirt and tie, and $1,000 white crocodile shoes just a bit chipped from the cobblestone streets—Johnny, dressed like Mark Twain, and Johnny's four bodyguards (one with three fingers, nicknamed Three Fingers) and the Bolivian and his bodyguards dine at the Executive Restaurant. The appetizer is ceviche, or fish marinated in olive oil, lemon juice, spices, the soup is bouillabaisse, or crabs, clams, scallops, shrimps, steamed fish, the entrée is Chinese mussels in a spiced tomato sauce: all added up, it's better than the clammy rice in the Golden Triangle. On stage is a tango dancer from Argentina, staring at his black-skirted partner as if relentlessly telling her, "You're under my power, señorita." After dinner, Johnny goes to the Hotel Camino Real ("If you want a Spanish girl . . ." "No, thank you, I'm tired") and in the morning flies to Paraguay with the Bolivian businessman.

ASUNCIÓN

"You want to taste it?" the Bolivian asks Johnny in English. His sample of Snow White (100-something pounds) arrived by car today as he arrived with Johnny by Aereo Boliviano. By now it's evening, and the two men are driving in circles around the terminal for dusty buses from cities like Caacupé, Caapucú and Caazapá. In every shop that they pass sit Paraguayans drinking maté, the drink of the gods, drinking it from gourds, wooden cups, silver chalices, drinking it through ornamented silver straws, drinking it to the last little drop, to the last little slurping sound. The maté, though everyone is addicted to it in Paraguay, is not proscribed in America, unlike the white powder like Johnny's familiar heroin that the Bolivian reaches under the driver's seat for a Ziploc bag of. "It's cocaine," the Bolivian says. "You taste it?"

"How taste it?" asks Johnny.

"Put on finger. Put on teeth."

Johnny complies. A boy behind the woodshed testing a Camel, he tentatively dips a finger into the Ziploc bag, then rubs the C-dust against his gums—his gums turn numb, and Johnny says, "Fuck! It's strong!"

"You feel right away?"

"Yes, they feel numb."

"Good quality cocaine."

"Whole shipment this good?"

"Whole shipment. But some got wet."

"Wet?" cries Johnny. "Water in heroin isn't good!"

"It isn't water. It's gasoline."

"Gasoline?"

"We put the cocaine in Ziploc bags. We put the bags in the gasoline tank. Some of the gasoline seeped in. But you don't worry about it. We—"

"I can't sell!" Johnny cries.

"To make cocaine, we—"

"Never do I fuck customers!"

"—we use kerosene. It's like gasoline. It goes away like steam. I guarantee," the Bolivian says. He drives to Johnny's two-story villa and, in the guest bedroom, lays out the Asunción newspaper *Ultima Hora* and the one-hundred-and-something pounds of Exxon-smelling cocaine. "Come back in forty-eight hours," the Bolivian says. "You'll see."

For the next forty-eight hours, Johnny visits brothers like Dopey, who, his Beretta sequestered, his $15,000 penalty paid, is truly watching the water behind the Itaipú Dam. He's just had a baby daughter that Johnny dandles, offers a rubber-nippled bottle to, and in Cantonese coos to,

"Don't cry. Don't cry. I'm here. Don't cry." Then, Johnny drives back to his villa and (one more nickname) to the Bazooka Bubble Gum, all purged of petrolic vapors. He takes out a vial of see-through liquid from the NYPD (by way of the brother with the Cowboys cap) and, with a coke spoon, puts in a little cocaine, shakes it for ten seconds, observes the liquid turn blue, sort of Dresden blue, compares this to an NYPD color chart, and tells the Bolivian businessman, "Good quality. Send to Panama City." In competition with the Colombians, Johnny now traffics (not counting alcohol)—in America's two most dangerous drugs.

PANAMA CITY

The double bubble goes by sea as Johnny goes by air to Tocumen International Airport, then by BMW to his hillside estate near President Noriega's. War has just broken out on a tin-soldier scale in Johnny's own living room, for his daughter enjoys the TV news and his son (her kid brother) enjoys the Japanese ninja flicks, and as Johnny comes home today, his daughter's at the TV remote control and his son's at the TV set, the kids zapping to and fro and yelling at one another in Cantonese, "Stop it!" Zap, and it's reality, the war in Nicaragua. Zap, and it's fantasy now, the war in Nagoya. "Daddy! Tell him to stop it!" or "Daddy! Tell her to stop it!" the kids cry in Cantonese to Johnny, who takes his daughter aside and says, "You're older, he's younger, be patient with him," and takes his son aside and says, "You're a boy, she's a girl, be gentle with her." "You two mustn't fight," Johnny tells them both, tells them as world-wearily as he once behaved at the Coliseum. "I'm more than a business-man now," Johnny tells them, "I'm now a Big Brother. You don't understand me, but I'm very busy and can't run around dousing fires."

Firemen, policemen, diplomats, Dragonheads: they put other people's fires out. And now there erupts another one: the telephone rings and it's Michael Jackson, the soft-spoken boss in New York, saying in Cantonese, "Big Brother. A war's about to break out in New York," and, saying goodbye to all five children and Jonquil, Johnny plods back to his BMW, to Tocumen International Airport, and to an airplane to the Big Apple, the Apple all his brothers want the most succulent bite of.

JohnSack

23

Stir-Fried Squid

The War of New York (a squabble right now, a war if Johnny can't stop it) was started in the early hours today by an incomparable soldier name of Wang, nickname of Big Banana. The underboss to the Star, last night he went to a crowded casino in Chinatown to play some poker—Chinese poker, thirteen cards to a hand—with fellow members of the Big Circle. At his table was Johnny's first convert, Fat Ass, smoking his Kents, chewing his toothpicks, spitting his jetsam, and at one in the morning discarding a card out of turn inadvertently, something like that. You and I would have said, "Whoa," but Big Banana (his nickname owed to his nose, which splatted across half his face) prided himself on how tough he was, tough as a tenpenny nail. A former Red Guard in Canton, he'd fled in the 1970s to Macao, robbed a glittering watch store, taken hits from the Macao Municipal Police. Bullets in his shoulders, bullets in his legs, he'd jumped from a second-story window of the Count of Saint January Hospital, he'd escaped on a fishing float to Kowloon, and, after recuperating, he'd become the Star's staunch bodyguard. When recently, in Monterey Park, the Star was shot during dinner, the soldier who grabbed for the gun and was himself shot was Big Banana, who recuperated in Massachusetts. A human bull's-eye, the Banana (as he's also called) is frightened of one little thing, nothing else: the suspicion by any living being that he isn't tough, tough, tough, and it was this fear that seized him in Chinatown when Fat Ass, his mind for a moment absent, discarded a card when he wasn't supposed to. Not telling Fat Ass "Whoa," Big Banana just jumped up, shouted in Cantonese, "You cheated me," and punched him.

The two started fighting. The others separated them. And now it's one day later, it's teatime at Johnny's vinyl-sided house on Austin Street, in Rego Park, and to and fro in the living room like an angry grizzly pads Fat Ass. "Everyone respects me, Big Brother. Everyone except Big Banana," he growls to Johnny in Cantonese. "He pulled down my face in Chinatown. So he thinks he's tough? Well, I'm tough too. If you let me, I'll shoot his brains out," says Fat Ass, slapping his hip, his black leather holster, and his Colt .45. "Did people tell you? He hit me in Chinatown. How *dare* he, Big Brother? Someone must be behind him. That man must be the Star. But how did the *Star* dare do it?" Of course the man behind the Star is Johnny, and Fat Ass is not-too-subtly asking him, "Are *you* behind him, Big Brother?"

"I don't think someone's behind him."

"Then let me kill him!"

"You'll be at war with the Star, then."

"I can just see it! Sitting inside a restaurant is Big Banana. I go to him and *bam,* and blow him away. I don't need anyone's help. Why can't I do it, Big Brother?"

"Because there'll be war with the Star."

"Peace! Always you're talking peace!"

"We're family, Fatty."

"Oh, how I wish it," says Fat Ass, and sits down at Johnny's coffee table. His half-smoked cigarette, he grinds out in Johnny's ashtray and, his hand not stopping, lights up another one. "Big Brother? Why are these motherfuckers in America, anyway? You bought them a $100,000 fishing float. You got them out of Kowloon, then Bangkok, then Los Angeles. You threw all your money into the sea. What have they done for you? Nothing but hurt you," says Fat Ass, and not too unreasonably. "Please excuse me, Big Brother," says Fat Ass, and grinds out his second half-cigarette. "But next time they hit me, I'll kill them right there." At *kill,* his hand slaps the coffee table, his hand is for once immobile, and on his hand his ever-patient auditor puts his own.

"Next time," says Saint Johnny. "Not this time."

NEW YORK

One fire out, one fire to go. Today Johnny waits in the parking lot of the Midway Motel, on Horace Harding Boulevard in Elmhurst. Up drive some former soldiers of Crew Cut's, Johnny gets into the car's back seat, and the soldier-driver stares at the rear-view mirror—at Johnny— while circling on 97th, 98th and 99th Streets. Twisting around, the soldier in the passenger seat commences a narrative as tangled as any in Agatha Christie. "Big Brother, the Star killed Crew Cut," the soldier says in Cantonese. "Now, that wasn't fair. If the Star killed Tony, that's fair, for Tony is the man who shot the Star. If the Star killed Tony's accomplice, that's also fair. But why did the Star kill Crew Cut? He was innocent, Crew Cut. He respected the Star. His closest friend was the Star. Big Brother," says the man in the passenger seat, slapping his hip and his gun, "I want to *lon* the Star. Will you approve it?"

"No," Johnny almost moans. "And don't even *tell* the Star you're aware that the Star killed Crew Cut. If the Star asks about him, tell him the last you heard was that he had passport problems in São Paulo. If the Star asks about White Snake, tell him the last you heard was that he left for New York. Act ignorant. Then these troubles will end. Day after day you won't try to kill the Star, and day after day the Star won't try to kill *you*. You can start making money again."

"As you say, Big Brother."

And drip. Another day ends for the New York Fire Department. His energies spent, Johnny goes home to Austin Street, a mile away in Rego Park. His black leather shoes coming off, his burgundy corduroy jacket coming off, his black leather belt a couple of notches looser, he falls on his bed supine. *Oh, what a rotten business drugs are,* Johnny thinks. His father would say it—his father was right. He sprawls on the bed recalling all the betrayals (how many were there? so far there were ten) and all the murders ensuing from them in the course of his periodic transactions in the Big H, the Big C. Fur, watches, diamonds, audiotapes—in each of his businesses were risks as well as rewards, but the risk-reward ratio in drugs was the least advantageous of all. Drugs brought money, money brought greed, greed more money, money more greed, and the whole endless daisy chain brought trouble with a ten-foot T. *Should I,* thinks Johnny, *close down the heroin-cocaine operation? should the Big Circle do just legitimate business? should we be stir-fried squids?* be dropouts in Chinese gangster slang? And even as Johnny lies pondering this, the answer appears in rainbow colors at the foot of his rumpled bed.

New York

The answer appears in cathode rays on Channel 4. This isn't the first time in Johnny's career that a newspaper, radio or TV story about the repercussions of heroin or cocaine has engaged the attention of their foremost importer to the United States. Often, Johnny has read, heard or seen how an American addict, devoid of a $10 bag, had fired a pistol, stabbed a knife, pulled a garrote—had murdered someone just to swipe a $10 bill from his or her wallet, and Johnny has thought morosely, *Ten bucks. That's what that person's life was worth.* One day in the New York *Daily News* he read of an addict who, for his $10 bag, his paper bag, his biz, had robbed and killed his own mother, and Johnny thought, *How could he do it? Even an animal knows that if it didn't have a mother it wouldn't survive. Why didn't the addict know it?* Another time in the *Daily News,* he read of an addict who, for his bag, had beat up his wife and robbed the coins she'd saved for the baby's milk. *Well, I suppose he's happy now,* Johnny thought. *His baby isn't happy, though. What will he feed the baby now? Water? Straight from the tap? Or will he put sugar in?* At the time, every pathetic story put a fissure in Johnny's heart, but the story tonight on TV is one that just shatters it. On the screen is a hospital nursery and in the cribs are babies: crack babies, born addicted to Johnny's new product, cocaine.

Are babies foredoomed. As slow as a bone-scan machine, the TV camera examines one of their meager bodies: its BB-shot toes, soda-straw legs, diapered waist, its sunken chest like a cigarette addict's, its O-

shaped mouth, incessantly wailing: wailing (if one may attempt to inter-
pret that *waa*) not "Mommy, I want your milk," but "Mommy, I want
another fix." One day old, and the babies in front of Johnny are trying to
shake their monkeys off, are trying to kick their nine-month habit. Like
the Professor's phony glasses, their eyes seem to focus on nothing this
side of infinity but on unimaginable galaxies beyond it. "It's tragic," a
nurse at the hospital tells a reporter for Channel 4: it is indeed, though
not in an Aristotelian way, for the babies don't suffer a tragic flaw, fault,
imperfection: no, what's tragic is sum and substance of who they are and
probably ever will be. Each little child is a gaping wound, nothing more,
a wound (like the face of a man with yaws) with no nonpathological tis-
sue around it. *I never knew this,* thinks Johnny, who never knew he had
customers one day old. *It's terrible, terrible.*

He always liked babies, Johnny did. He dandled them even if half their
genes derived from a not-too-beautiful donor like Dopey. The brothers
who told him, "If I betray you, I'll accept death without complaint,"
meant much, much less to Johnny than Jonquil's son, the one who told
him, "I'm daddy's boy." That boy and his younger brother died in Cambodia, died innocently, and it was to avenge them that Johnny shipped
half a ton of heroin and a projected ton of cocaine to their assassins in
America: it *wasn't* to commit a copycat crime and to abuse other innocent children, children as yet unconceived during the war in Vietnam,
Cambodia, Laos. It wasn't to put this or that white powder into a Ziploc
bag and to cart it halfway around the planet into an infant's arteries at
Fifth Avenue Hospital. *Thump thump!* The infant's heart beats, and to his
toetips, fingertips, brain goes a dollop of Johnny's heroin, Johnny's
cocaine—no, Johnny's intention wasn't that. The story on TV concluding,
commercials commencing, Johnny, supine on his bed, his head on his
hands, his eyes on his plaster ceiling, prays to his virtuous father, his
father who told him, "Never touch opium! Never!" "Daddy," whispers
Johnny now in Shanghai dialect. "You were right about drugs. I'm sorry
I disobeyed you. My children are dead, and I can't bring them back, but
I can save other children. Daddy, I'll stop selling drugs."

By his bed is an ivory telephone that Johnny doesn't dare use. Putting
his black leather shoes back on, he walks to a booth at Alexander's

department store, on Queens Boulevard, and, one after another, calls up the quarreling bosses. He summons them to a site that isn't quite under the clock at the Biltmore (teacakes, that's what the Biltmore would serve them) but under the crystal-chandeliered lobby of the Penta, once Pennsylvania, Hotel.

NEW YORK

To the Penta the bosses come with an agenda that's the inverse of Johnny's. For one and one half years, none of their drugs have eluded the American customs inspectors. The first contretemps was in Seattle, 138 ice buckets seized. The next was in New York, at Kennedy, four brass fishes seized, fishes full of heroin where the caviar ought to be. The latest was in Manila, untold dozens of chairs, armchairs, microwaves and refrigerators grounded in an American warehouse. The heroin trade in America is still being run by Chinese secret societies—the Gang of Loyal Tranquillity, the Gang of Righteous Tranquillity, the gangs that Johnny recruited, telling them, "We can take over," but it's not run to the slightest degree by Johnny's Big Circle. "Big Brother. We're starving," say Fat Ass, Wrist Watch, Michael Jackson, the Movie Star, the ABC with the Cowboys cap, Big Banana, and a half-dozen others in Cantonese at lunch at the Penta today. "We need some goods. We need them now."

The bosses and Johnny are underground, under the Penta's resplendent lobby in the Globetrotter Restaurant. They may be its only customers who aren't in the fashion world, for the Penta stands on Seventh, or Fashion, Avenue, the Globetrotter is a popular place for designers, photographers, models, all of them dressed in *le dernier cri,* and in this chichi environment even the ABC wears his Cowboys cap pointed forward. In thin brass frames on the walls, sketches of what was *à la mode* in every decade since the flappers look down upon the Big Circle. For the 20s it's Fortuny, for the 30s it's Vionnet, for the 40s it's Patou. For the 50s it's Balenciaga, two evening dresses, one of green satin with a halter neckline, one of green layered chiffon with a gathered hemline, each with an added hairpiece: one a coq-feather question mark, one a Maltese cross. For the 60s it's Gernreich, the topless bathing suit. For the 70s it's

Zandra Rhodes, a dress with an open ellipse, exposing a daring navel, and for the 80s (the present decade) it's Channel, a beaded *traje de luces* like a proud matador's, except with a V-neck. It's under the stares of these stately models that Johnny addresses the bosses now, the indigent bosses who told him, "We need some goods." "I'm your Big Brother," Johnny begins in Cantonese, a Schiaparelli behind him, a jacket of shocking pink with a bow of black-and-white stripes. "It's wrong if my neighbors eat shark's-fin soup and my little brothers eat hot dogs," his brothers, in fact, are chomping on filets mignons at the Globetrotter now. "You say you need goods? Well, you're getting goods. I haven't told you," Johnny continues, "but in the pipeline right now is white powder worth $3,000,000, white powder worth $12,500,000, and *colo,*" cocaine, "worth $32,000,000. Soon they'll be in New York. But when they're here," Johnny continues as the incomparable bosses gasp, "we'll quit, we'll stop selling drugs, we'll become legit. We'll invest the $47,500,000."

"Invest?" asks a boss, unused to this high-faluting word.

"We'll put all the $47,500,000 into legitimate businesses."

"What businesses?" asks someone.

"Like restaurants?" someone else.

"A nice idea," Johnny compliments him. "We could open a restaurant up in Times Square. A restaurant, though, is a pretty piddling business. We'd have to get up at four every morning to buy the fish, meat, vegetables. By midnight we'd have to sell every sole—no, we'll want to sell something grander."

"Like—?" asks someone, mystified.

"Like anything at all. Like ketchup," says Johnny, hoisting a Heinz bottle off the pink-tableclothed table. "Like this knife, fork, spoon," he continues, brandishing every one. "Medicine," meaning drugs, "isn't the only thing you can sell. You can sell these matches, even."

"How can I make money from matches?"

"Buy them low. Sell them high. Look," Johnny perseveres, brandishing a book of Globetrotter matches. "Say the cardboard costs an American cent. Say the phosphorous costs an American cent. Say the labor costs an American cent, and say the transportation from the production point costs an American cent. All right: these matches cost four American cents. But you can sell them to the Globetrotter Restaurant for *five* American cents. *Ye,"* says Johnny, a Cantonese word that means *voilà*. "You make one American cent."

"That's what I mean, Big Brother. How can I make *money* from matches?"

"Simple. You sell one hundred million matchbooks. That's $1,000,000."

Some bosses squint. Others stare vacantly at the Schiaparelli in back of Johnny, the jacket, the black satin sheath. *Who do I know,* they think as in their minds' eyes they scan their connections in Chinatown, Brooklyn and Queens, *who'd buy a hundred million matchbooks, matchbooks imprinted the Globetrotter Restaurant?* Speaking for all the bewildered people around him, one boss says in Cantonese, "Whatever you say, Big Brother."

"No," Johnny says, sensing why no one has fathomed him. "You don't sell the matches in Chinatown. You sell them in Ohio, Iowa, California, all across the United States. Yes," he continues, observing the still-squinting people. "You sell them in English. You'll have to learn it."

"We know English already," says someone in Cantonese.

"You know *good morning, good afternoon*. Can you say in English, I manufacture matchbooks? Can you say in English, $1,000,000?"

"One miyyon dowwas," the man says in English.

"How about $10,000,000? Can you say that?"

"No," the man confesses in Cantonese.

"I'll teach you English. I'll teach you," says Johnny, "all about capitalism. Say you sell matchbooks. The *profit,"* continues Johnny, saying *profit* in English, "for one book is one American cent. The *profit* for one hundred million books is $1,000,000. *One million dollars,"* continues Johnny in English, acknowledging the man who originally said, "One miyyon dowwas." "A knife, fork, spoon, a Paraguay watch, there's *profit* from every one. Not from white powder alone. Not from cocaine alone. Does everyone understand me?"

"Whatever you say, Big Brother."

"Now," says Johnny, "your *cost* is $4,000,000, your *profit* is $1,000,000, your *profit margin* therefore is? Is twenty-five percent. Some items, like Paraguay watches," and Johnny holds one of the bosses' wrists as an audiovisual aid, "have a high *profit margin*. Others, like Coca-Cola," and Johnny raises one of the bosses' glasses, "have a low *profit margin*. Of course we'll want a business with a high *profit margin*."

"If you say so, Big Brother."

"Next," says Johnny, and his class in Capitalism 101 continues till Johnny says, "We will make money by *using* money, that's what our future will be."

"We're for it, Big Brother," the bosses say, but in their minds they're picturing the $3,000,000 shipment, the $12,500,000 shipment, and the $32,000,000 shipment, and in their minds they're computing that $47,500,000 will finance a full year's gambling—finance, that is, if they manage to hold their losses to $1,000,000 per week.

After dessert, Johnny goes to Kennedy International Airport and boards an Asia-bound airplane. How sweet it would be if Johnny could run his new legitimate businesses (and live with his loved ones) in Hong Kong! Johnny Kon Ketchup, Limited! Johnny Kon Tableware, Limited! But Johnny's a fugitive from the Royal Police, the unstatutory owner of Johnny Kon Passports, and it's not Hong Kong but Singapore that he's bound for. He can't go home till he neutralizes the one willing witness against him, the tattletale navigator of his ill-starred fishing float, the *Victory*.

CHIANG MAI

And where is that sky-eyed sailor? Shh. With help from the witness protection people in Hong Kong, he has sailed to faraway places like Amsterdam, Rotterdam, Hamburg and Capetown, but, on hearing in every port that Chinese men were searching for him, he's hiding out far from the briny blue on a lichee and longan honey farm here in Thailand. He doesn't know that at every such farm in Thailand, Chinese men have been dropping in, looking around, buying (say) ten jars of luscious sunflower honey, asking, "Does someone speak Cantonese?" He doesn't know that in back of his honey truck one day, two Chinese men on a motorcycle tailed him, strayed off the road, toppled down the mountain, broke their heads. But one day, walking out to his gate, stretching, picking up a Chinese newspaper, glancing at Chinese headlines saying, "More Vietnamese Refugees," leaving the gate an inch ajar, and starting back to his home, he hears someone call him in Cantonese, saying, "Hey, Steven!"

Turning around, the navigator asks, "Who are you?"

"I'm from Hong Kong," his visitor says, then pulls out a .38 revolver. As dolls at Disneyland say, it's really a small world, after all, for the visitor is another of Johnny's incomparable bosses, named Crazy Chun. Though born in Taiwan, Crazy looks more like a Japanese gangster (another nickname of his is Little Yakuza)—he's fluent in Japanese, his neck to his ankles is swathed in red, green, black and blue dragon tattoos, and he runs clubs, casinos, brothels (the girls are Chinese) in Tokyo. For the last half-dozen years he's smuggled for Johnny, smuggled his fur, counterfeit currency, diamonds, watches, and his well-liked white powder into Tokyo. He almost worships Johnny, bowing to him as Japanese do to Emperor Hirohito: eyes facing the floor, while he whispers to him in Mandarin, "Big Brother." He once opened a red silk bag and gave him a $300,000 necklace: thirteen pearls, all of them natural, none of them cultured, one of gumball diameter, the rest incrementally smaller, gave them to Johnny saying, "These are for Jonquil," Jonquil who (not even knowing that Crazy had robbed it) wouldn't really want to gad about town in a $300,000 necklace. Of all the bosses, the one most ready to die for Johnny in the line of secret-society duty is Crazy. Once, while sitting at an etched window (etched with a bamboo forest) eating some Japanese noodle soup at the Café Royal Park in Tokyo, Crazy told him in Mandarin, "I'll never betray you. If I'm arrested, I'll kill myself." It was three months ago a soldier of Crazy's met the low-lying navigator serendipitously, met him at breakfast at a white formica table full of papayas, pomelos, pineapples, rambutans at the Hotel Narai Coffee Shop in Bangkok, the navigator mentioned that he raised honeybees and Crazy has practically combed every comb in Thailand in search of the man since then. And now he's found him and says, "I'm from Hong Kong," and pulls out a .38 and fires once, twice, thrice, and, one eye east and one eye west, the navigator falls on his doorstep, dead.

For sure? Up from the gate runs another boss, a man dressed like

Crazy in a Thai farmer's cotton clothes, conical hat, but armed with a .45 automatic instead of a .38. And *bam!* into each other crash the two bosses, almost falling, recovering, and boss number two says, "Did you kill him?"

"I killed him!"

"I'll make sure!" the second boss says, he too fires once, twice, thrice, the navigator flops like a fish on the deck of a fishing float, then, as down from upstairs come the witness protection people, firing at the atmosphere around the second boss and Crazy, hitting the atmosphere, missing the men, the two men rush through the gate, jump into a Japanese pickup truck, cry in Mandarin, "We did it!" do an American snappy high-five, pedal to the metal, and disappear into the dizzying traffic (trucks, taxis, cars, and tuk-tuks like three-wheeled golf carts) in the streets of Chiang Mai.

SINGAPORE

Ding dong! The witch is dead! In the heretofore solemn lobby of the Mandarin Singapore Hotel, the marble wall engraved with a giant gilded drawing of the Empress of Heaven (the Mother of God)—the Empress receiving birthday gifts like a flute, recorder, mandolin, scroll, and a serving of long-life dumplings, the gifts being borne to her by the Eighty Immortals, the Chinese inscription saying,

> *Empress of Heaven,*
> *The poet writes that*
> *You're beautiful —*

in the heretofore decorous lobby are Crazy, the second murderer, and Johnny, and at the door the Sikh in white turban, black jacket, white breeches, probably wonders, *Who are these people, long-lost brothers?* as the three brothers hug and dance circles around the *faux* glass fountain and cry in Mandarin, "We did it!" Still ecstatic, they take the pink-granite-floored elevator up to the thirty-fifth floor and the Pine Court, the Chinese restaurant there. In front of it stands a carved wooden screen to intercept all evil spirits (which, according to *feng shui* consultants, can't turn left or right) and in front of this barrier stands a rosewood statue of Kuan Kung, the God of Loyalty, that Johnny and the two bosses now bow to. Inside the Pine Court, its decor like that of the Palace of Celestial Purity, in Beijing, its carpet by the same people who did Windsor Castle, its tables rosewood, its chairs rosewood, its walls painted with Chinese flowers, with plum blossoms, peonies and pines, its ceiling festooned with Chinese lanterns, six to a cluster, dozens of clusters—inside it the brothers have beer and Johnny crows in Mandarin, "Now I'll return to Hong Kong!"

If wishes were horses. On the way out of the Pine Court, the brothers pass a stonemason's wall with the Chinese inscription,

> *The clear wind blows for me,*
> *But sprinkled on the stones*
> *Is frost,*

and soon there comes to Singapore a very important person from Hong Kong. A crony of Johnny's, tonight he's Johnny's guest at the Compass Rose, the breathtaking restaurant on the seventieth floor of the skyscraper hotel the Westin Stamford. From its circumferential windows he (and the Singapore girl that Johnny provides him) see the whole shining city-state: the yellow lights along the river and in its ripples, reflected, the white lights of cars on the freeway, approaching, the red lights of cars on the freeway, receding, the white lights of after-hours offices, some as high as this restaurant, the red, white and blue neon advertisements ("IMPERIAL") on these buildings, the red lights to tell the pilots they're flying too low: the VIP sees all this and Malaysia and Indonesia, too. "I heard what happened," the VIP whispers to Johnny in Cantonese.

"You heard about Chiang Mai?"

"Everyone's heard in Hong Kong."

"I can return to Hong Kong, then?"

"You could return today. *Except,"* says the VIP, and from his suit pocket he pulls a white paper, a photocopy of a computer printout. On it in dot-matrix letters are

332

Kon Yu-Leung
Lau Shu-Ming
Yin Cheng-Ling,

etcetera, the names of Johnny, Wrist Watch, the Ghost, and four other brothers, also to Johnny's horror the name of Jonquil. "Some men came to the Royal Police," the VIP says as Johnny, his shrimp paste in fried sashimi still in his chopsticks, untouched, listens as if his life depended upon it. "They carried this list. They asked to see the dossiers of every-one on it. They took those dossiers. They left."

"Who were the men?"

"I don't know their names."

"They were from Hong Kong?"

"No," the VIP whispers. "They were Americans."

24
Ghost Chaser

BANGKOK

No longer Ivory white, more like Dial yellow, more than a hundred white-powder bricks (120, to be exact) stand as though they're a wall inside the frosted-window house next door to the Wanakarm Restaurant. "They faded, Big Brother," the brothers told Johnny in Cantonese recently. "Eggs, bread, powder, they must be white in New York. Off-white, people don't want in New York." By order of Johnny, the brothers take twenty old Dial bricks, forty new Ivory bricks, crumble them up and jumble them up, put the not-quite-white powder in two dozen hollow marble slabs, put the red-flecked marble in two dozen carved redwood frames, ship this as "24 antique chairs" to Panama City.

PANAMA CITY

Philistines! The brothers in Panama smash up the antique chairs, and into a tub they pour sixty bottles of (oh, enough's enough)—of Chivas Regal that Johnny bought at a duty-free store in Colon. The empty bottles, the brothers then use a hair drier to dry the insides of, then they refill these bottles with the not-quite-white powder. They put the bottles into twelve-bottle cartons along with 10,700 authentic bottles of Chivas Regal, and with invisible ink they put an "O" on every adulterated carton.

They ship this as "Chivas Regal" up to Miami, and night after night they dip their glasses into the tub of Chivas Regal in Panama City ("Not bad").

MIAMI

Into this port come 10,700 bottles of Chivas Regal and sixty bottles of "Chivas Regal," and, paying the tax, the brothers use the tools of technology (ultraviolet lights, bombarded onto invisible ink) to discriminate between the two powerful drugs. They sell the Chivas Regal in Miami, then load up the "Chivas Regal," drive it up Interstate 95, unload it on Austin Street, put one pound apiece into Ziploc bags, and sell it to Chinese middlemen instead of to Mafia, Mexicans, Dominicans, blacks. And bingo—that's $3,000,000 (and this year 1,572 people will die).

BANGKOK

That leaves a hundred bricks, all Dial, in the warehouse next to the Wanakarm Restaurant. The talented courier, Four Eyes, takes eighty bricks, crumbles them, takes 160 new Ivory bricks, crumbles *them,* mixes the two, and spoons them into Ziploc bags. He sandwiches these in thousands of T-shirts (none with inscriptions like "I♥NY") that he puts into cartons, labels as "T-shirts," ships to the Port of President Stroessner, Paraguay. But stingo—the Thai police intercept them. They seize the not-quite-white powder, worth $12,500,000. They arrest Four Eyes and imprison him in a real cesspool, excrement up to his shoulders. They beat him, break his ribs, and, when he passes out, throw water on him and torture him further, yelling in English, "Who are you working for?"

"No one!" cries Four Eyes, who's taken the oath of the Flaming Eagles, the oath that if he ever betrays, he must accept death without complaint. "I'm just working for me!"

PORT OF PRESIDENT STROESSNER

The T-shirts were consigned to Johnny's accountant at the Champion watch factory here. A quintessential accountant, a timid, polite, soft-spoken man, a Chinese cousin of Mr. Milquetoast, he doesn't know beans about the not-quite-white powder (which Johnny was to off-load in Panama City) or how this white powder differs from Johnson & Johnson's talcum. No matter: he too is arrested, imprisoned, tortured, this time by the Paraguayan police. He isn't extradited to the United States: too time-consuming, too many motions in Asunción, too many meddlesome lawyers saying, *"Señor juez,"* saying in Spanish, "Your Honor." He's simply thrown out of Paraguay, conveniently on a plane to Miami.

MIAMI

How coincidental! Wearing Dockers and waiting for the accountant at Miami International Airport are two DEA men who, not beating him, not breaking his ribs, handcuff him and accompany him on a plane to New York. There they will ask him, "You worked in Paraguay?"

"Yes."

"You worked at Champion Watches?"

"Yes."

"You worked for Johnny Kon?"

"Yes," the timid accountant will say. He also doesn't know beans about the Flaming Eagles and its "I'll accept death" drastic oaths.

ASUNCIÓN

A delicacy here is the soft white hearts of banana trees. They come in pint-sized cans that Johnny's cocaine connection, the Bolivian businessman, has filled with his foo-foo dust instead (not all the $32,000,000, only a $2,000,000 sample) and has shipped via Buenos Aires or as far as possible from Colombia to Panama City to Miami. But stingo again—the Paraguayan police arrest the Bolivian and imprison, torture and ask him, *"¿Por quien trabajas?* Who are you working for?"

"¡Por Johnny Kon!" says the Bolivian, who probably thinks that a Flaming Eagle is a Hot-Shot Two-Under-Par.

PANAMA CITY

Ten cartons, containing 240 cans, of scrumptious banana hearts stop en route to Miami and (as Johnny didn't pay the $4,000 per kilo or $240,000 to President Noriega) are seized by the Panamanian police. Then these efficient police come for Johnny, who, fleeing his mango-surrounded estate, speeding by BMW to Tucumen International Airport, boarding the blue-seated business class of Royal Dutch Airlines, receiving a tiny blue chinaware house with a jigger of Bols, and taking off to Santo Domingo, Amsterdam, Kuala Lumpur and Tokyo, is now a fugitive from Panama, too, from Panama as well as Hong Kong and (not even Johnny knows) perhaps the United States.

HAKONE

Heiwa. The word means peace in Japanese, means *shanti, salaam, shalom.* In the tranquil lake is an image of Fuji, upside-down, of Fuji totally dormant, of Fuji assuring the bass, smelt and trout that its last little drop of lava dripped out 280 years ago. The frame to this mirror is pine, snow-covered pines, to trod underneath them is *(crunch)* to trod on the softly moaning snow, on snow from which there mystically rises the steam of meandering springs. In the mist is a snow-roofed hotel, and in a suite in a spring-water-nourished tiled tub is Johnny, thinking, thinking, the skin on the bridge of his nose scrunched up, his eyes seeming tighter together, thinking. In the hot sulfur-smelling water with him is a Chinese girlfriend, not Dominique, a girl aged twenty-seven sipping a tall glass of orange juice asking in Shanghai dialect, "What are you thinking about?"

"My business," says Johnny.

"Can I massage you?"

"Not now."

His hand a gossamer fan, he not impolitely dismisses her. The object of Johnny's stubborn concentration is *Who is the ghost? the golden finger?* or, as we say in America, the snitch, the sneak, the stoolie inside the Big Circle? Who (for clearly there's someone, thinks Johnny, thinks Johnny correctly, because the multiple busts in Asia and the Americas can't be

337

just serendipitous)—who in his gang is ratting on him and his top-secret shipments, ratting to the DEA and its counterparts in Bangkok, Asunción, and Panama City? Among the blood brothers, there isn't one even in prison who Johnny isn't suspicious of, nor is there one he isn't *ashamed* he's suspicious of. Fat Ass, Fat Cat, Three Fingers, Four Eyes, Wrist Watch, Green Snake, Big Banana, Michael Jackson, Crazy Chun, Dopey, Tiger, Tony, Tommy, Tony's accomplice, the ABCs, the Star, the General, the Ghost—all these brothers (and hundreds unnamed) could be and certainly *couldn't* be the poltergeist who is sounding off to Asia's and the Americas' hats. The skin on his nose-bridge squeezes, it emits little drops like a lemon, clenched, beneath it his brain becomes crushed pulp, a tangle of incompatible thoughts. An hour of this lemon-pressing at last produces seeds, and Johnny in his tub concludes that the man most likely to be the traitorous ghost is the Ghost himself: the Eurasian, the man whose mother was Asian, his father an American marine: either that or an Arab, he can't remember, whose name at birth was Yin: or wasn't, he can't remember, who carries passports from the United States, China, Thailand, Japan, France, Switzerland, Brazil, Bolivia, Colombia, Costa Rica, the Dominican Republic, and Saudi Arabia, who lost two passports (two different names, two different birthdays, one red-haired photograph) once in a taxi in Hong Kong and, to get them, bribed a sergeant in the Royal Police, who when Johnny first met him six years ago at the New Miramar Hotel (Johnny ordering borsht, the Ghost a ham-and-egg sandwich) admitted in Shanghai dialect, "I'm confused. I don't know who I am, but I don't care."

He cannot be counted on, the Ghost. At the Miramar, Johnny gave him $500,000 of counterfeit traveler's checks to cash in Tokyo: these the Ghost did, but when he returned with the $45,000 profit he called up Johnny, told him in Shanghai dialect, "I'm in my room at the Miramar," and, pooped by too many *sake*-salutes, passed out, the telephone still in his dangling hand. *He's sick, he's dead,* Johnny worried, hearing a busy signal buzz for the hundredth time. *He's been arrested, he's fingered me, and the hats are looking for me.* A bellboy at the Miramar at last arousing him, the Ghost called Johnny past midnight and said in Shanghai dialect, "No, I was just tired."

"All night I've been worried!"

"I took sleeping pills, too."

"If you were tired, why?"

"Also some Scotches."

"I'm angry about this!"

"It won't happen again."

But happen it almost always did. Japan, Bolivia, Brazil—wherever Johnny sent the Ghost, force majeure interfered, and the Ghost overstayed by days, sometimes months. Once, Johnny sent him to Bangkok, and after ages the Ghost returned with a beautiful girl who, soon after that, slit her wrists with a razor blade in a room at the Fortuna Hotel and was rescued by Johnny's worried bosses. Taken to Johnny's kangaroo-carpeted office, handed a Kleenex, she started sobbing in Mandarin, "I love Ronny," I love the Ghost.

"Is he your lover?" Johnny asked.

"Yes. He took my money, too."

"And now you're penniless?"

"He told me I could smuggle."

"Why did you attempt suicide?"

"He left me for someone else."

Appalled, Johnny called the Ghost (his hair that day red, the roots brown) onto the kangaroo carpet and said, "I'm ashamed! You aren't a standing guy," his left fist hitting his chest, his Shanghai dialect meaning "A righteous guy." "What if the girl were your sister? What if a guy had diddled with *her?* How would you feel? We're gangsters, but also we're human beings!"

"It won't happen again."

At times Johnny had to rescue the Ghost. One time, the Ghost had borrowed $50,000 to buy some stolen traveler's checks. He'd borrowed the $50,000 from a gangster, but he hadn't repaid it. The gangster had phoned him ("Come see me") but he hadn't come. "Why do you cheat the *bad* guys?" Johnny asked him in Shanghai dialect.

"I don't cheat them, Big Brother."

"They call you and you don't come."

"If I did, they would kill me."

"Why don't you cheat the *good* guys?"

"They won't do business with me. I ask them for $50,000 to buy some stolen traveler's checks. They don't trust me."

Johnny laughed. He lent him the $50,000, but one year later the Ghost owed another gangster $150,000 ("I'll break your Achilles tendon") and Johnny had to lend him the $150,000, too. Even brothers like Four Eyes, who once was the Ghost's associate, and the Sergeant wanted to kill him. Once, Johnny fired him: took him to lunch at the Empress Hotel in Hong Kong (black pepper steak for Johnny, grouper fish for the Ghost) and told him, "You can't be counted on. You always come back late. In front of my store are a thousand customers, and the sign on my door says CLOSED. I can't wait for you, Ronny. You must quit this business. You aren't suited for it."

"All right," said the Ghost, his hair that day red, the tips purple. "I'll open a coffee shop in Taipei."

"Good," Johnny said. "You have enough money for one. If you need more, just call me," but Johnny thought too, *I should kill him. He knows too much. If he's ever arrested, he'll squeal to the DEA.* And now in Hakone, Japan, among the sulfur-smelling steaming springs, a land once known as Oojigoku, the greatest hell, but tactfully changed to Oowaku-dani, the greatest waterfall, when a Japanese emperor visited it, Johnny sits thinking, *Who is more liable to sell out his brothers than (as they call him) the Tardy Ghost? Yes, the traitor's the Ghost,* Johnny thinks. He climbs from the tub, wraps a great towel around him, asks his Chinese girlfriend in Shanghai dialect, "What time is it?"

"It's after six."

"Let's eat," says Johnny, and he, she, and her ineffectual chaperone (her mother) go out for sukiyaki, cooked at their varnished table.

SINGAPORE

"Ronny," Johnny begins, interrogating the Ghost in Shanghai dialect in an oh-so-casual way at the New Otani Hotel, at a table by a golden four-paneled screen full of red-headed black-necked cranes at the River Terrace Restaurant. "I think there's a traitor among us."

"So do I. We have such bad luck. Do you know who he is?" asks the Ghost, his hair brown, the tips red, his eyes shifting possibly guiltily to the pentagonal swimming pool past Johnny's left ear. Faxes, phones, scramblers-unscramblers—Johnny has wires around the civilized world, but he hasn't any to this man's mind, eighteen inches away.

"I think it's the Star. Do you?"

"Maybe it is," says the Ghost. A waitress in a sarong approaches, and from the lilac-and-lavender menu and its *laksa lemak* and *rojak* (jellyfish with lotuses, pineapples, peanuts, and prawn paste) the Ghost chooses coffee-and-cream.

"This traitor," Johnny continues. "I'm chasing him. What if I find him?"

"Don't let him go, Big Brother. You've got to kill him. I'll help you."

"Thank you, Ronny," Johnny concludes, Johnny who's thinking, *This motherfucker. Why did he tell me, "I'll help you"? He wouldn't kill a chicken.*

TAIPEI

Scoping out the Ghost tonight is Johnny's frequent bodyguard Tiger, who spotted him at that fabulous pleasure palace the Fuhao (Luxurious) Night Club. With the Ghost are two tall men: two Americans, as Tiger learns when a girl onstage sings in Taiwanese,

Olive tree, I'm not going home tonight,

and the two men in long-sleeved white shirts start dancing with two Chinese slit-skirted girls. Walking onto the Fuhao's floor, Tiger beckons the Ghost, shoves his shoulder roughly, yells at him in Cantonese, "You brought Americans here. Why?"

"They—they're my *friends.*"

"You can't afford them. You owe me $10,000."

"I—I'll pay you *tomorrow.*"

"Don't bullshit with me," Tiger tells him, then leaves, then calls up Johnny in Tokyo, saying in Cantonese, "You know who the traitor is? It's the Tardy Ghost."

TOKYO

Slipping a plastic card into one of the intricate telephones lined up like slot machines at Narita International Airport is Johnny. In the next booth, he spots a man with ridiculous red-dyed hair, and he taps the Ghost's shoulder—startled, the Ghost jumps around. "Why are you scared?" asks Johnny in Shanghai dialect.

"I—I was calling Taipei," whispers the Ghost, implying he was calling about drugs.

"What are you doing?" asks Johnny, meaning what drugs?

"Amphetamine," whispers the Ghost.

"Is there money in it?"

"Yes, $10,000 per kilo," whispers the Ghost. Amphetamine, made in Taipei, and not heroin or cocaine is the most sought-after drug in Japan, sought by 600,000 restless addicts. "I've got eighty kilos in Tokyo," whispers the Ghost. "Do you want them?"

"Yes," says Johnny instantly. It isn't that uppies, uppers, leapers, rippers, thrusters, bumblebees, call these amphetamines what you will, are a major missing ingredient in Johnny's pharmacopoeia. It's that if Johnny can buy these cartwheels from the Ghost, then Johnny will know that the Ghost hasn't blabbed to the DEA, for the DEA doesn't let its informers deal drugs. For $800,000, quickly recouped, Johnny will know that the ghost, the golden finger, who has disabled his heroin-cocaine operation in Asia and the Americas is some other scoundrel than the Ghost. "Yes," Johnny tells him. "Get a one-kilo sample. Take it to the Washington Hotel. Rent a small locker in the lobby, second floor. Put the sample inside it. I'm staying at the Washington, bring me the key."

"I will," says the Ghost, departing to his amphetamine den, then to the Washington Hotel. As far as the Ghost can see, the same sort of Japanese man who designed the Narita telephones and the Nintendo games designed the three-keyhole lockers in the Washington's lobby. Seeing that (1) a green light is on, the Ghost opens (2) a locker door, and, the pep pills going in, he starts dropping coins into (3) a slot as he keeps watching (4) a gray light-emitting diode change from 3^{00} to 2^{50} to 2^{00} to 1^{50} to

1^{00} to 0^{50} to 0^{00}, meaning yen outstanding, and, not overpaying, he doesn't need to palpate (5) a coin-return slot. He twists (6) a key counterclockwise ninety degrees, pulls out the key, closes the door, sees (7) the green light go off and (8) a red light come on, doesn't push (9) a button, having no earthly idea what the jutting button is for, and brings the coral-colored-handled key to (10) Johnny's room. Johnny, in turn, takes the key a half mile to the mezzanine of the Century Hyatt, and to muted piano music he casually hands it (as casually as, in Nara, he once handed him a chocolate cookie to feed an importunate deer, explaining, "It brings good luck") to Crazy Chun, his much-tattooed boss in Tokyo, who brings it back to the Washington and reverses the Ghost's punctilious operations: turns it clockwise ninety degrees, and, the red light going off, the green light going on, the 50-yen coins soaring out, no, not really, takes out the waiting lightning. He has his people test it and reports to Johnny, "It's good," and Johnny buys the Ghost's eighty kilos.

All his suspicions voided, he then throws a dinner party for the man he unjustly suspected, for the DEA noninformer. He throws it here in Tokyo's Century City: in Shinjuku, though not in one of its awesome hotels but in a "hot pot" restaurant in Shinjuku's crowded southeast corner, full of loud restaurants, bars, pussy-shoot shows, sexual-paraphernalia shops, video-vertiginous arcades, raucous pachinko parlors—more on pachinko later on—and swarms of Japanese men. The "hot pot" in Johnny's restaurant squats on top of some orange flames on Johnny's table, inside it is boiling water that Johnny, the Ghost, and the other guests use a utensil like a tea strainer to dip their pork, chicken, shrimp, fish, tofu and vegetables into, then to dump on their rice and eat, all the while drinking sake as though it's Asahi Beer. *"Motto osakeo kudasai.* More sake, please," cries Crazy Chun in Japanese at lesser and lesser intervals, and the Ghost's once-white face gets red (his hair, though, is brown today) from the warm rice wine. His table a foot above the floor, his legs extended like in a Porsche, the Ghost stays seated while raising his sake precariously and, in Mandarin translation, singing,

> *You and I will be as free,*
> *As the birds up in the trees,*

Oh, please stay by me,
Diana,

then, after applause, singing a Mandarin song of Taiwan,

This green island
Is a little ship,
Rolling, rolling,
In the moonlight.

My dear island,
Let my song flow,

then, after more lively applause, singing songs from the Peking opera.
The next sake-sodden singer to compete in the Big Circle Amateur Hour
is Crazy Chun, who renders the Taiwanese hit *One Little Umbrella* and
gets ecstatic applause from all the Big Circle *and* from the Japanese at
the tables around him, the Japanese raising their sakes and Crazy Chun
thanking them, *"Domo arigato gozaimasu!"* "Big Brother!" the Big Circle
cries in Cantonese, and Dominique, who is Johnny's companion tonight,
cries too. "Now you sing!"

"No, I don't sing," Johnny laughs, then tells Dominique, "Well, someday maybe I'll sing for *you.*" He's happy tonight, Johnny is, relieved that
his old colleague the Ghost, the Ghost in a T-shirt inscribed "I♥NY" and
(it's cold tonight) in a chocolate-colored corduroy jacket, the Ghost who,
in coming months, will sell him speed worth $6,000,000, hasn't turned
traitor against him. But also Johnny is saddened in his sake-proof cerebrum that now the most probable traitor is the brother he selflessly rescued from Hong Kong, Bangkok, Los Angeles. *Is the ghost really the
Movie Star?* Johnny wonders, while in New York, in Chinatown, something melodramatic happens that in a matter of months will give to
Johnny an unambiguous yes or no.

New York

It's Christmas Eve in Chinatown. The snow becomes dew on the neon signs. Some bosses, including the Movie Star, are at a Chinese poker, pai-gow and fan-tan casino that's run by one of the "Chamber of Commerce" tongs, run by a brown-fedora-wearing man and protected by the neighborhood gang the Flying Dragons. At the next table, a Dragons leader waves to the Star hospitably, saying in Cantonese, "Welcome, I'll pay the bill."

"I've got money, I can afford it," the Star says huffily.

"What? You won't let me treat you?" says the Dragon.

"Don't talk to Muy that way! Shut up!" says Big Banana, the Star's number-two, the man with the pancake-batter nose. As the Dragon stands angrily up, Big Banana, who lives for one thing: to show everyone he is tough, tough, tough, takes out his gun, and the Dragon takes his. At the nightclub *all* the Dragons take out their guns and, the singers silenced, the taxi dancers suspended, tell the Banana, "If you shoot, we'll shoot too."

And all this rancor from "Welcome"! Thank goodness the Dragon didn't tell the Star "Go jump in the goldfish bowl"! As the air curdles, the soft-speaking big-stick-carrying boss, Michael Jackson, says, "You're getting high, Big Banana. And Joe," to the Dragon, "you are too," his palms down, his hands moving outward as though they're smoothing a rumpled bedspread. "Let's keep cool."

"As long as I pay the bill," says the Dragon.

"No," says the casino manager. "You don't pay and *you* don't pay—*I* will pay," and he shoos these lions, unicorns, out of his frightened community center. And here everything would end, except that the Star concludes that the Dragons are gunning for him. Just after Christmas, he's being driven across the Brooklyn Bridge and along the Brooklyn-Queens Expressway, a trench sometimes, an elevated highway other times, at his eye level television antennas, satellite dishes, water towers, and MOE'S MART signs, the Star is being driven along when *bang! bang!* his car backfires and his driver cries, "It's the Dragons!" And *screech!* the driver stops, the soldiers storm out to stop other people's cars, and the Star (on his face true terror, just as he had in a tell-tale frame when a gun went off on his movie set)—the Star jumps behind a corrugated-steel side wall. Alas, the Star's on a bridge, and he falls to a surface street in Brooklyn.

He's paralyzed. Just like in Monterey Park, he's taken to an emergency room, afterwards to his home near the Elmhurst Tanks. In pain, on pain-killing heroin, he receives acupuncture in his bladder-eleven point and his gall-bladder-thirty-nine point as his dubious bodyguard watches the steel needles go in. His soldiers, his girlfriend, desert him, and even his bodyguard employs a knife (not a sterilized needle) to puncture his own left thigh, meaning *My oath—I'm breaking it and I'm paying for it,* and telling the Star in Cantonese, "I'm loyal. But also I'm broke. I beg you, let me leave you."

"If you do," says the Star, putting his gun to his poker-faced head, "I'll kill myself."

At last his physical and psychological pains (psychological: *What's happened to me, I'm responsible for*) are too much for the Star, who calls up his ex in Hong Kong, who calls Dominique in Hong Kong, who calls Johnny in Tokyo, who calls the Star at his home near the Elmhurst Tanks. "Father," the Star laments in Cantonese, "I've hurt you. I know you're angry at me. Don't blame yourself, I deserve it. Can you forgive me?"

"I'm from the Triad tradition," says Johnny. "Once you're my brother, you're my brother forever. I forgive everything."

"Thank you. Father," the Star still laments, "I can't stay in America now. Please let me leave it."

"And go to—?" asks Johnny.

"To Shanghai. To a top-notch acupuncturist. To one who can cure paralysis. Father, may I leave America?"

"Yes, you may," says Johnny.

TOKYO

"Yes, you may," Johnny says, and at that instant sees, *The traitor isn't the Star. If he worked for the DEA, it wouldn't let him go to Shang-hai. That means the traitor is— Who?* Johnny wonders. He hangs up the pay phone, walks out to Shinjuku's clean streets, walks by the loud zelkova trees, creaking with cicadas, *crick, crick, crick, crick, criii . . . ck,* walks by the gray, black and glassy skyscrapers, some of them square, some circular, some buttressed by X's five stories high, X's across office windows, X's like bars sinister, walks out in Shinjuku thinking, *Who?* He walks to the southeast corner and its Japanese, Chinese, French, Italian and Haitian restaurants, its "EET" signs, "EET" signs, "EET" signs, "EET," its stores for Hohner harmonicas, Eterna pianos, Yamaha guitars, *Glory, glory, hallelujah* is what the Yamaha's strumming, its Sony stores whose loudspeakers shout in Japanese,

> *Why don't you try it? Why don't you buy it? We guarantee you'll be satisfied by it!*

he walks by this ear-ripping part of Shinjuku thinking, *Who?* He walks by the bars, pussy shoots, sexual accessories—*life-size woman! inflatable rubber! velvet vagina!*—video arcades, pachinko parlors: pachinko, something like pinball, at every moment two to ten balls falling past a few hundred pins, *clink,* to the left, *clink,* to the right, *clink clink,* down the drain, *sayonara,* the pinballs clinking, the music echoing, the whistles shrilling, the loudspeakers shouting in Japanese,

> *Try machine number forty! Try machine number forty! It's about to pay twenty thousand balls! Try machine number forty!*

the lights flashing, the lights saying in English, "FLASH," "HERE WE GO," "ZUSEEEEN," the TV screen in the midst of these clinking pinballs showing a lion, tiger, elephant, death's head, stone head on Easter Island, or pillar at Stonehenge, *help, I'm imprisoned in a kaleidoscope, rrrrr,* the balls in a landslide into the jackpot container, the Japanese (they don't flip flippers, they don't tilt machines)—the Japanese watching impassively like Buddhists contemplating mandalas, but Johnny still thinking, *Who has betrayed me? Who?* Once, Johnny took Dopey to the Sportsland Pachinko Parlor, *clink clink,* every second the Disney character got off one, two, three tumbling balls, *clink clink,* he lost $100 an hour and now Johnny thinks, *Is it Dopey? No, he's too dopey. Is it Michael Jackson? No, he's too*

smart. Is it the General in prison in Toronto? Tommy in prison in Beau-
mont, Texas? Fat Cat in prison in Hong Kong? Four Eyes in prison in
Bangkok? No no no. Is it Wrist Watch in prison in Los Angeles? The elegant
messenger, arrested with white powder worth $1,000,000? No. Is it Tiger?
No, he's always with me. Is it Crazy? No, he took the Yakuza oath, "If I'm
arrested, I'll kill myself." There's only one man who the traitor could be.

Clink.

Clink.

Clink.

And with heavy heart, Johnny concludes that the man who strutted
into the Miramar, who put his palms together and said, "I pray I'll be
loyal like you, Kuan Kung," who turned up his palms as though offering
fruits and said, "Big Brother? Will you be our leader?" and who five years
ago was Johnny's first disciple was now his Judas. *I didn't promote him,*
Johnny concludes. *I let his best friend tell him to watch the water in South*
America. I let his worst enemy punch him in public in Chinatown. He
even insinuated to me, "Are you behind it, Big Brother?" The man who's
telling tales to the DEA is Fat Ass. The traitor, alas, is Fat Ass.

To catch him, Johnny books a flight to New York.

25
Ghost Catcher

TOKYO

Run, Johnny! Run! At your heels are the blackfeet, chasing you, the NYPD is chasing you, but Johnny runs into a Chinese grocery store. Runs past ginger. Runs past ginseng. Runs past jars like formaldehyde jars. *"Ai!"* cries the grocer in Cantonese, and Johnny (the cops almost catching him)—Johnny climbs onto a chair, jumps out a window, runs down an alley, into a building, upstairs, into a third-floor apartment, whew! At the window, breathless, he watches the cops in the alley run by. In the bedroom, breathless, he wakes up, it was a nightmare, he turns to the woman beside him, it's Dominique, they're still in bed in a darkened room at the Holiday Inn Crowne Plaza in Tokyo, and Johnny tells her in Shanghai dialect, "I dreamt the cops were chasing me."

"That doesn't bode well," says Dominique. "You shouldn't go to New York."

"I've got to. But," says Johnny, still spooked, "I'll leave my briefcase with you. Burn everything in it if anything happens to me." With a suitcase (a Louis Vuitton, its fabric full of LV's) he drives to Narita International Airport and walks onto Northwest Airlines.

LOS ANGELES

It's Friday in the United States. "WELCOME," "BIENVENIDO," "BIEN-
VENUE," say the many-colored walls at Los Angeles International Airport.
A woman immigration inspector looks at Johnny's passport (it's from
Costa Rica, his name is Wong) and at the American visa that the Ghost
got him for thirty $100 bills. On the visa is a slanted blue line ("What
does this mean?" Johnny asked the Ghost, but the Ghost didn't know)
that the immigration inspector looks at, then looks at Johnny with eyes
that say, "Well, what sort of queer bird are you?" Or does Johnny imagine this? He hurries to another terminal, where a man on a barstool
swivels around to observe him. Or does Johnny (his name now is Lee)
imagine this, too? He waits in the bar until the last moment, when, the
gate almost closed, he hurries onto Eastern Airlines.

NEW YORK

The plane having taken him to Newark International Airport, the
bus having taken him to the Port Authority Terminal, a Mercedes now
takes him (his name once again is Wong) to the Doral Park Avenue
Hotel, on the northwest corner of Park and 38th. In its lobby are two can-
delabra upheld by two massive bronze boys. Between them is an oval
mirror so elegantly antique that a man who confronts it won't recognize
his gray, silver-splattered, shriveled cheeks, also a brown leather bench
that (as Johnny recalls) recently bore the weight of the presumptive traitor, bore Fat Ass. One night he sat there smoking his Kents when he was
supposed to be sitting on a brown plastic chair at a much more flatter-
ing mirror in the lobby of the Hotel Kitano, on the southwest (not northwest) corner of Park and 38th. At the Kitano, he was to meet a Chinese
woman courier to pick up four brass fishes full of what wasn't caviar
from Bangkok, but without warning the DEA arrested her. "I waited for
her. She didn't show up," Fat Ass told Johnny in Cantonese later.

"You waited on Park Avenue?"

"Yes, on the corner of 38th."

"You waited at the Kitano?"

"No, at the Doral Park."

"Wrong hotel," Johnny told him, Johnny who now perceives, He knew. He knew that the DEA was waiting at the Kitano. He set it up. At the Doral Park, Johnny goes to his tenth-floor room adorned in Italian Provençal to drop off his Louis Vuitton.

NEW YORK

"Big Brother? Why did you come to New York?" asks Fat Ass in Cantonese. It's one hour later, it's late Friday night, Saturday morning, and Johnny and all the local bosses are at the Fireside Bar, a wood-floored, wood-walled neighborhood bar (a regular here is Soupy Sales) on the southeast corner of Third and 35th. Near their round table is an old upright where an old pianist (he's ninety) is batting out

> *A-tisket, a-tasket,*
> *A green and yellow basket,*

and other oldie-goldies. "It's dangerous in New York," says Fat Ass in Cantonese solicitously.

"What's dangerous about it?" asks Johnny.

"A lot of arrests in Chinatown recently."

"I'm only here three days, then Brazil."

"You shouldn't have come, Big Brother."

"I miss you, Fatty," says Johnny, looking at Fat Ass searchingly. "I miss you all," he continues, looking around the table like King Arthur. "Long time. No see." He turns back to Fat Ass to see him staring intently over his—Johnny's—shoulder, and he follows those eyes to the bar and two well-built customers, one of them white, blue-suited, black-shoed, the other a Chinese, windbreaker-jacketed, neither of them singing along to *A-Tisket, A-Tasket.* "Do you know these two?" Johnny asks Fat Ass.

"No, I don't know them," says Fat Ass.

"Does anyone know them?"

"No, we don't."

"It's three o'clock. I think they're policemen. I was tailed," Johnny reports, "in Los Angeles, and I think I was followed here," *or,* Johnny thinks, *I was informed on by Fat Ass.* "Let's leave," Johnny says, and, downing their Michelobs, the brothers all do.

NEW YORK

It's Saturday now, Saturday noon, and Johnny and all the bosses revolve at the rate of one half inch every second eight floors above Times Square in the Broadway Lounge of the Marriott Marquis. Some going forward, some going backward, they sit at round plastic tables eating beefburgers as Times Square, like driftwood, passes by the curved picture window of their revolving restaurant: first the headlines like DUKAKIS DANCES BOUZOUKI, then the marquee for *Prison,* a new horror movie, then the red billboard for tickets to *Cats, Cabaret,* and *Oh! Calcutta!* then the cool chaser:

ENJOY COCA-COLA

ENJOY THE REAL THING.

The city's cacophony (jackal packs of taxis, fire engines, ambulances) horn in through the window in competition with a girl at a grand piano fifty feet away, a girl who's tinkling tunes about a more idealized city, tunes like *East Side, West Side, All around the Town.*

Among the revolving brothers today is Dopey, an illegal alien in the United States, in whose vinyl-sided home in Queens are the last twenty heroin bricks from Bangkok. These bricks, all Dial, have been crumbled and jumbled with thirty-nine new Ivory bricks, making a total of fifty-nine units (as they're called) that on Friday arrived in a false-walled shipping container at the Port of New York and, soon after that, at Dopey's cottage in Queens. In his hand today is a white envelope with a small sample that, as the jackals bray and the tots play ring-around-rosie, he slips under the table to Johnny, who slips it into his black leather shoe, the shoe that's farther from the wide window. "You shouldn't carry it, Big Brother," says Fat Ass in Cantonese solicitously, Fat Ass who's sitting opposite him, Fat Ass who doesn't add "I'll carry the heroin for you, Big Brother," Fat Ass who *can't* carry heroin if he's informing for the DEA.

"I'm taking it to Big Banana," Johnny says levelly.

"How many of the fifty-nine will Big Banana get?"

"Thirty," says Johnny. "And you'll get twenty-nine."

"He doesn't deserve it. He does nothing for us."

"He supplies the Star's customers now."

"Whatever you say, Big Brother."

After lunch, Johnny (heroin in his black leather shoe) and the bosses sip coffee on this same eighth floor in the Clock Lounge, a giant clock on a golden chain laying claim to the Biltmore's business, the Biltmore having become the Bank of America. Above the gangsters rises an atrium thirty-six balconies high, as well as twelve see-through elevators full of people, perhaps plainclothesmen, looking down on their mischievous business (this year 2,480 writers, rockers-and-rollers, businessmen and bums, nine hundred more than last year, will die). The high visibility isn't a problem for Johnny, who's done deals at the Peninsula, Dusit Thani, and Philippine Plaza, why not the Marriott Marquis? One shoe with heroin in it, he walks out to Broadway, where a Chinese artist asks him in Mandarin, "May I draw your portrait?"

"You draw very well," says Johnny.

"I also draw very quickly."

"But thank you, I haven't time."

NEW YORK

Back at the Doral Park Avenue Hotel, in the green-walled bar off the Doral's lobby, Johnny has beer in a pilsner glass with Big Banana, who now runs the Star's operations in the Big Apple. Johnny doesn't quite trust the Banana, whose square-shaped face is a "traitor's face" according to a Chinese book ("Big ears are good, small ears are bad") that Johnny in his twenties bought from a fortune-teller in Hong Kong. But the Banana can't be the traitor today, for he accepts the white envelope against the DEA's rules (he also once murdered someone against the DEA's rules) and he takes it to Queens, tests it, calls up Johnny, and in

Cantonese says, "It's perfect. When can you meet me?" Meaning "When do I get the thirty units, worth $2,250,000?"

"Eight o'clock," Johnny tells him.

NEW YORK

"Take thirty units to Big Banana," Johnny tells Dopey in Cantonese as the bosses eat Boston lobsters in the VIP room in the basement of one of the Chinese restaurants near Third and 33rd, and Dopey (who has his own driver, for he has crashed cars in Bangkok, Bolivia and Paraguay) leaves via the Midtown Tunnel to Queens. He fetches the not-quite-white powder, takes it to Big Banana, and calls up Johnny in the VIP room.

"I met him," says Dopey.

"Then come here for lobster."

"No, I'll see you tomorrow."

NEW YORK

"All right, tomorrow," Johnny confirms in the VIP room as Fat Ass sits silently eating scallops. A man Johnny's never seen (he's white and well-built) comes downstairs, passes by Johnny, goes to the toilet, passes by Johnny again, goes upstairs. *That's strange,* thinks Johnny. *Why didn't he use the toilet upstairs?*

NEW YORK

It's Sunday now, Sunday noon, and Johnny's again in the atrium of the Marriott Marquis, he's having lunch with a Chinese friend under the mounted cattle horns at JW's Steakhouse. In the name of this long-time friend are all Johnny's motion-picture theaters, shopping centers, supermarkets, buildings in the United States, and Johnny's dining on cream of chicken soup while telling him in Cantonese, "Sell them." He then hops to the table where all the bosses are and says, "We're selling things in New York, Los Angeles and San Francisco and buying the

Hotel Sasimi," meaning sesame, a many-acres resort hotel, its price $200,000,000, "in Taipei. All of you will work for it, and the Ghost will manage it. So that will be the future for the Big Circle."

"Is there a casino there?" asks Fat Ass.

"Yes."

"Can I run the loan-sharking counter?"

"Yes."

"Good, I'll make money," says Fat Ass.

NEW YORK

"Ronny," says Johnny in Shanghai dialect, pointing to the Ghost's diamond DuPont pen at dinner that evening at the Café New York, on the Hilton's lower level. "This pen I gave you."

"Yes, Big Brother. The pen's very nice."

"And Ronny," says Johnny, pointing to the Ghost's diamond Rolex. "This watch I gave you too. Your pen, your watch, your house in Taipei, they're gifts from me."

"Yes, Big Brother. You gave me me."

"And now, Ronny," says Johnny. "I'm giving you a $200,000,000 company. I'm making you the manager of the Hotel Sasimi in Taipei."

"Thank you, Big Brother."

The two are sitting in one of the restaurant's bright booths. Its walls are of glass that's etched with scenes of New York: the skyline, the Statue of Liberty, the Brooklyn Bridge, the Empire State, and the old Madison Square Garden, looking quite like the Kremlin: these and their shiny brass frames secluding the two Chinese from the chattering tourists around them. The table is salmon-streaked marble. On it in sunrise-sunset shades is a menu depicting the Statue of Liberty bearing a torch like an ice-cream cone with a flame like a swirl of peach frozen custard, a menu from which the two have chosen chicken in a wicker basket for Johnny and black coffee for the Ghost. No appetite has the Ghost tonight. He came down to dinner a half-hour late, a half-hour that Johnny spent at a nearby souvenir shop, Leonardo's, looking at Statues of Liberty made of green plastic, black plastic, and black-tainted copper (sometimes adorned with thermometers)—looking at cups, ashtrays and bells inscribed "I♥NY," looking at "wallet stuffers" that said,

> *Take a first step to tomorrow,*
> *Start in the course of your choice,*
> *Look at what life has to offer,*
> *Listen to your inner voice,*

and buying a pack of Wrigley's Doublemint Gum. At half past eight, when finally the Ghost appeared, his hair was Moroccan red and his face was too, the Ghost confessing to Johnny in Shanghai dialect, "I've been drinking." He has the jitters (shaking hands, shifting eyes, tremolos in his voice) tonight. At one point when Johnny excuses himself, steps to a telephone, drops in some quarters from Leonardo's, calls up a brother in Asia, and says in Mandarin, "It's here," meaning the not-quite-white powder—when Johnny comes back the Ghost has a shirt button open and a hand under it, and Johnny asks him in Shanghai dialect, "What are you doing?"

"My— My stomach itches," says the Ghost, startled.

"Have some more coffee."

"No, I've been flying all day. I'm tired," says the Ghost.

"Go to sleep," says Johnny, and the Ghost departs.

Alone, Johnny has his last fried potato sticks. He rises, pays the check, takes the up escalator, crosses the Hilton's burgundy-carpeted lobby, exits by a revolving door: exits onto a cobblestone driveway off the Avenue of the Americas. A doorman in silver-braided charcoal opens a fare-printed taxi door, but Johnny opts for a postprandial constitutional. He strolls south across West 53rd. On the corner is a sort of Venus de Milo, her arms absent, her head absent, what's left of the lady cadaverous green, and at one of three telephone booths is a man who's saying (to Johnny? to the other party?)—saying, "Mr. Kon?" From habit Johnny looks up, he sees two pedestrians turn, they seize him and pin his arms behind him, and the man at the phone, showing his wallet, showing his badge, sounding triumphant, says, "Mr. Kon, I'm DEA. You're under arrest."

It's March 1988. *Oh no*, thinks Johnny, age forty-five, thinks Johnny correctly. *The traitor wasn't Fat Ass. All along, the traitor was the Ghost.*

Part Four

26
Sick Man

NEW YORK

By foot, autos, horses, helicopters, hovering mother ships, all the humans at this intersection (hundreds, if Johnny's eyes don't lie) turn to Johnny, converge on Johnny, put handcuffs on Johnny, pat Johnny down. He feels as an American does when he's playing quarterback and he's sacked. He doesn't say *"Oof,"* but his English acquires a sudden unprecedented fracture as he protests to the DEA, "I name not Kon! I name is Wong!"

"No, Mr. Kon," says the DEA man who was making the pseudo telephone call. "We don't make mistakes. Where's your gun?"

"I no have gun!" Johnny protests.

"Where are your papers?"

"I no have!"

A tiny frown crosses the DEA man's forehead. The man was brought up in Pittsburgh in the Italian (Italian like him) and Irish district and, in his childhood, played catcher for a hard-hustling team in the Little League. Some of his teammates, some of his little competitors, grew up to be heroin addicts, a boy becoming a sunken-socketed derelict, another becoming an armed robber, then a convicted prisoner, another (a boy on the DEA man's team) overdosing, succumbing to cardiac arrest, dying. By now the DEA man abominates dealers, but if he hopes to arrest someone with a Beretta, a briefcase, a vest-pocket book with the names, addresses, telephone numbers of all of Manhattan's middlemen, or (for argument's sake) a white envelope in a black leather shoe, he's sorely disappointed, for all Johnny yields him is a pager that in the next hour will flash unincriminating digits like 33, 88 and 99 and a passport for Mr. Ricky Wong of San José, Costa Rica. Johnny's business cards, his $1,200 in American money, and his Bolivian bolivianos, Brazilian reals, Colombian pesos, Dutch guilders, French francs, German marks, Japanese yen, Malaysian dollars, Panamanian balboas, Philippine pesos, Singapore dollars, Swiss francs, and Taiwanese dollars stay in his right pants pocket in a fat wallet from Christian Dior, a wallet the DEA unprofessionally overlooks. Its hands on Johnny's shoulders, the DEA pushes him into the back of a Chevrolet Impala and at thirty-two mph (in sync with the staggered traffic lights) drives him up the Avenue of the Americas toward Central Park.

Oh, stupid me, Johnny in the Chevvy thinks. *The day I met him, the Ghost admitted, "I don't know who I am." I should have told him, "Come back when you do."* Johnny still doesn't know, but the Ghost has considered himself a DEA secret agent for one and one-half years, approximately since the birthday party (the paper hats, the paper horns) in Panama City for Johnny's son. As the boy blew the candles out, the Ghost was flying from Tokyo into the Sea-Tac International Airport, in Seattle, the city that Johnny had said stay away from, inspectors are too meticulous there. No heroin, cocaine or amphetamine was in the Ghost's luggage, but a customs inspector arrested him on the grounds that he was conspicuously like Tommy, the man who had one year earlier brought the ice buckets into Seattle and said, "Why must you see one? What must you see one for?" Like Tommy, the Ghost was an Asian (actually, a Eurasian) who had often brought flying-flower-embellished buckets from Tokyo to New York, this according to the custom inspector's improvement on Kojak: the customs inspector's computer. When the customs inspectors caught Tommy, they used their modern magnifying glass to examine hundreds of thousands of customs declarations by Asians, and they found fourteen men (ten were couriers for Johnny, they later would learn) who had Tommy's profile. The first one to saunter into Seattle unaware that he had been tagged by a customs inspector's infernal machine was the Ghost. Arrested, he sat nonchalantly in the same eight-foot-wide, eight-foot-long, eight-foot-high cubic room that Tommy had, sat there until the DEA man whose friend died in Alphabet City (and lay three weeks in the morgue, unidentified) walked in. "I'm with the DEA," the DEA man said immediately. "I want to know about buckets. You either tell me or go to prison the rest of your life." What color there was to the Ghost and (it seemed) to the heart in his "I♥NY" disappeared, and the Ghost promised the DEA man his fickle allegiance. A half year ago, the Ghost testified to a grand jury in Brooklyn, then went to Japan and sang,

> *I love you with all my heart,*
> *I got hope we'll never part,*
> *Oh please stay by me,*
> *Diana,*

in Mandarin translation while the jury was handing down a sealed indictment of Johnny. As for drugs, the Ghost stopped dealing them in the United States, it was against the DEA's rules, but in Japan he started dealing amphetamines, the DEA didn't concern itself with Japanese speed freaks. *Why didn't I kill the Ghost long ago?* Johnny in the Chevvy thinks. *It was my kind heart.*

The car turns west on West 57th, it passes by Carnegie Hall and the studios for the *The Young and the Restless,* it stops just short of the Hudson River. The man who made the pseudo telephone call ("Mr. Kon?") now escorts him to a brick building and up the elevator to the DEA's poster-walled office. He seats Johnny on an armless plastic chair and says, "Your name's Johnny Kon?"

"No," says Johnny. "My name Wong."

"No, we know you, Mr. Kon."

"What you know?"

"We know you're a big drug dealer."

"Drug? Why you talking about?"

"Now don't kid me, Mr. Kon."

"Why you talking? I don't know nothing about. I furrier, I do business with fur. I legitimate business man."

"You're smart, Mr. Kon . . ."

"I don't know nothing, drug."

". . . But we finally got you. Your pager," says the DEA man as a 33, 88 or 99 appears on it. "Who's paging you?"

"They leave telephone number?"

"No."

"Then how I know?" asks Johnny. He feels he's sitting pretty in spite of the recent unpleasantness on the Avenue of the Americas. He was patted like Lassie there, but he provided no items of evidence, none (at any rate) detected by the DEA, not even a card confirming he's Johnny Kon. His brothers, eating in Chinatown, paging him again and again, getting no callback, certainly knew he was incommunicado, knew to go underground themselves. The only witness the DEA had—the Ghost—could admittedly dye his hair some acceptable color and sit in a courtroom pointing his golden finger at Johnny and testifying in English, "That man is Johnny Kon. I once worked for him. He smuggled drugs to America," but the Ghost was arrested seventeen times in Taipei and his word isn't worth the Monopoly money the Chinese drop upon dead men. *They won't convict me,* Johnny thinks, Johnny correctly thinks, but he doesn't recognize that the DEA and the prosecutors, judges, jailers, the "they" of American justice do not *intend* to convict him or (it would take many weeks) even try him. They know that Johnny flouted our law, that Johnny brought poison into America and misery to Americans, that Johnny in justice should be imprisoned for many, many years—they know this as well as I do, as well as you readers do, and they don't intend to do DNA analyses to prove it to twelve benighted jurors. Not unlike in the Middle Ages, they just intend to lean on Johnny, to put him under extreme duress, to make him an offer he can't refuse, to more or less torture him till, of what's left of his own free will, he rises in court as he rose thirty years ago at the self-criticism sessions in Gongjalu, in Communist China, and says, "Your Honor, I'm guilty." The rack being banned by the Eighth Amendment, the "they" of American justice intend to use a psychosomatic one on Johnny instead.

"Mr. Kon," says the DEA man tonight. "You have the right to remain silent. Anything you say . . ."

New York

Lights. Camera. Action. At the courthouse in Brooklyn the following morning are CBS, NBC, ABC, the *Times, News, Post,* the Associated Press. Reliable sources tell them that all the heroin in the United States, the Chinese are now bringing in. Reliable sources tell them that Johnny's the DEA's most wanted man, that Johnny's the world's second biggest smuggler—the first is a general in the Golden Triangle—that Johnny imported heroin into America, *quote,* in mind-boggling amounts, the total was one half ton. The cameras roll, the ballpoints roll, the kingpin himself comes into the courtroom. He wears what he wore on the Avenue of the Americas: black leather shoes, black trousers, black belt: a white silk shirt, a red silk tie, an Oxford gray corduroy jacket. His hands, recently cuffed lest he punch out the DEA men accompanying him, are now more correct for a somber federal courtroom: uncuffed. He thinks, *So this is an American courtroom.* A man tells Johnny in English, "I represent you."

"You represent me?"

"Yes."

"Thank you."

"Do you speak English?"

"Yes."

"Today you say, 'Not guilty.'"

The judge, in his sixties, walks in. The marshal says, "Everybody rise," and the public, press and Johnny do. The judge sits down, then they do. The prosecutor, a brown-haired woman, the scourge of Chinese criminals here, says that Johnny violated the United States Criminal Code, Title 21, Section 952(a), he imported heroin into the customs territory of the United States. The judge says, "How do you plead?" and Johnny says, "Not guilty." The judge pulls his glasses down, looks at Johnny like Kilroy, and says—but Johnny can't understand him. The man who told Johnny, "I represent you," disappears, and Johnny is escorted out by a

DEA man who chews a toothpick and tells him, "Ha! At last I nailed you. The rest of your life you'll be in some fuckin' prison." In the basement the DEA man, who also abominates dealers, among the one thousand addicts he has encountered is one whose babies subsisted in dirty diapers, another (a woman) who let men defecate onto her, all for the $10 bag—the DEA man slides the toothpick to the molars that haven't yet tasted it and says, "Yeah, I nailed you. You'll never get out of the fuckin' jail." *This man,* Johnny thinks, *is acting just like a gangster,* and Johnny tells him, "I Buddhist. I good guy, and I no die. Just bad guy die." This the DEA man will report to the woman prosecutor, known to Chinese criminals as the Dragon Lady, who'll threaten to add to her indictment that Johnny violated Title 18, Section 115(a), he threatened to murder a DEA special agent.

Johnny is brought to a 12-story prison near City Hall, in Manhattan. His wallet, minus his business cards, which he has torn up, tossed into a toilet, and irretrievably flushed, is taken from him. So are his coins, lest he sharpen them into "Chinese stars" and cast them at prison guards à la Bruce Lee. So are his $50,000 diamond Piaget watch, lest he barter with it, and his $400 gold-buckled belt, lest he hang himself with it. "Hey, Johnny!" cries a prison lieutenant with a tattoo that says "U.S. Marines." "What are you doing here? Hey, sir!" the lieutenant cries to a prison captain. "This man was my buddy in Hong Kong!" Furtively, Johnny nudges him.

"You boss here?" Johnny asks.

"Yeah."

"Let me out," Johnny laughs.

"Nooo," the lieutenant laughs.

Johnny is put in solitary confinement although he's just a suspect, just a *sick man* in Chinese gangster slang. He isn't allowed any telephone calls, newspapers, or TV news, isn't allowed any TV at all. He's only allowed to exercise (to walk around aimlessly) for one hour every other day. He isn't allowed to shower if he showered the day before. He's only allowed to send letters if the warden approves them, but on a scrap of paper he surreptitiously writes to a brother in Tokyo, in Chinese characters,

> *I'm here because of the Ghost. Let him go west,*

meaning "Kill him. Or he will testify against me." He rolls this into wad and gives it to an attorney, but a guard finds it and forwards it to the Dragon Lady, who, having added to her indictment that Johnny violated Title 21, Section 848(b), he led a continuing criminal enterprise, threatens to add furthermore that Johnny violated Title 18, Section 1512(a), he attempted to murder a government witness. In fact it's Johnny, just Johnny, who'll testify that Johnny is blatantly guilty if the American government has its way.

Hong Kong

The turn of the screws commences. Five months pregnant, wearing pajamas, one of Johnny's three younger sisters (one who once worked for Imperial Fur) is at her apartment in Kowloon, is walking to her kitchen to steam some fish, barbecue pork, and fry bok choy for her husband and daughter, seven years old. It's six o'clock: suppertime, and as she passes through her small living room, the door to the hallway suddenly opens and ten men in civilian clothes burst in. "We are police," says one man in Cantonese.

"What's happened?" gasps Johnny's sister.

"Come with us," says the man, as Johnny's sister's daughter cries, really cries, her tears streaming down, "Mommy, where are they taking you?"

"Don't worry. Your father will cook for you," says Johnny's sister. She changes into a flowered dress and says, "I'll be home soon," in no way anticipating that it will be thirty months before she's home. As ten men guard her, she takes the elevator down, and as her husband cuts the bok choy, she's whisked away in a Honda to the Hong Kong Correctional Center.

It's suppertime one mile away. One of Johnny's two younger brothers (one who once worked for Champion Watches) is at his apartment, thick with the odor of a Nanking duck, China's most succulent kind. He recently bought it in Beijing and brought it back on Air China, and now its vapors saturate the apartment as, in the kitchen, his wife starts steaming it. But *knock,* there's a knock on the door, and ten men in civilian clothes crowd in. "We are police," says one man in Cantonese.

"What's wrong?" asks Johnny's brother.

"Come with us," says the man, and, the Nanking duck turning cold, Johnny's brother and his loyal wife are whisked away to the Hong Kong Correctional Center.

It's suppertime in Jonquil's apartment another mile away. Jonquil (like Johnny's sister and brother) doesn't know white powder from Domino's confectioner's sugar, but ten police come for her and whisk her away to the Hong Kong Correctional Center. Six months later, Johnny's sister delivers her baby (a daughter) there, then the authorities call for the U.S. marshals, and Johnny's sister, Johnny's brother, and Jonquil are hand-cuffed, leg-chained, taken to Kai Tak International Airport, and walked up a stairway onto Northwest Airlines. Then they're extradited to the United States.

NEW YORK

They're put into Johnny's prison. They're brought to court by the Dragon Lady, who says that they violated the United States Criminal Code, Title 21, Section 963, they conspired with Johnny to import heroin into the customs territory of the United States. The judge says, "How do you plead?" and Johnny's sister, brother and spouse, stunned to be on the other side of the planet accused of doing something more than invoicing weasels, invoicing watches, and "chopping" or rubber-stamping the incoming checks or, in Jonquil's case, of doing anything at all in the import-export business, say, "Not guilty." Then they're returned to Johnny's prison, where Jonquil sits day after day on the edge of her cot, squeezing her handkerchief, sobbing.

At last she's allowed to meet in a third-floor attorney's room with Johnny, her orange-clothed co-conspirator in *United States versus Kon*. Her eyes in this cell-sized room seem focused on something far outside the prison, something across the Hudson, something probably in Hong Kong. Still twisting her handkerchief as if she were wringing out yesterday's tears so as to accommodate today's, she asks Johnny in Shanghai dialect, "What did I do that's wrong?"

"You didn't do anything wrong," says Johnny.

"Then why am I in this prison?"

"They got you so they can get me," says Johnny.

"But I didn't do anything wrong."

"You're right, sweetheart. You didn't but I did."

"Then why am *I* in this prison?"

"They want me. They're holding you hostage."

"But what did I do that's *wrong?*"

Again and again (repetition: it's Jonquil's flaw) this delicate woman goes to the glass-walled attorney's room, sits with Johnny, wrings her security handkerchief as a housekeeper wrings a mop, and rings all conceivable changes on her two exigent questions, *ding* and *dong*. His arm around her, Johnny accords her his two standard answers until, when the handkerchief looks like a rag that's been in and out, in and out, of the barrel of a Beretta, often his patience frays and he cries to Jonquil, "Listen to me!" He squeezes her shoulder emphatically, and Jonquil pulls back and says, "You hurt me! You promised you wouldn't ever hurt me!" and Johnny, mortified, strokes her and Jonquil cries, "Don't touch me!" Then Johnny says, "I love you. They know I love you. They know I'll do anything for you. That's why they imprisoned you," and Jonquil bursts into tears and asks, "But what did I do that's wrong?" At night, Jonquil (the orphaned daughter, bereaved mother, oblivious moll, the woman who twenty years ago told Johnny, "We need each other. What do we need after that? Just rice," the woman whose diamonds don't adorn *her* but the dark insides of a box at the Hang Seng Bank, in Hong Kong)— Jonquil the Buddhist goes to her iron cell, iron cot, she takes a Seconal but lies awake thinking, *I'll take them all, I'll kill myself,* as four floors above her Johnny lies thinking too. *How dare they arrest her?* Johnny thinks. His wife didn't commit conspiracy, but if she did (and she didn't) she clearly didn't commit it in the United States but in Hong Kong, and there is no law against conspiracy in Hong Kong. How dare the Americans, Johnny thinks—how dare they export their laws to another sovereign country just as they arrogantly export their Coca-Cola, McDonald's, Roseanne? How dare they be so high-handed as to reach across oceans to hammer a "Yes, you may" and a "No, you may not" onto the walls of Hong Kong? Or onto the walls of Panama, where in a year they'll arrest its President Noriega for violating the United States Criminal Code, Title 21, Section 952(a), he imported cocaine into the customs territory of the United States? Or onto the walls of Arabia, where in five years they'll board a Chinese ship, the *Silver River,* for violating the United States Criminal Code, Title 22, Section 6503, it may be exporting chemical weapons to Iran? What, Johnny thinks, would Americans do if China arrested an American writer, editor or senator on the streets of New York for speaking ill of its Chairman Deng in violation of Chinese law? The Americans killed Johnny's kids, and Johnny's thinking that when he seeks justice, they try to kill the kids' disconsolate mother, too. *Myself, I did wrong,* Johnny thinks. *But the Americans, they're doing worse.*

And thinking this, Johnny falls asleep and, in the morning, goes down to the aching attorney's room, and Jonquil tells him in Shanghai dialect, "I didn't do anything wrong."

"I know it, and Buddha knows too."

"Then why am I in this prison?"

"The Americans know I'd die for you."

"But what did *I* do that's wrong?"

"You married the wrong man."

TOKYO

And now the American government plays its ace. In her modest apartment in Tokyo, Dominique, Johnny's girlfriend, dresses in slacks, a sweater, and (it's winter) a black leather coat to go out for shark's fin soup at the Phoenix Hill Restaurant. Walking three flights to the lobby, walking outside, she stops at a corner telephone booth to call her grandmother in Shanghai and say in Shanghai dialect, "How are you?" "Take care of your health," "Goodbye." As she hangs up, a Japanese man in civilian clothes seizes her left wrist, another seizes her right wrist, and a third wields a copy of Dominique's passport photo and says in English, "Excuse me. Is this picture you?" The man doesn't say "We're police," but Dominique knows about Johnny, his sister and brother and Jonquil, and she assumes that they are.

"No, it's not me," says Dominique in English.

"She's a very beautiful woman," says the policeman in Japanese.

"Yes, but she isn't me," says Dominique in Japanese, not falling for flattery.

"She is so beautiful, we were afraid to approach you."

"You needn't have been. She isn't me."

"Is your name Dominique?"

"No," says Dominique.

"Are you Chinese?"

"No, Korean."

"Excuse me, but you must come with us," says the policeman, and, a hand on each wrist, he and the others whisk her into a Nissan and to a Tokyo jail. They seat Dominique at a small desk in a small room and ask her in Japanese, "Do you know Johnny Kon?"

"No," says Dominique.

"You don't know him?"

"No," says Dominique, as loyal as any brother to the oath of the Flaming Eagles. In her apartment months ago, she stood among clouds of choking smoke to burn up the contents of Johnny's briefcase, as Johnny had asked her to.

"The heroin dealer, Johnny Kon?"

"No, I don't know him."

"Do you know we can imprison you?"

"Go and imprison me."

"We can imprison you for many years."

"Imprison me for fifty years. Imprison me for one hundred years. And still I don't know Johnny Kon."

"You don't know about heroin?"

"No!" cries Dominique, shoving the wooden desk onto the Japanese. They question her for twenty-eight days and, her answers not changing, call for the U.S. marshals to extradite her to the United States.

NEW YORK

"We'll fight and win, Mr. Kon," says Johnny's attorney in English. He's sitting on a one-piece plastic chair, the plastic curved for his sacral spine, two circular holes for his buttocks, the rest of the chair colored dragon's-blood red. He's sitting at a black plastic table—sitting at it side-wise, for he's six foot three and, if he faces it, isn't able to get his legs under it. His right knee rests on his left one, and his right leg swings to and fro like a pendulum, *tick, tock,* he earns from ten to ten thousand cents every second, the rate's indeterminate because he has charged his affluent client a flat $500,000, trial or no trial, win it or lose it, Johnny gets off or Johnny gets life. Johnny had already paid this $500,000 when the Dragon Lady or one of her colleagues accused the tall attorney of vio-lating the United States Criminal Code, Title 26, Section 6651, he failed to file income tax. The judge called for Johnny and told him, "He may have a conflict of interest now." "How conflict interest?" asked Johnny. "He may not fight for you." "How not fight for me?" "Have you seen his wife?" "No, I not seen her." "I've seen her. She's very beautiful. And she may tell him, 'Don't fight for Mr. Kon. Cooperate with the United States.' Mr. Kon," the judge continued, "you may appoint another attorney." "How can? I pay this one. He not pay back," answered Johnny, who's sit-ting tonight on a one-piece, two-holed, plastic chair across from his tall, well-paid, entrenched attorney in a white-painted concrete attorney's room with a red-painted steel water pipe like at the Pompidou Museum, all this in Johnny's prison near City Hall. "We'll fight and win, Mr. Kon," says Johnny's attorney in English, sipping a Diet Pepsi.

"No. We not win," says Johnny. A sense of humor (of gallows humor) seizes him, a wide smile stretches across him, a twinkle lights up his nar-row eyes, and Johnny laughs, "This really joke. They want me too bad. Why they don't give you indictment last year? Why they don't tell me conflict interest last year? If government want, they put you in jail and give me $5,000 public defendant. This really fucking joke," says Johnny. He shakes his finger teasingly at his long-legged attorney and says, "Don't tell me we win."

"We'll fight and win, Mr. Kon."

"What happen if we fucking up? What happen if we really losing? What then my wife will get?"

"At least fifteen years, maybe thirty."

"How 'bout my sister and brother?"

"At least ten years, maybe twenty."

"How 'bout Dominique?"

"Ten years."

"And how 'bout me?"

"Two life sentences, probably."

"The one life," says Johnny, laughing, "isn't enough? They don't satisfy one, they want two? Maybe when I rebirth again, I owe them another next life."

"Don't worry. We'll win, Mr. Kon."

"You are good lawyer, but I worry."

"You shouldn't. Oh, about Dominique," says Johnny's optimistic attorney. His leg is a pendulum still, *tick, tock*. "She's coming here."

"Where they will put her?"

"Upstairs in fifth floor south."

"Will put her in fifth floor south?"

"Yes. In the women's ward."

"Will put her and Jonquil together?"

"Possibly in the same cell."

"What what?" says Johnny, his smile collapsing. "Will to killing my Jonquil? She never knows about Dominique. She very very depressed already. Will to giving her nervous breakdown? No, that I can't allow to do. If I plead guilty," he says histrionically, his fist hitting himself where his heart is, "will they let Dominique stay Japan?"

"No, Mr. Kon," says Johnny's attorney. "They already pressured the Japanese. They told them that Dominique's important, that they must have her. If they tell the Japanese forget it, the Japanese will never extradite anyone else. No, Dominique has to come to New York."

"And fuck with Jonquil," Johnny groans.

"She's coming very soon, Mr. Kon."

"What if I plead guilty before?"

"Before she's here?"

"Yes, before."

"Then," says Johnny's attorney, "if Jonquil pleads guilty too, and your sister and brother plead guilty too, I think I can get Jonquil into another prison, and Jonquil and Dominique won't meet."

The neurons in Johnny's head start tying themselves into knots. "The stupid Japanese," he says, buying time. "Ronny," the Ghost, the man who informed against him—"Ronny sold half ton ice in Japan. Americans probably told him do it, Americans want me to trusting him. Americans then, Americans import half ton ice to Japan, but Japanese no stop bowing to Americans. Americans say, 'We want Dominique,' and Japanese say, 'Here she is.' Stupid Japanese!"

"What do you want to do, Mr. Kon?"

"I must make smart decision. I don't want sorry all my life. If," says Johnny, still posing hypotheticals—"if I plead guilty and Jonquil, sister, brother and Dominique plead guilty, what Jonquil will get?"

"She'll be out about a year from now."

"What my sister and brother will get?"

"They'll be out in about six months."

"How 'bout Dominique?"

"About six."

"Then how 'bout me?"

"You, probably nineteen years."

"How many nineteen years should I do?"

"Maybe around about ten."

"Please," says Johnny, now bargaining, as (in his unimprisoned life) he so often did in matters of fur, wood, paper, pewter, watches, secret society turf. "I am 101 percent not innocent. My family and Dominique are 101 percent not guilty. What is if I plead guilty and my family and Dominique plead not? What is if—"

"No, Mr. Kon. The government wouldn't accept it. It already pressured the governments of Hong Kong and Japan. It has to show them everyone's guilty."

The neurons in Johnny's head untie. They lie as if magnetized, lined up, and point in just one direction. In all their crackling amperes is the Morse code for *I'm guilty, guilty at least a hundred percent. But,* their message continues, *there is no way the Americans can prove it.* Against Johnny Kon, the government has no evidence: not a heroin mote, not a drug-money cent, not a telephone tap, not a home, hotel or restaurant tap, not even (a year after telling him, "Mr. Kon, you're under arrest") an

ID card for a Mr. Kon. The government failed to "turn" or to turn against him his brothers in the Big Circle. The General in prison in Toronto, Tommy (the aspiring spiderman) in prison in Beaumont, Texas, Fat Cat in prison in Hong Kong, Four Eyes in prison in Bangkok—all stayed loyal to Johnny and didn't elect to go home to their wives by testifying against him. Crazy Chun, the tattoo-coated boss in Japan, who was lured to New York and put in a cell in Bayonne, New Jersey, and who was asked to testify against the man he'd told while eating noodle soup in Tokyo, "I'll never betray you. If I'm arrested, I'll kill myself," well, Crazy didn't betray him but stripped his bed and, with the bed sheet, hanged himself in his Bayonne cell. Only the Ghost and two other people close to Johnny—the timid accountant for Champion Watches and Wrist Watch, the elegant messenger, both in prison in New York—only those impeach-able people opted to solemnly swear that Johnny imported heroin into the customs territory of the United States. A smoking gun, the American government didn't have, what it had through its legal maneuvers were Johnny's disordered wife, Johnny's postpartum sister, Johnny's bewil-dered brother, Johnny's indignant girlfriend. *They're hostages,* Johnny tells himself in this cell-like attorney's room, *they're hostages like the American embassy people in Tehran, the American airplane passengers in Beirut, the American passengers on the Achille Lauro.* If now the ter-rorists were the Americans, that wouldn't negate the obstinate fact that for Jonquil, Johnny's sister, Johnny's brother, and Dominique the only available angel was Johnny himself. It was what? twenty years ago? that Johnny told Jonquil, "I'll never leave you. I'll never hurt you. As long as I live I'll care for you—this I promise." No acts of America's relieved him of his promise to Jonquil or of his obligations to his sister, his brother and Dominique. If it weren't for Johnny and his semisuccessful revenge against the United States, all four innocent people would be home in Asia now. *I didn't mean to,* Johnny thinks, *but I got them into this, and I'm honor bound to get them out.* "So now I'm smart," Johnny tells his long-legged attorney. "I will give up, and I will plead guilty."

"Good, Mr. Kon." Johnny's attorney sits back in his dragon's-blood plastic chair. He takes his right knee off his left one and rests his left knee on his right one. He swings it to and fro like a pendulum, *tick, tock,* his rate at the end of this case might compute to $10,000 per hour, plus expenses. "You made a very wise decision," says Johnny's wealthy attorney, and Johnny looks at him wryly, thinking, *I paid you $500,000. This very wise decision, I should have made back then.* The attorney sees Johnny's slight scowl, and he adds hastily, "We can still win, Mr. Kon."

"No. I made my mind. If," Johnny says—"if my family home, I already win." He stands up and leaves the white-painted concrete room.

NEW YORK

It's April 1989. The man who pleaded guilty thirty years ago at a self-criticism session in Gongjalu ("You did something wrong," "Yes, I ate one peanut") and the man's wife, sister, brother stand in front of the judge's carved desk in his law-book-papered chambers in Brooklyn. To their left stand the tall attorney and the short prosecutor known as the Dragon Lady. A look-alike of the femme fatale in *Terry and the Pirates*— not, the Dragon Lady is short, buck-toothed, brown-haired, black-spectacled, unmarried, unattached. She isn't Asian but Boston Irish, a woman whose sum and substance of life outside of her briefcase consists of the Boston Red Sox. All her life she's rooted for the Boston Red Sox. Her childhood hero was Carl Yastrzemski, the man who amassed the most games, at-bats, hits and runs for the Boston Red Sox and who the Dragon Lady, age six, wrote towers of fan mail to, Dear Yaz, Dear Yaz, Dear Yaz, Dear Yaz, and who Yastrzemski considerately wrote back to, "Thanks for the interest." The reddest of red-letter days for the Dragon Lady isn't today but was Sunday, October 1, 1967, when she was ten and Yastrzemski (three years older than Johnny, who was pushing fur in Vietnam) hit four for four in the year's last game and won "the impossible dream" for, yes, the Boston Red Sox. In these chambers today, the Dragon Lady (her name is Palmer) isn't wearing a baseball cap, but in her office around the corner are caps, baseballs and bats for the Boston Red Sox, and on her desk amidst the 14-inch-paperwork is a baseball signed by Yastrzemski, the wonderful fielder for the Boston Red Sox.

As far as it impinges on Johnny, all American justice in all its convolutions is the Dragon Lady. It was she who, when the four brass fishes were seized at Kennedy, prosecuted the Chinese woman courier. It was she who, when the Ghost was arrested at Sea-Tac, in Seattle, *didn't* prosecute him on condition that he'd inform on Johnny. It was she who inflicted duress on Johnny by extraditing his wife, sister, brother, girlfriend—a girlfriend who yesterday rode in a van, one car ahead of her, one car behind her, the red lights flashing, the sirens wailing, through most of Tokyo to Narita International Airport and to United Airlines, a girlfriend in handcuffs who even now is riding from Kennedy International Airport and who, if Johnny has second thoughts, if Johnny chooses the trial by jury guaranteed by the Constitution, will be eyeball to eyeball with Jonquil tonight. "It won't be pretty," the Dragon Lady (who's feeling feisty, for Roger Clemens got his one thousandth strikeout yesterday and won for the Boston Red Sox) has just told Johnny's attorney. And lastly it will be the Dragon Lady, who, if Johnny pleads guilty, chooses how much time he'll do, for her "recommendation" will be the judge's sentence, invariably.

"How old are you?" the judge asks Johnny.

"Forty-six," Johnny says.

"Where were you born?" the judge asks Johnny.

"Shanghai," Johnny says.

"Are you," the judge asks Johnny, "under the influence of any drug that might cause diminution of your mental capacity?"

"No," Johnny says.

"Do you understand the charge against you?"

"Yes."

"Has your attorney explained it?"

"Yes."

"Have you read it?"

"Yes."

"Tell me in your own words what you did to bring about the charge against you."

"I conspiracy," Johnny says in words that his old English teacher in Kowloon would be proud of, "to importation more than a hundred grams of heroin to the United States."

"Do you plead guilty?" the judge asks Johnny.

"Yes," Johnny says.

"I find that you're pleading guilty because you're guilty, and I accept your plea. Do you plead guilty?" the judge asks Jonquil, who yesterday told Johnny in Shanghai dialect, "I'll say whatever you tell me to."

"Yes," Jonquil says.

"Do you plead guilty?" the judge asks Johnny's sister, who yesterday told Johnny in Shanghai dialect, weeping, "I'll never plead guilty. I never knew about drugs. Brother, did you ever tell me? Forget I'm your sister, I'm your employee. Sir, did you ever tell me?" "No," Johnny answered yesterday, "but you can't fight the Americans. If you fight them you'll be in prison twenty years. You must plead whatever they say."

Johnny's sister nods, and the court interpreter says, "She says yes."

"Do you plead guilty?" the judge asks Johnny's brother.

"Yes," Johnny's brother says.

"I find that you're pleading guilty because you're guilty, and I accept your plea," says the judge, and, as Jonquil is quickly spirited off to a prison (a prison hospital) in Lexington, Kentucky, the others go back to their high-rise prison near City Hall. They arrive coincidentally with Dominique, who greets them in Shanghai dialect and takes Johnny's hand.

"We all pleaded guilty," Johnny tells her.

"But why? You should have fought it."

"You don't know the Americans. They swear on the Bible, but they tell lies. To put me in jail they'd swear anything. If I had a baby they'd swear it conspired with me. Dominique, you must plead guilty too."

"No! I didn't conspire with you! I'll fight it!"

"We all know you're innocent but—"

"I told you you must retire!"

"But they will prove you're guilty."

"But this is America! I heard there's justice!"

"I heard that too," says Johnny. "And I believed it."

27
Man In Box

The Chinese character for *man* stands abandoned inside the Chinese character for *box*. A convict, Johnny's a *man in box* in Chinese gangster slang, he's a jack-in-the-box who's counting the years until he'll pop out, he's a brown-suited man in the VIP ward of his prison near City Hall. Across from him is John Gotti, who's sitting reading the hundreds of letters the U.S. postal service delivered today (as it delivers every day) from Gotti groupies around the civilized world. Old organized crime: that's Gotti. New organized crime: that's Johnny, and the old and the new are surprisingly similar, starting with the great ceremony where Gotti said, *"Omerta,"* and Johnny said, "I'll keep these secrets. If I don't, may I be killed by a thousand swords." "If I were you," Johnny tells Gotti now, "I'd leave the United States. They will try you one after one. If you win this one, they will give you another one. Leave. Come China. Come visit me."

"Maybe," says John Gotti.

PETERSBURG

On New Year's Eve (and New Decade's Eve) Johnny's behind white bricks at a prison in Virginia that looks like a college campus, marigolds all around it. Most of his fellow prisoners, as in all of America's prisons, are the jetsam of the war against drugs: the users (a Texan got twenty-five years for one wrinkled marijuana cigarette) and the thieves, robbers, muggers and murderers who, to get their imported delights, need $20 or more per day, also the dealers, middlemen, mules: the tourists who go through customs carrying drugs in Crest tubes, whatever, but not many kingpins like Johnny, not many at all. Nor has the deportation of so many people removed the heroin, cocaine, marijuana from America's streets. All this year, Johnny didn't deal, but in the booming heroin business the Colombians replaced the Chinese, and this year in America 2,743 people died, two hundred more than last year.

LEWISBURG

A crucial question: will Johnny be killed before he's set free? It's one year later, it's 1990, and he's behind thick brick at a prison in Pennsylvania that looks like a rook in a chess set. A tattooed man from Taipei, tattoos on his arms, legs, shoulders, is Johnny's best friend here. Both were in Chinese secret societies: the tattooed man in United Bamboo and Johnny in Tranquil Happiness. Both were approached seven years ago by the Taiwanese CIA: the tattooed man in a canteloupe-colored house near Golden Gate Park, in San Francisco, and Johnny under the plaster busts of Bacchus and Venus in the pink-and-plum-carpeted lobby of the Peninsula, in Hong Kong, the tattooed man and a CIA man eating kiwis, kiwanos and passion fruits ("They look like toys," said the tattooed man) and Johnny and a CIA man eating walnut cake. Both were asked to do "wet work" for the Taiwanese CIA: the tattooed man to kill an American newspaperman in Daly City, California, and Johnny to kill the tattooed man in Manila, to kill him before he could blab that he killed the newspaperman on behalf of the Taiwanese CIA. The tattooed man did his job (and was imprisoned for it) but Johnny purposely didn't and now tells the tattooed man in Mandarin, "Small world. As small as a Buddhist prayer wheel."

Even smaller. Two months later, the Taiwanese CIA (or someone else, who can say?) attacks the tattooed man in a prison corridor. His heart stabbed, his head swollen, his head becoming pumpkin size, he dies in the prison hospital and Johnny, for his own safety, since he's on the CIA hit list, enters solitary confinement. One hour's exercise every two days. One shower every two days.

LOMPOC

It's four years later, it's 1994 and Johnny, for his own safety, enters a prison in California that's the New Rock, the New Alcatraz, so proclaimed by an enormous boulder in front of it. No sooner is he inside than the Taiwanese CIA (or someone) spreads the word about him, and for his own safety he's put in the prison hospital's crazy-ward. All day the crazy prisoners bang their doors. Some walk in circles, waving their hands, talking to walls, screaming, *"Aaagh,"* and others scream back, "Keep quiet!"

DUBLIN

It's still 1994, and for his own safety he enters another prison in California.

PHOENIX

It's still 1994, and for his own safety he enters another prison, in Arizona.

TUCSON

It's still 1994, and for his own safety he enters another prison in Arizona. Made of adobe, apparently, and colored like iron ore, it looks like a hacienda that is entirely inhabited by Mexicans and Mexican-Americans who obviously don't work for the Taiwanese CIA. By the giant saguaros, their arms in the air like traffic cops signaling *stop,* the swallows are swooping purposefully. The swallows are in a fight to the finish with the pitiless prison warden, and Johnny (who was just three when his grandmother told him, "Swallows bring good luck") is on the swallows' side.

A couple of swallows started this. Their nest was over (and their droppings were *on*) the warden's adobe door, and the warden destroyed their nest. "Why did the warden do?" Johnny asked the Mexican prisoners in English, looking forlorn. "Why he will kill the baby bir's? Why he won't let the bir's will live?" Their nest wiped out, the swallows now build another one, and to Johnny's (and some of the Mexicans') consternation the warden destroys that, too. The swallows then build *another* nest, and the warden destroys it and lays some strands of barbed wire on the cornice above the swallow-stained door. And still the swallows come back, they somehow dodge the barbed wire, they start still another nest, and Johnny approaches them like Saint Francis and, in English, the swallows being domestic ones, tells them, "Little bir's! You fly away! You make your nest somewhere else! Will," says Johnny, shaking his finger meaningfully—"will be more safe than here!" The swallows not heeding him, Johnny, that night, under cover of darkness, takes the dangerous barbed wire off. The next day the warden puts it on, the next night the convict takes it off. The next day the warden puts it on, the next night—enough, and the next day the convict confronts the warden in his captain-of-industry office and, not disrespectfully, lest he (Johnny) be ordered to go and demolish rocks, says, "Now there are three baby bir's. Are protection by federal government."

"Protected? I didn't know."

"Are dangerous species," says Johnny, and the chastened warden lets the swallows (they're the most common ones: barn) stay on the U.S. government cornice. One month later the three little babies, bigger, their throats adobe-colored, their tails scissors-shaped, are swooping up and down with their mother and father, at age one month they're feeding another brood. At the warden's stained door is Johnny, his face radiant, his eyes as wide as a boy's who's watching a new toy train take the curves of a figure-eight track. Go, blithe spirits. Go.

NEW YORK

It's one year later, it's 1995 and Johnny is behind bricks at a prison in Brooklyn that looks like the warehouse it recently was. It's Sunday, and Johnny's in the prison chapel watching a Catholic priest in a streaming stole say, "Hail Mary, Mother of God." Like most other prisoners here, Johnny hasn't come to hail the Mother of God but to hail other prisoners that he can do business with only at Sunday services. Johnny's broke. His money, his fair-weather friends embezzled years ago. His $20,000,000 building in Chinatown, his Chinese friend sold, then spent the proceeds at all six positions at a blackjack table in Atlantic City. His $2,250,000 from the not-quite-white powder that, via Dopey, he sent to Big Banana, Big Banana kept, then bought a nightclub in Bangkok. Another $1,000,000, a Chinese multimillionaire kept, a Chinese criminal who (as fate would have it) is sitting right now in this prison chapel on the steel folding chair next to Johnny. "Where is my $1,000,000?" asks Johnny in whispers and Cantonese.

"I gave it to Fat Ass, Michael Jackson and Muy," whispers the Chinese man.

"Not according to Fat Ass, Michael Jackson and Muy," whispers Johnny.

"Are you trying to extort it from me?" whispers the Chinese man.

"Are you saying that I, Johnny Kon, am trying to extort from you? In that case," whispers Johnny, just as he did to Mahogany before the Irish policeman murdered him, "I'll just forget it."

"Pray for us sinners," says the Catholic priest.

OTISVILLE

Nothing that Johnny said in his eight prior prisons was as momentous as what he says now behind barbed wire at this ninth prison in New York State near Sing Sing, West Point, and Vassar. It's two years later, it's 1997 and Johnny is on a pay phone talking (via an attorney's office) to a Thai friend in the warehouse prison in Brooklyn. "Hello," says Johnny in Mandarin.

"Hello," says the Thai.

"How are you doing?"

"I'm not bad lately."

"Two months ago," says Johnny, "I had someone bring you some soy sauce." Big quart bottles of Kikkoman, oyster sauce, octopus, salmon, clams—the Chinese going from here, in Otisville, where there's a commissary, to Brooklyn, where there isn't, load up with food that isn't served in the messhall there. "Did you get it?"

"I did, I did."

"Two weeks ago," says Johnny, "a young brother named Chen, from Foochow, went to your place. He brought ten to twenty bottles of soy sauce."

"Ah," says the Thai.

"Tell him that Kon has asked him to give you two."

"Which guy again?"

"Last name is Chen."

"What is his full name?"

"He's just called Little Chen."

"How was it? You asked him to—"

"He brought ten to twenty bottles of soy sauce. Tell him I asked him to give you two."

"Aw, it's too much trouble," says the Thai. And that's it: two bottles of Kikkoman, then they talk of Johnny's scheduled release and Johnny's scheduled return to Asia, seven days hence. The soy sauce really exists. It stands in eleven bottles in Chen's cell in Brooklyn. Chen's personal property record, signed by a prison officer, says, "11 soy sauce." But the DEA, listening in on this conversation, proud of having its most wanted man, not satisfied with his nine-year stay in New York, Petersburg, Lewisburg, Lompoc, Dublin, Phoenix, Tucson, Brooklyn and Otisville, not wanting him in his old haunts in Asia—the DEA concludes (or pretends it concludes) that Johnny and the Thai are speaking code, that two bottles of soy sauce from Otisville to Brooklyn mean two kilos of heroin from Bangkok to somewhere secret in the United States.

NEW YORK

It's one week later, and Johnny's again in the prison near City Hall, he's booked on a midnight flight to Hong Kong, he's waiting for the steel-barred bus to the court in Hauphauge, New York, to the judge who'll release him. The bus comes, but the marshals don't call out "Kon." He's taken instead to a room full of caps, baseballs and bats for the Boston Red Sox, of Boston memorabilia, a map of Thailand, and a wood-framed photo of Johnny Kon: the unforgettable office of the Dragon Lady. Her eyes, grotesquely magnified by her black-rimmed glasses, are like two burning coals. She says Johnny pleaded guilty. She says Johnny made a deal with her. She says Johnny broke that deal by importing heroin—"soy sauce"—into the customs territory of the United States. She says she can now renege on the deal and Johnny won't get an early release.

"Miss Palmer," Johnny begins.

"No, Mr. Kon," says Johnny's long-legged attorney, who's in this base-ball museum too. "You're here to listen to Miss Palmer. Not to tell her anything."

"That's it, Mr. Kon," says the Dragon Lady and, palms down, sweeps her hands to her left and right as if to clear her desk of this odious mat-ter forever. Johnny will pass a lie-detector test ("Is soy sauce a code word for anything else?" "No") but it won't placate the Dragon Lady.

OTISVILLE

"Father, I've been counting," says Leopard, an unsmiling soldier in the Big Circle, in Cantonese. "Do you realize how many brothers died?" It's three years later, it's 2000 and Johnny is still behind barbed wire at the prison near Sing Sing, West Point, and Vassar, and Leopard's impris-oned here too. The two men are wearing sweats today: they're in the gym, but, unlike the man who's jogging, his sneakers slapping the var-nished wood, his *slap slap* echoing from the rafters, unlike the man on the stand-still bike, his *whirr* like a distant insect swarm, unlike these men the Chinese are in the stands, seated, smoking cigarettes, watching the smoke-whorls, contemplating. Leopard, a former soldier of the Star's, his face crushed as though by Jupiter's G's, his face creased like a bull-dog's, horizontally lined, Leopard who fought in the "Saturday Night Gang War," who stayed underground in Hong Kong, who sailed, then swam, by the pearly-toothed sharks to the Isthmus of Kra, who, to take the next bullet, jumped in front of the Star in Monterey Park, who stormed from the Star's screeching car on the Brooklyn-Queens Expressway, who guarded the Star as a steel needle stabbed his bladder-eleven point, who, in time, stabbed *himself* in his own left thigh and said, "Let me leave you," but who didn't leave the Star—Leopard the loyal soldier has let some smoke escape from his lips, and as it slowly decomposes, becomes a few cirrus-cloud strands, fades, he says to Johnny in Cantonese, "We had such grand plans. But Father, I've been counting. Do you realize how many brothers died?"

No, Johnny doesn't. Nor does he want to tally them even now. If he could, he would reminisce about the quick instead of the dead, reminisce about the brothers still on the street and, for the most part, still in the amicable embrace of the Big Circle. There are exactly twelve. Michael Jackson, the man who lay in a tire compartment like a fetus enduring contractions to get to New York and run Johnny's office there, is a Red Pole (a Double Flower Red Pole) in Bangkok. Fat Cat, the man on the *Victory* who, in the great typhoon, cried like Columbus, "Sail on!" is out of his prison in Hong Kong and running a Chinese poker, pai-gow and fan-tan casino in Macao, and the *Victory*'s captain who said, "We're dead," is out of his prison and is retired in Hong Kong. Tony and Tony's accomplice, whose name is Charles, the men who thought, *He didn't invite us!* and who used guns to chasten the Star in Monterey Park, are soldiers in New York and, with their pupils—a whole second generation of the Big Circle in New York, Toronto, Vancouver, San Francisco and Los Angeles—are keeping the old ways alive as muggers, murderers, your-home-is-my-home invaders, extortionists, pickpockets, counterfeiters of credit cards, yellow-slavers, and of course smugglers, not of heroin (though there's still some) but of Chinese illegal aliens, many of them already in the Big Circle. Three Fingers, the three-fingered bodyguard in Santa Cruz, Bolivia, and Dopey, the quick-fingered soldier in Bangkok, his toy (his Beretta) again in his unpredictable grasp, are soldiers in São Paulo, Brazil, and Ah Dat, the man who was shot in the stomach when Baldie was shot in the heart in Bangkok, is a soldier in Amsterdam, the headquarters for the Big Circle in Europe. The rest of the twelve, though they're on the street in Asia or the Americas, at one time betrayed the Big

Circle and were without ceremony expelled from it. Wrist Watch, the elegant messenger, who testified to a grand jury that Johnny imported heroin into the customs territory of the United States, and the Jap Man, the right-hand man to the Professor, who even when the Professor was dead didn't switch sides to Johnny, are on the streets of Hong Kong. Old Fox, the man who made vases for Johnny, who then double-dealt with him, and who Johnny ordered a hit on, is fortuitously alive on the streets of Bangkok, and Green Snake, who, with White Snake, if you remember, murdered the man who'd have made a billionaire out of Johnny—murdered Crew Cut—is still alive on the tango-happy streets of Buenos Aires.

No, Johnny doesn't care to add up the brothers who died. He'd rather add up the brothers who are still drawing breath even if they're drawing it in Asian and American prisons. Again, there are exactly twelve. The Star, who for top-notch acupuncture went to Shanghai but who, for the pain, took heroin, too, was convicted of heroin possession and is on Death Row in Canton. Of the Star's soldiers, Big Banana, the tough guy, was seized in Bangkok, spirited off to New York, and convicted of heroin conspiracy and is in prison in Los Angeles, and Leopard, the loyal guy, was convicted of heroin conspiracy and is, of course, in prison here in Otisville. Four Eyes, the talented courier who said, "I'll pay the tax," and who was convicted of putting heroin into T-shirt sandwiches, is half-insane in his miserable prison in Bangkok. Four other couriers are in four other prisons: in one in Toronto is the General, caught with the Ziploc bags, in Texas is Tommy, caught with the flying-flower buckets, in New York is the Chinese woman, whose name is Chen, caught with the fat brass fishes, and in Florida is the ABC who doesn't wear a Cowboys cap: his name is Sing, and he was convicted of kidnapping three Florida millionaires. The Sergeant, the fat, full-jowled, full-bellied man from the NYPD, was arrested when Johnny was ("I'm on the job," the Sergeant told the DEA men who came for him in Montclair, meaning "I'm a cop myself," but the DEA men slapped handcuffs on)—the Sergeant was convicted of heroin conspiracy and is in prison in Ray Brook, New York, near the site of the Winter Olympics of February 1980. Buddhahead, the man who flexes his biceps, triceps, infiniticeps, and who vanished with

$2,500,000 from Johnny's safe-deposit box, was convicted of heroin conspiracy and is in prison in Los Angeles. Tiger, Johnny's bodyguard, the one who told him, "You know who the traitor is? It's the Tardy Ghost," was arrested in Hong Kong and convicted of heroin conspiracy in New York, and, not ceasing to be Johnny's shadow, is in prison with him in Otisville. The twelfth jailbird is Johnny, who doesn't want to torture himself with the memory that of the robust young men he led for six rambunctious years, a total of one, two, three, whatever the number was, died.

"I've counted twelve," says Leopard.

"No. That isn't possible," Johnny says.

"And most of them, other brothers killed."

"No. How did you calculate twelve?"

"Number one was Dead Man."

No, Johnny thinks, *number one was Mahogany,* the man whose throat the Irish policeman cut in New York, a murdered man who Leopard wouldn't know about.

"He was shot," says Leopard, still referring to Dead Man, "by the Professor. Number two was the Professor, and number three was the Professor's bodyguard. They were shot by Crew Cut. Number four was Crew Cut. He was shot by White Snake and Green Snake. Number five," says Leopard, by now these numbers drop onto Johnny's ears like kettle-drum thuds, like *boom, boom, boom,* "was White Snake. He was killed but I don't know how. Was White Snake shot?"

"No. He was hammered," Johnny groans.

"Also, I don't know who by," says Leopard.

"Paul," Johnny groans. A brother in Paraguay.

"Number six," says Leopard, "was the Snake."

"The Snake? Did someone kill him?"

"No one told you?" asks Leopard. "He was Muy's driver," the Star's automobile driver. "He was the one on the Brooklyn-Queens Expressway, the one who when there was a backfire cried, 'It's the Dragons!' That's when Muy jumped out and Muy was paralyzed. He told us to kill the Snake."

"I didn't know," Johnny groans.

"Number seven," Leopard begins.

"We're only halfway?" Johnny asks.

"—was Baldy. He was shot by Dopey. Number eight was Steven," the *Victory*'s sky-eyed navigator. "He was shot by Crazy Chun. Number nine was Crazy Chun. He—"

"He hanged himself," Johnny groans.

"Number ten was Golo," the hit man who Johnny ordered hit, who was recently shot in Amsterdam. "Number eleven was Eddie," the ABC with the Cowboys cap, who was recently stabbed in Atlanta. "Number twelve was Little Lee," the soldier of Tiger's, who was thrown from an eighth-floor window in Bangkok. "That's twelve," says Leopard.

No, Johnny thinks, *he left out Mahogany.* No, Johnny thinks, thinking of three minor brothers in Asia and the Americas, *he left out Lee, he left out Lau, he left out Lau's bodyguard.* No, Johnny thinks, *he left out the man who made vases in Bangkok,* his head was cut off and thrown in the Chao Phraya River. *No,* Johnny thinks, *he left out the man who betrayed me: the Ghost,* he was poisoned by parties unknown in La Paz. "I've counted eighteen," Johnny groans, Johnny who hasn't counted the two who died of natural causes: not Fatty, his former mentor, who died of heart disease in Bangkok, and not Fat Ass, his first convert, who died of a heart attack in New York.

"And most of them, other brothers killed," says Leopard.

"Leopard, I never wanted that," Johnny says.

"What went wrong?" asks Leopard.

Johnny doesn't answer him. He exhales his cigarette smoke, and he watches it dissipate like a tenuous ghost, a ghost that's saying, "Adieu, adieu." "A tree, that's what I wanted," says Johnny, recollecting some words of wisdom from long ago. "A tree that grows branches. A tree that grows stronger. Not one whose branches die." Oh, what high hopes he once harbored for the Big Circle! And how close he came to making them real! He did take his sweet revenge, sweet as ten spoonfuls of honey, spoonfuls enough to be sickening, against the arrogant swaggerers of the United States. He did get his pistols, silencers, rounds, to the very approaches of Hong Kong for the great revolution against the Royal Police. He did operate in sixteen countries: in Belgium, Bolivia, Brazil,

Canada, France, Hong Kong, Japan, the Netherlands, Panama, Paraguay, the Philippines, Singapore, Taiwan, Thailand, the United Kingdom, the United States. His profits, but for a gunshot in Paraguay, would have been $600,000,000 per year, more than the profits of General Dynamics, Bethlehem Steel, Barnes & Noble, Motorola, Hilton Hotels, Sunoco, Texaco, Office Max, Apple, Compaq, Kellogg, Costco, Kmart, J.C. Penney, B.F. Goodrich, Nike, Reebok, Schwab, Mitsui, Mitsubishi, Mattel, CBS, Time-Warner, or *The New York Times*. Profit for profit, among the top two hundred corporations in our new global economy would have been Johnny's Big Circle. How close Johnny came!

"What went wrong?" asks Leopard.

"Very little, Leopard," Johnny says.

"What was it? Do you know?"

"The fault lay in me," Johnny says. "The brothers believed in me. They entrusted their lives to me. And when all's said and done, I didn't deliver, I let them down. But," Johnny says, "if I had known then what I know now, we'd have succeeded. And this I promise, Leopard. That when I'm let out," and Johnny, sentenced to twenty-seven years, at last awarded an early release, will go back to Hong Kong in the People's Republic of China at age fifty-eight in July 2001—"when I'm let out, I'll stay loyal to the brothers even as they have stayed loyal to me. The dead ones I can't help, but I'll help their families. The imprisoned ones I'll release. The free ones I'll reunite. When I'm let out," says Johnny, still sitting, a prisoner jogging, a prisoner cycling, a prisoner shooting baskets, *swish*, "I'll rebuild the Big Circle. I don't know what we'll do. But this time we'll succeed."

Sources

My sources for most of *The Dragonhead* were Chinese criminals. For one dozen years I hung out with them—some, like Johnny, in prisons from New York to California but most on mean streets from New York to Hong Kong. I lived in their bullet-proof-windowed homes in New York, and they lived in my more porous one in the Rocky Mountains. I invited them to a Fourth of July celebration that, if freeze-framed, would be a glorious cover for *The Saturday Evening Post,* and they invited me to a watch-store robbery that my conscience told me, "Don't go to." Chinese criminals and I saw movies together. Often we ate together, ate the plastic-wrapped burritos at a prison in New York and the scallops with walnut halves at a restaurant in Los Angeles and the eels, abalone, grouper (it lay on its side open-mouthed, looking aggrieved) in the VIP room of a restaurant in Hong Kong. At this last site I was with the Dragonhead of all Dragonheads, the grand panjandrum who, when I asked for his secrets, apologized in Cantonese and said, "I can't answer that."

"I apologize for asking you."

"Please don't apologize," said the Dragonhead, who, I discovered, couldn't answer because he hadn't time—he had many, many secrets—and who assigned a White Paper Fan to spill them to me over coffee on the mezzanine of the International Hotel.

For five hundred hours with Chinese criminals, I took notes. With minor exceptions that I didn't use in *The Dragonhead,* I believed what the criminals told me and without exceptions what Johnny told me. Of course I double-checked on Johnny's accounts, and I always discovered that he'd been honest with me. He'd told me, for instance, about the rain-cloud-colored movie in the colonel's trailer in Danang, the movie of American missiles hitting a bridge, an oil, gas or water tank, and a train backing halfway into a tunnel—so Johnny had said. He'd said the colonel's name was Bresser or Bressler, something like that, and I spent weeks tracking down Colonel Frederick C. Blesse, Jr., by then a retired lieutenant general playing golf in Florida. I asked him if he remembered a Johnny Kon. "No," said General Blesse. I asked him if he remembered a Chinese furrier. "No," said General Blesse. I asked him if he remembered a man who one winter night in Danang was in his trailer watching a black-and-white movie of American missiles hitting Vietnamese targets. "No," said General Blesse. *Well,* I thought, *either Johnny lied or in his pre-criminal days was a quite forgettable character,* and I asked General Blesse if he'd ever shot a black-and-white movie. "Yes," said General Blesse and said that it showed the American missiles hitting a bridge, an oil, gas or water tank, and a train backing halfway into a tunnel, exactly as Johnny reported it.

Johnny's crimes as reported by Johnny were, with a major exception, consistent with Johnny's crimes as charged by the Dragon Lady. The major exception was the complicity (if there was any) of Jonquil, Johnny's brother and sister, and Dominique. Johnny told me, and I believed him, that Chinese criminals, like Italian criminals, do not risk their private lives by even so much as confiding to wives, children, brothers and sisters what they do when away from home—or at home if Jonquil's asleep. But the Dragon Lady not only indicted the four adults nearest and dearest to Johnny but, perhaps inevitably, convinced herself that the four adults deserved this, that Jonquil, for one, had been one of Johnny's couriers, that Jonquil "did import heroin" in violation of Title 21, Section 952(a), that Jonquil "did distribute heroin" in violation of Title 21, Section 959(a), and that Jonquil flew several times from New York to Hong Kong with suitcases stuffed with American bills in violation of Title 31, Section 5316(a). "She was ruthless," insisted the Dragon Lady, her jaw almost hammering me, her buck teeth almost chomping me in her baseball-embellished office.

"Johnny says she's 101 percent innocent."

"Bullshit," said the Dragon Lady. "She wasn't running money for him? She wasn't laundering money for him? She pleaded guilty, for God's sake!"

"Johnny says he told her to, told everyone to."

"He says they aren't guilty? He's so full of it!"

"Also he says that *he* pleaded guilty for *them.*"

"Oh, please! We'd have creamed him! That's why he pleaded guilty!"

"You told *The New York Times* he took the fall for his family's sake."

"Listen," said the Dragon Lady. "I'm not going to sit and debate with Johnny Kon," and she said *Johnny Kon* as though she could taste him and he tasted terrible. "We had the evidence to convict him. He'd have gone down. Big time," said the Dragon Lady, who has been called ferocious (called this in federal court) by the judge in *United States versus Kon*. The lady clearly believed what she said, but I believed Johnny.

Someone else who didn't concur with Johnny and who I didn't believe was the Sergeant. Sitting with me in his prison near the site of the Winter Olympics, the Sergeant didn't deny that he eagerly flew to Hong Kong, to Johnny, but called it an out-and-out lie that he stayed at the Royal Garden: he stayed at a cheaper hotel, said the Sergeant. He said that what Johnny wanted to "move" wasn't money, watches or heroin but fur, fur (as I noted) that Johnny was already moving at Macy's, Gimbel's, Alexander's, Broadway, Bullock's, Penney and Sears. He said that he went to Toronto not to get heroin but to get two dozen furs, and he said that he went to the Mirage Bar of the New York Hilton, in Manhattan, to get expensive jewelry to sell to the jewelers on West 47th. He got this jewelry, said the Sergeant, in three brown grocery bags that he stashed (two in the trunk and one behind the spare tire) in his Lincoln. He drove, said the Sergeant, to a hotel and not a motel in Times Square and had sex with the pretty brunette he'd met at the Mirage Bar by asking her, "You waiting for someone too?" He then drove, said the Sergeant, to the Market Diner, and when with two cups of coffee he returned to the Lincoln he was robbed of the Lincoln, the grocery bags, and the expensive jewelry. His account of his interrogation at the Regal Airport Hotel, in Hong Kong, was much like Johnny's (and one other brother's) account, but he maintained that his red-ribboned daughter wasn't with him in Hong Kong.

"The grocery bags," I asked him. "Why did you put one behind the spare tire?"

"Don't ask," said the Sergeant, his fingers intertwined, his thumb rubbing his knuckles. "I do a lot of stupid things." As with the Dragon Lady, I didn't believe the Sergeant, I believed Johnny.

I first met Johnny at Lewisburg. Four years later, I started taking notes at Lompoc—mental notes, for I couldn't bring a pen, pencil, paper or tape recorder and, like a spy, had to type up these notes after coming home. A guard at last gave me a pencil stub, and I started writing notes on the napkins by the burrito machine, then Johnny and I went to Tucson and I was permitted a pen and pad but not a tape recorder, lest Johnny's fellow prisoners think he was squealing to the FBI. My notes, four times as long as this book, four secretaries and I typed up and Johnny fact-checked, but Johnny had no say whatsoever about what I wrote in *The Dragonhead*. We stipulated this at our first meeting at Lewisburg, and only once did Johnny renege: at Otisville, when he asked me to cut three critical sentences. I refused, and it was with almost watery eyes that Johnny told me, "My people will have to kill you."

"Here's where they'll find me," I said rather melodramatically, writing down my address in the Rocky Mountains but knowing that Johnny had promised that I could write what I chose to and knowing that Johnny's word was gold. The sentences stayed in *The Dragonhead*.

One request of Johnny's, I willingly agreed to. It was that I write nothing a man might be murdered because of, and I omitted (among other things) the name of the man who said in Chiang Mai, "Did you kill him?" and "I'll make sure!" and who fired once, twice, thrice at the navigator, lest that man be murdered by the navigator's relatives. I changed the names of Johnny's women to "Isabel," "Jonquil," and "Dominique." I changed the name of Johnny's son to "Jerry," and I regretfully changed a few other names and identifying characteristics. But mostly I used real names, including the names and nicknames of almost all Chinese criminals. I didn't collapse characters, though I confess that the USO man in Saigon wasn't the USO man who was sweating in Hong Kong. I didn't invent dialog. When Johnny says in *The Dragonhead*, "I can carry more mud for the People's Republic," then that's what Johnny said in Gongjalu, although—forgive me—he said it in Gongjalu in Shanghai dialect. I did translate currencies into American dollars, centigrade into Fahrenheit, kilometers into miles. I didn't invent gestures. When Fatty says in *The*

Dragonhead, "Feel them!" and Johnny chooses a $100 bill and pats the long-haired head of Benjamin Franklin, then that's what Fatty said and Johnny did in Hong Kong. I didn't invent thoughts. When, in *The Dragonhead,* the General brushes his fingers on Johnny's carpet, lifts them up to his gold-rimmed glasses, checks them for any unwelcome dust as Johnny thinks, *Why? No one walks here but Jonquil and me,* be confident that the General did it and Johnny thought it, or so Johnny told me and I believed.

All that said, I'll ask for some slack, about a half-inch of it. When, in Hong Kong, Johnny said his first words in English, I can just about guarantee they were "Madam, can I help you?" but I can't guarantee that Madam replied precisely, "Oh, I'm just looking." She may have replied, "No, I'm just looking," or "No thanks, I'm just looking," or "No thanks, I'm just looking around." I can't guarantee that in New York, Johnny said precisely in Pidgin English, to Mahogany, "And then you die," for Johnny may have said, "And now you die," or "And now today you die," or "And now today, motherfucker, you die." Nor can I guarantee that this or any other conversation in *The Dragonhead* is in the same sequence it was originally in in New York or in Oslo or anywhere else. Be confident that in Hong Kong, in the Peninsula's pink-and-plum-carpeted lobby, Johnny told the Movie Star, "We should *kill* him," and be confident that in the string quartet's repertoire was

> *I don't stand*
> *A ghost of a chance,*

but should you be confident that Johnny said *kill* and the string quartet played *a ghost of a chance* simultaneously? No, you shouldn't, and I hope this doesn't disappoint you. If it does, please consider that the dialog in *The Dragonhead* is as verbatim as any you have relied on in *The Peloponnesian War,* by Thucydides, or (please trust me, for I've been quoted in it) in *The New York Times.*

A word about time. A rough, not a rigid, chronology sometimes occurs in *The Dragonhead.* Johnny didn't go to Taipei, Bangkok, Singapore, Manila, São Paulo, Asunción, La Paz, Quito, Bogotá, Panama City, Los

Angeles, San Francisco, Toronto and New York in that smooth order but in a sort of Brownian motion. And one prison scene is out of sequence at the request of the Bureau of Prisons. A word about place. I went to almost all of the sites in *The Dragonhead,* but I described them as they appeared in Johnny's time, not as they appear nowadays. If, to live life as Johnny did, you try to sit under the totem of the Colombian god at the Café Colombia of the Sheraton Center, in New York, now you'll sit in the gym of the Sheraton Manhattan. If you try to sit by the two stone sphinxes in the Mirage Bar of the New York Hilton, now you'll sit by the steel bolts in the Bridges Bar, nor can you sit downstairs anymore in the Café New York. In Queens, Alexander's now is Sears, the beige-and-brown booths at Sizzler's are pea-green-and-mauve booths at Sizzler's, and the waitresses aren't in UPS uniforms but in raspberry shirts, black pants. At the Penta, once again Pennsylvania, there is no Schiaparelli of shocking pink at the Globetrotter Restaurant, for there is no Globetrotter Restaurant. There is no bar at the Doral Park, on the corner there is no Fireside Bar, the new has evicted the old in Asia and Europe, too, and coca leaves aren't sold on the sidewalk in South America. One confession: Johnny's house on Austin Street, in Queens, may really have been on Booth Street or Wetherly Street.

We live in misty climates these days. Our world becomes blurred as fictions trespass on facts, obscuring a city's skyline, a person's silhouette, an event's particulars—obscuring, in the end, our world as it actually is. I hope no fictions intrude on *The Dragonhead,* but I confess there's an alien element that I (like every writer, even an AP reporter who, at the very minimum, chooses what's in the first paragraph) cannot keep out, and that is my own predilections. The best I can do is, I can cop to them here and now. I'm against murder. I'm against mayhem. I'm against running guns into Hong Kong and running them into America's dresser drawers. I'm against kidnapping, counterfeiting, robbery. I'm against fraud as committed by Johnny and as committed by Publishers Clearing House, and I'm against extortion as committed by Johnny and as committed by the IRS. I'm against Rolexes, and I'm against all other glitter that no one who knows that less is more would add to his impedimenta if his taste weren't corrupted by ten thousand hours of commercials to the effect that he'd be a lesser human being without them. I'm against toilet paper from Florence, toilet paper imprinted with Botticelli's *The Birth of Venus,* toilet paper that a certain heroin-and-cocaine exporter uses in some (though not all) of his 140 great estates in Colombia. I'm against cigarettes. I'm against processed foods. Pay what you will, I won't inflict a fat-filled burger, a sugar-filled cereal, or a salt-filled soup on any innocent fellow man. I'm against heroin. If in our society other people sell Marlboros, other people sell Macs, Cap'n Crunches, Campbell's, other people poison us with impunity, do I think, *Well, so what if Johnny does too?* No, I don't. If other people aren't in prison, do I think that Johnny's inculpable too? No, I devoutly don't, but I do understand why Johnny at one time thought so.

I like Johnny. At our first meeting, in Lewisburg, I instinctively hugged him. My predilections aren't those in *Reader's Digest,* where Johnny was written up (by someone who never met him) as crafty, ruthless, dangerous, notorious. But like *Reader's Digest,* I do deplore what Johnny's done. I deplore what's done every day by the Chinese Mafia and the Japanese, Vietnamese, Russian, Ukrainian, Israeli, Italian, Nigerian, Dominican, Jamaican, Cuban, Colombian, Mexican and Afro-American Mafias. While writing *The Dragonhead,* I often wondered where is the White Man Mafia? Are palefaces such perfect saints that we never, never team up into organized criminal enterprises? At last I saw, we white men are so entrenched in Congress, in state legislatures, and on city councils that we can and do pass laws declaring that our own favorite crimes aren't illegal. A crime, by our definition, is what the unwashed races out to usurp our authority commit, at least until (as with drinking, gambling and, in some states, smoking pot) we decide to do it ourselves. A predilection that I confess I couldn't keep out of *The Dragonhead* is, I deplore what's done every day by· the White Man Mafia.

About the Author

John Sack has been a journalist for fifty-five years. He was a news-paper reporter in North and South America, Europe, Africa and Asia, a contributor to *Harper's*, *The Atlantic* and *The New Yorker*, a contributing editor of *Esquire*, a writer, producer, and special correspondent for CBS News and its bureau chief in Spain, a war correspondent in Korea, Vietnam, Iraq and Yugoslavia, and the author of ten nonfiction books, including *An Eye for an Eye* and *M*. You can visit him at www.johnsack.com.